Shojo Beat

THE GENTLEMEN'S ALLIANCE CROSS

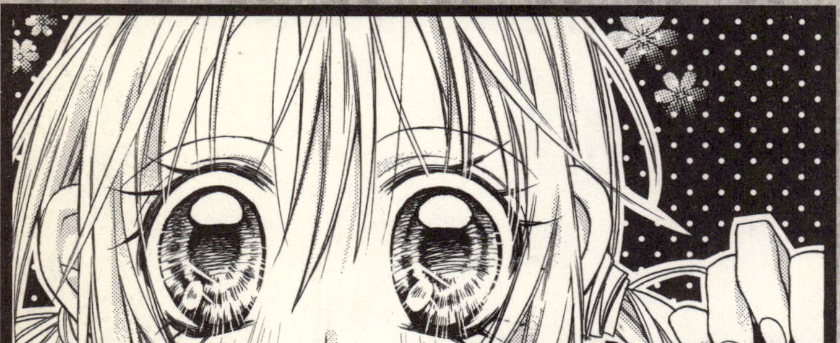

Story & Art by

Arina Tanemura

Vol. 7

CONTENTS

Chapter 28: The Rush of My Heartbeat: Cherry Blossom Gateway 3

Chapter 29: Opening Heart Fantasia 37

Chapter 30: Like Singing a Melody Under Your Breath.................... 71

Chapter 31: Hydrangea Always Bloom in the Rain 105

Chapter 32: Reminiscence, the Canary's Song................................139

Bonus Funnies 172

Bonus Story: Maora's Mind Oracle Generation ☆ 174

Notes on the Text..181

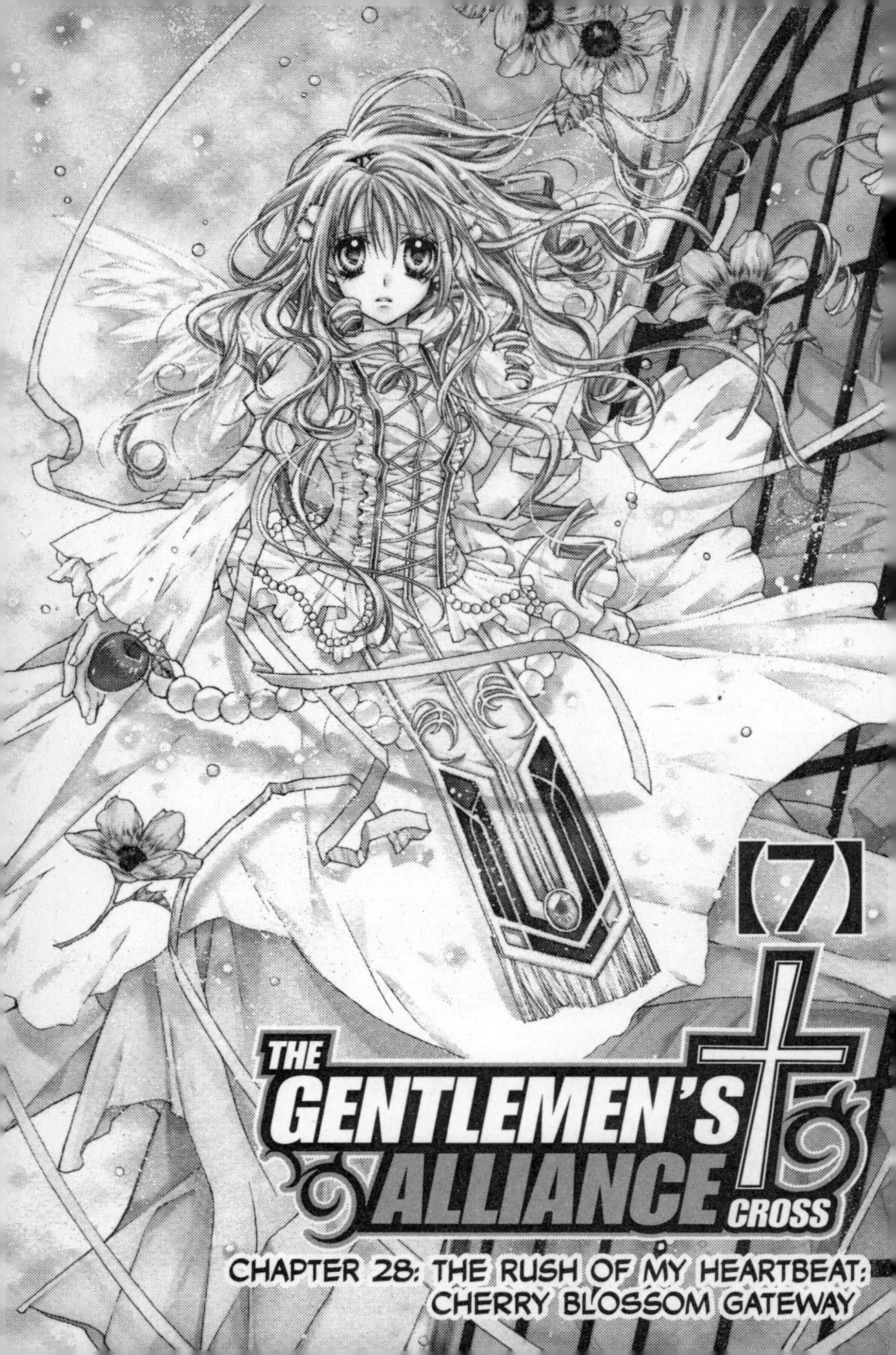
[7]
THE GENTLEMEN'S ALLIANCE CROSS
CHAPTER 28: THE RUSH OF MY HEARTBEAT: CHERRY BLOSSOM GATEWAY

CHARACTER INTRODUCTIONS

THE REAL SHIZUMASA (Younger Twin)
An illness prevents him from attending school. He helped Haine mend her yanki ways.

TAKANARI TOGU (Elder Twin)
Student Council President
The double. Referred to as "the Emperor" and is the highest authority in school. Wrote Haine's favorite picture book.

HAINE OTOMIYA
Bodyguard & General Affairs
A cheerful girl who is in love with Shizumasa-sama. Former juvenile delinquent. Adopted into the Otomiya family in fourth grade.

MAGURI TSUJIMIYA
Vice President
In love with the Emperor.

POSTMAN ↔ **MAORA**
The Same Person!!

He appears in the most unexpected places.

Planning Events & Accounting
Childhood friend of Maguri.

USHIO AMAMIYA
Clerk
Haine's friend. Haine is dearer to her than anyone.

THE GENTLEMEN'S ALLIANCE CROSS

Haine Otomiya is a former juvenile delinquent who attends Imperial Academy. One day, she is appointed the rank of "Platinum" as Emperor ShizumasaTogu's fake girlfriend in order to ward off the other girls. Now having found out that there are two Emperors, Haine's heart sways between Shizumasa and Takanari.

The members of the student council performed *Cinderella* for the graduating students, and Haine tried to keep her distance from Takanari. Witnessing this, the Postman revealed who he really is—Maora! Maora then said he would run to become the new Emperor so Haine will become his!

While Takanari considered what was best for the academy during the election, Maora tried to cheat by rigging the votes. Haine found out what Maora was up to and challenged him to a duel! Realizing that Haine was truly worried about him, Maora had a change of heart...

Takanari returns to the position of Emperor, and finally, the student council is back to its usual self again...

STORY THUS FAR

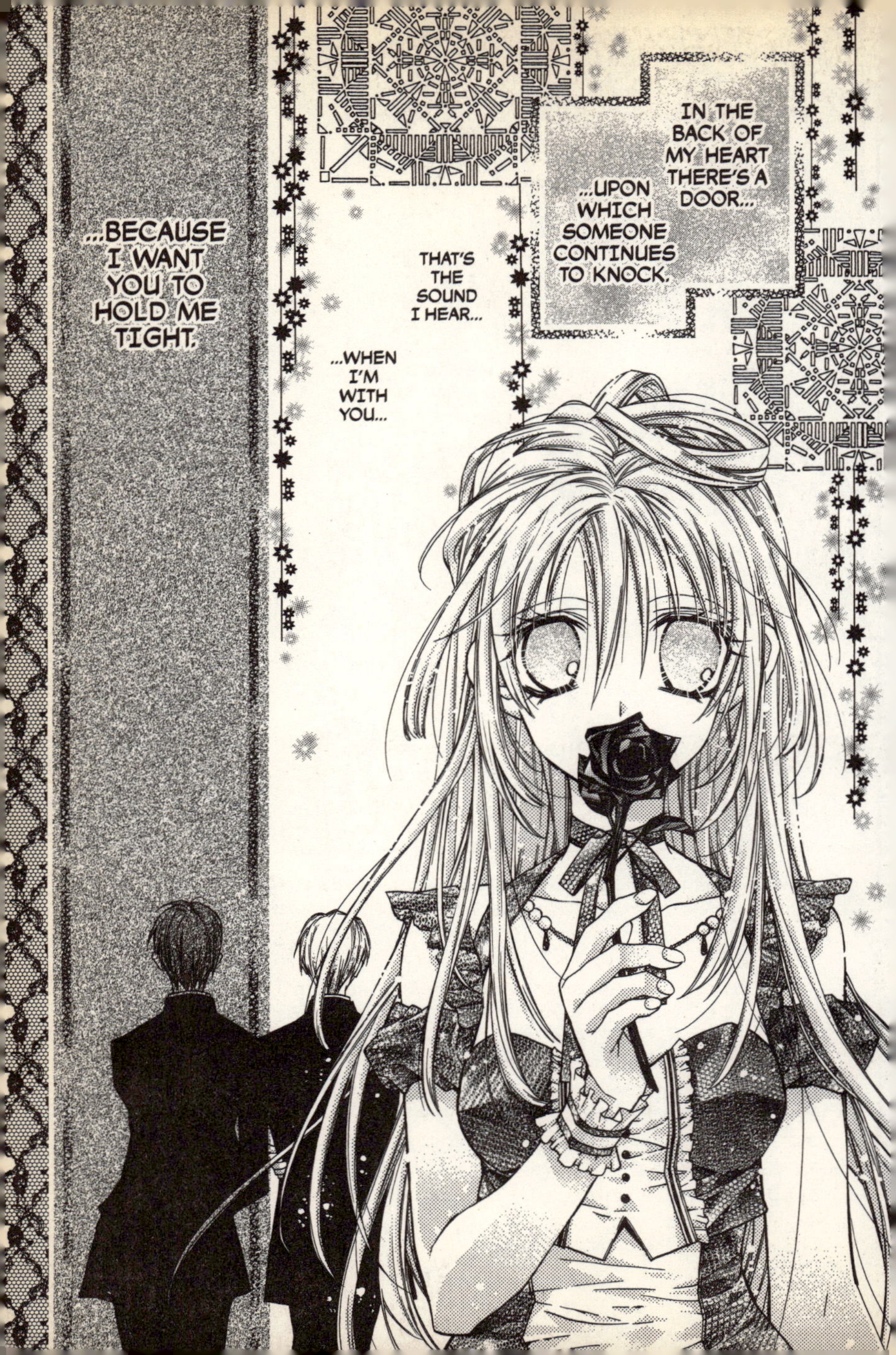
IN THE BACK OF MY HEART THERE'S A DOOR...
...UPON WHICH SOMEONE CONTINUES TO KNOCK.
THAT'S THE SOUND I HEAR...
...WHEN I'M WITH YOU...
...BECAUSE I WANT YOU TO HOLD ME TIGHT.

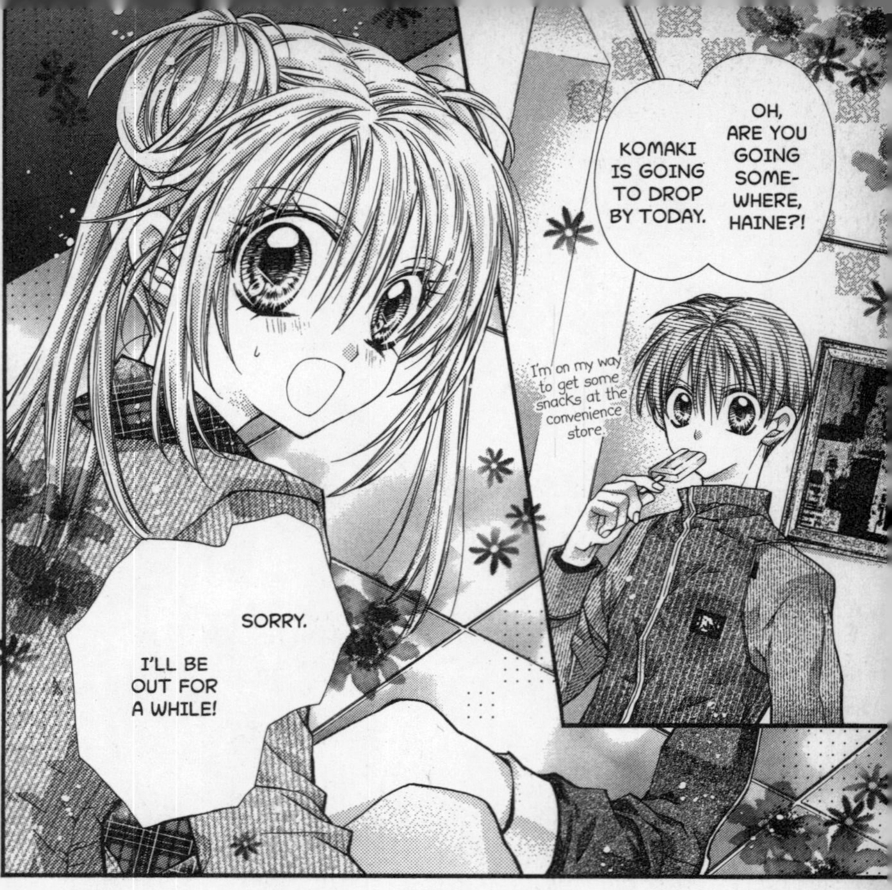
OH, ARE YOU GOING SOME-WHERE, HAINE?!
KOMAKI IS GOING TO DROP BY TODAY.
I'm on my way to get some snacks at the convenience store.
SORRY.
I'LL BE OUT FOR A WHILE!

Chapter 28: The Rush of My Heartbeat: Cherry Blossom Gateway

Lead-in My voice and heart are like two opposing mirrors...

This is a one-shot, which is rare for *The Gentleman's Alliance †*. I wrote it because I wanted to draw the Togu mansion.

To differentiate between Shizumasa and Takanari... Well, I try to make Shizumasa look slightly younger, so I draw his eyes larger. (But when I hurry, I end up drawing Takanari's eyes pretty large too...)

This is one of those chapters where you see Hainekko agonizing over her worries, so I tried drawing her in a mini form in those scenes so that the drawings don't all look the same.

Actually, the bonus story about Kusame and Komaki that was included in volume 5 takes place a little after this chapter, so Kusame and Komaki are not going out yet at this point.

Kusame goes down to the convenience store claiming to get snacks while eating an ice cream. And even after Komaki arrives, he continues to play computer games. I really like the fact that Kusame is an average middle schooler. (laugh)

And his favorite drink is Fanta Grape!!

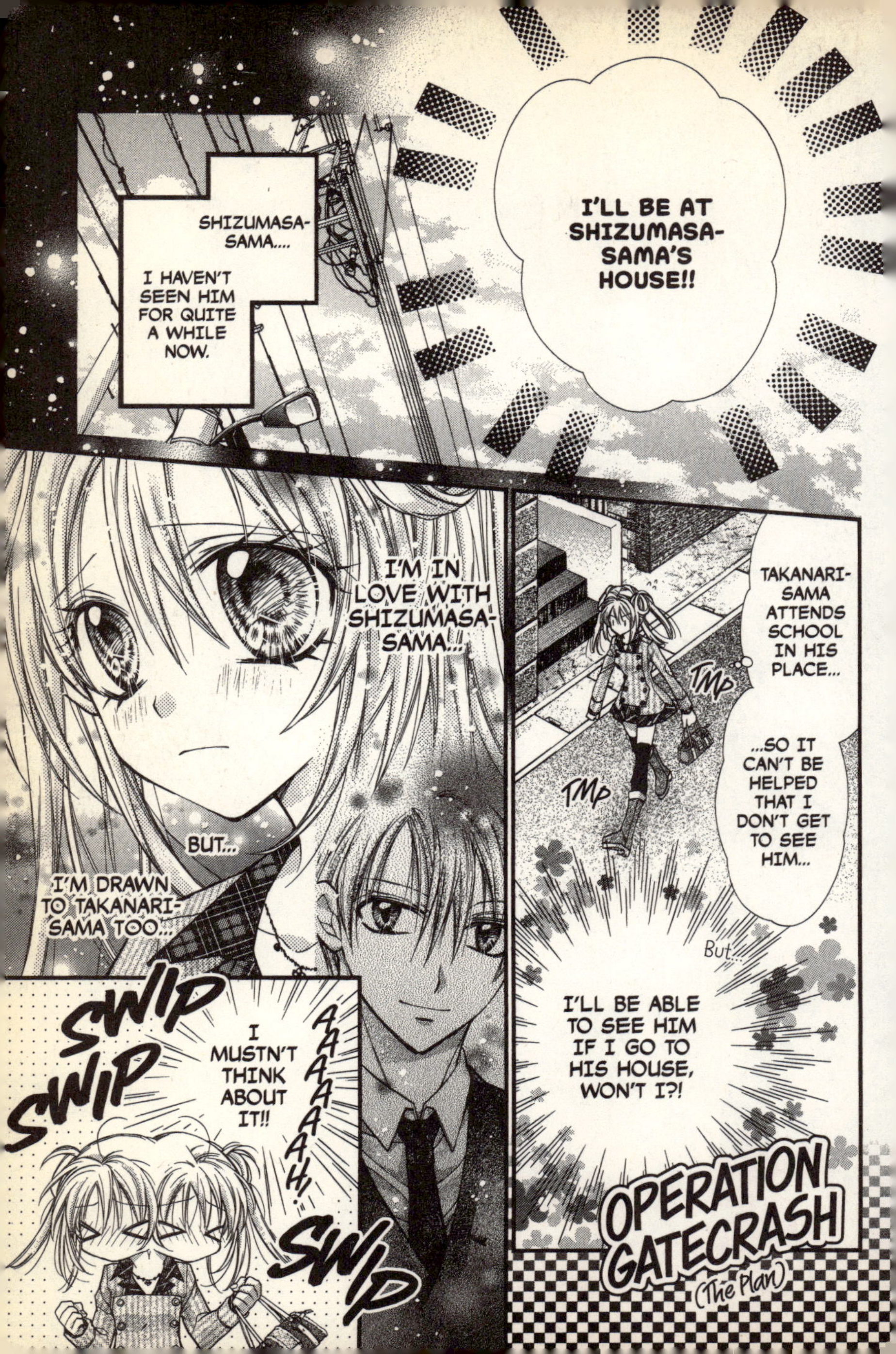
I'LL BE AT SHIZUMASA-SAMA'S HOUSE!!
SHIZUMASA-SAMA....
I HAVEN'T SEEN HIM FOR QUITE A WHILE NOW.
TAKANARI-SAMA ATTENDS SCHOOL IN HIS PLACE...
TMP
TMP
...SO IT CAN'T BE HELPED THAT I DON'T GET TO SEE HIM...
But...
I'LL BE ABLE TO SEE HIM IF I GO TO HIS HOUSE, WON'T I?!
OPERATION GATECRASH
(The Plan)
I'M IN LOVE WITH SHIZUMASA-SAMA...
BUT...
I'M DRAWN TO TAKANARI-SAMA TOO...
SWIP
SWIP
I MUSTN'T THINK ABOUT IT!!
AAAAAAAH!!
SWIP

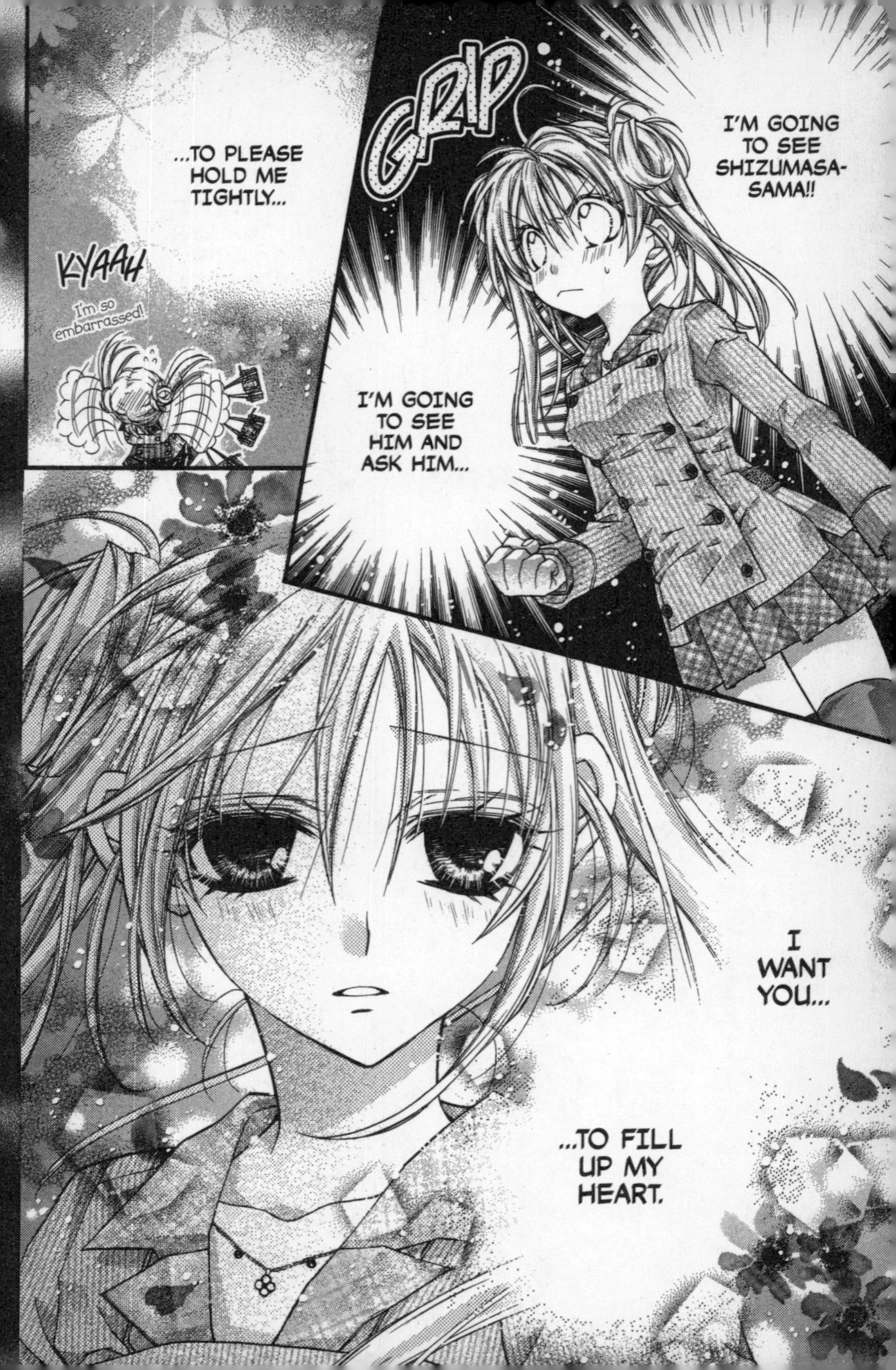
I'M GOING TO SEE SHIZUMASA-SAMA!!
GRIP
I'M GOING TO SEE HIM AND ASK HIM...
...TO PLEASE HOLD ME TIGHTLY...
KYAAH
I'm so embarrassed!
I WANT YOU...
...TO FILL UP MY HEART.

Hello.

Tanemura here. Here is volume 7 of the *The Gentleman's Alliance †*.

Hm, this is something a little personal. My longest manga series were *Jeanne* and *Full Moon*, but now *Gentlemen's Alliance* is scheduled to be longer than those two... (Actually, it's already longer.)

And that is all thanks to all you fans who have supported this series, and to the work of all the staff and members of the editorial office.

I'm going to continue working hard on the series, so please support me along with Haine and the others. ♥

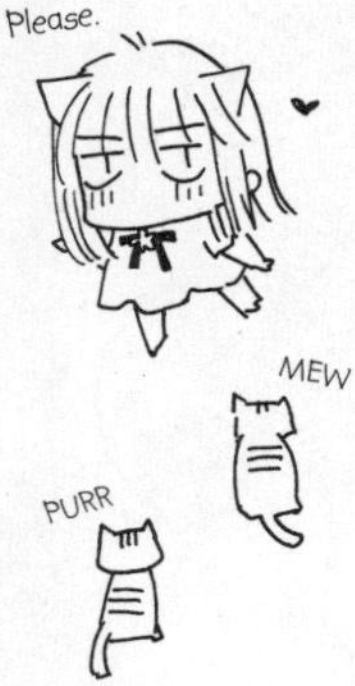
Please.
MEW
PURR

Now back to volume 7... ♪

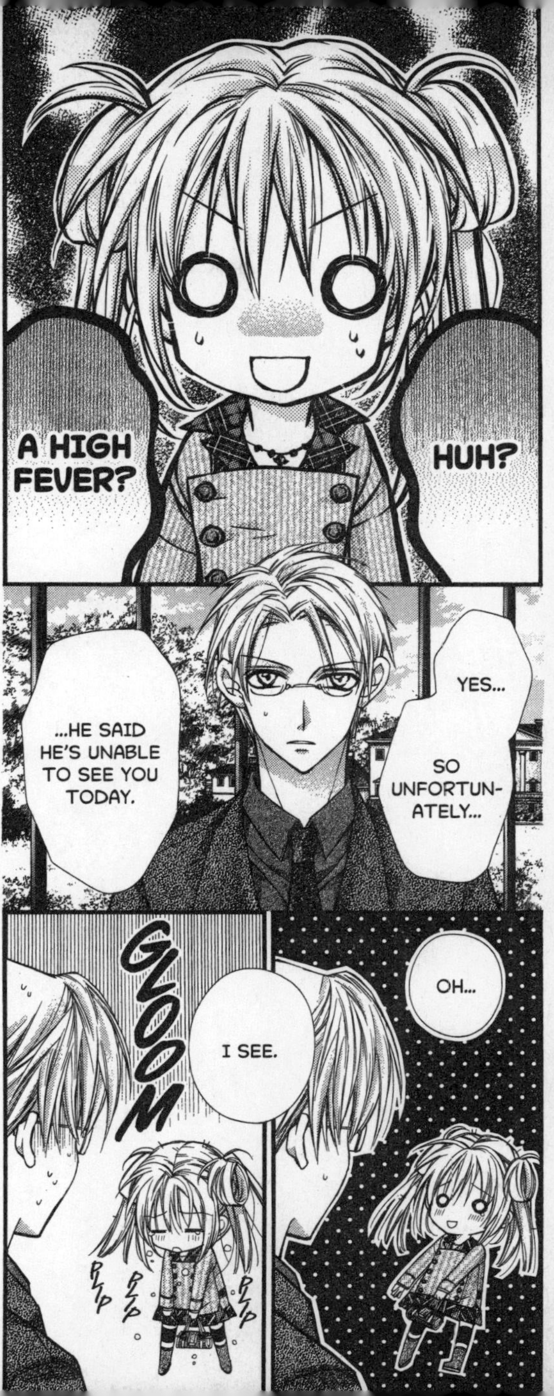
HUH?
A HIGH FEVER?
YES... SO UNFORTUNATELY...
...HE SAID HE'S UNABLE TO SEE YOU TODAY.
OH...
I SEE.
GLOOM
PLIP PLIP PLIP

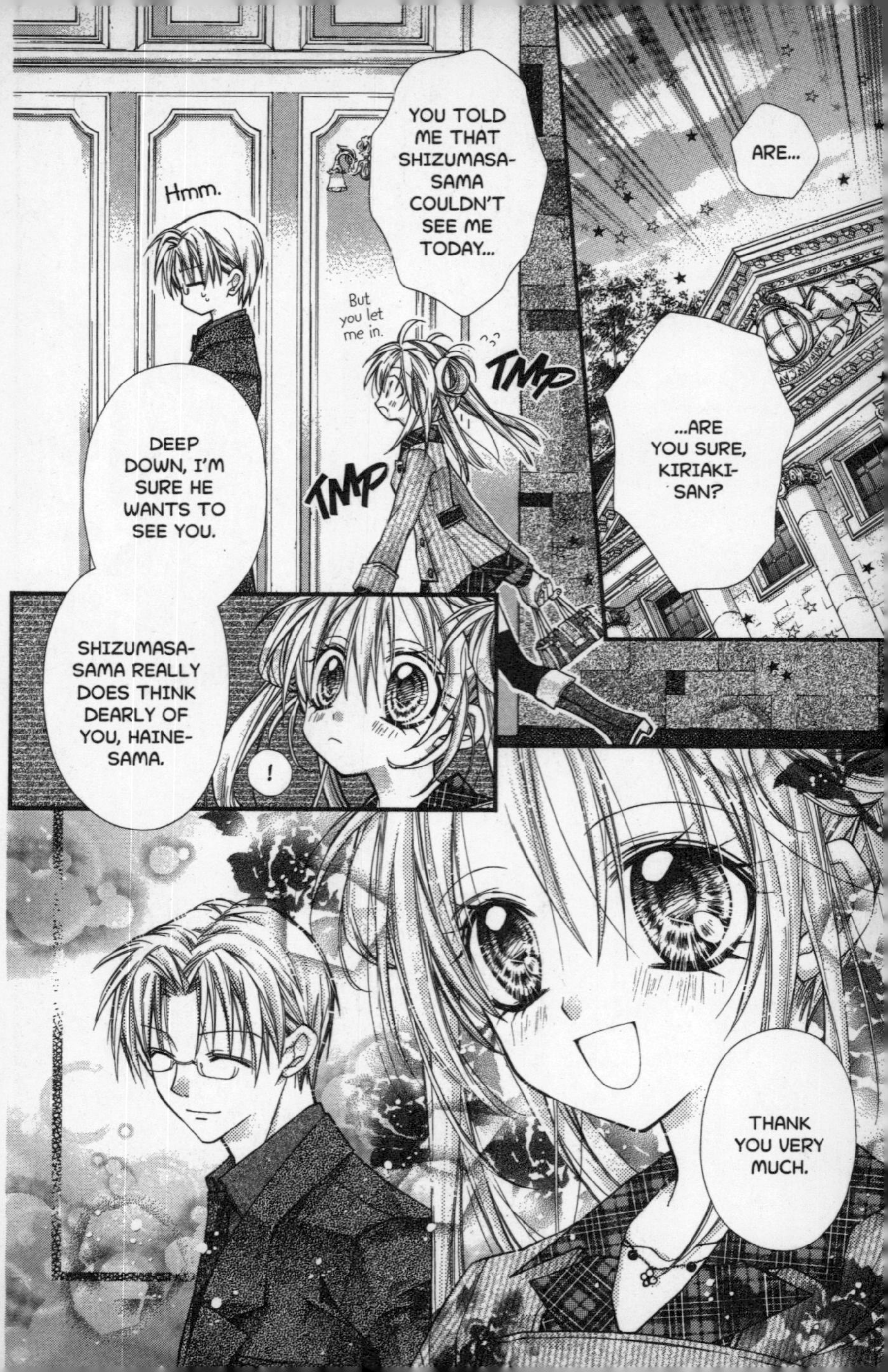
ARE...
...ARE YOU SURE, KIRIAKI-SAN?
YOU TOLD ME THAT SHIZUMASA-SAMA COULDN'T SEE ME TODAY...
But you let me in.
TMP
TMP
Hmm.
DEEP DOWN, I'M SURE HE WANTS TO SEE YOU.
SHIZUMASA-SAMA REALLY DOES THINK DEARLY OF YOU, HAINE-SAMA.
!
THANK YOU VERY MUCH.

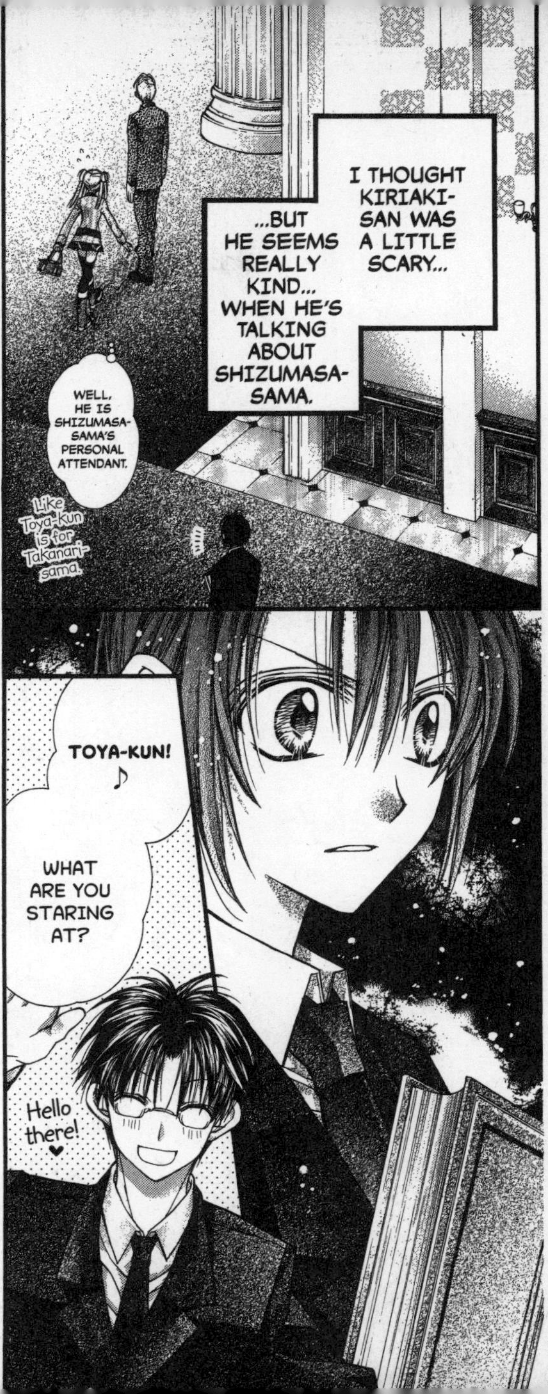
I THOUGHT KIRIAKI-SAN WAS A LITTLE SCARY...
...BUT HE SEEMS REALLY KIND... WHEN HE'S TALKING ABOUT SHIZUMASA-SAMA.
WELL, HE IS SHIZUMASA-SAMA'S PERSONAL ATTENDANT.
Like Toya-kun is for Takanari-sama.
TOYA-KUN! ♪
WHAT ARE YOU STARING AT?
Hello there! ❤

Animal Crossing: Wild World

This is a game for Nintendo DS, and though I happen to be a little lazy, I have been able to drop by the village every day.

By the way, the village is called "Tane Village."

My favorite friend is Blaire-chan (squirrel). ❤

I have fun creating Haine-chan's school uniform and whatnot in the game.

It's a lot of fun to see the seasonal changes like the cherry blossom trees blooming and the snow falling.

By the way, my room is in the classical theme, and my second floor has black and white furniture with a wallpaper night scene to give it a urbanized look.

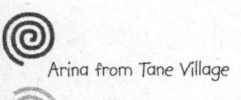

Arina from Tane Village

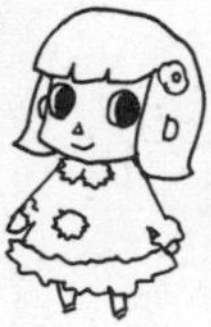

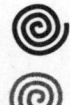

A young girl who like to change shoes. I like the boots. ❤

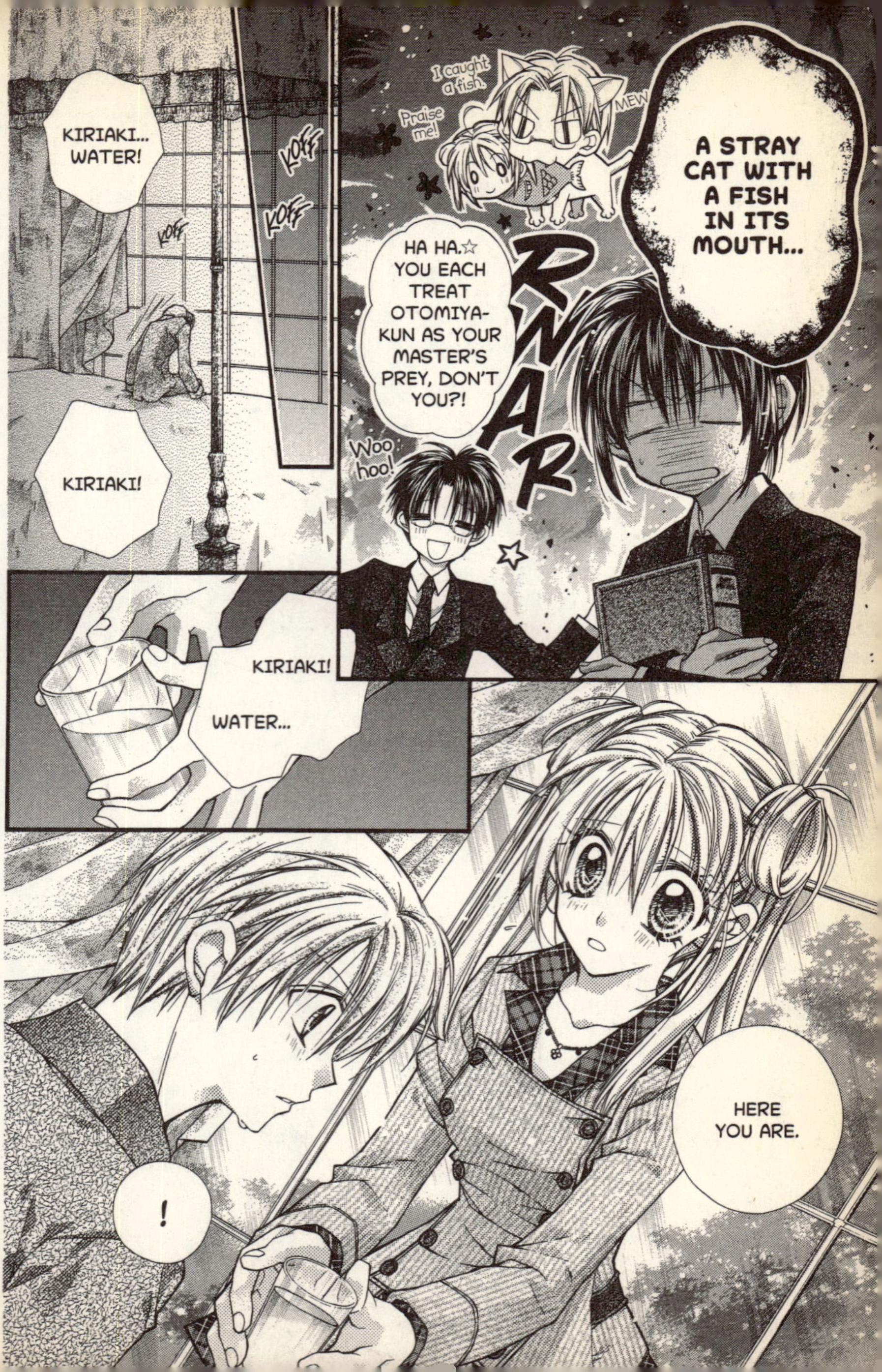
A STRAY CAT WITH A FISH IN ITS MOUTH...
I caught a fish.
MEW
Praise me!
HA HA.☆ YOU EACH TREAT OTOMIYA-KUN AS YOUR MASTER'S PREY, DON'T YOU?!
RNAR
Woo hoo!
KIRIAKI... WATER!
KOFF
KOFF
KOFF
KIRIAKI!
KIRIAKI!
WATER...
HERE YOU ARE.
!

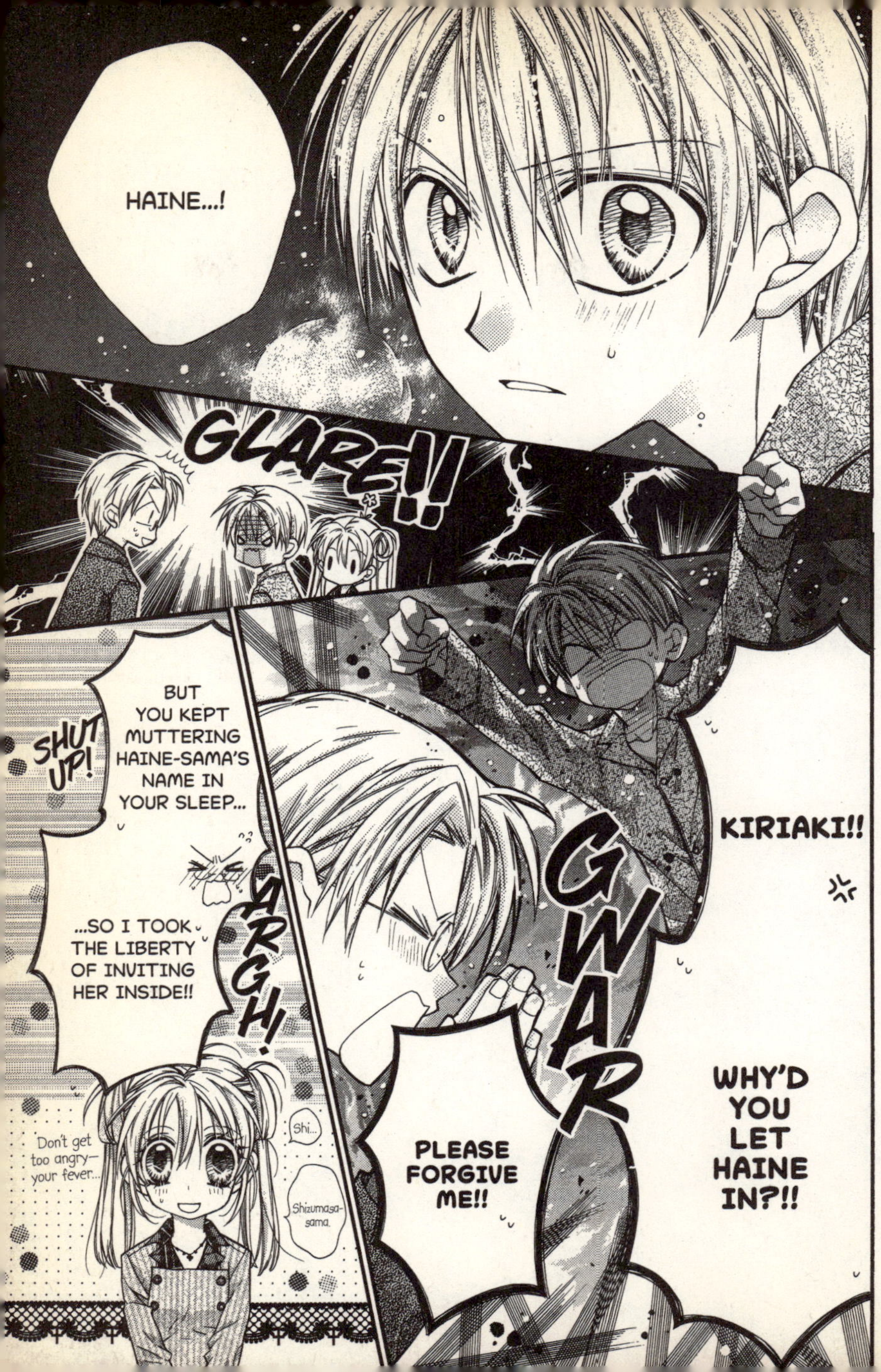
HAINE...!
GLARE!!
KIRIAKI!!
WHY'D YOU LET HAINE IN?!!
GWAR
PLEASE FORGIVE ME!!
BUT YOU KEPT MUTTERING HAINE-SAMA'S NAME IN YOUR SLEEP...
SHUT UP!
...SO I TOOK THE LIBERTY OF INVITING HER INSIDE!!
ARGH!
Shi...
Shizumasa-sama.
Don't get too angry—your fever...

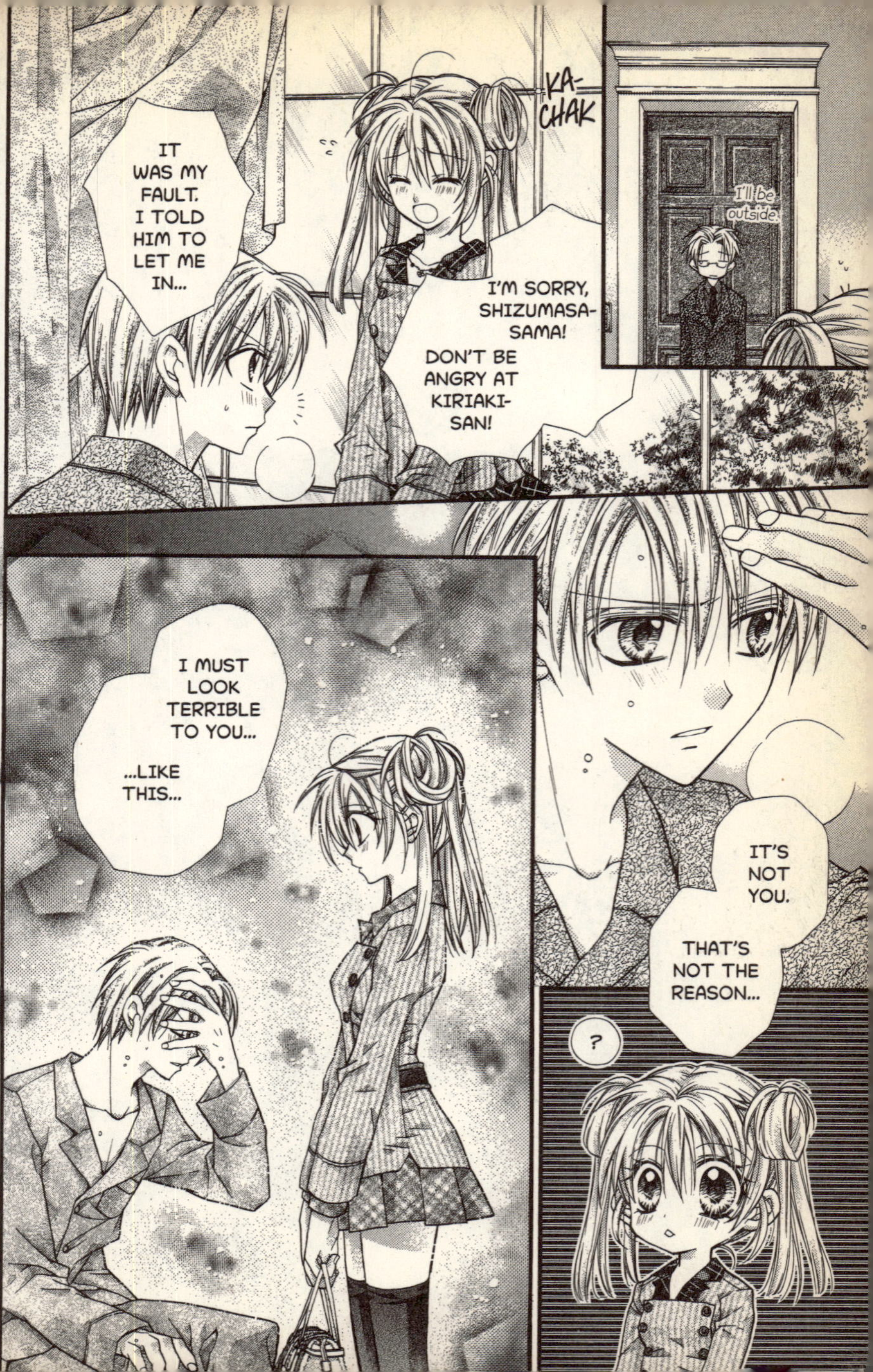
KA-CHAK
I'll be outside.
I'M SORRY, SHIZUMASA-SAMA!
DON'T BE ANGRY AT KIRIAKI-SAN!
IT WAS MY FAULT. I TOLD HIM TO LET ME IN...
IT'S NOT YOU.
THAT'S NOT THE REASON...
?
I MUST LOOK TERRIBLE TO YOU...
...LIKE THIS...

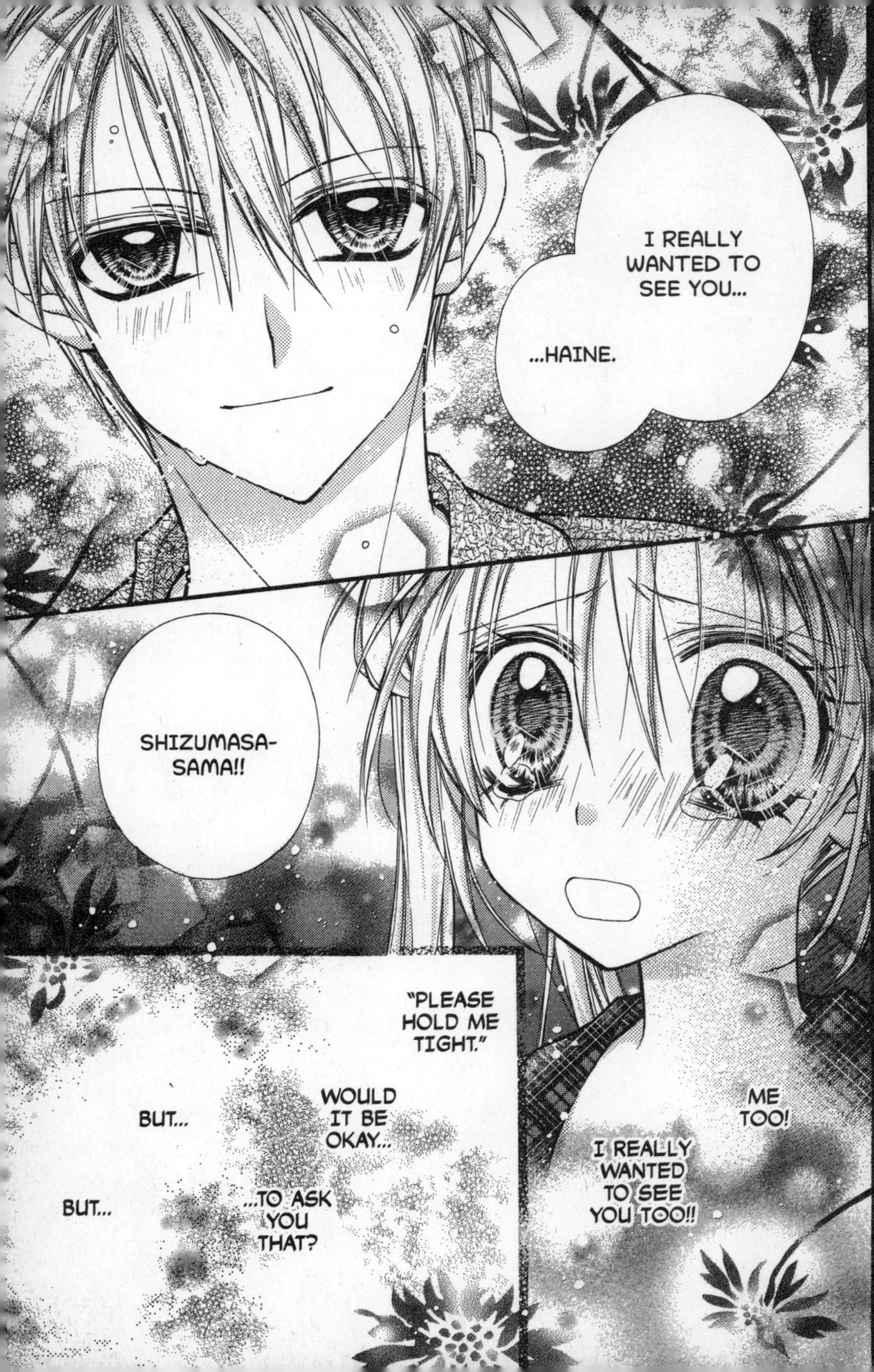
I REALLY WANTED TO SEE YOU...
...HAINE.
SHIZUMASA-SAMA!!
ME TOO!
I REALLY WANTED TO SEE YOU TOO!!
"PLEASE HOLD ME TIGHT."
WOULD IT BE OKAY...
BUT...
...TO ASK YOU THAT?
BUT...

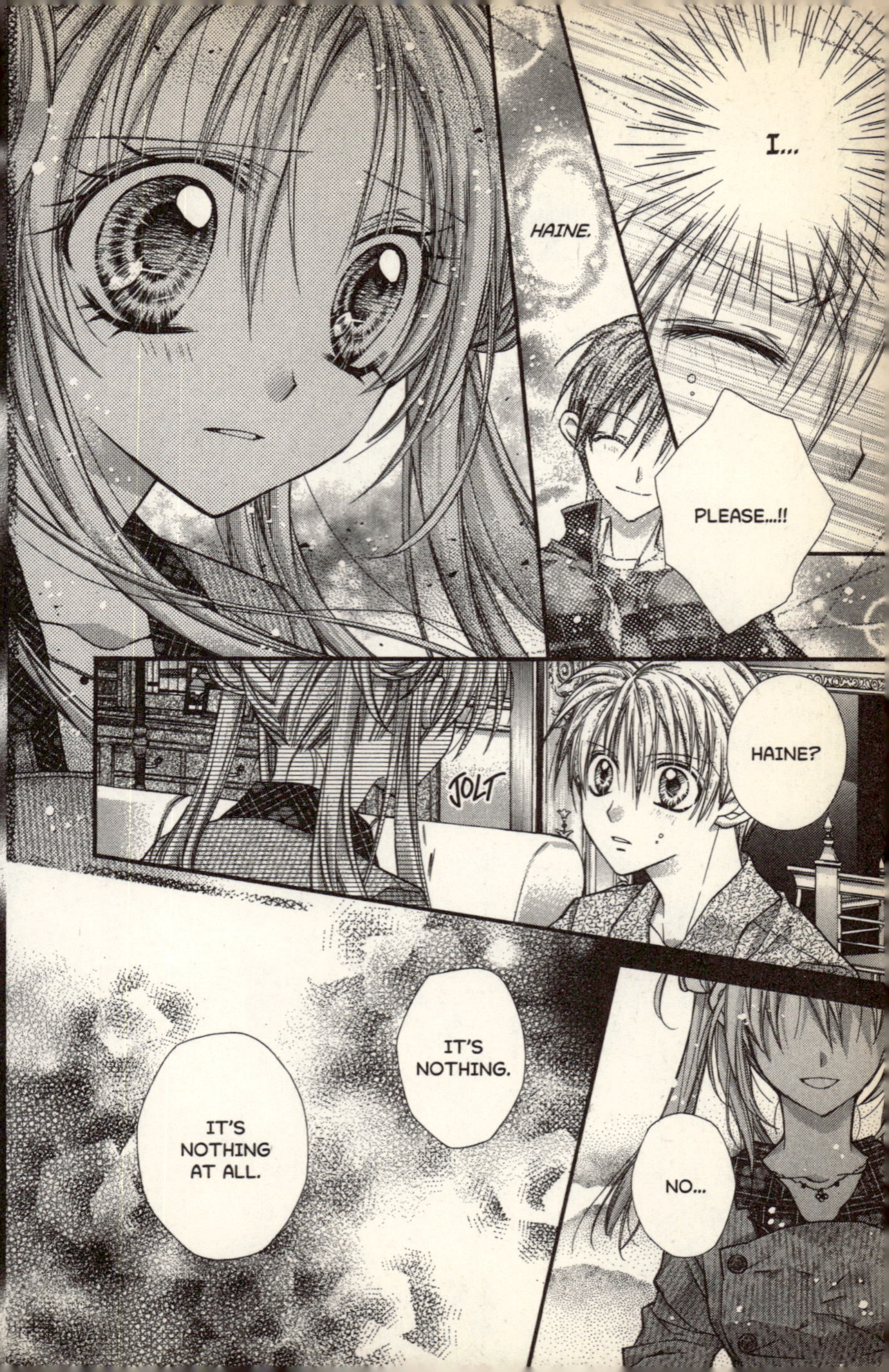
I...
HAINE.
PLEASE...!!
HAINE?
JOLT
NO...
IT'S NOTHING.
IT'S NOTHING AT ALL.

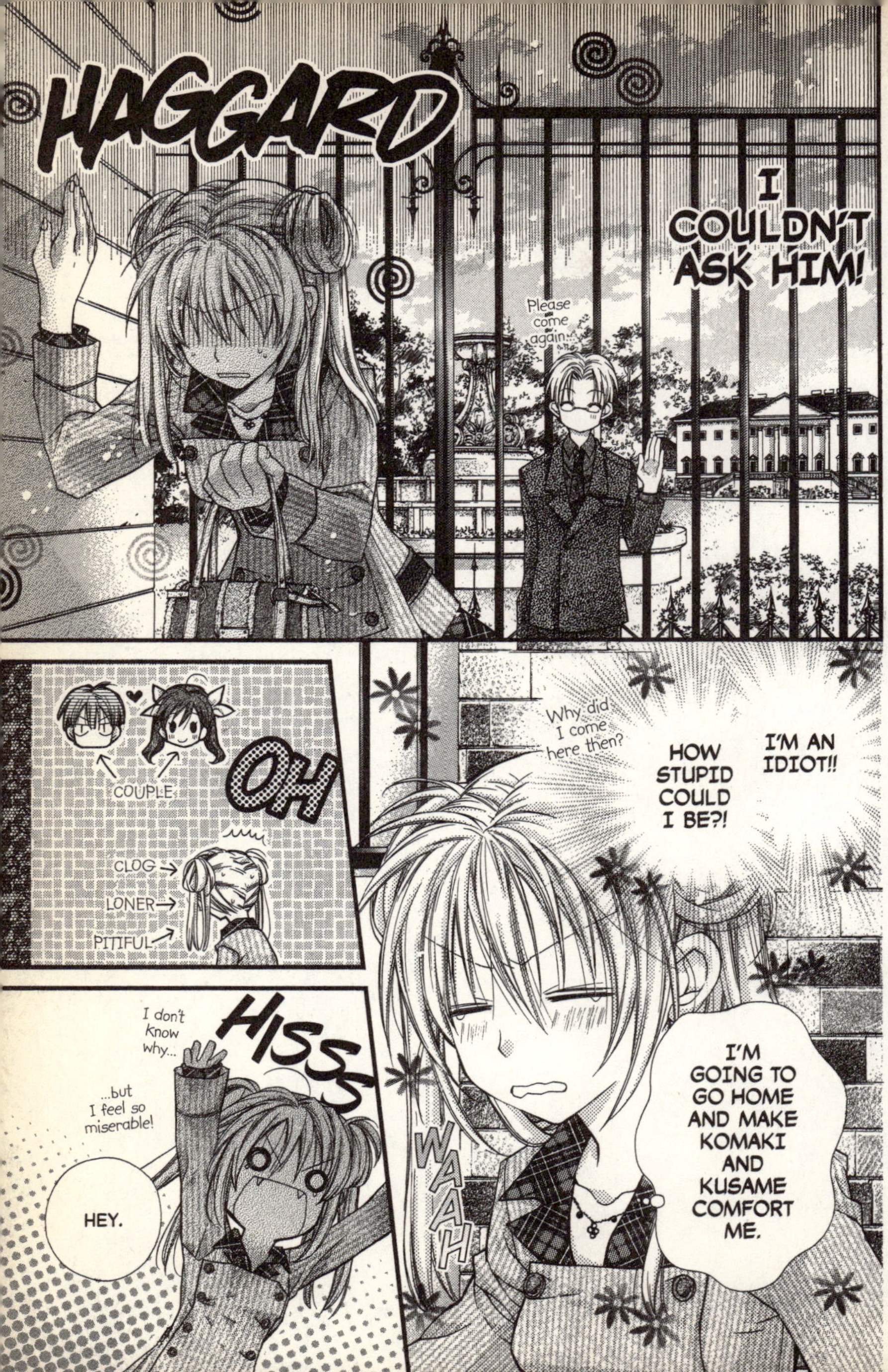
I COULDN'T ASK HIM!
Please come again...
HAGGARD
I'M AN IDIOT!!
HOW STUPID COULD I BE?!
Why did I come here then?
I'M GOING TO GO HOME AND MAKE KOMAKI AND KUSAME COMFORT ME.
WAAH
OH
COUPLE
CLOG
LONER
PITIFUL
HISS
I don't know why...
...but I feel so miserable!
HEY.

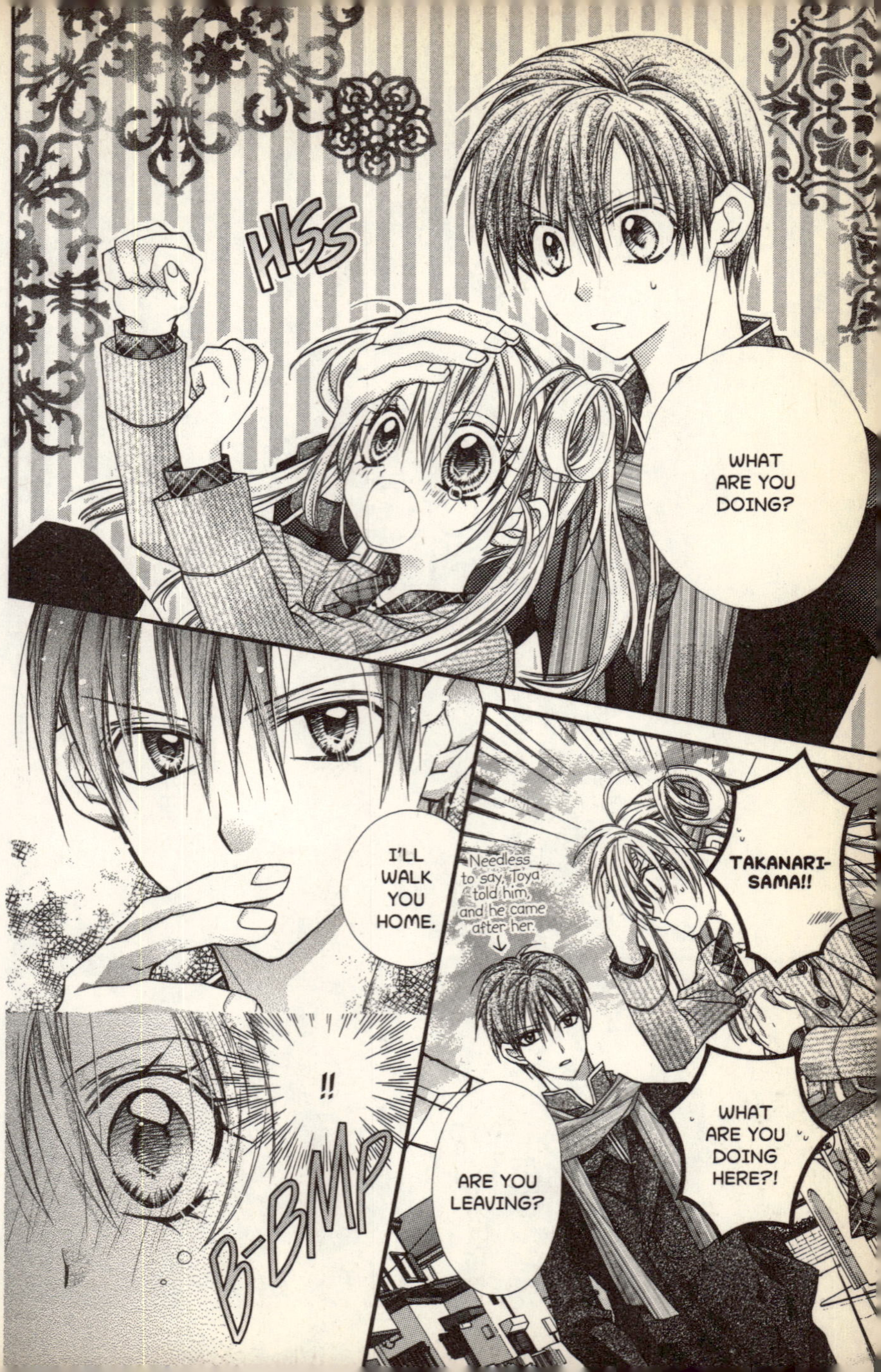
HISS
WHAT ARE YOU DOING?
TAKANARI-SAMA!!
Needless to say, Toya told him, and he came after her.
WHAT ARE YOU DOING HERE?!
ARE YOU LEAVING?
I'LL WALK YOU HOME.
!!
B-BMP

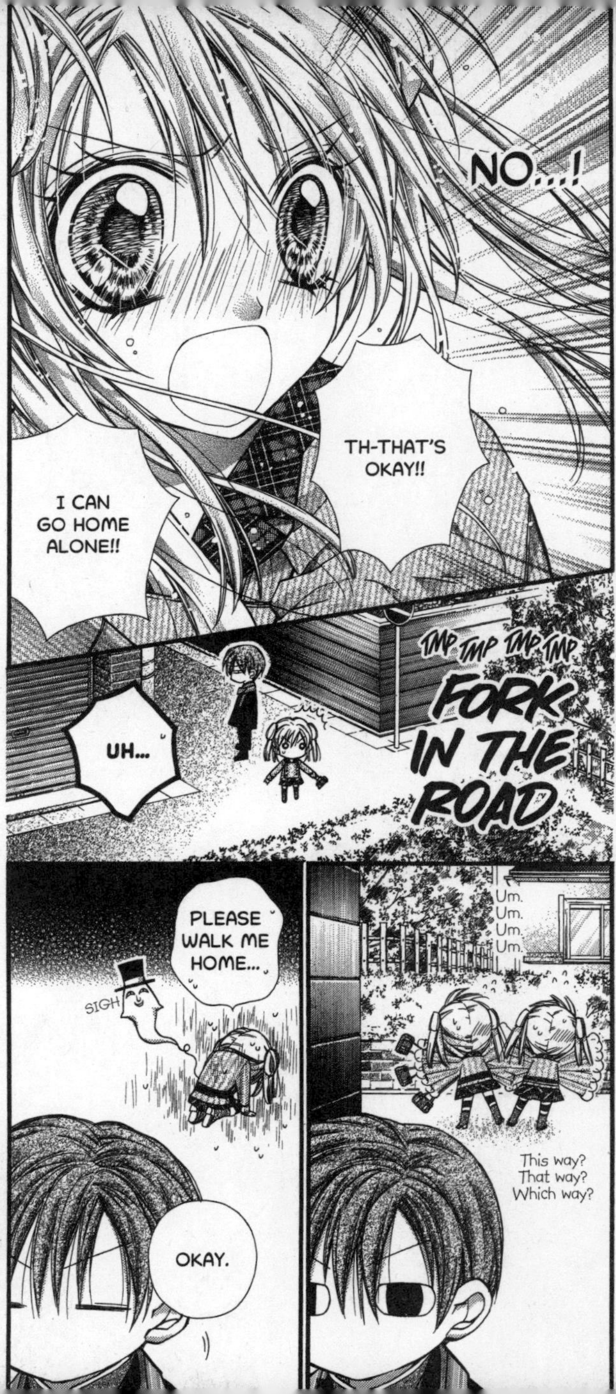
NO...!
TH-THAT'S OKAY!!
I CAN GO HOME ALONE!!
TMP TMP TMP TMP
FORK IN THE ROAD
UH...
Um. Um. Um. Um.
This way? That way? Which way?
PLEASE WALK ME HOME...
SIGH
OKAY.
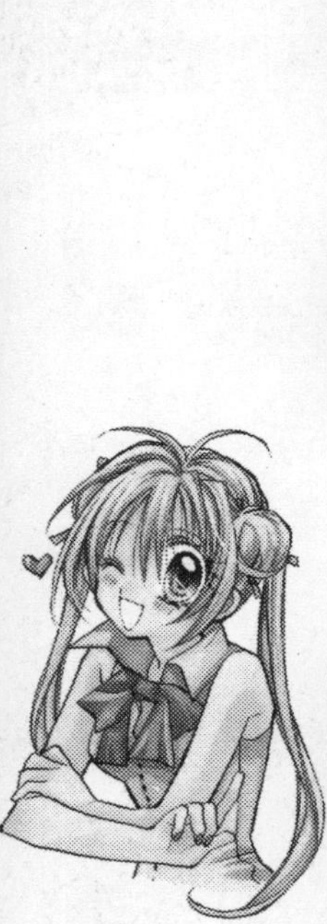

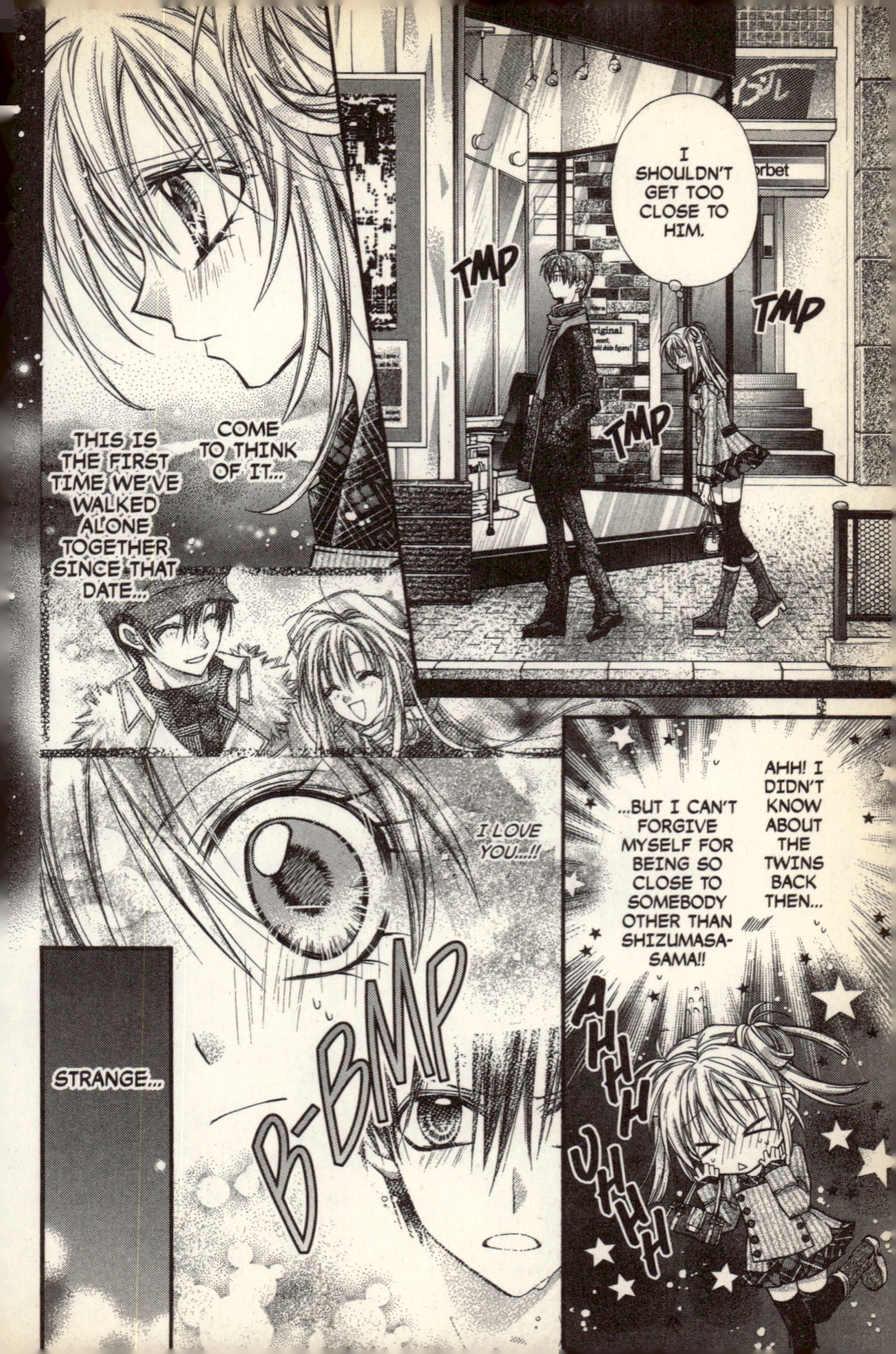
I SHOULDN'T GET TOO CLOSE TO HIM.
TMP
TMP
TMP
COME TO THINK OF IT...
THIS IS THE FIRST TIME WE'VE WALKED ALONE TOGETHER SINCE THAT DATE...
AHH! I DIDN'T KNOW ABOUT THE TWINS BACK THEN...
...BUT I CAN'T FORGIVE MYSELF FOR BEING SO CLOSE TO SOMEBODY OTHER THAN SHIZUMASA-SAMA!!
AHHHHHH
I LOVE YOU...!!
B-BMP
STRANGE...

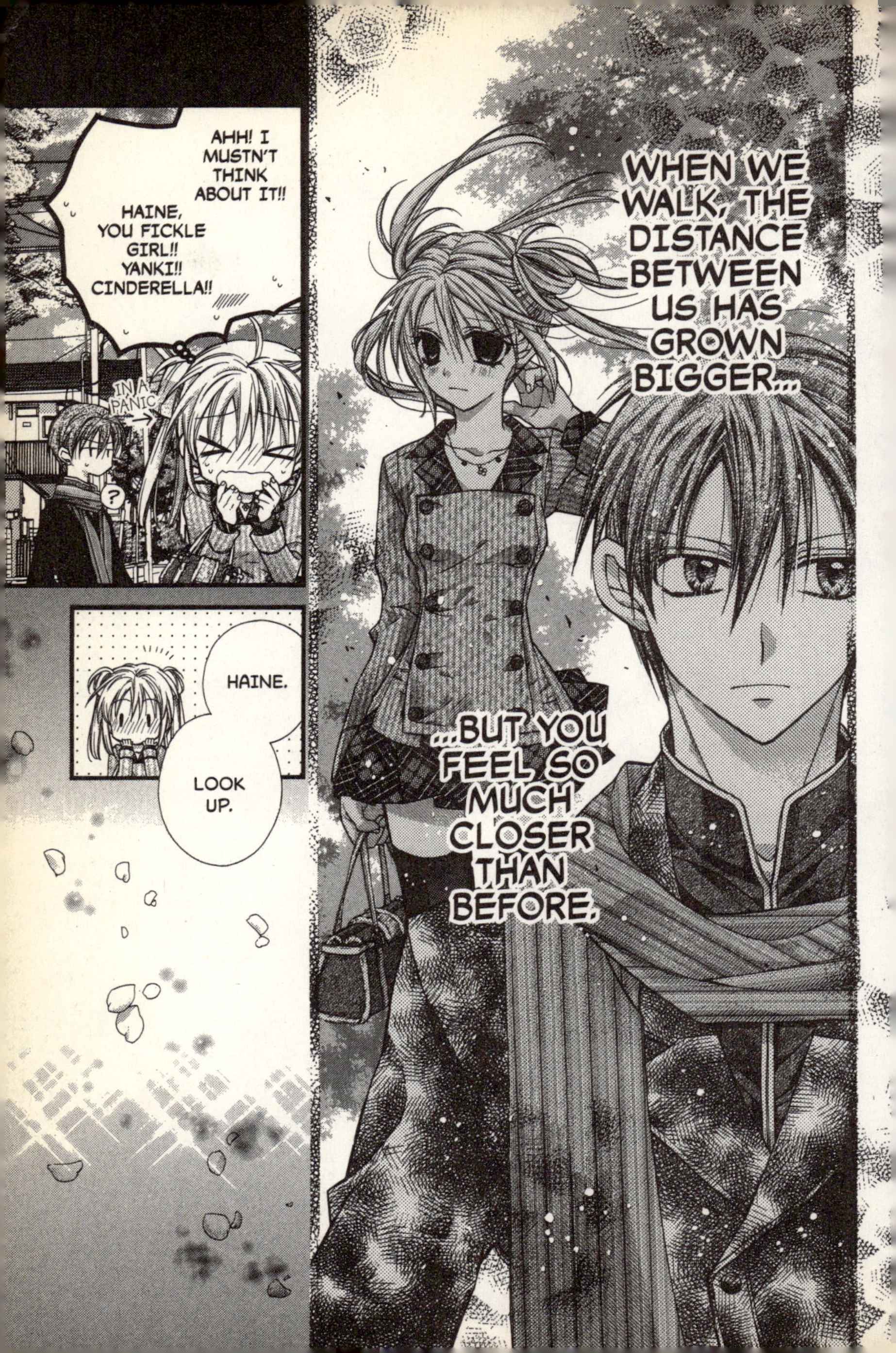
WHEN WE WALK, THE DISTANCE BETWEEN US HAS GROWN BIGGER...
...BUT YOU FEEL SO MUCH CLOSER THAN BEFORE.
AHH! I MUSTN'T THINK ABOUT IT!!
HAINE, YOU FICKLE GIRL!! YANKI!! CINDERELLA!!
IN A PANIC
?
HAINE.
LOOK UP.

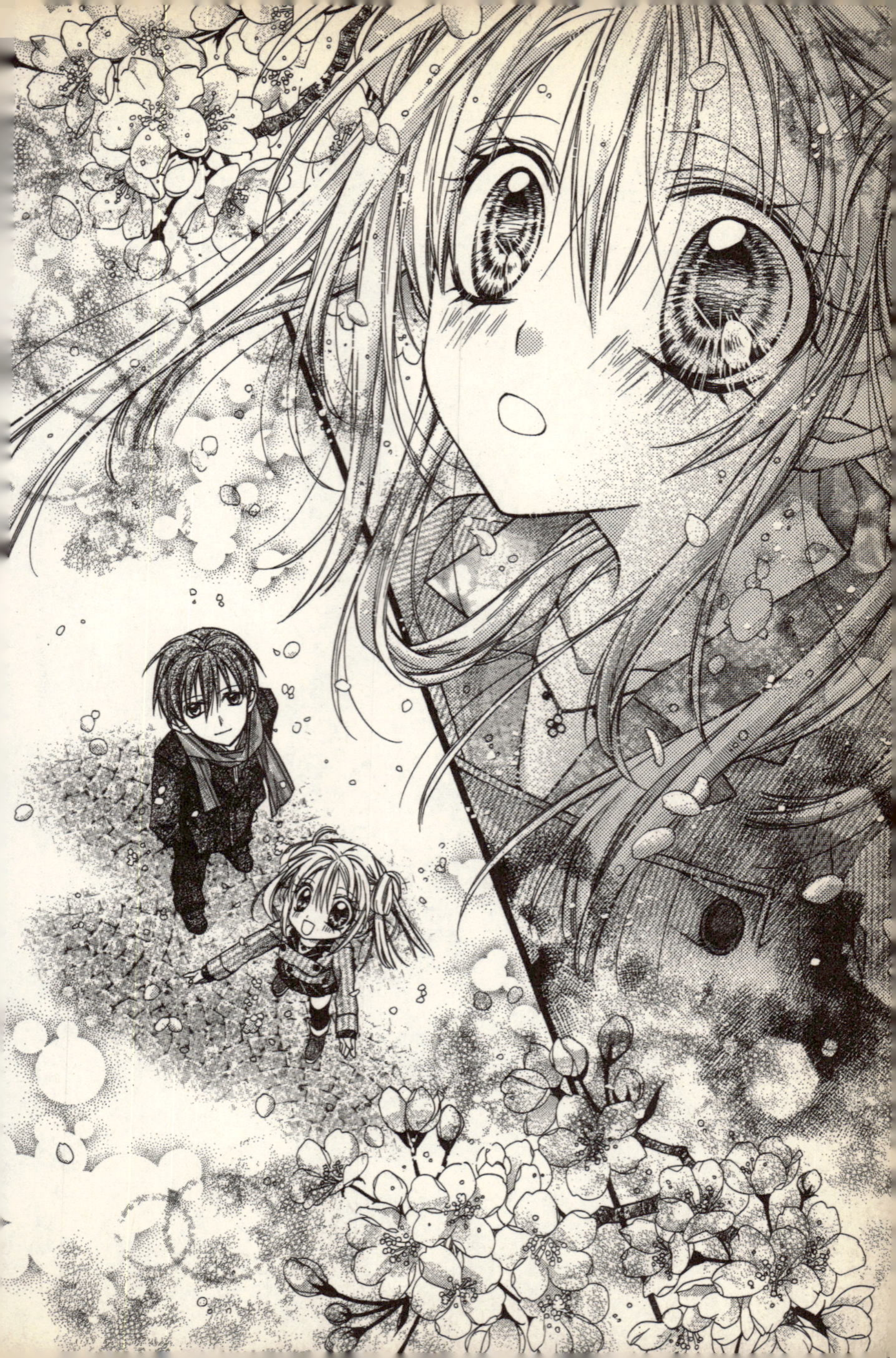

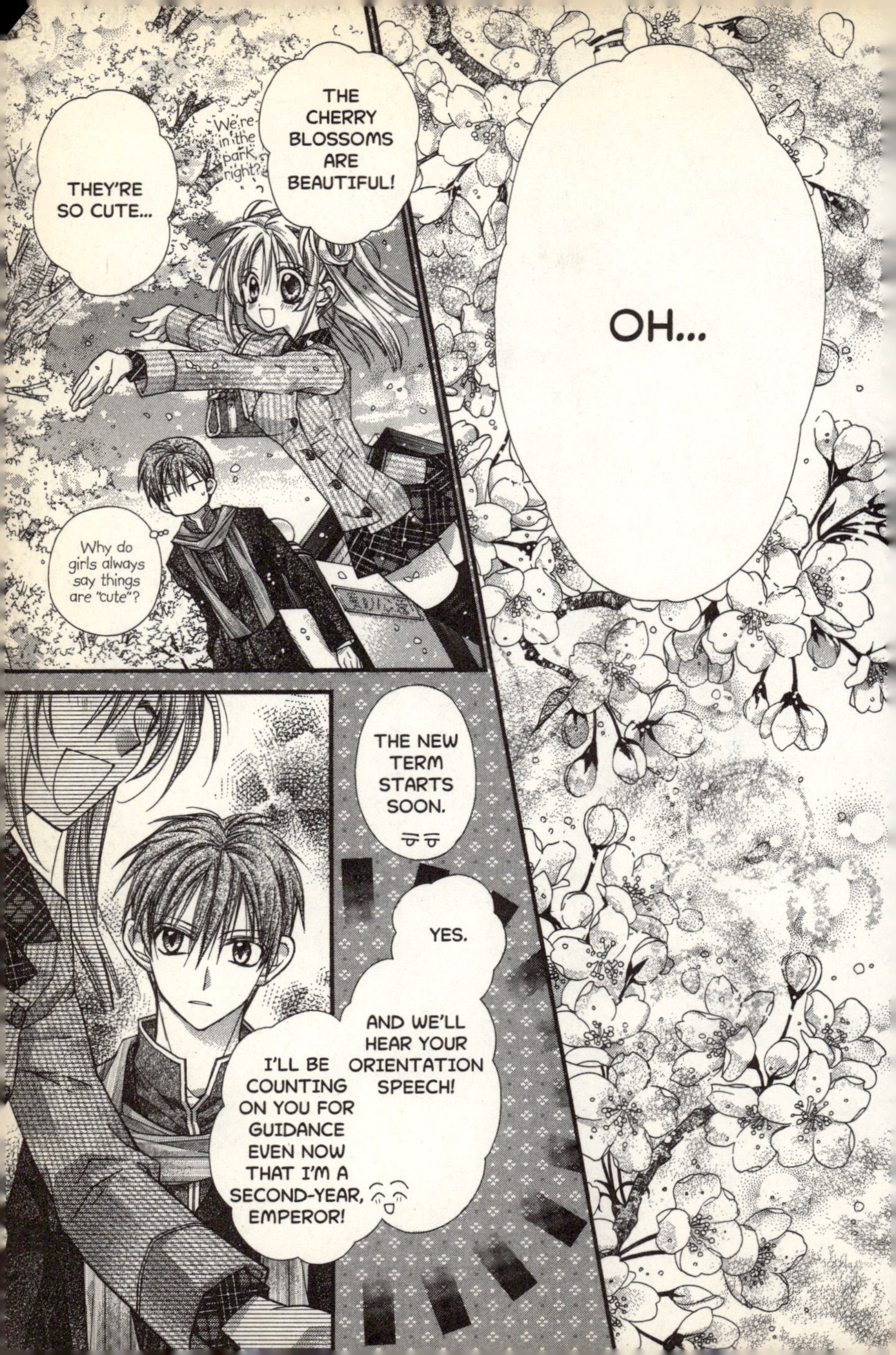
OH...
THE CHERRY BLOSSOMS ARE BEAUTIFUL!
We're in the park, right?
THEY'RE SO CUTE...
Why do girls always say things are "cute"?
THE NEW TERM STARTS SOON.
YES.
AND WE'LL HEAR YOUR ORIENTATION SPEECH!
I'LL BE COUNTING ON YOU FOR GUIDANCE EVEN NOW THAT I'M A SECOND-YEAR, EMPEROR!

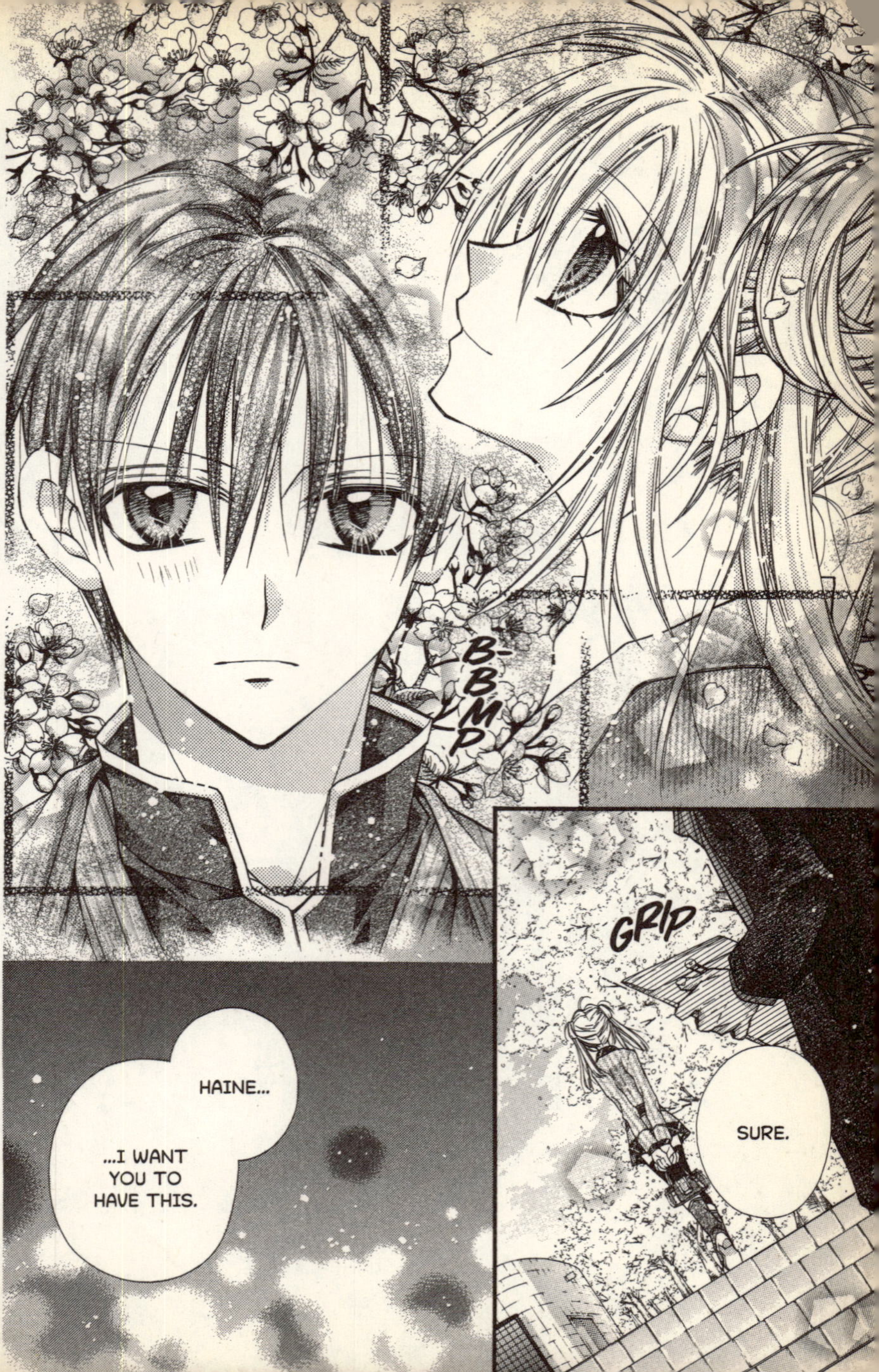
B-BMP
GRIP
SURE.
HAINE...
...I WANT YOU TO HAVE THIS.

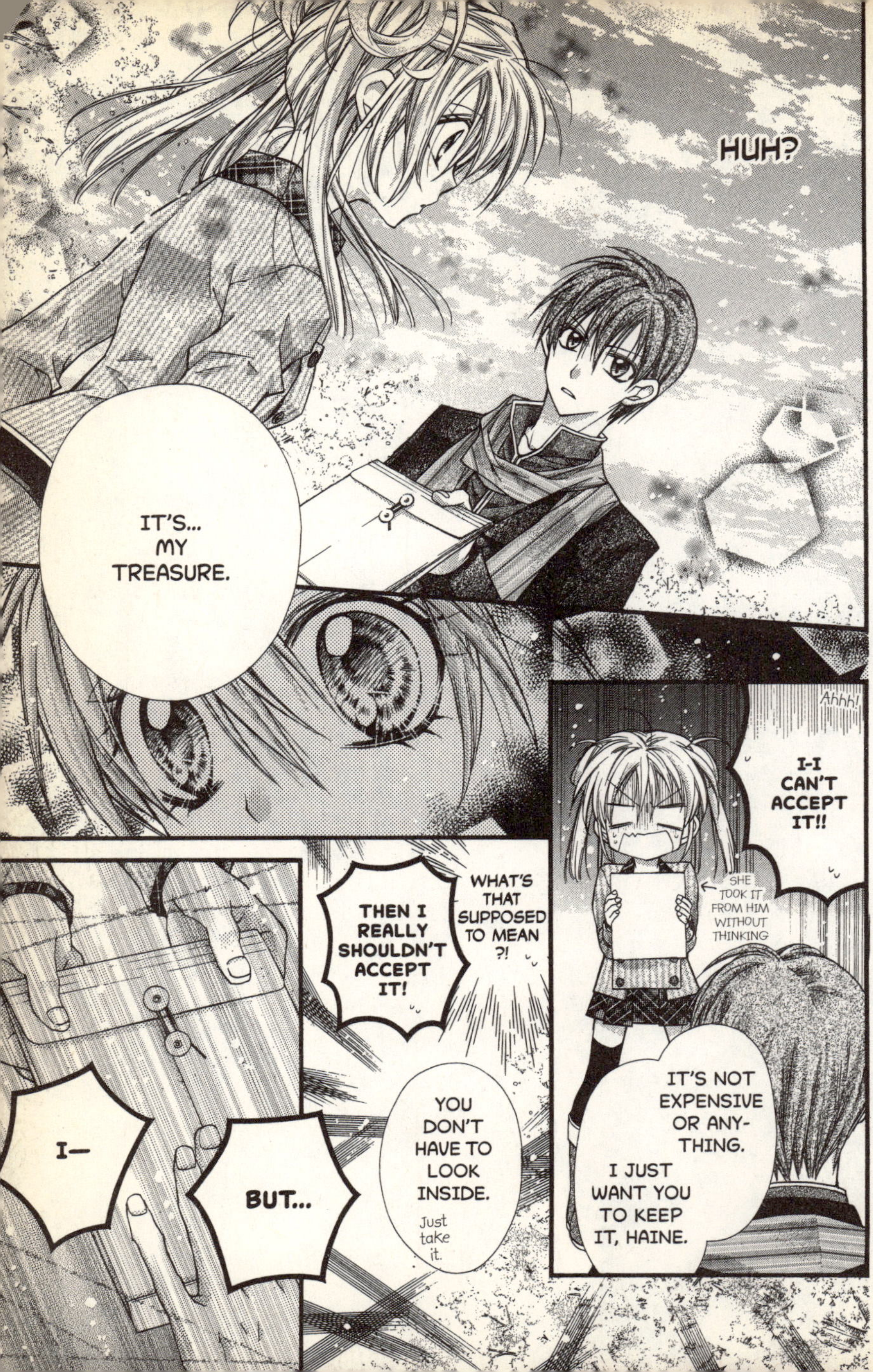
HUH?
IT'S... MY TREASURE.
Ahhh!
I-I CAN'T ACCEPT IT!!
SHE TOOK IT FROM HIM WITHOUT THINKING
IT'S NOT EXPENSIVE OR ANY-THING.
I JUST WANT YOU TO KEEP IT, HAINE.
WHAT'S THAT SUPPOSED TO MEAN ?!
THEN I REALLY SHOULDN'T ACCEPT IT!
YOU DON'T HAVE TO LOOK INSIDE.
Just take it.
BUT...
I—

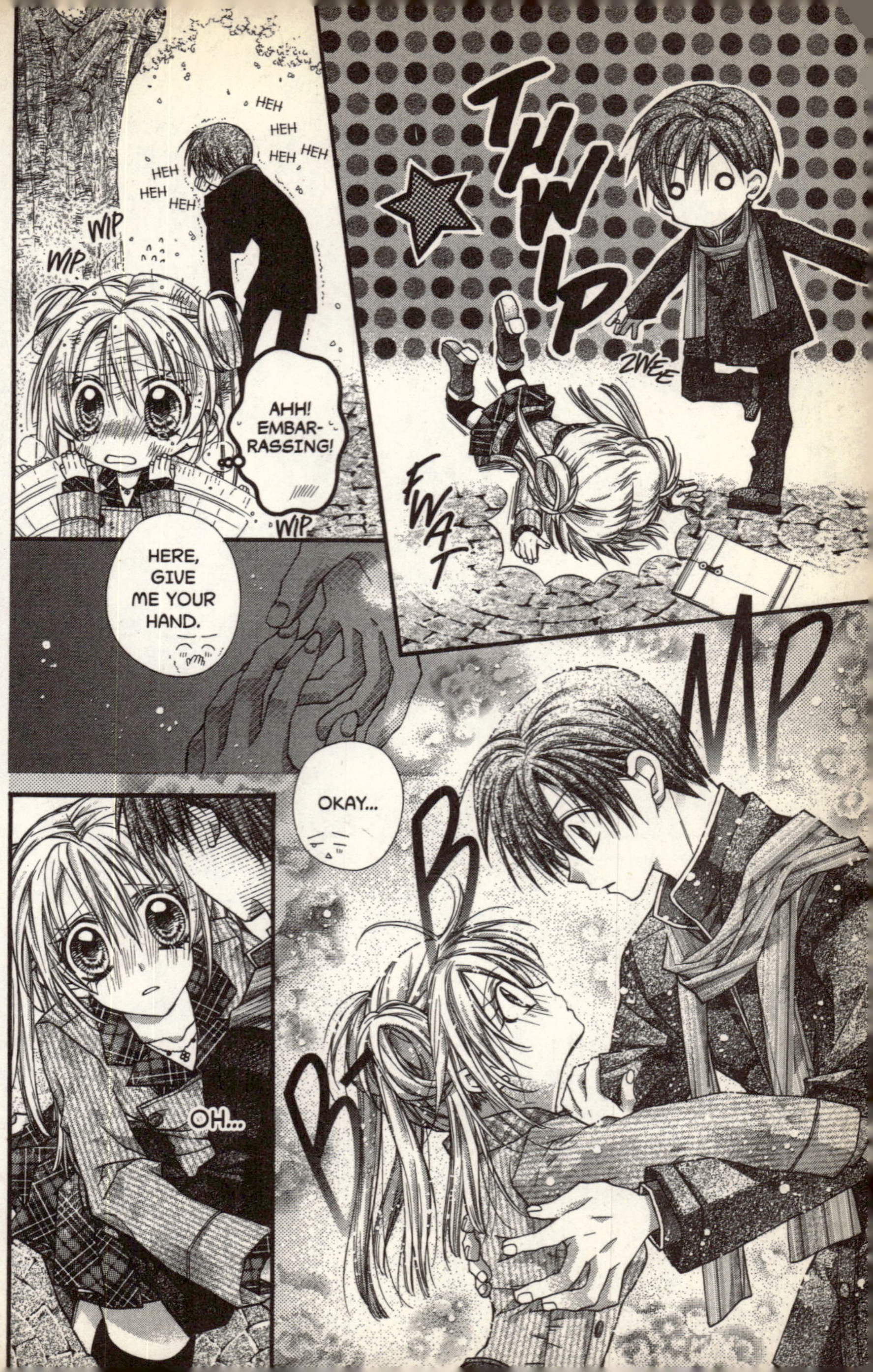
THWIP
ZWEE
FWAT
HEH
HEH
HEH
HEH
HEH
HEH
HEH
WIP
WIP
AHH! EMBARRASSING!
WIP
HERE, GIVE ME YOUR HAND.
OKAY...
B-
B
MP
OH...

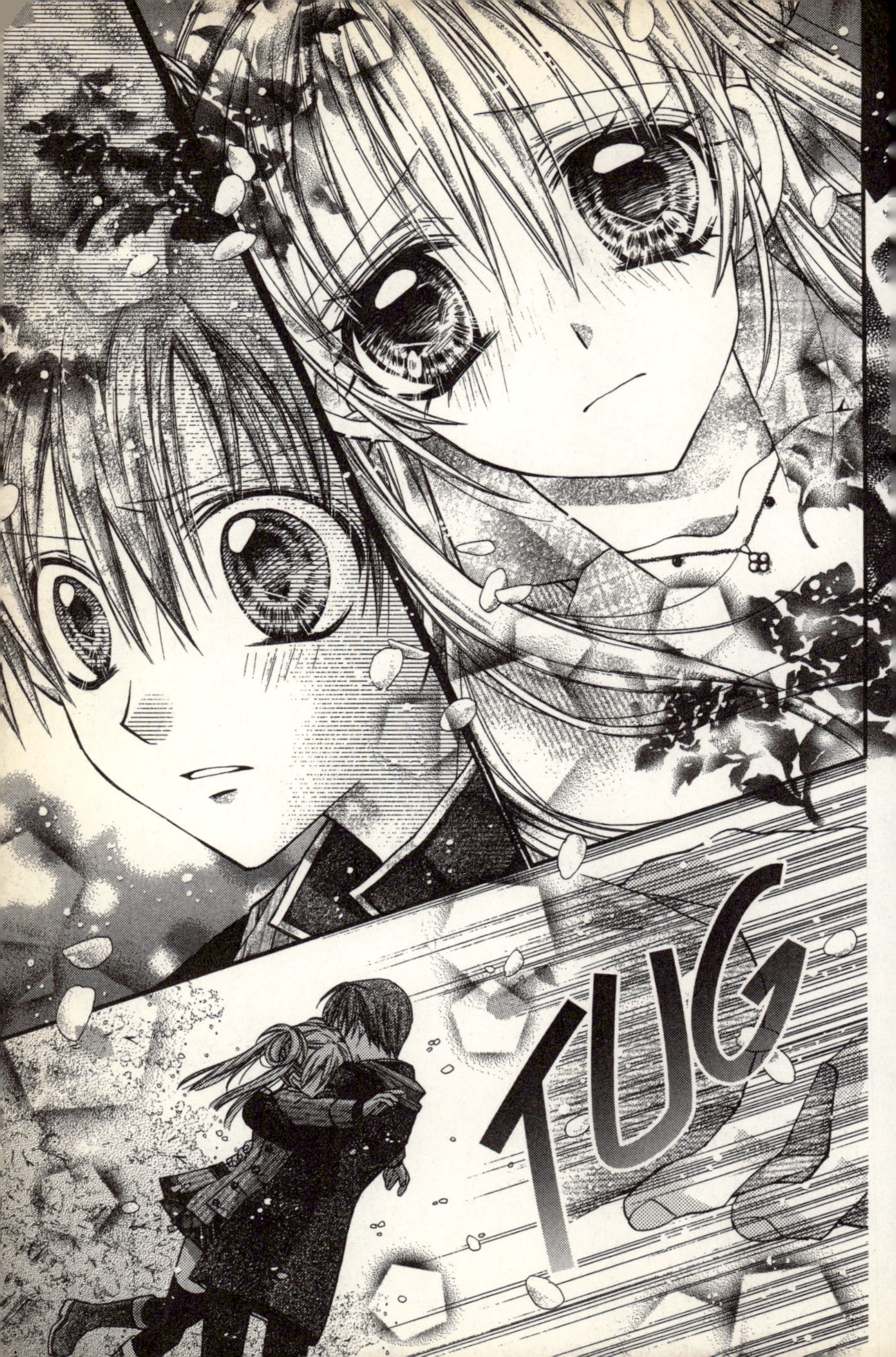
TUG

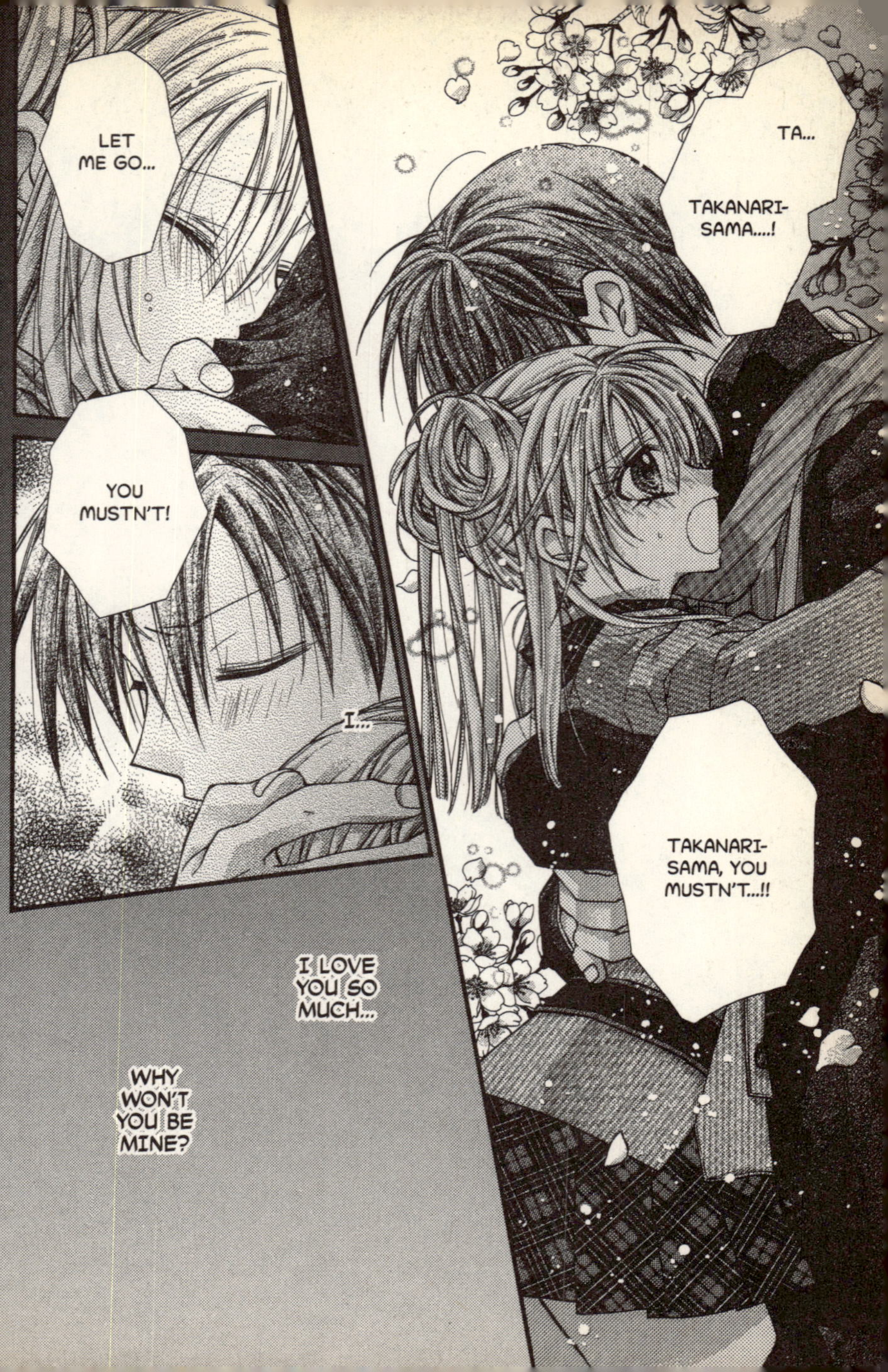
TA...
TAKANARI-SAMA....!
TAKANARI-SAMA, YOU MUSTN'T...!!
LET ME GO...
YOU MUSTN'T!
I...
I LOVE YOU SO MUCH...
WHY WON'T YOU BE MINE?

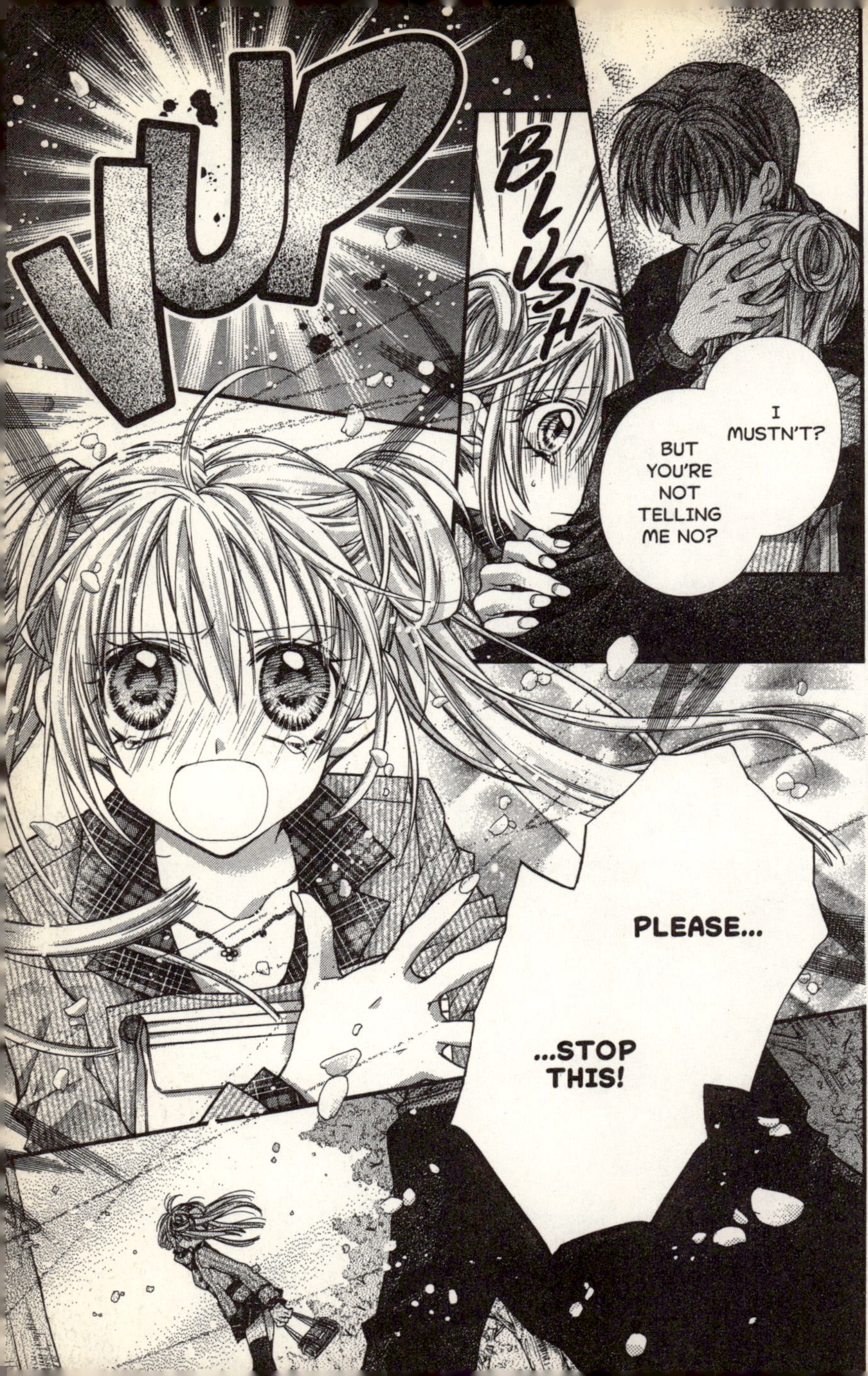
BLUSH
I MUSTN'T? BUT YOU'RE NOT TELLING ME NO?
VUP
PLEASE...
...STOP THIS!

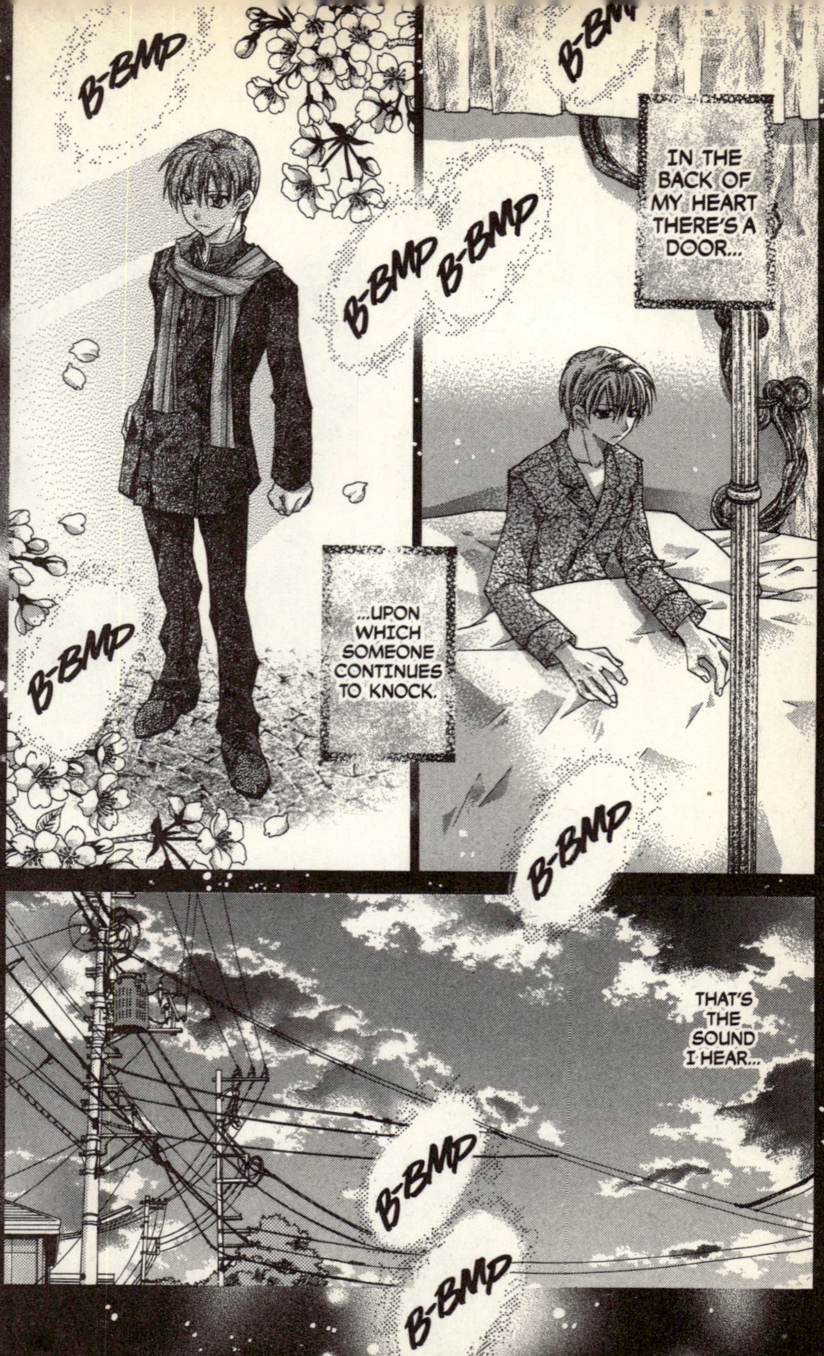
B-BMP
IN THE BACK OF MY HEART THERE'S A DOOR...
B-BMP
B-BMP
B-BMP
...UPON WHICH SOMEONE CONTINUES TO KNOCK.
B-BMP
B-BMP
THAT'S THE SOUND I HEAR...
B-BMP
B-BMP

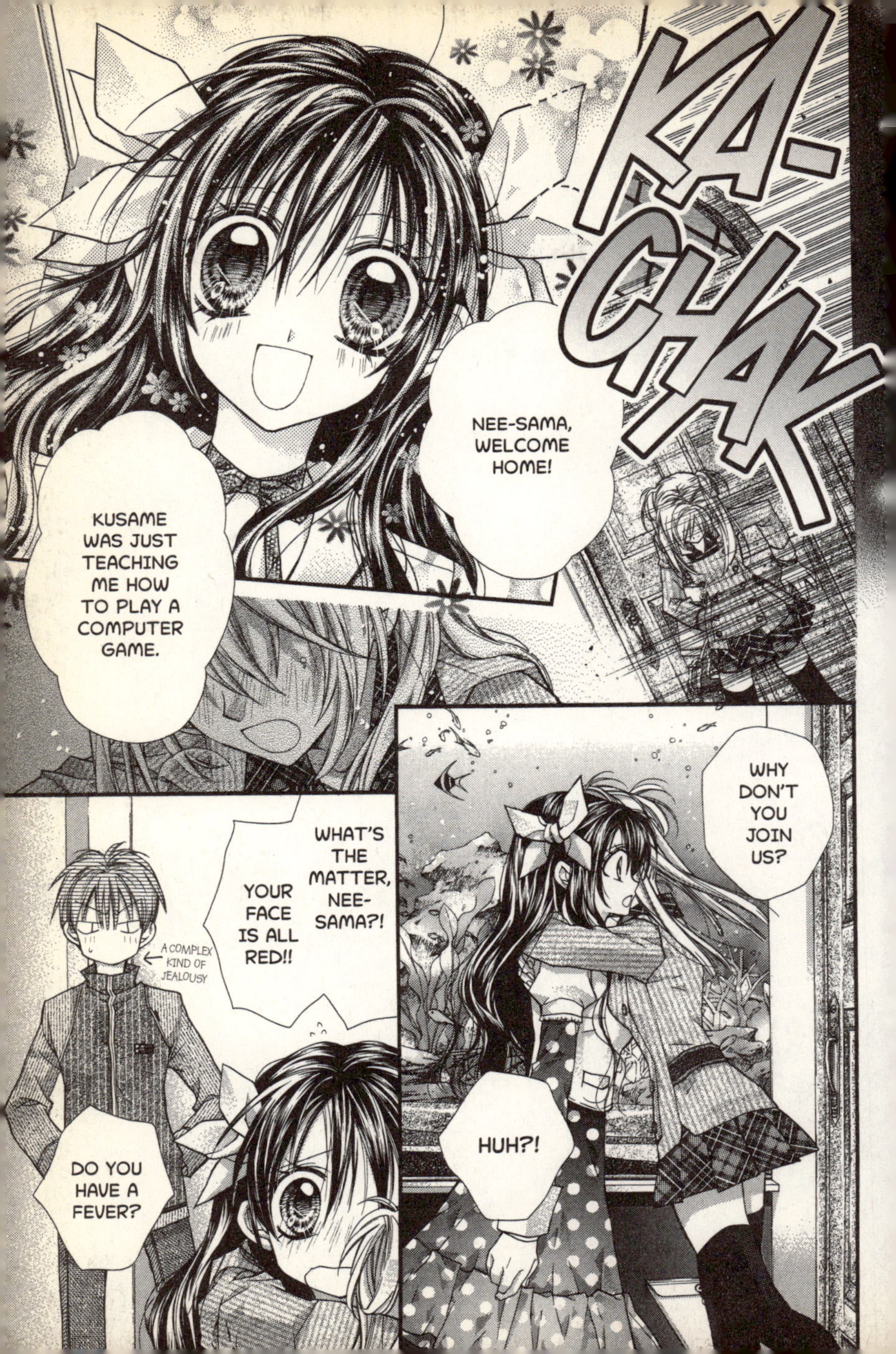
KA-CHAK
NEE-SAMA, WELCOME HOME!
KUSAME WAS JUST TEACHING ME HOW TO PLAY A COMPUTER GAME.
WHY DON'T YOU JOIN US?
HUH?!
WHAT'S THE MATTER, NEE-SAMA?!
YOUR FACE IS ALL RED!!
A COMPLEX KIND OF JEALOUSY
DO YOU HAVE A FEVER?

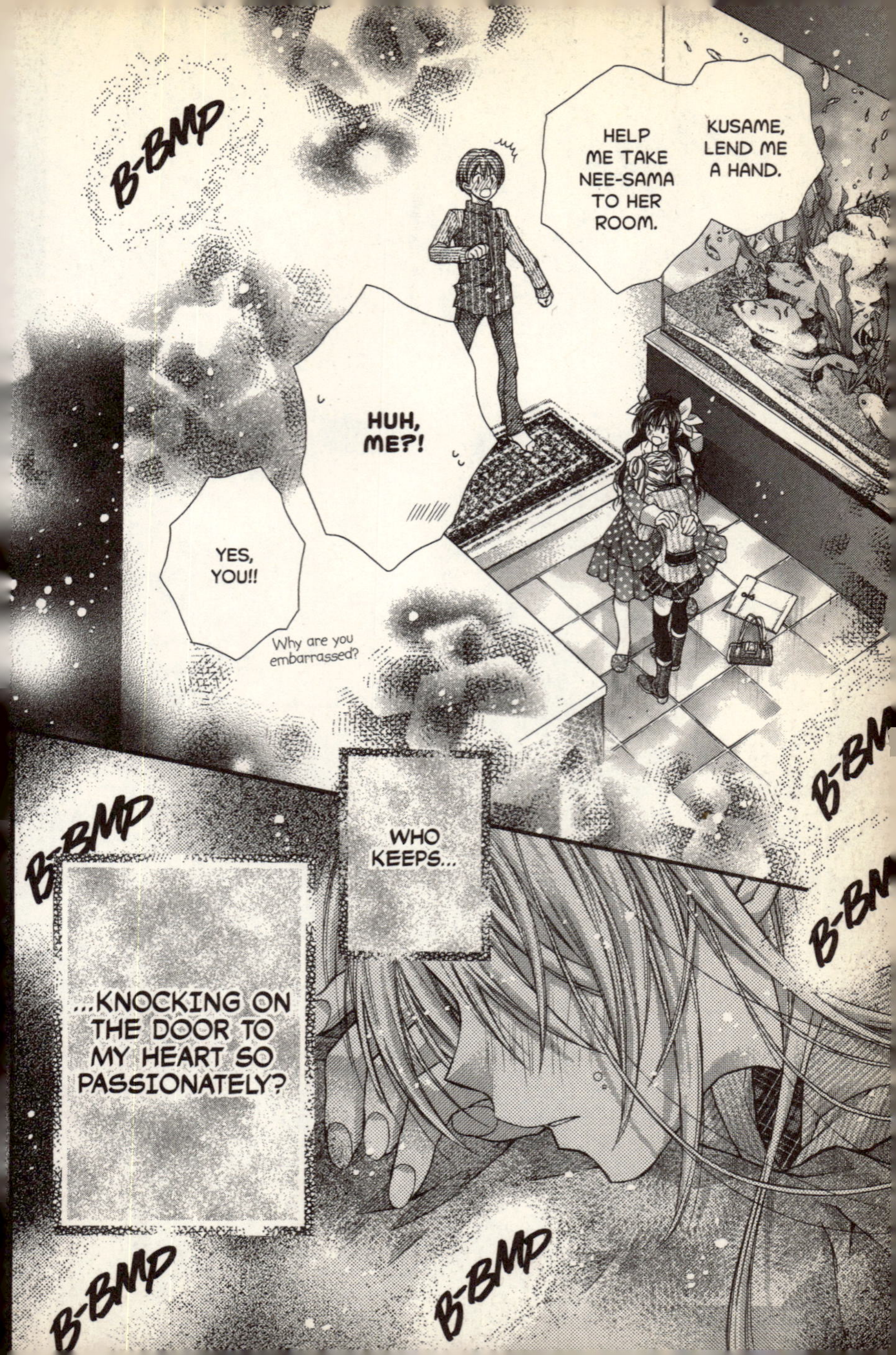
KUSAME, LEND ME A HAND.
HELP ME TAKE NEE-SAMA TO HER ROOM.
B-BMP
HUH, ME?!
YES, YOU!!
Why are you embarrassed?
B-BMP
B-BMP
WHO KEEPS...
B-BMP
...KNOCKING ON THE DOOR TO MY HEART SO PASSIONATELY?
B-BMP
B-BMP

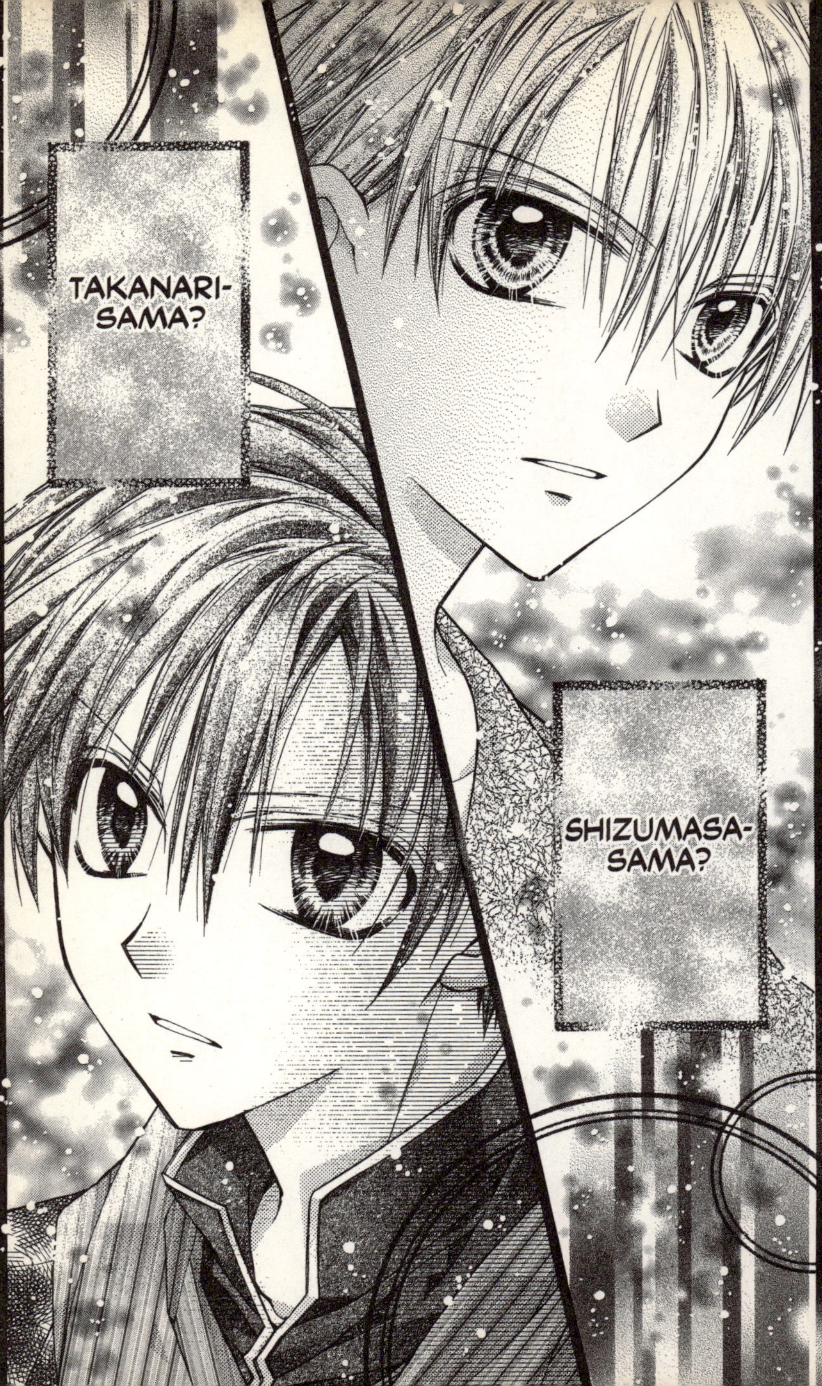
SHIZUMASA-SAMA?
TAKANARI-SAMA?

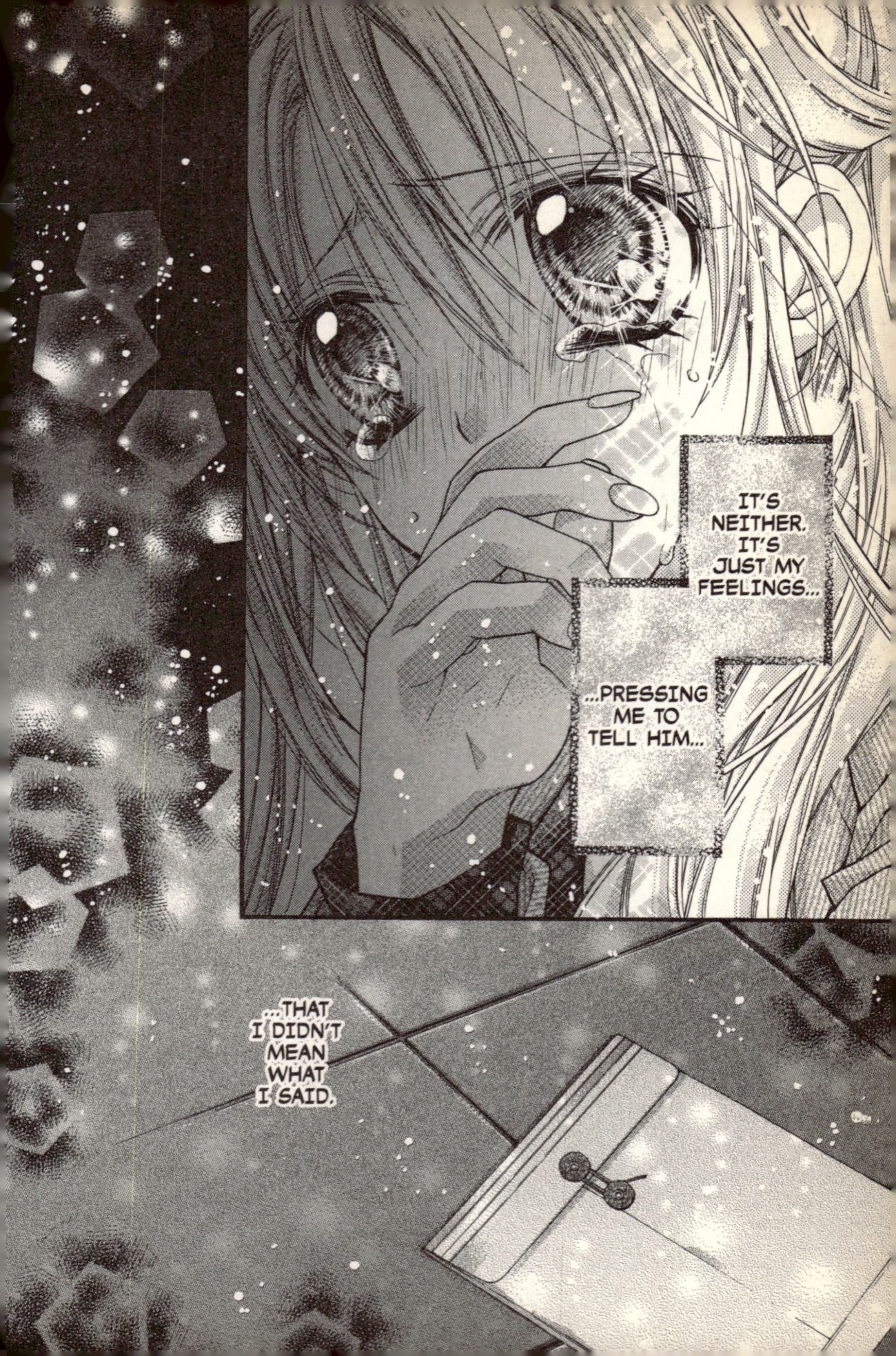
IT'S NEITHER. IT'S JUST MY FEELINGS...
...PRESSING ME TO TELL HIM...
...THAT I DIDN'T MEAN WHAT I SAID.

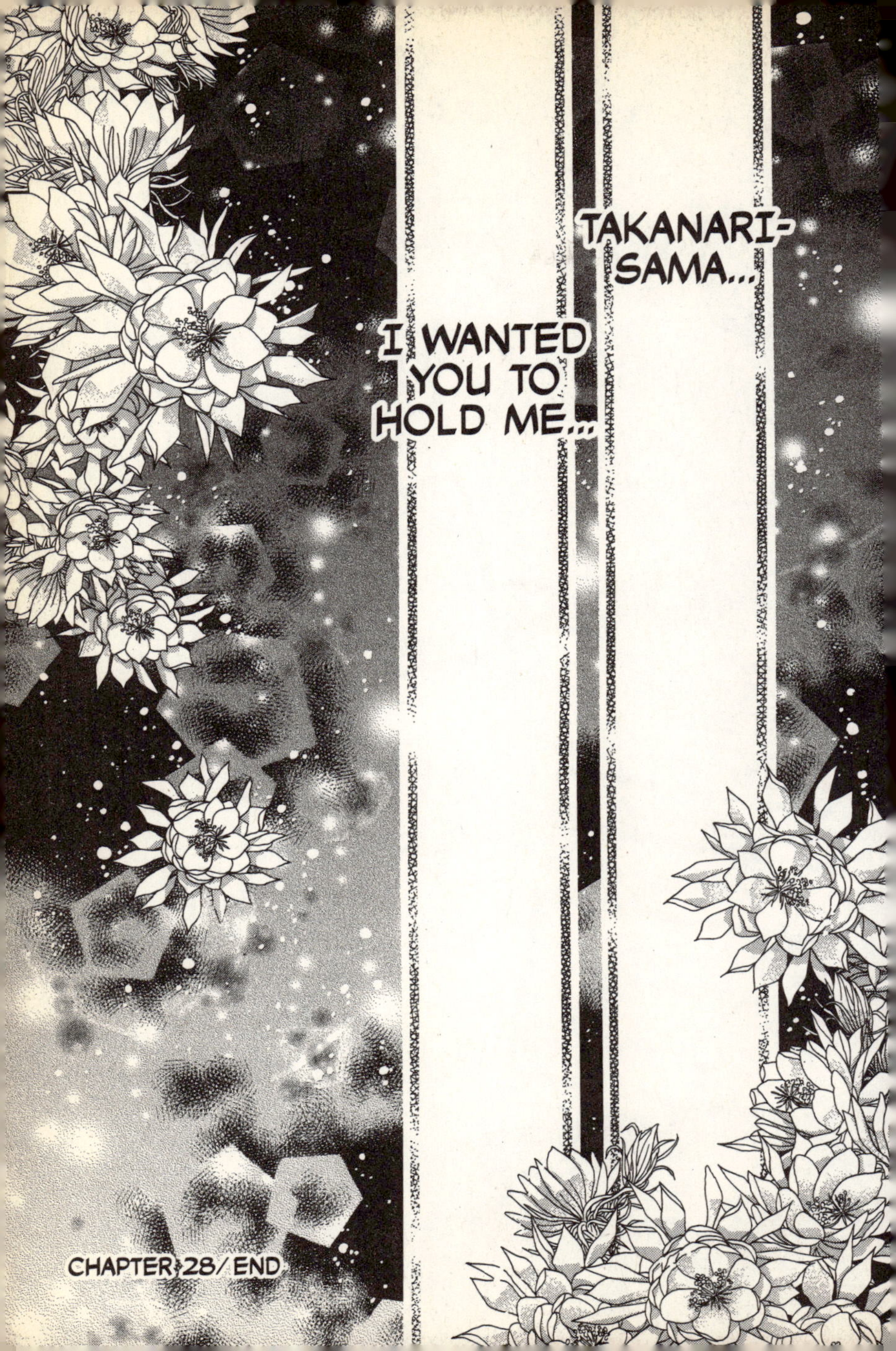
TAKANARI-SAMA...
I WANTED YOU TO HOLD ME...
CHAPTER 28/ END

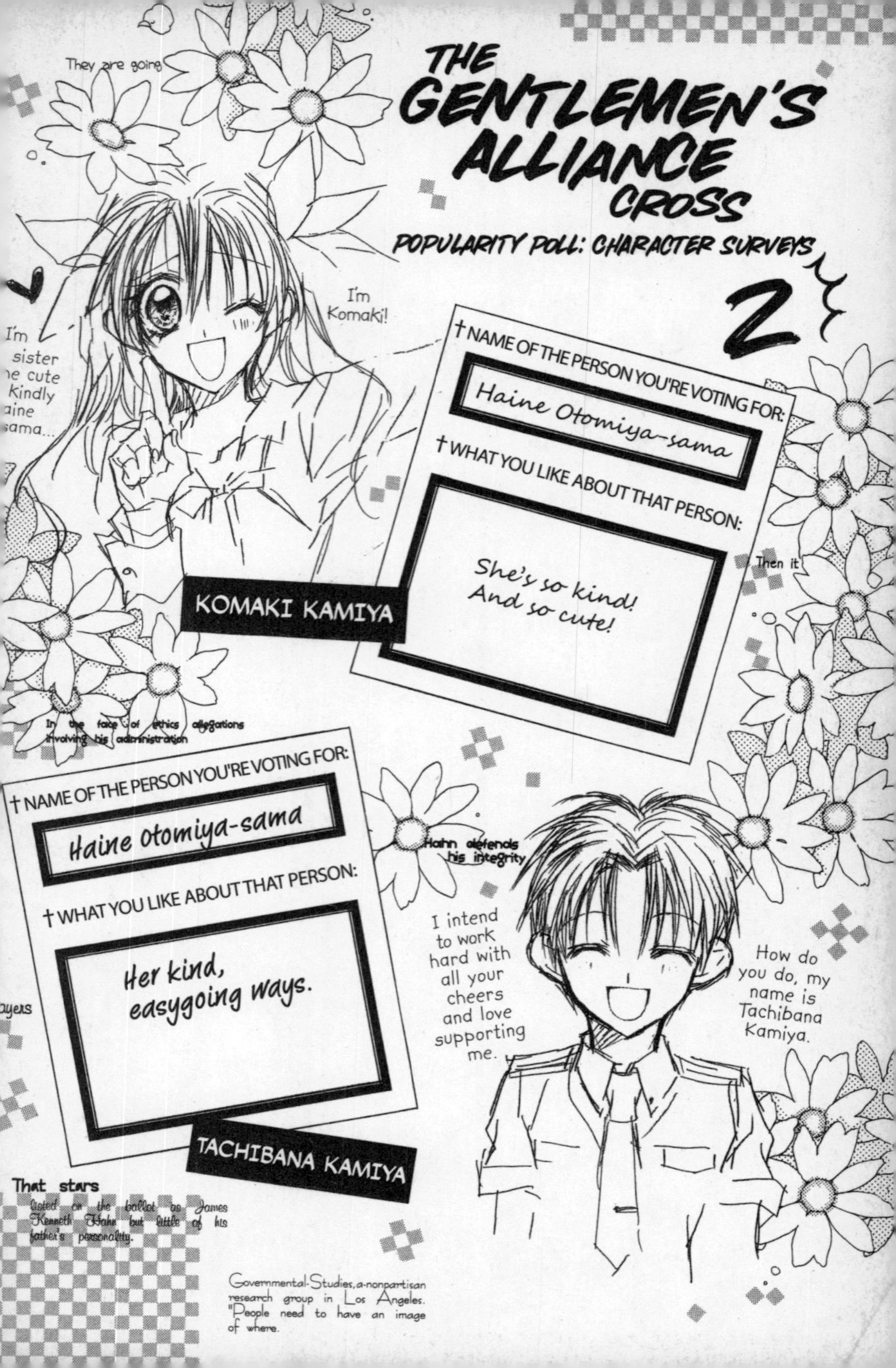

THE GENTLEMEN'S ALLIANCE CROSS
POPULARITY POLL: CHARACTER SURVEYS
2
I'm Komaki!
I'm sister the cute Kindly aine sama...
†NAME OF THE PERSON YOU'RE VOTING FOR:
Haine Otomiya-sama
†WHAT YOU LIKE ABOUT THAT PERSON:
She's so kind! And so cute!
KOMAKI KAMIYA
How do you do, my name is Tachibana Kamiya.
I intend to work hard with all your cheers and love supporting me.
†NAME OF THE PERSON YOU'RE VOTING FOR:
Haine otomiya-sama
†WHAT YOU LIKE ABOUT THAT PERSON:
Her kind, easygoing ways.
TACHIBANA KAMIYA

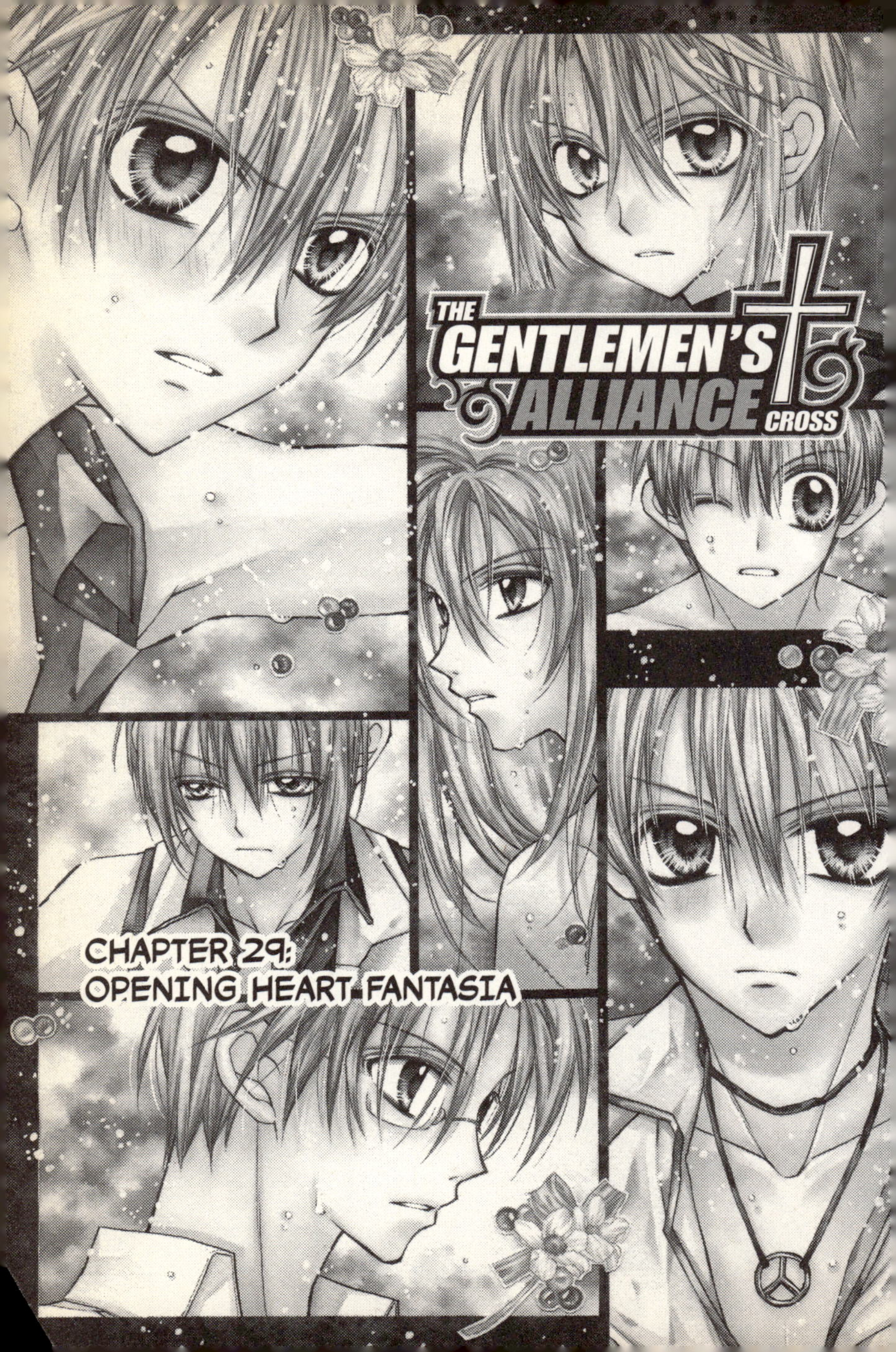
THE GENTLEMEN'S ALLIANCE CROSS
CHAPTER 29:
OPENING HEART FANTASIA

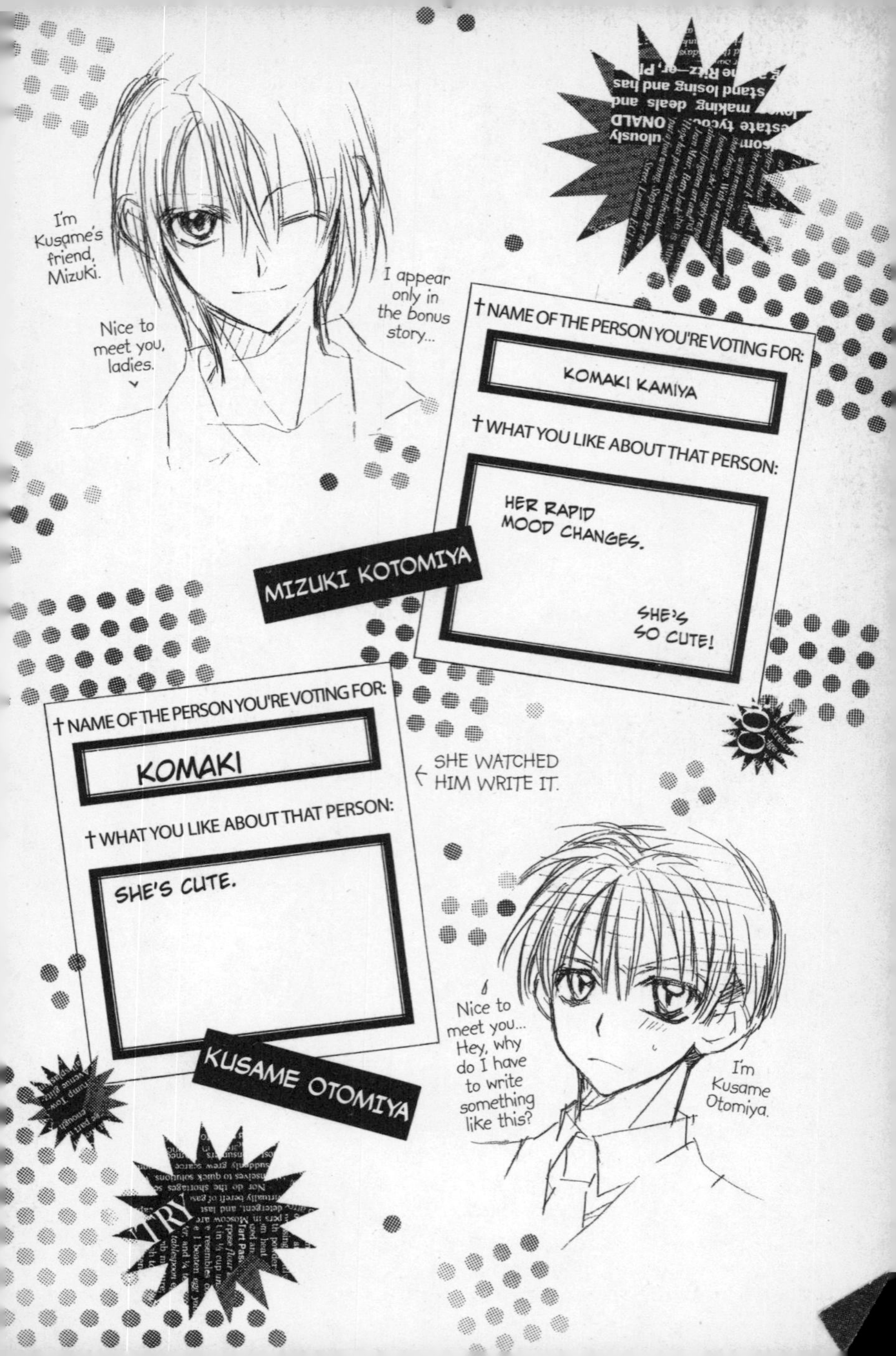
I'm Kusame's friend, Mizuki.
Nice to meet you, ladies.
I appear only in the bonus story...
† NAME OF THE PERSON YOU'RE VOTING FOR:
KOMAKI KAMIYA
† WHAT YOU LIKE ABOUT THAT PERSON:
HER RAPID MOOD CHANGES.
SHE'S SO CUTE!
MIZUKI KOTOMIYA
† NAME OF THE PERSON YOU'RE VOTING FOR:
KOMAKI
← SHE WATCHED HIM WRITE IT.
† WHAT YOU LIKE ABOUT THAT PERSON:
SHE'S CUTE.
KUSAME OTOMIYA
Nice to meet you... Hey, why do I have to write something like this?
I'm Kusame Otomiya.
TRY

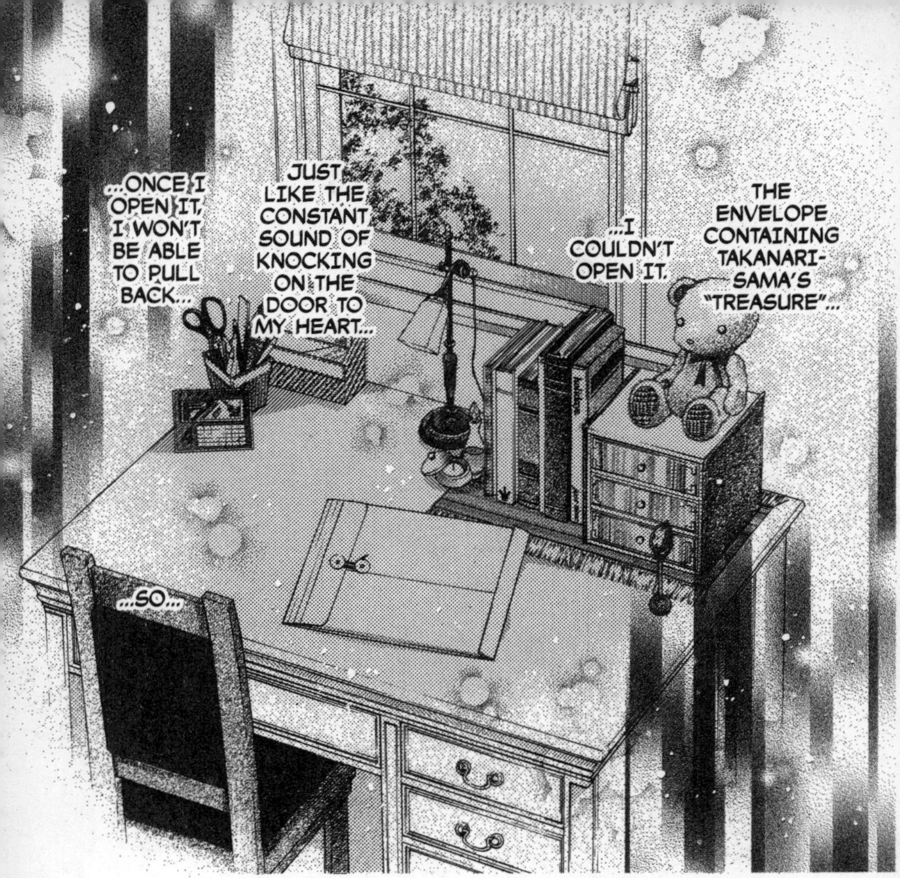
THE ENVELOPE CONTAINING TAKANARI-SAMA'S "TREASURE"...
...I COULDN'T OPEN IT.
JUST LIKE THE CONSTANT SOUND OF KNOCKING ON THE DOOR TO MY HEART...
...ONCE I OPEN IT, I WON'T BE ABLE TO PULL BACK...
...SO...

Chapter 29: Opening Heart Fantasia

Lead-in This fever is your fault...

Spoilers! I'm giving away the story!

In this chapter I challenged myself to draw a dream—an incomprehensible dream. And yes, it turned out to be pretty hard work...(laugh) My blood type is A (though I don't know if that has anything to do with this), so my ideas tend to be sensible. They don't turn out to be as surreal as I would wish them to be...

Sorry, I really don't know if having blood-type A has anything do with this or not.

In the chapter in which Haine was kidnapped, I drew Maora, Maguri, and Ushio as pigs—and I liked the pigs a lot. I decided to draw them as pigs again. The latter half of the dream is probably Haine's wish that everything would be so peaceful if it was like this...

Also, the kiss scene at the end, well... "The girl kissing the guy" is taboo for me. //// I know it's silly, but it happens to be a no-no in my manga series...

But I'm trying to break my personal taboos in *The Gentlemen's Alliance †!* So I gave it a try... Well, I tried to stop her, but Haine wouldn't listen...(laugh) I wanted to focus on Haine's inner battle in this chapter. (The last line is supposed to express how she's surrendered to her feelings.)

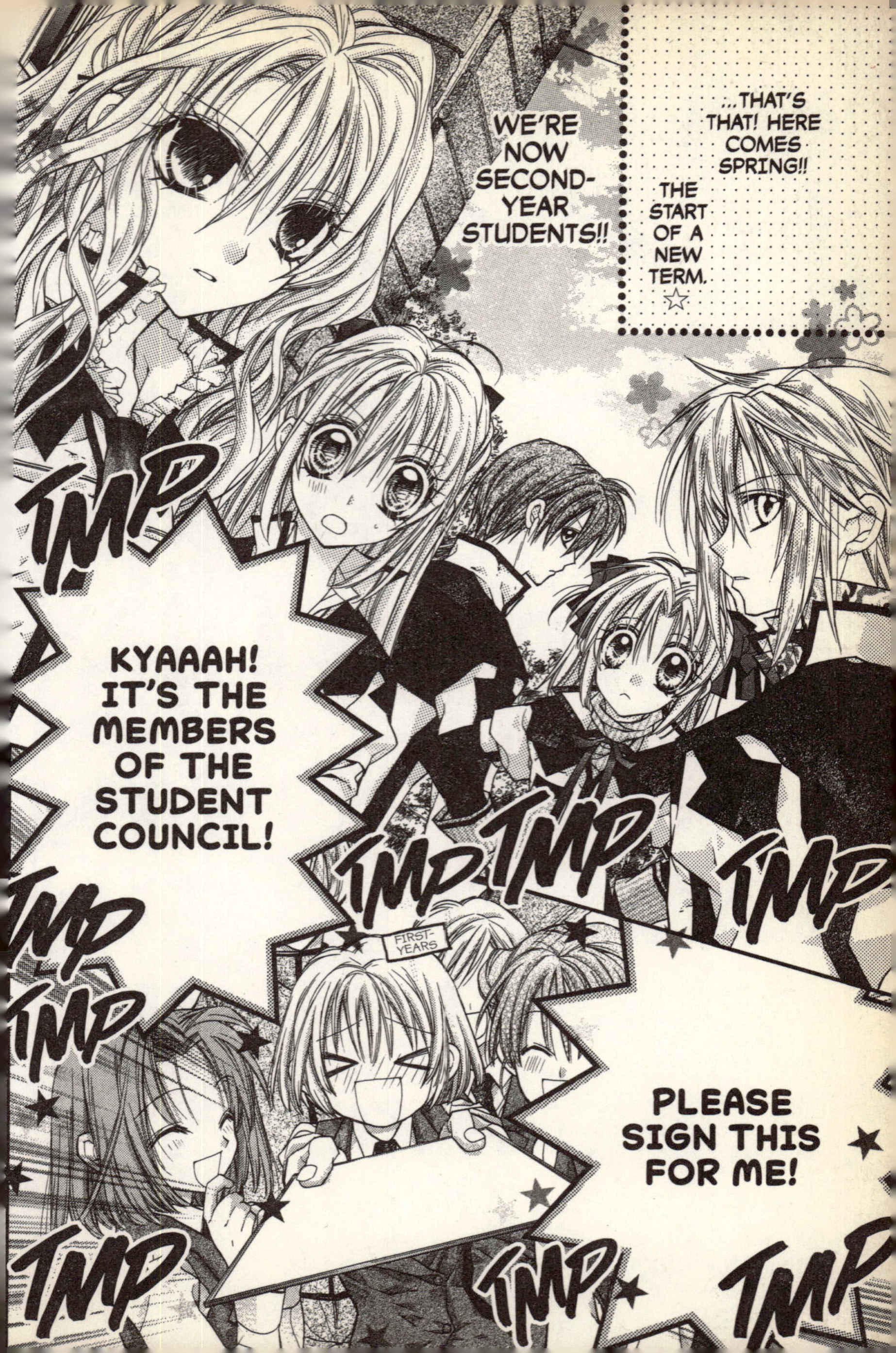
...THAT'S THAT! HERE COMES SPRING!!
THE START OF A NEW TERM. ☆
WE'RE NOW SECOND-YEAR STUDENTS!!
TMP
KYAAAH! IT'S THE MEMBERS OF THE STUDENT COUNCIL!
TMP TMP TMP
TMP TMP
FIRST-YEARS
PLEASE SIGN THIS FOR ME!
TMP TMP TMP

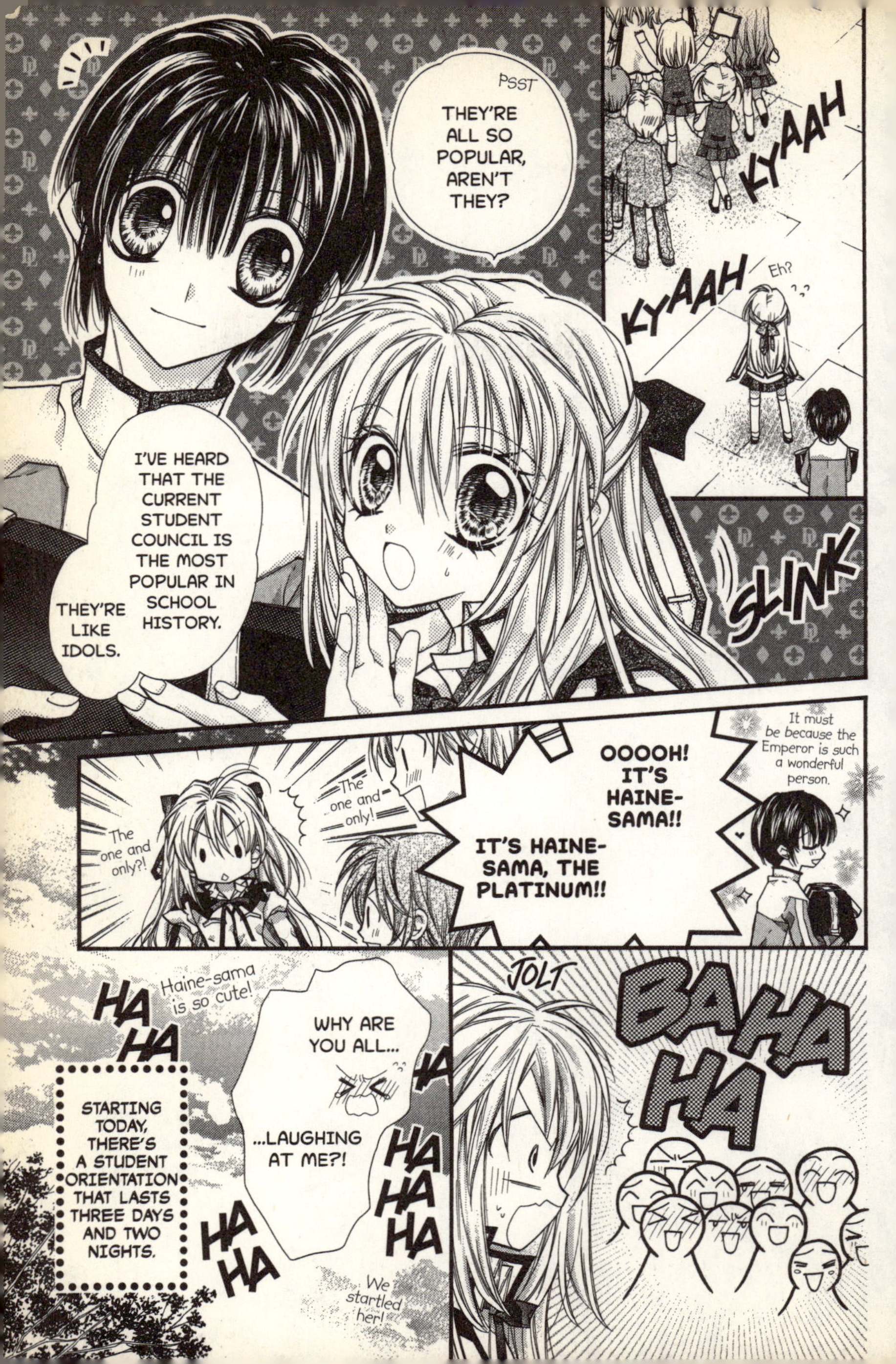
KYAAH
KYAAH
Eh?
SLINK
PSST
THEY'RE ALL SO POPULAR, AREN'T THEY?
I'VE HEARD THAT THE CURRENT STUDENT COUNCIL IS THE MOST POPULAR IN SCHOOL HISTORY.
THEY'RE LIKE IDOLS.
It must be because the Emperor is such a wonderful person.
OOOOH! IT'S HAINE-SAMA!!
IT'S HAINE-SAMA, THE PLATINUM!!
The one and only!
The one and only?!
JOLT
BAHAHA
HA
WHY ARE YOU ALL...
...LAUGHING AT ME?!
HA HA HA
HA HA
Haine-sama is so cute!
HA HA
HA HA
We startled her!
STARTING TODAY, THERE'S A STUDENT ORIENTATION THAT LASTS THREE DAYS AND TWO NIGHTS.

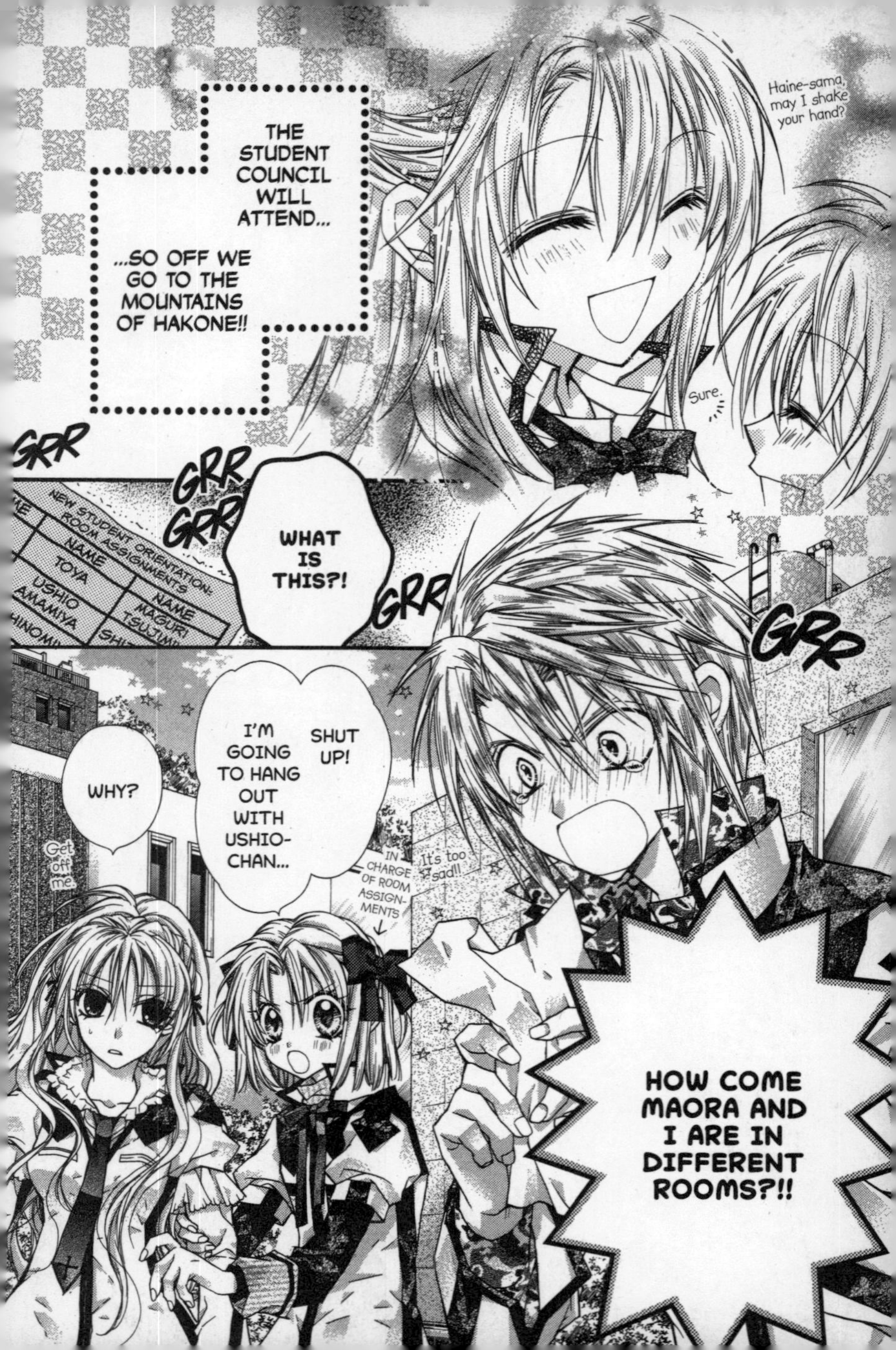
Haine-sama, may I shake your hand?
Sure.
THE STUDENT COUNCIL WILL ATTEND...
...SO OFF WE GO TO THE MOUNTAINS OF HAKONE!!
GRR
GRR
GRR
GRR
GRR
WHAT IS THIS?!
NEW STUDENT ORIENTATION: ROOM ASSIGNMENTS
NAME
MAGURI
TSUJIMI
NAME
TOYA
USHIO
AMAMIYA
HOW COME MAORA AND I ARE IN DIFFERENT ROOMS?!!
It's too sad!!
IN CHARGE OF ROOM ASSIGNMENTS
SHUT UP!
I'M GOING TO HANG OUT WITH USHIO-CHAN...
WHY?
Get off me.

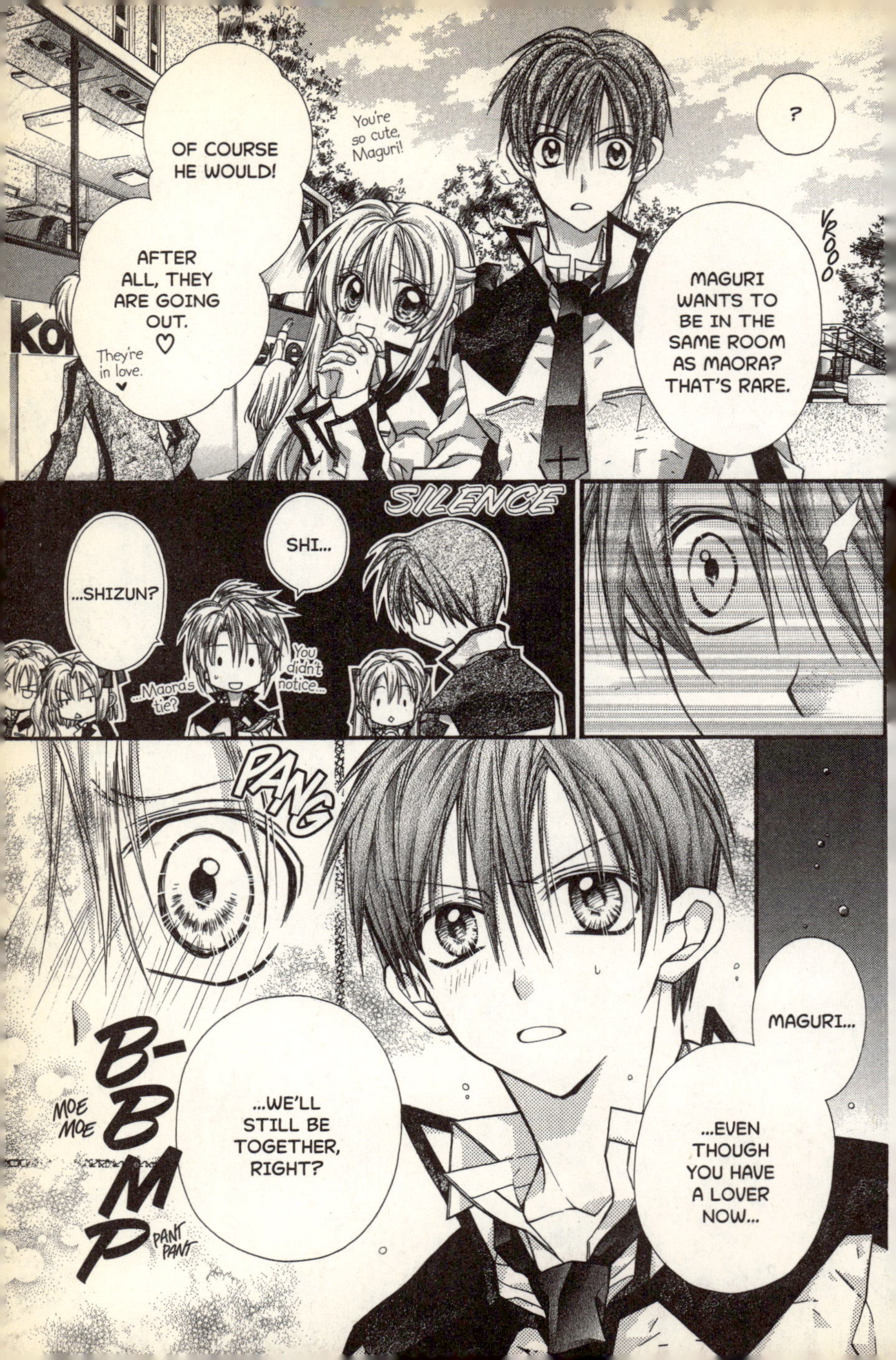
?
MAGURI WANTS TO BE IN THE SAME ROOM AS MAORA? THAT'S RARE.
VROOO
You're so cute, Maguri!
OF COURSE HE WOULD!
AFTER ALL, THEY ARE GOING OUT. ♡
They're in love. ♥
SILENCE
SHI...
...SHIZUN?
You didn't notice...
...Maora's tie?
PANG
MAGURI...
...EVEN THOUGH YOU HAVE A LOVER NOW...
...WE'LL STILL BE TOGETHER, RIGHT?
B-BMP
MOE MOE
PANT PANT

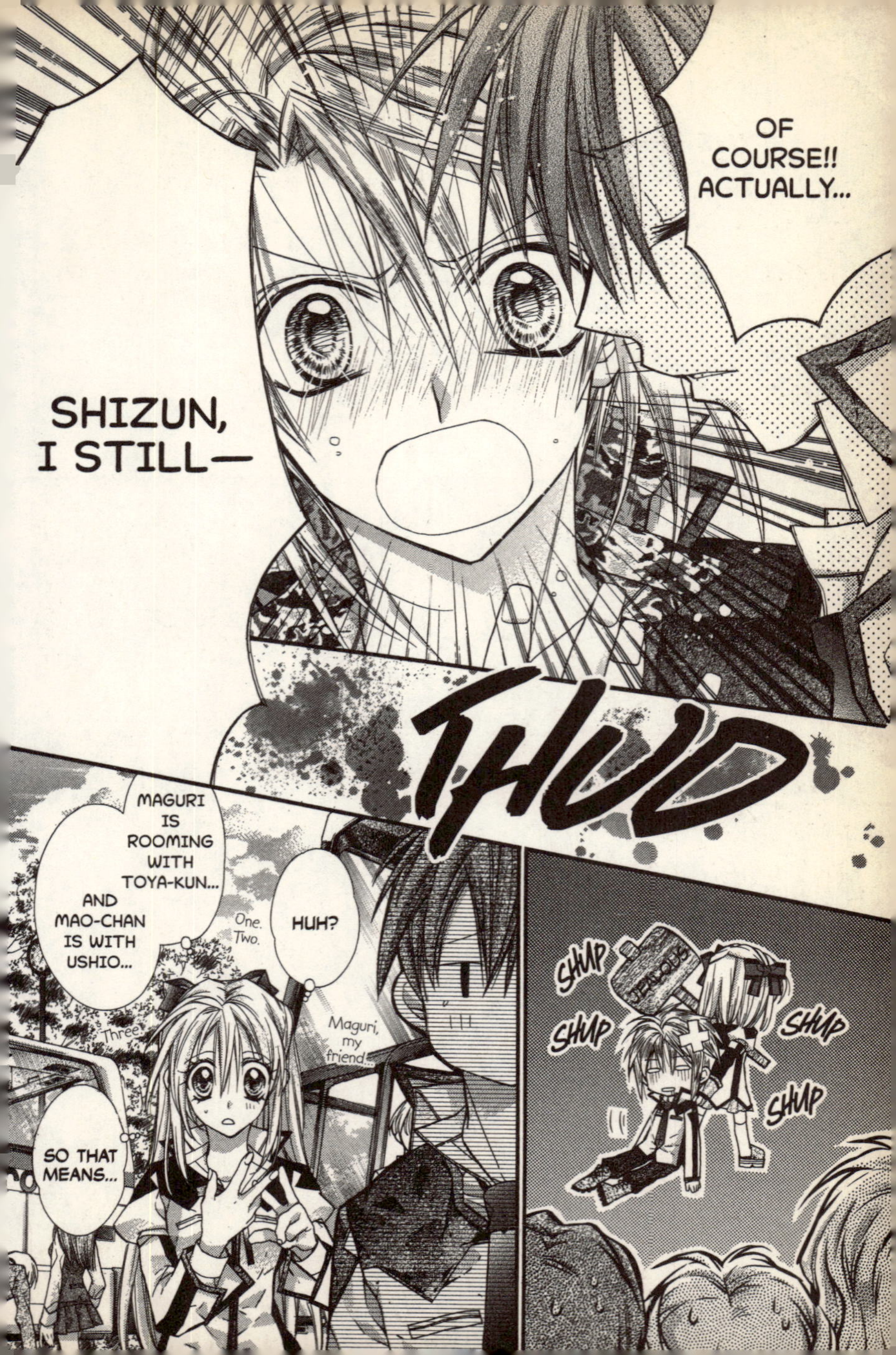
OF COURSE!! ACTUALLY...
SHIZUN, I STILL—
THUD
SHUP
SHUP
SHUP
SHUP
JEALOUS
HUH?
One. Two.
Maguri, my friend.
MAGURI IS ROOMING WITH TOYA-KUN... AND MAO-CHAN IS WITH USHIO...
Three.
SO THAT MEANS...

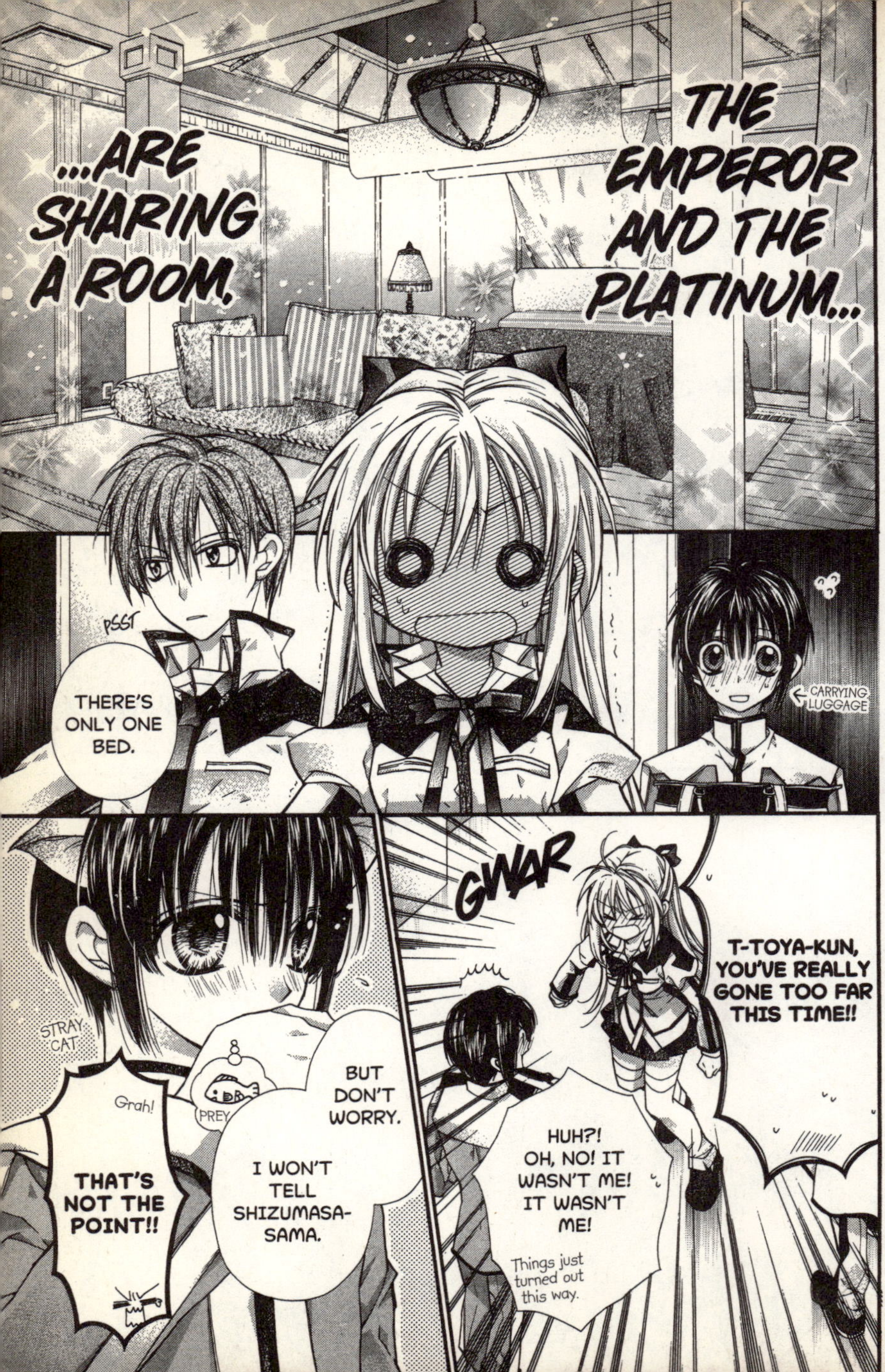
THE EMPEROR AND THE PLATINUM...
...ARE SHARING A ROOM.
CARRYING LUGGAGE
PSST
THERE'S ONLY ONE BED.
GWAR
T-TOYA-KUN, YOU'VE REALLY GONE TOO FAR THIS TIME!!
HUH?! OH, NO! IT WASN'T ME! IT WASN'T ME!
Things just turned out this way.
BUT DON'T WORRY.
I WON'T TELL SHIZUMASA-SAMA.
PREY
STRAY CAT
Grah!
THAT'S NOT THE POINT!!

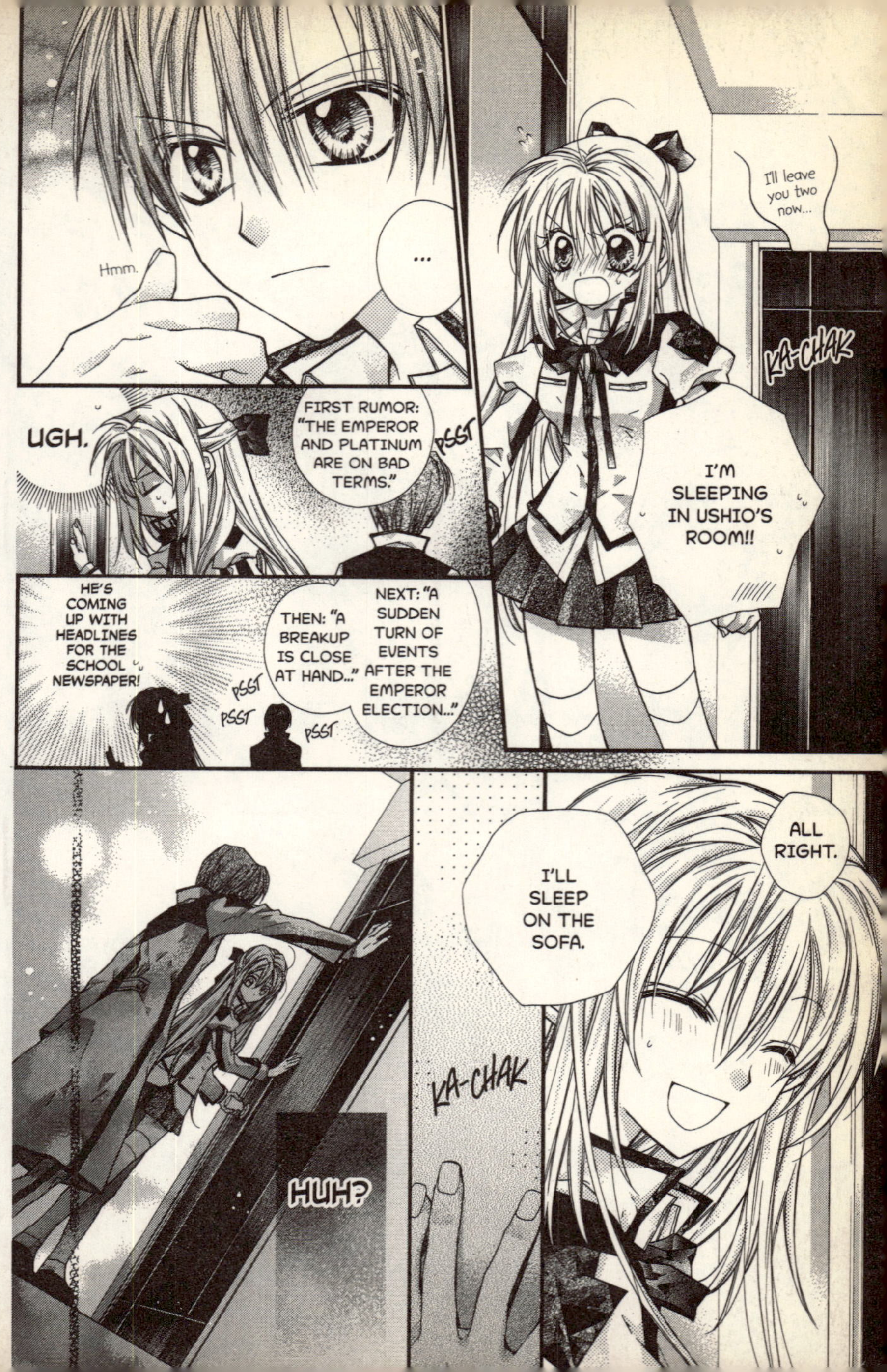

I'll leave you two now...
KA-CHAK
I'M SLEEPING IN USHIO'S ROOM!!
...
Hmm.
FIRST RUMOR: "THE EMPEROR AND PLATINUM ARE ON BAD TERMS."
PSST
UGH.
NEXT: "A SUDDEN TURN OF EVENTS AFTER THE EMPEROR ELECTION..."
THEN: "A BREAKUP IS CLOSE AT HAND..."
PSST
PSST
PSST
HE'S COMING UP WITH HEADLINES FOR THE SCHOOL NEWSPAPER!
ALL RIGHT.
I'LL SLEEP ON THE SOFA.
KA-CHAK
HUH?

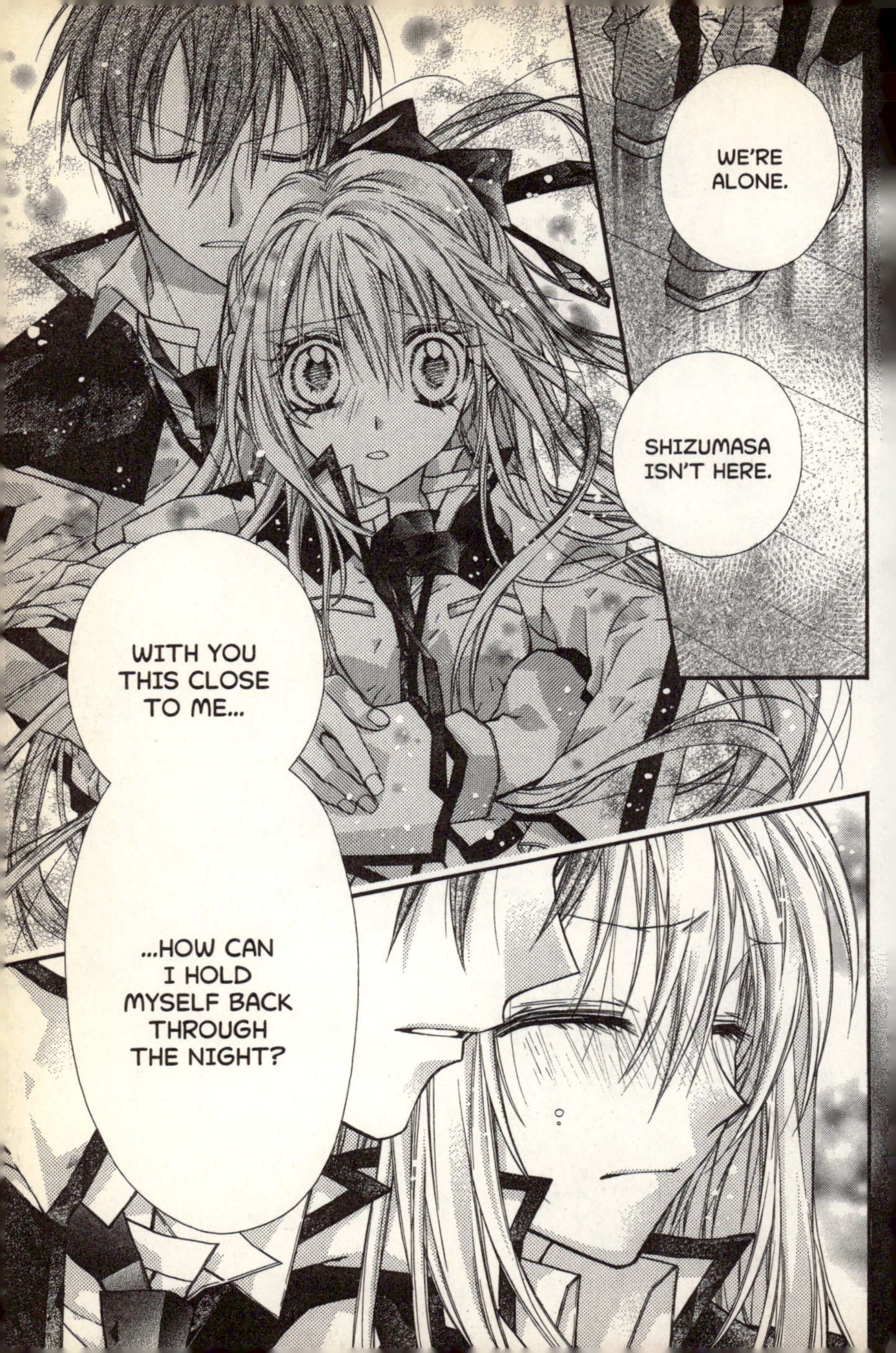
WE'RE ALONE.
SHIZUMASA ISN'T HERE.
WITH YOU THIS CLOSE TO ME...
...HOW CAN I HOLD MYSELF BACK THROUGH THE NIGHT?

TONIGHT...
...I'LL MAKE YOU MINE.
KA-CHAK

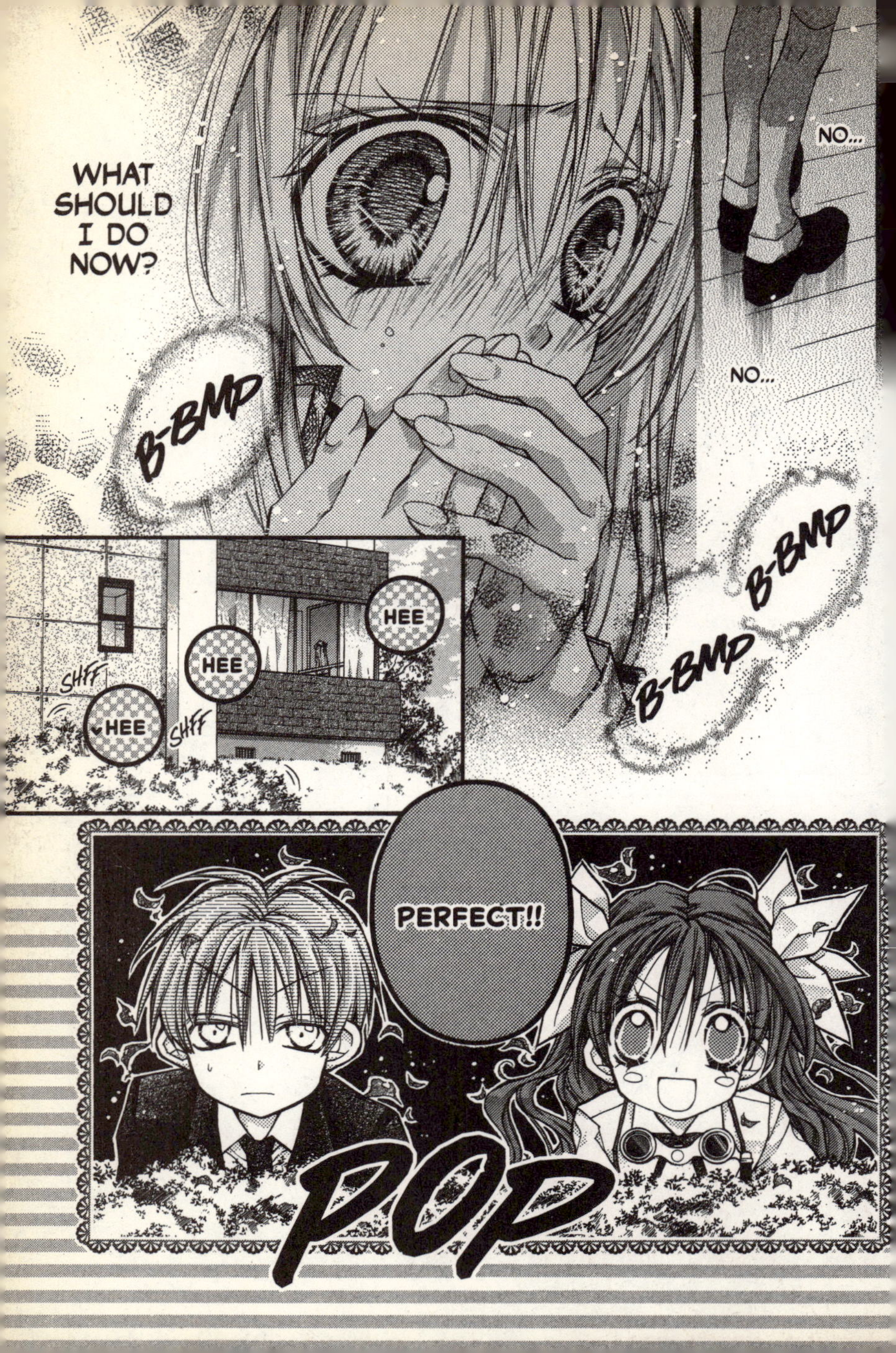
NO...
NO...
WHAT SHOULD I DO NOW?
B-BMP
B-BMP
B-BMP
HEE
HEE
HEE
SHFF
SHFF
PERFECT!!
POP

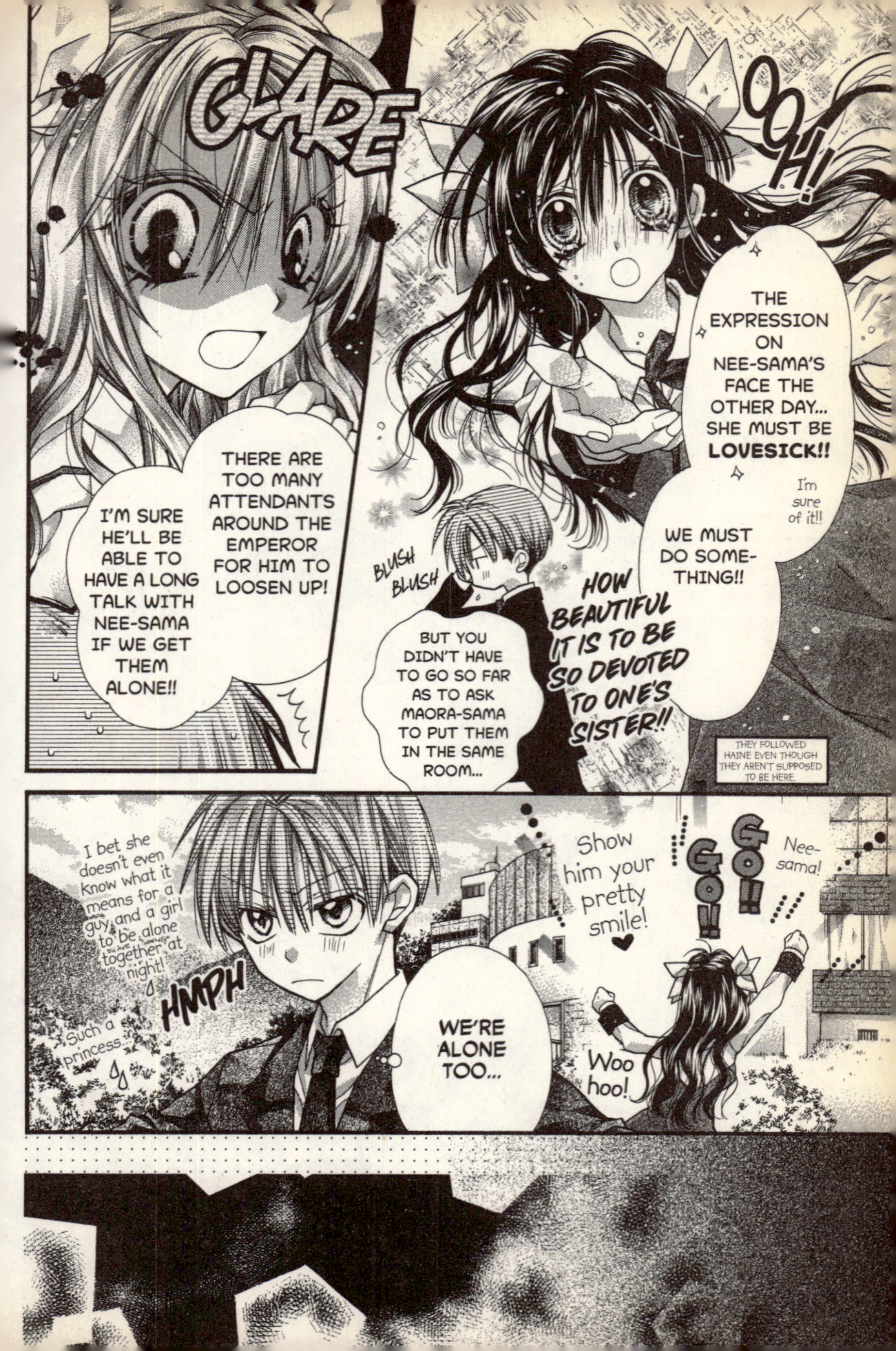
OOH!
THE EXPRESSION ON NEE-SAMA'S FACE THE OTHER DAY... SHE MUST BE **LOVESICK!!**
I'm sure of it!!
WE MUST DO SOME-THING!!
HOW BEAUTIFUL IT IS TO BE SO DEVOTED TO ONE'S SISTER!!
BLUSH BLUSH
BUT YOU DIDN'T HAVE TO GO SO FAR AS TO ASK MAORA-SAMA TO PUT THEM IN THE SAME ROOM...
THEY FOLLOWED HAINE EVEN THOUGH THEY AREN'T SUPPOSED TO BE HERE.
GLARE
THERE ARE TOO MANY ATTENDANTS AROUND THE EMPEROR FOR HIM TO LOOSEN UP!
I'M SURE HE'LL BE ABLE TO HAVE A LONG TALK WITH NEE-SAMA IF WE GET THEM ALONE!!
Nee-sama!
GO! GO!!
Show him your pretty smile!
Woo hoo!
WE'RE ALONE TOO...
I bet she doesn't even know what it means for a guy and a girl to be alone together at night!
HMPH
Such a princess.

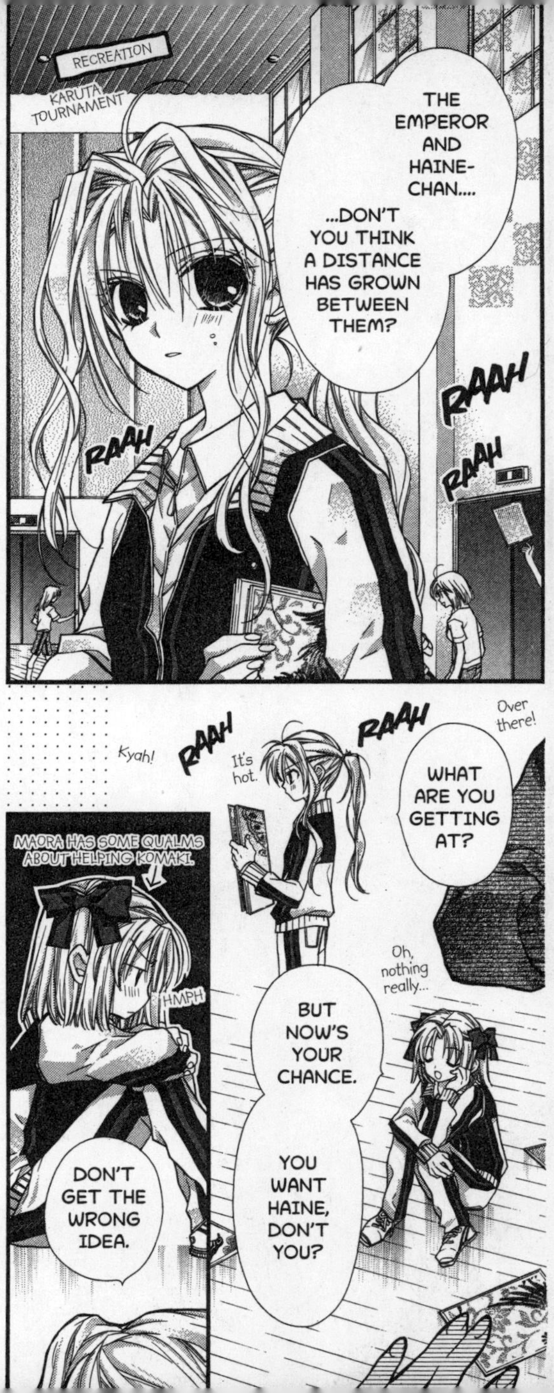
RECREATION
KARUTA TOURNAMENT
THE EMPEROR AND HAINE-CHAN....
...DON'T YOU THINK A DISTANCE HAS GROWN BETWEEN THEM?
RAAH
RAAH
RAAH
Over there!
RAAH
WHAT ARE YOU GETTING AT?
It's hot.
RAAH
Kyah!
Oh, nothing really...
BUT NOW'S YOUR CHANCE.
YOU WANT HAINE, DON'T YOU?
MAORA HAS SOME QUALMS ABOUT HELPING KOMAKI.
HMPH
DON'T GET THE WRONG IDEA.

★Kamikaze Kaito Jeanne

My second manga series, *Kamikaze Kaito Jeanne* will be published in a collector's edition in Japan!

It will be six volumes total. They will have newly drawn covers, illustrations, and an essay manga!

The final volume will include a bonus story!

We're also planning a little gift for the readers.♥

By the way, the bonus story will probably take place after the main story. It will be about Shinji and Natsuki.

It's been a while since I drew Maroyan!!

Please look forward to it.♥♥♥

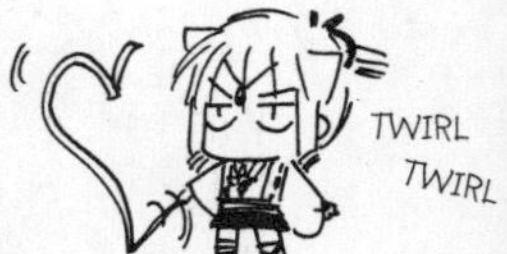
TWIRL
TWIRL

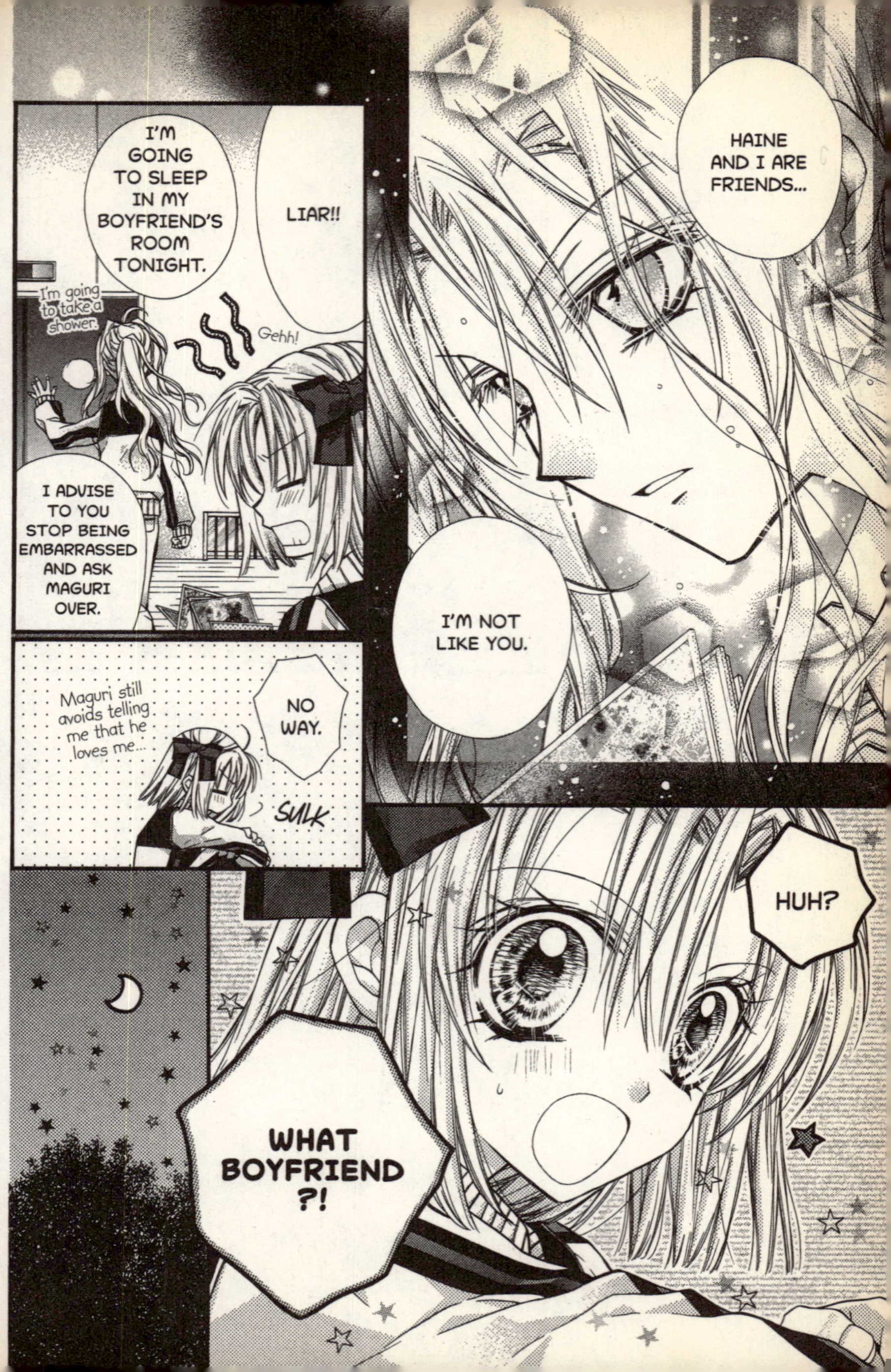
HAINE AND I ARE FRIENDS...
I'M NOT LIKE YOU.
I'M GOING TO SLEEP IN MY BOYFRIEND'S ROOM TONIGHT.
LIAR!!
Gehh!
I'm going to take a shower.
I ADVISE TO YOU STOP BEING EMBARRASSED AND ASK MAGURI OVER.
NO WAY.
Maguri still avoids telling me that he loves me...
SULK
HUH?
WHAT BOYFRIEND ?!

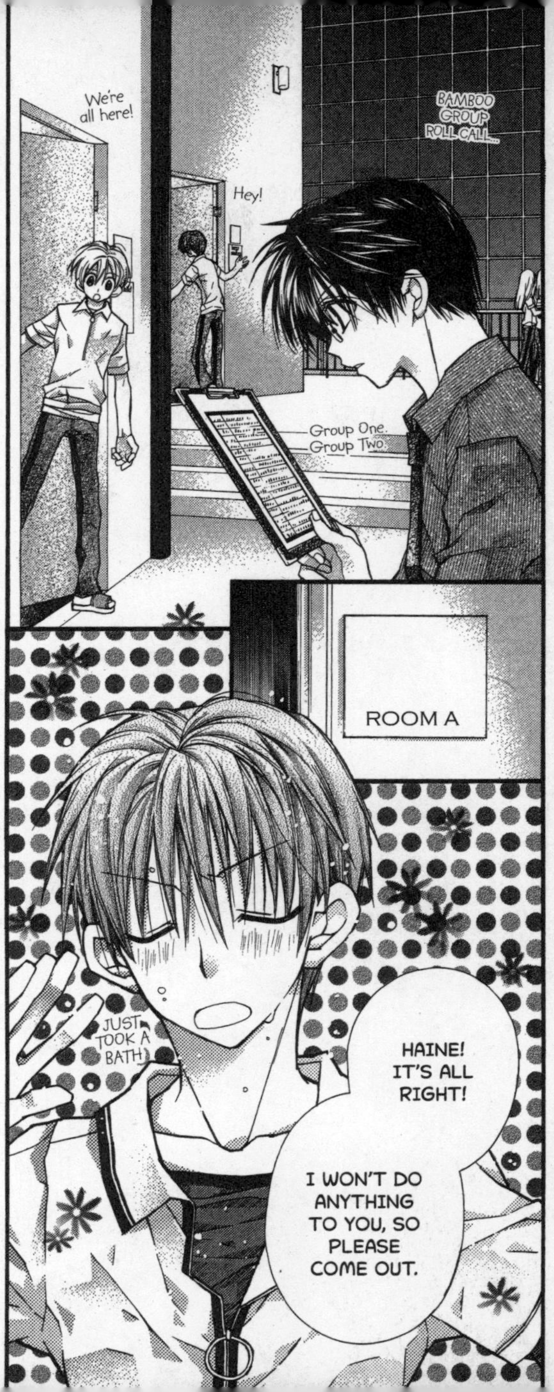
BAMBOO GROUP ROLL CALL...
Hey!
We're all here!
Group One.
Group Two.
ROOM A
HAINE! IT'S ALL RIGHT!
I WON'T DO ANYTHING TO YOU, SO PLEASE COME OUT.
JUST TOOK A BATH

Special Thanks♪

Nakame Saori

Meech
Yuko-chan
Chihiro-chan
Ooka-san

Hina-chan
Ibuki-chan
Sakura-chan
Toma-chan
Negami-san
Kona-chan

Asa-chan

Riku & Kai

Ribon Editorial Department
Shueisha

Ammonite Ltd

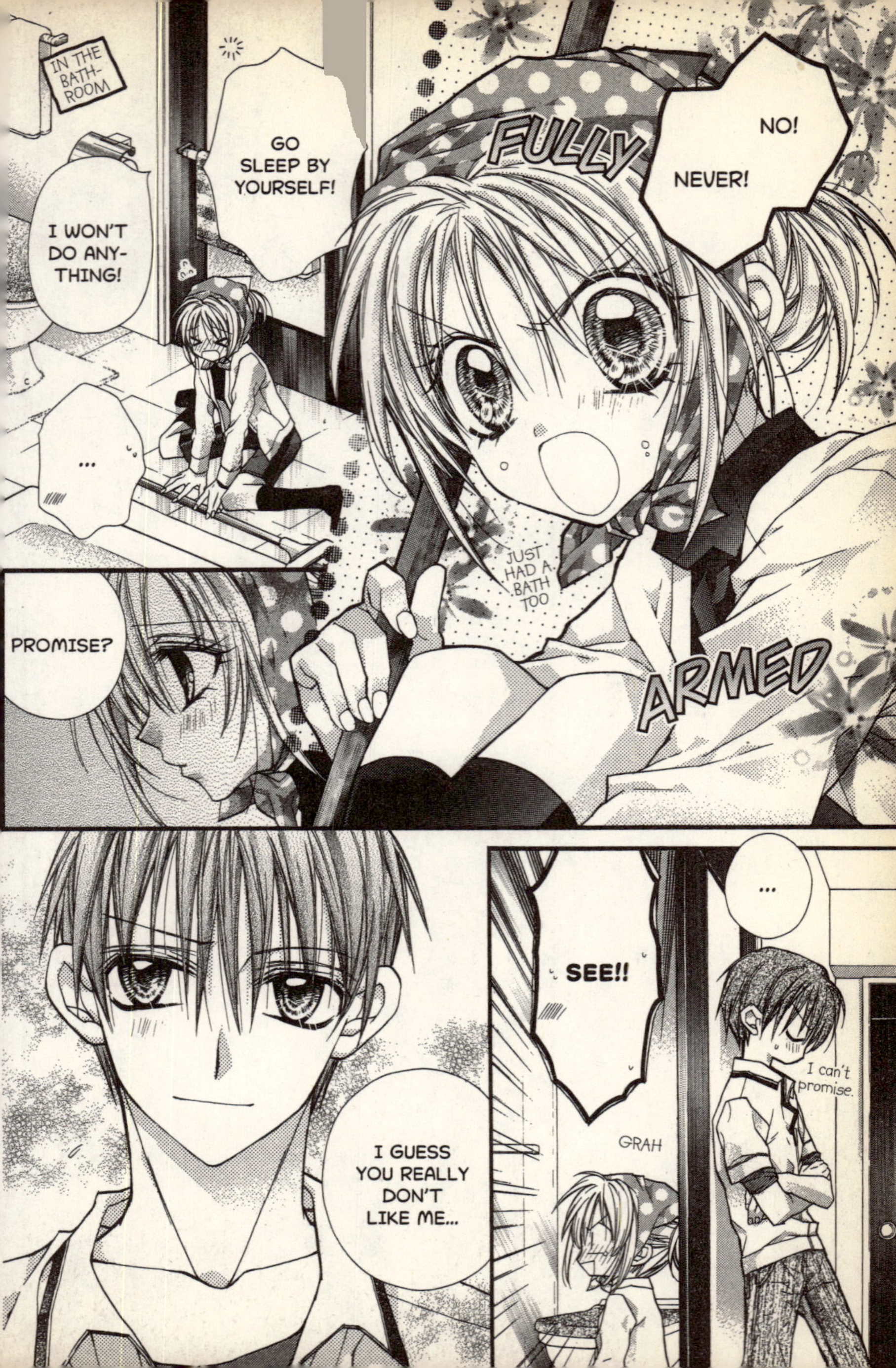
IN THE BATH-ROOM
I WON'T DO ANY-THING!
GO SLEEP BY YOURSELF!
NO!
NEVER!
FULLY
ARMED
JUST HAD A BATH TOO
...
PROMISE?
...
I can't promise.
SEE!!
GRAH
I GUESS YOU REALLY DON'T LIKE ME...

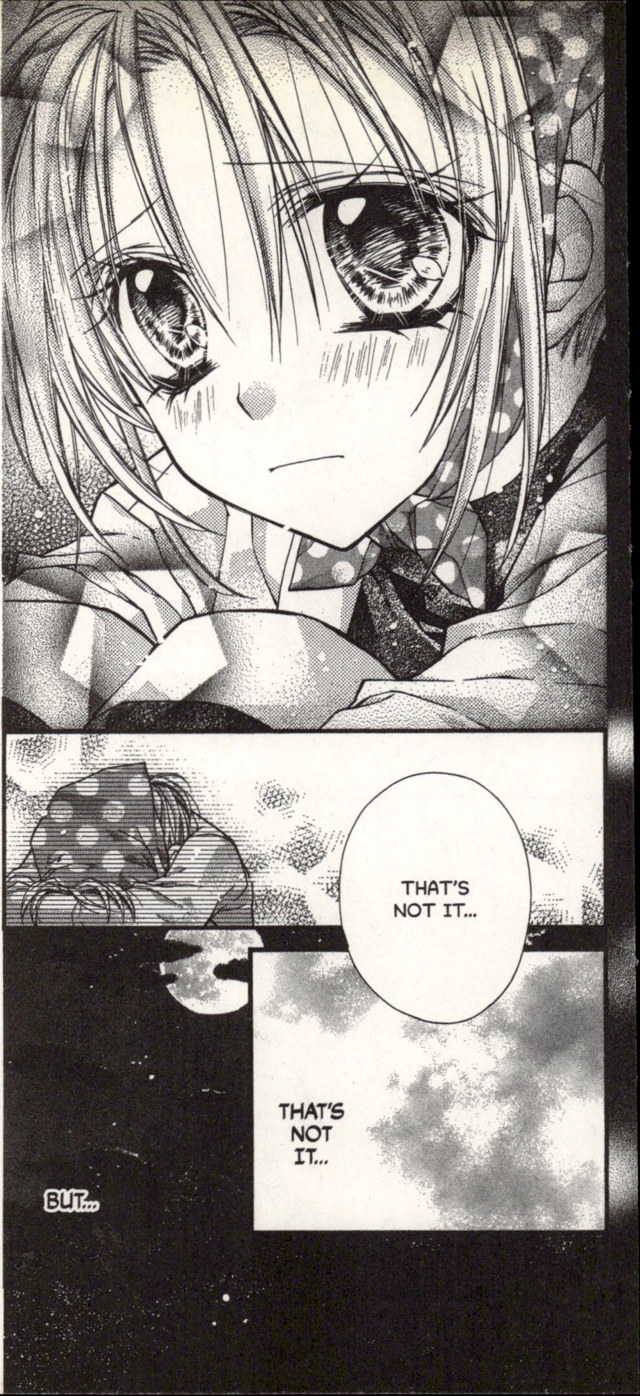
THAT'S NOT IT...
THAT'S NOT IT...
BUT...
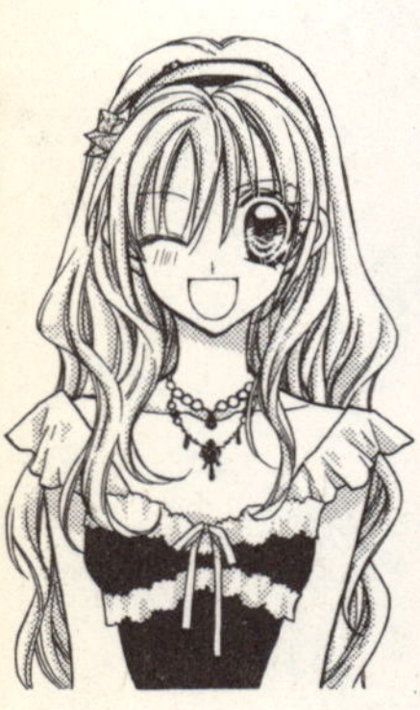

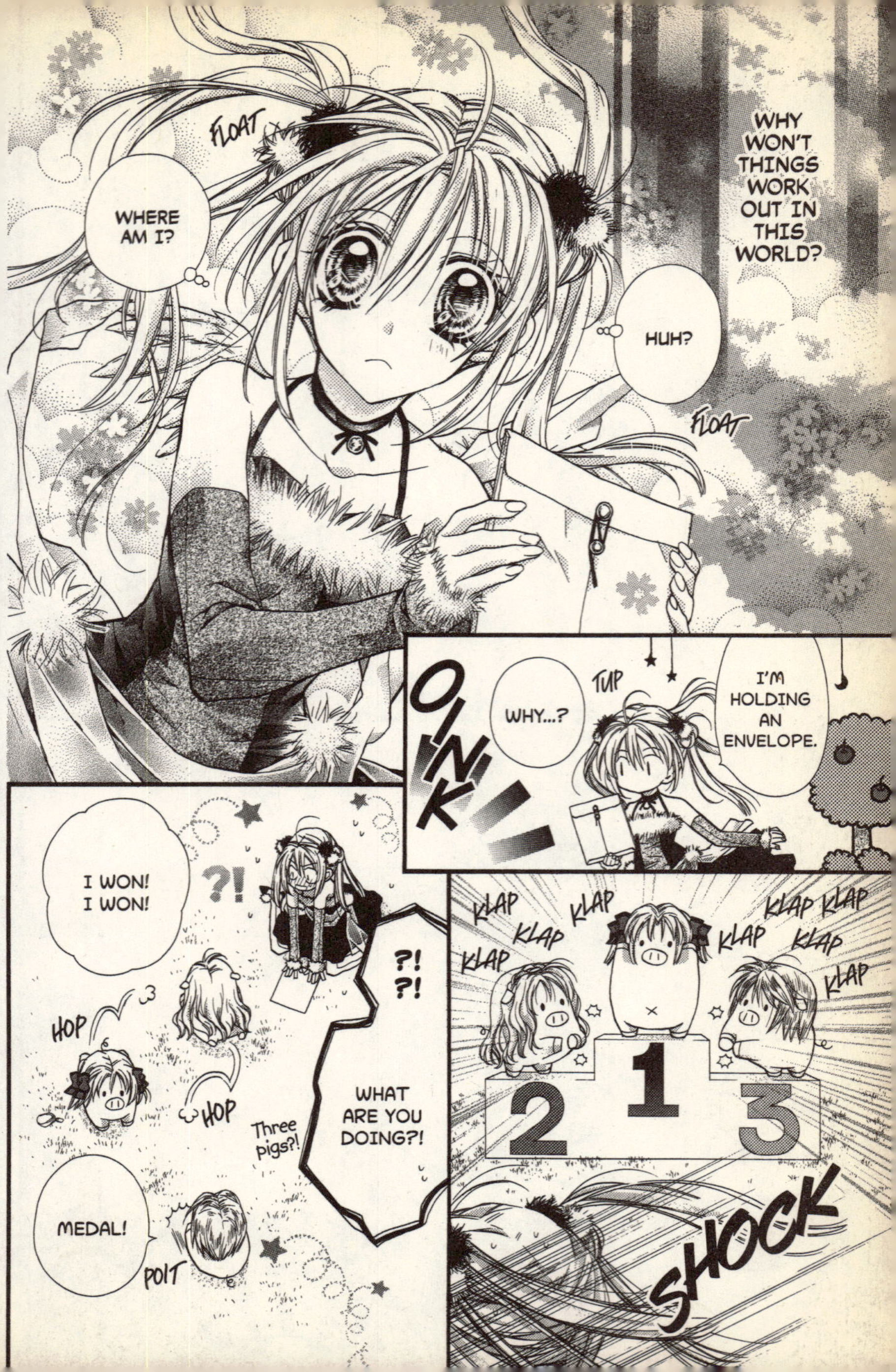

WHY WON'T THINGS WORK OUT IN THIS WORLD?
HUH?
FLOAT
FLOAT
WHERE AM I?
I'M HOLDING AN ENVELOPE.
TUP
WHY...?
OINK
KLAP KLAP
KLAP
KLAP
KLAP
KLAP
KLAP
KLAP
1
2
3
SHOCK
WHAT ARE YOU DOING?!
?! ?!
?!
I WON! I WON!
Three pigs?!
HOP
HOP
MEDAL!
POIT

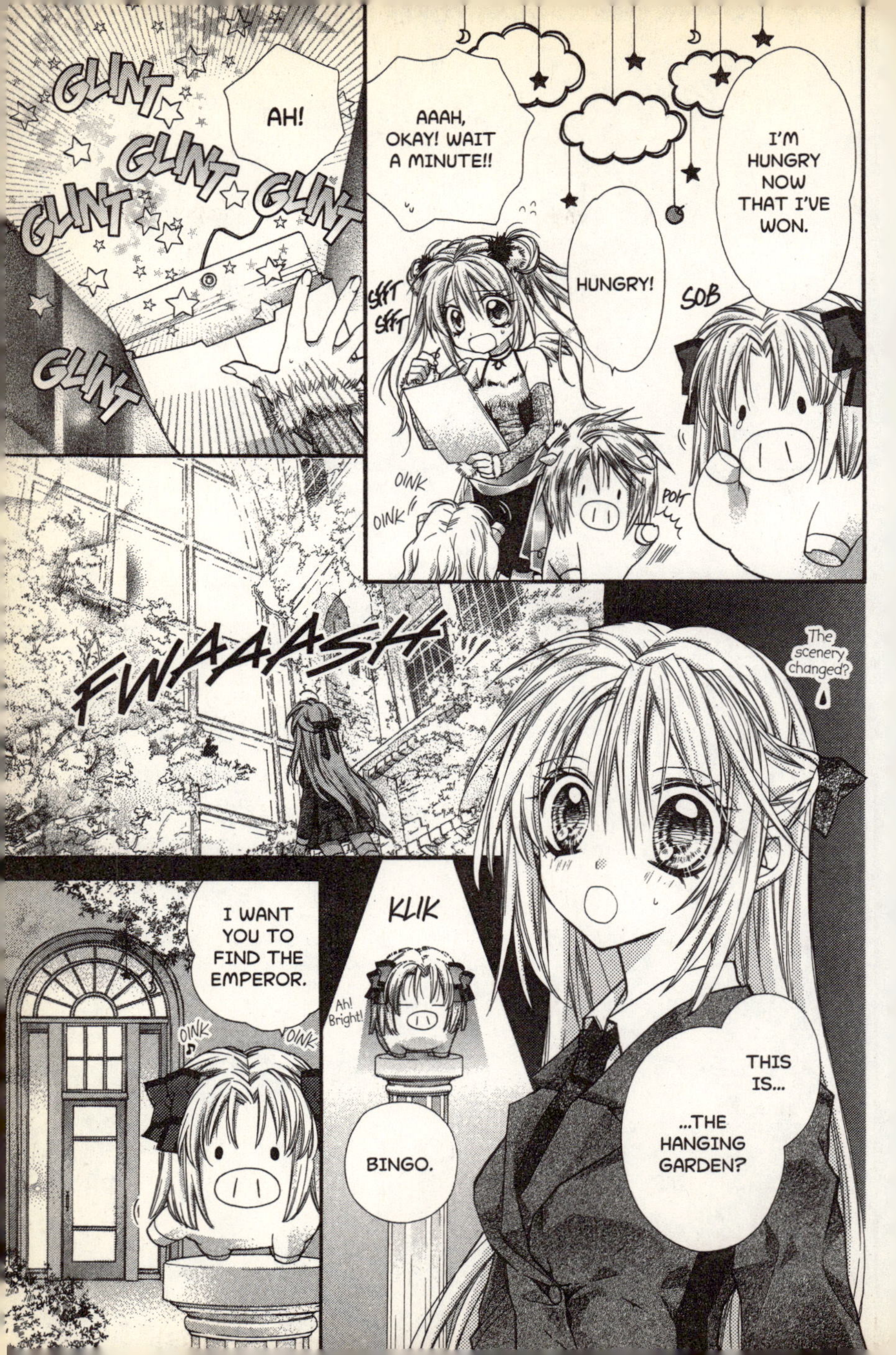
I'M HUNGRY NOW THAT I'VE WON.
SOB
HUNGRY!
AAAH, OKAY! WAIT A MINUTE!!
SFFT SFFT
POK
OINK OINK
AH!
GLINT GLINT GLINT GLINT
GLINT
FWAAASH
The scenery changed?
THIS IS...
...THE HANGING GARDEN?
KLIK
Ah! Bright!
BINGO.
I WANT YOU TO FIND THE EMPEROR.
OINK OINK

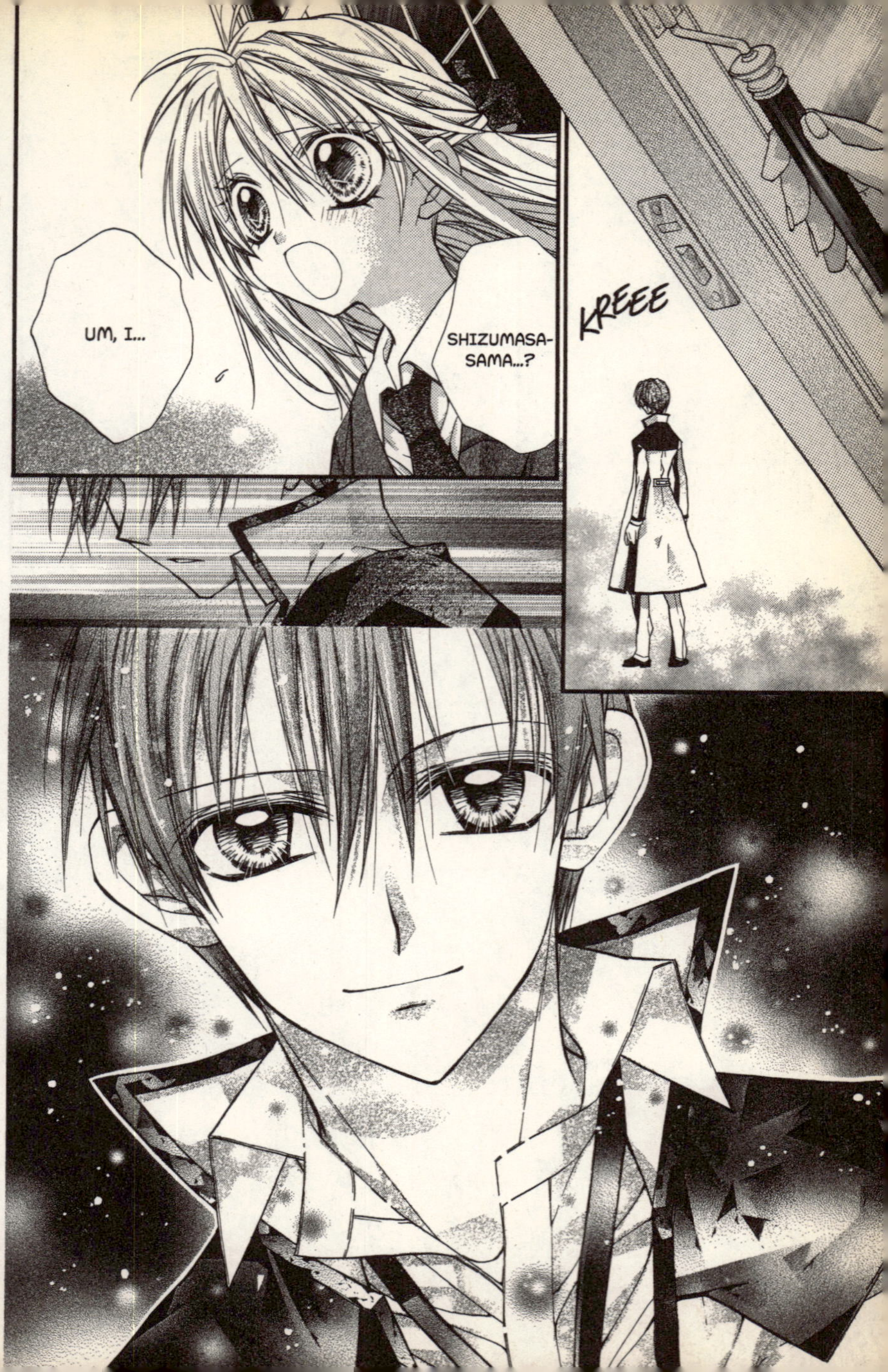
KREEE
SHIZUMASA-SAMA...?
UM, I...

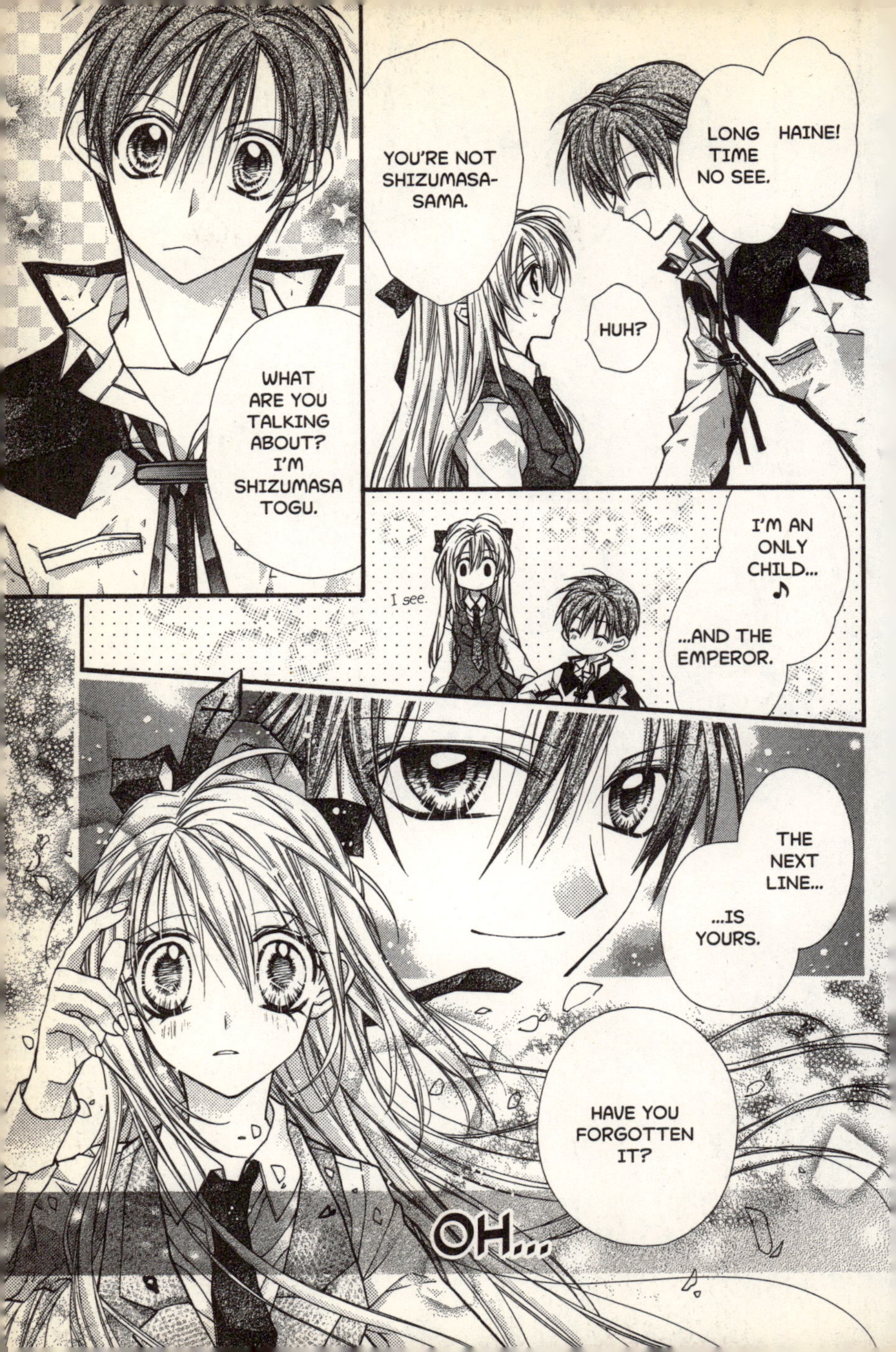
HAINE! LONG TIME NO SEE.
HUH?
YOU'RE NOT SHIZUMASA-SAMA.
WHAT ARE YOU TALKING ABOUT? I'M SHIZUMASA TOGU.
I'M AN ONLY CHILD... ♪
...AND THE EMPEROR.
I see.
THE NEXT LINE...
...IS YOURS.
HAVE YOU FORGOTTEN IT?
OH...

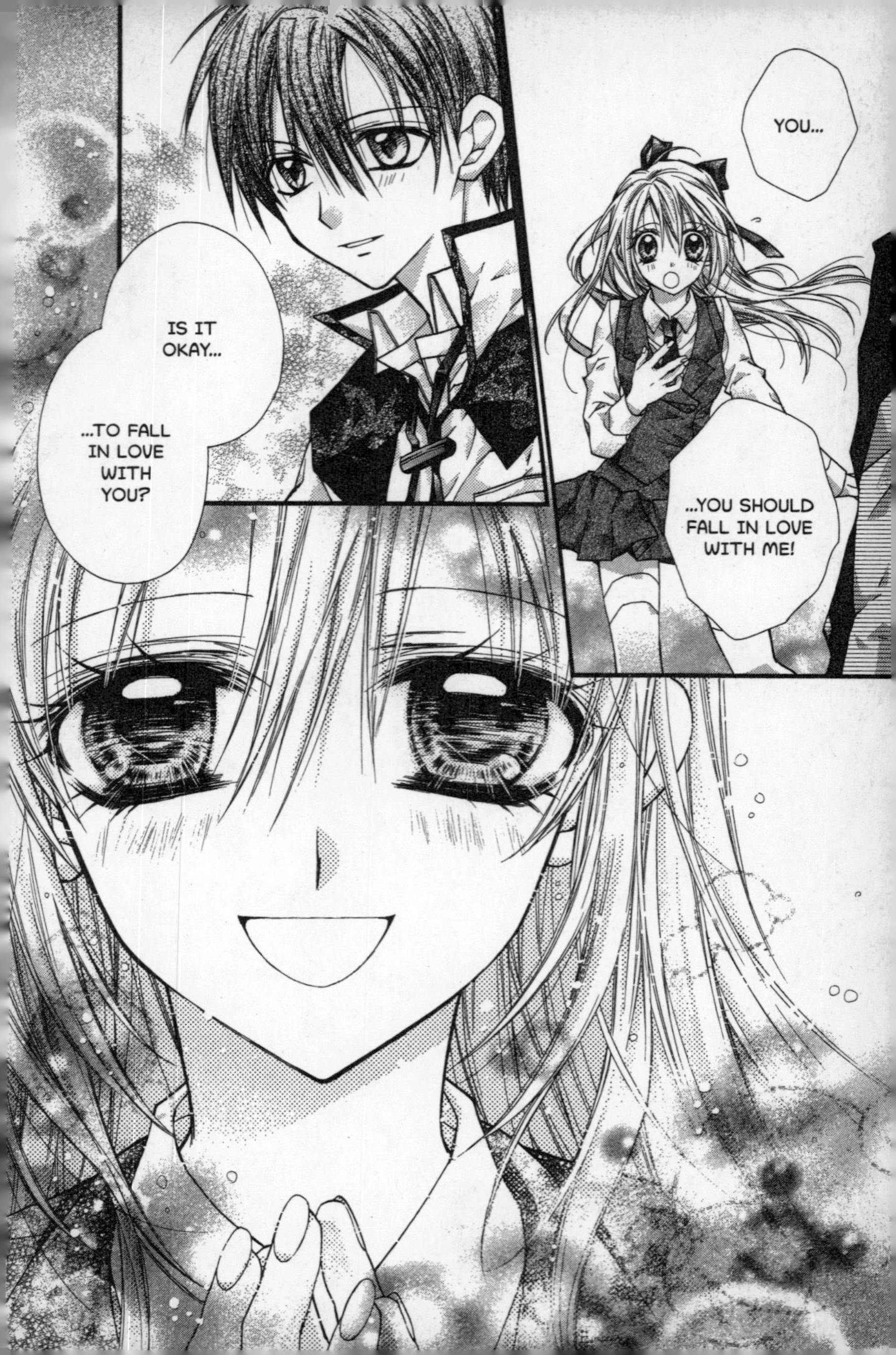
YOU...
...YOU SHOULD FALL IN LOVE WITH ME!
IS IT OKAY...
...TO FALL IN LOVE WITH YOU?

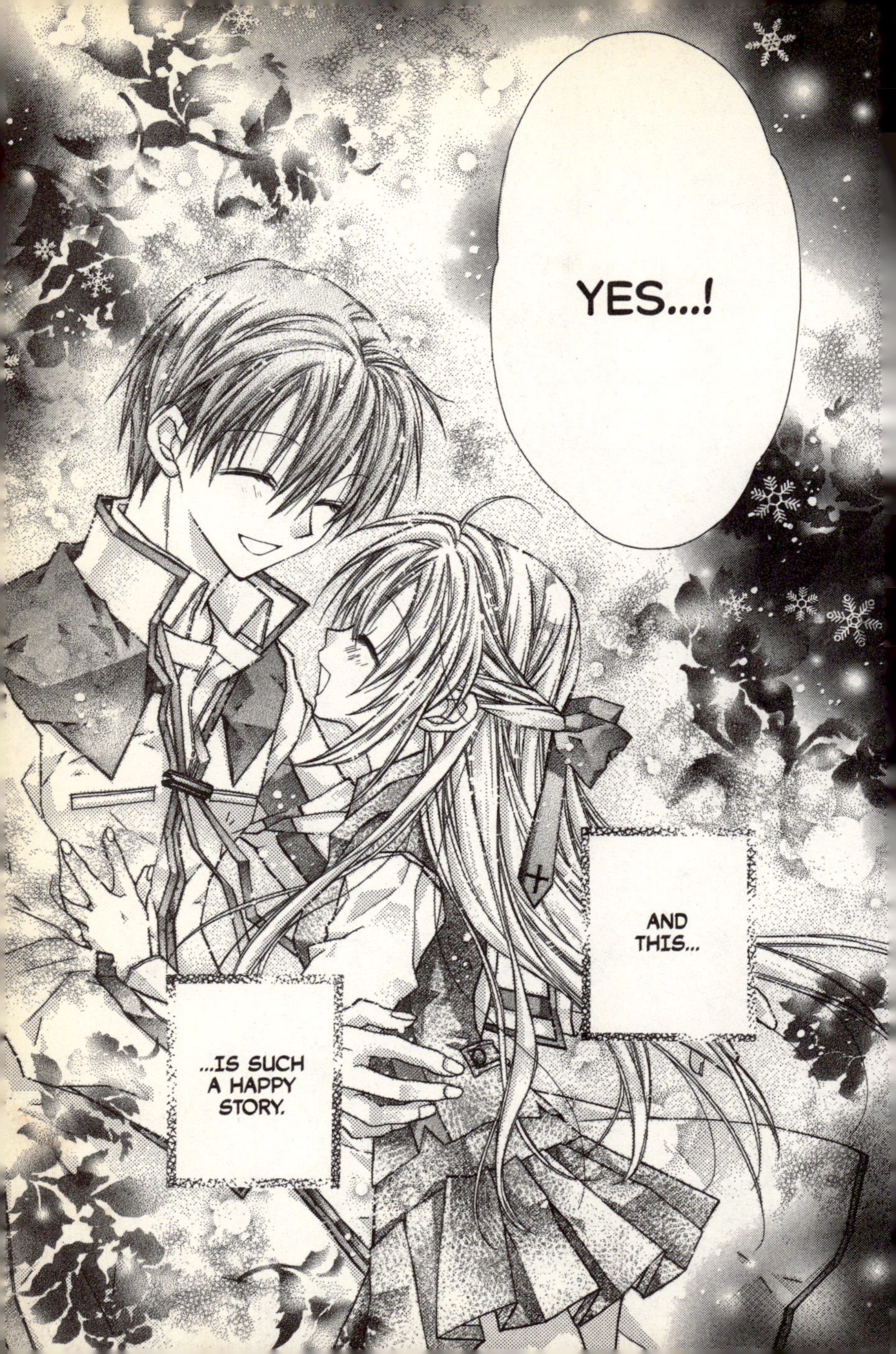
YES...!
AND THIS...
...IS SUCH A HAPPY STORY.

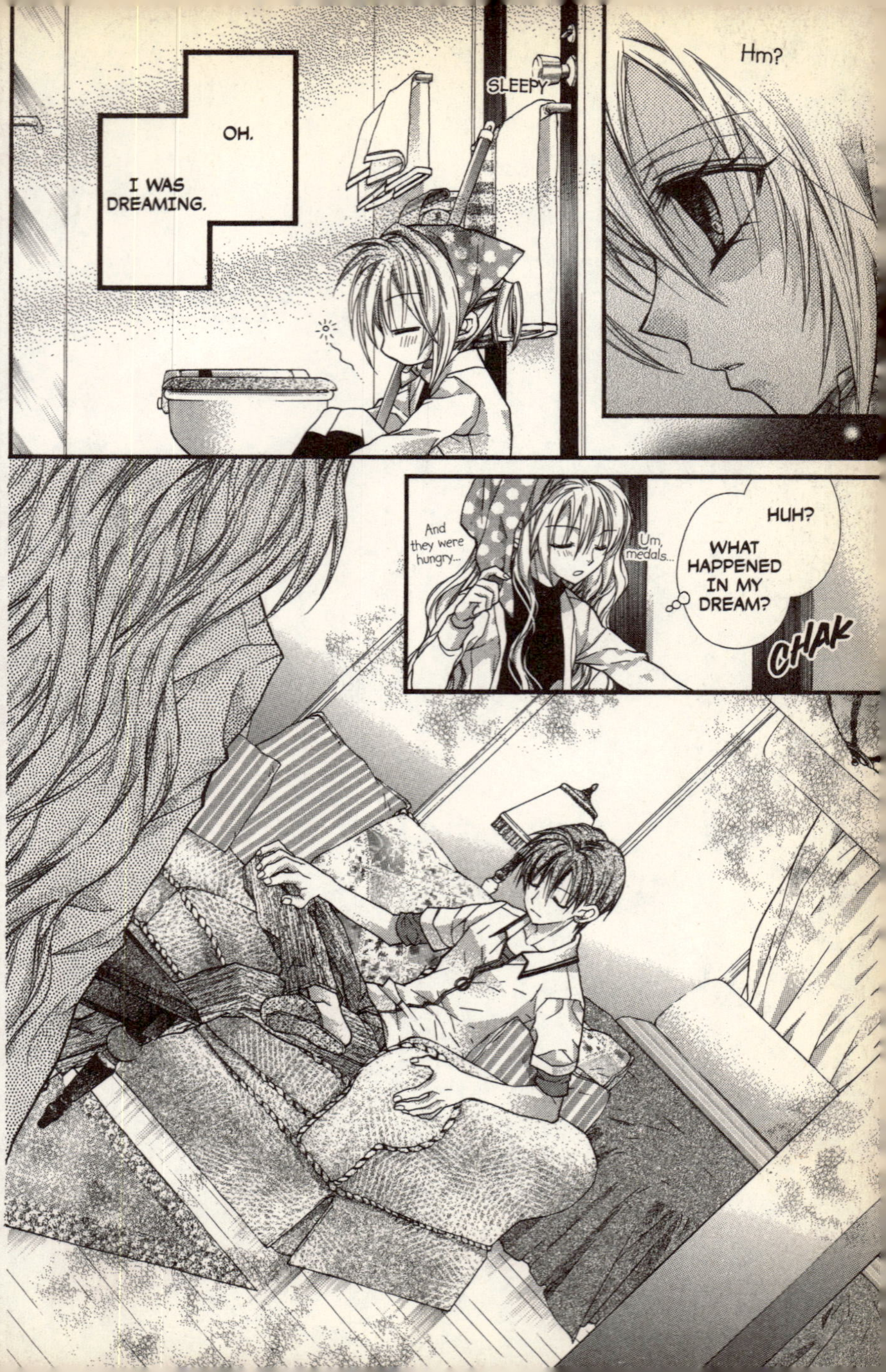
Hm?
SLEEPY
OH.
I WAS DREAMING.
HUH?
WHAT HAPPENED IN MY DREAM?
CHAK
Um, medals...
And they were hungry...

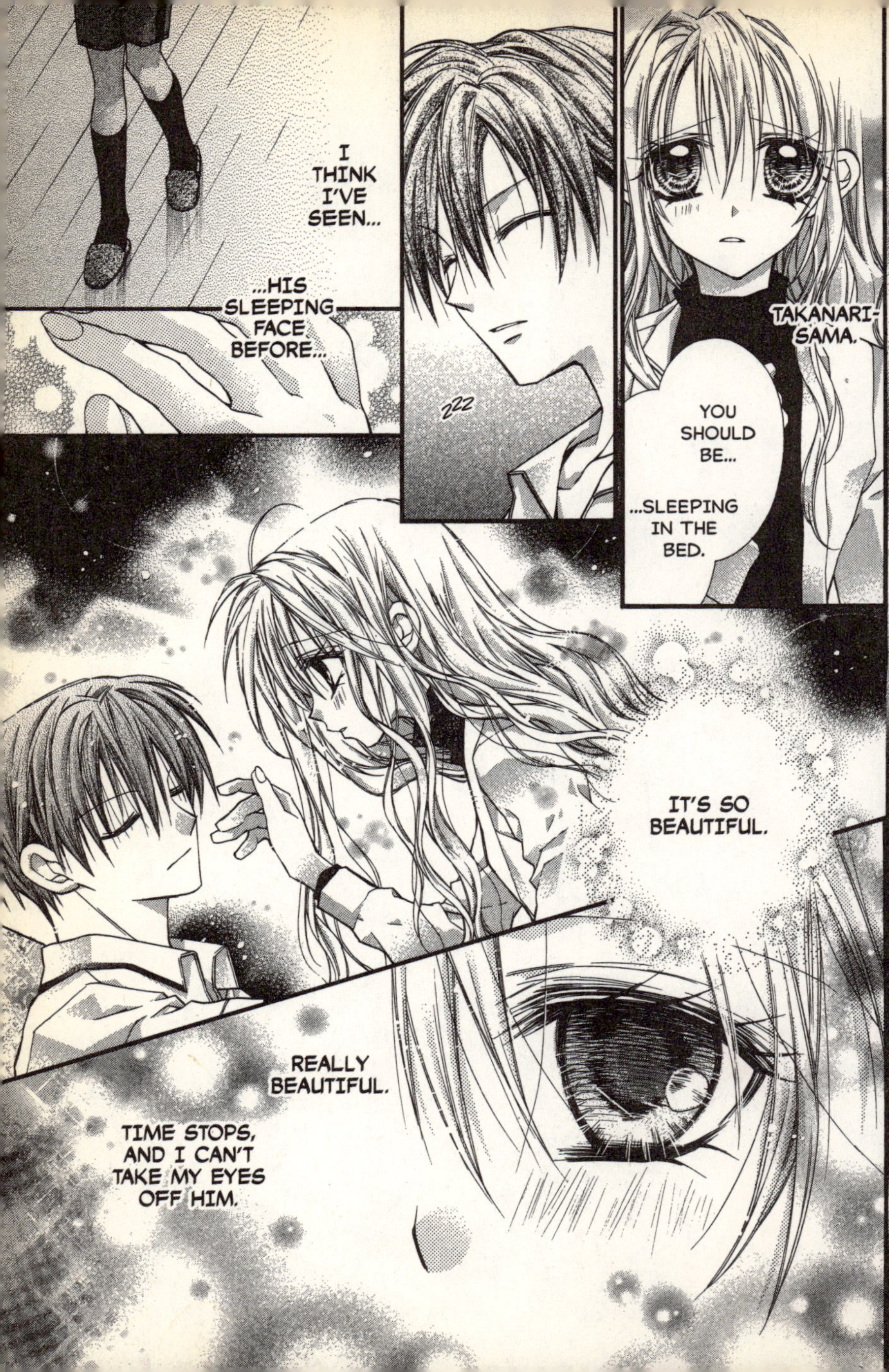
TAKANARI-SAMA.
YOU SHOULD BE...
...SLEEPING IN THE BED.
zzz
I THINK I'VE SEEN...
...HIS SLEEPING FACE BEFORE...
IT'S SO BEAUTIFUL.
REALLY BEAUTIFUL.
TIME STOPS, AND I CAN'T TAKE MY EYES OFF HIM.

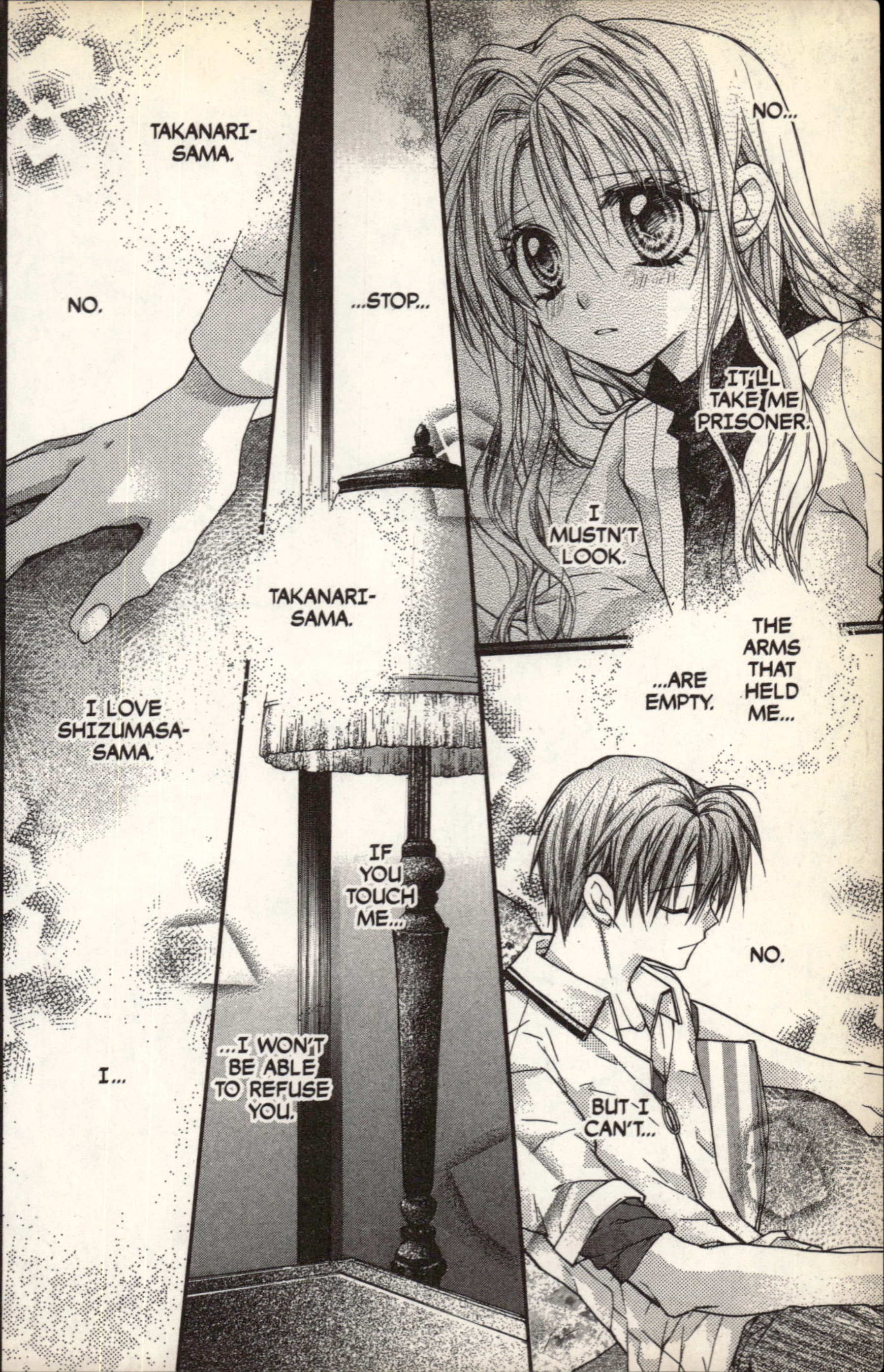
NO...
IT'LL TAKE ME PRISONER.
I MUSTN'T LOOK.
THE ARMS THAT HELD ME...
...ARE EMPTY.
NO.
BUT I CAN'T...
...STOP...
TAKANARI-SAMA.
IF YOU TOUCH ME...
...I WON'T BE ABLE TO REFUSE YOU.
TAKANARI-SAMA.
NO.
I LOVE SHIZUMASA-SAMA.
I...

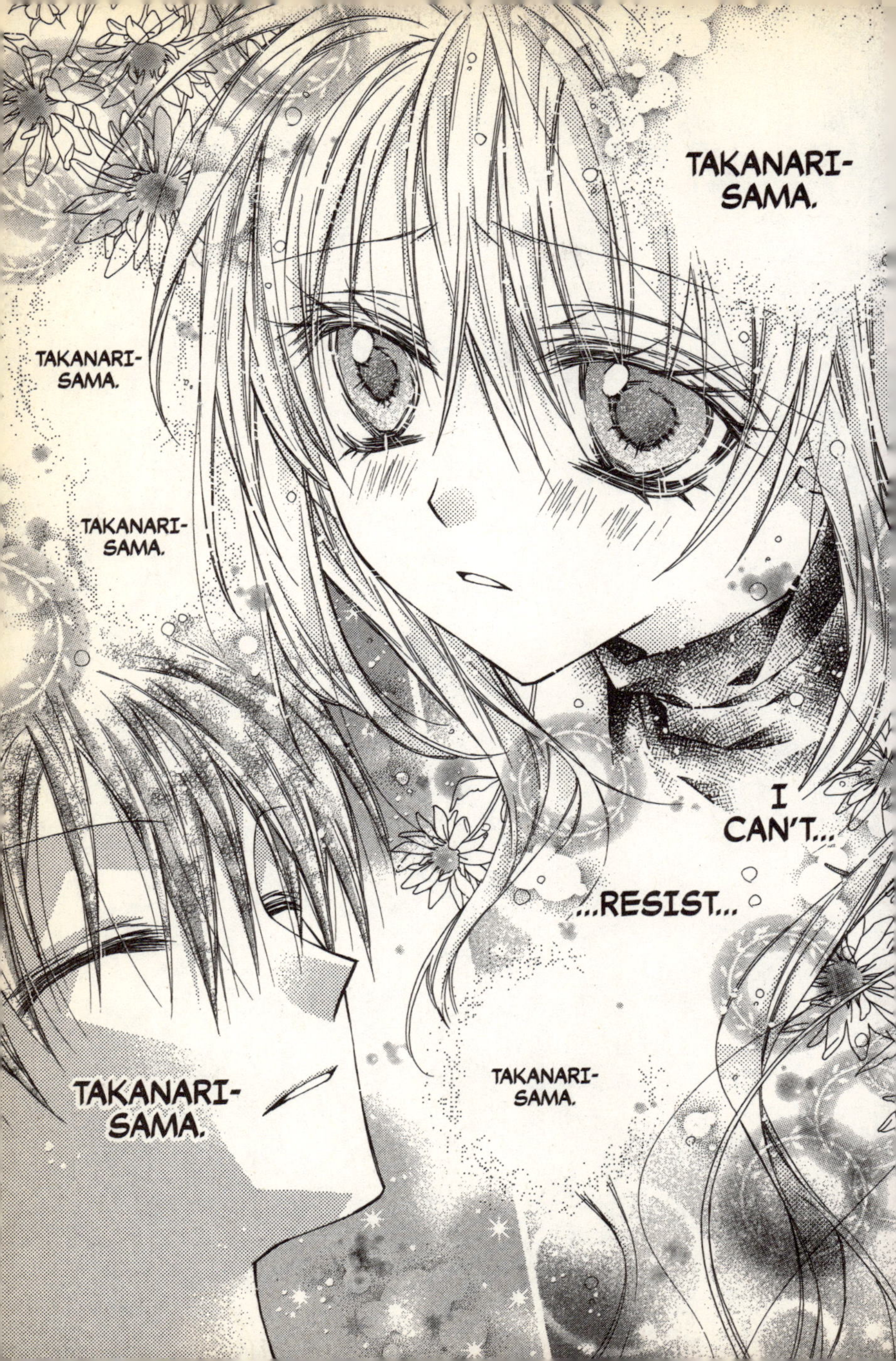
TAKANARI-SAMA.
TAKANARI-SAMA.
TAKANARI-SAMA.
I CAN'T...
...RESIST...
TAKANARI-SAMA.
TAKANARI-SAMA.

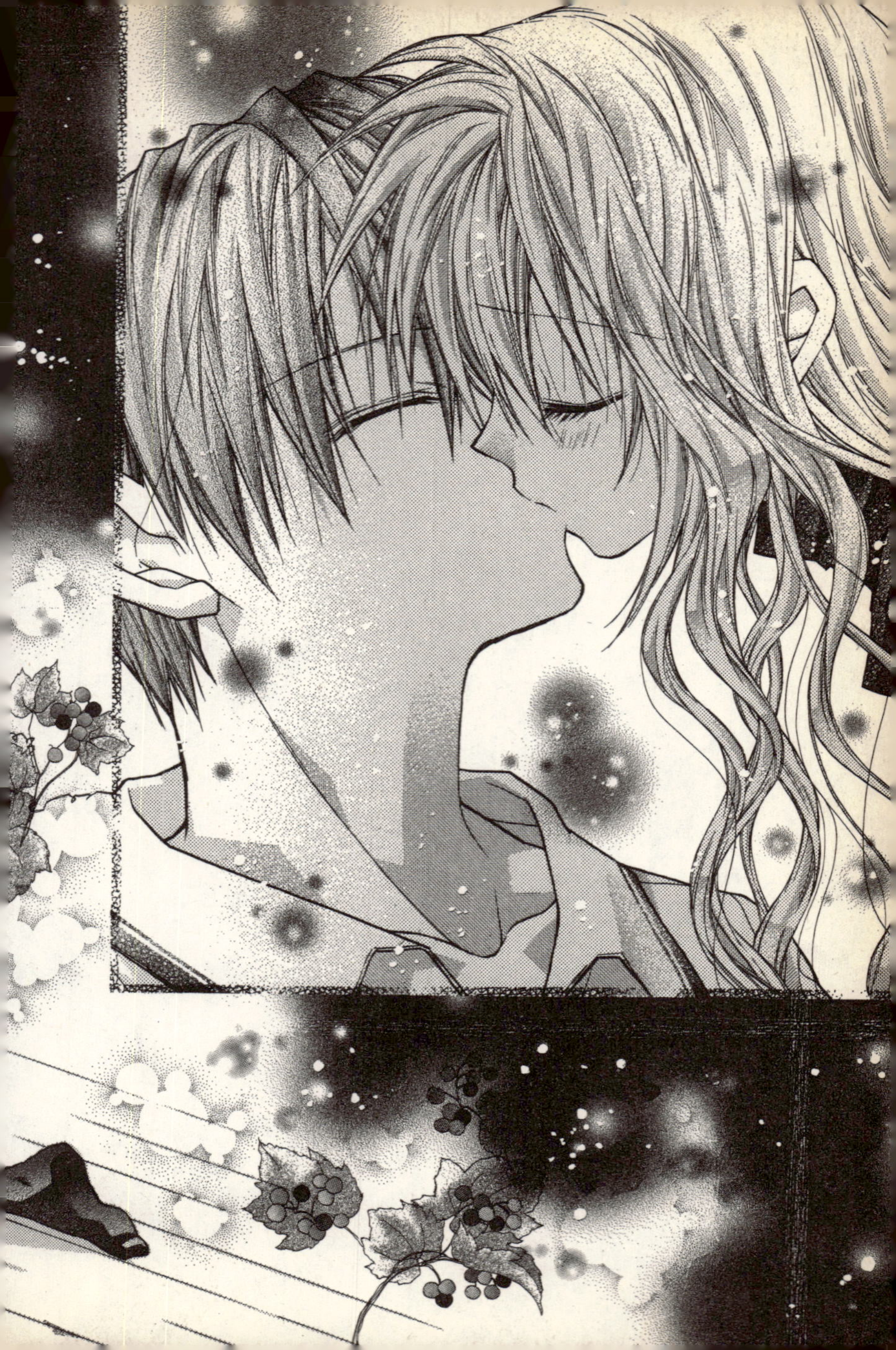

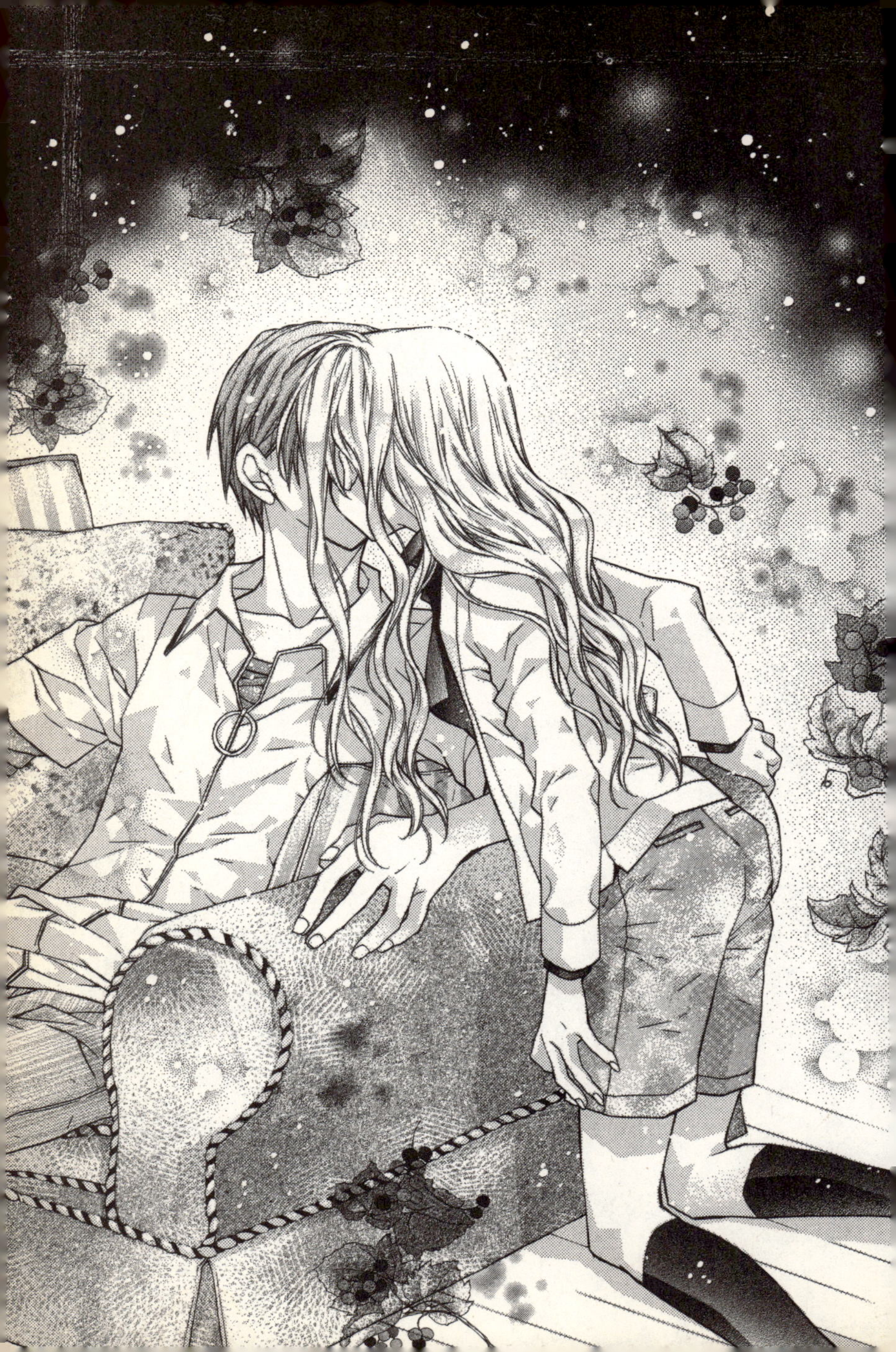

Growers Council has mounted Kodak had violated seven of of fats and oils in food an information campaign and Polaroid's key patents on to acts in the last year but

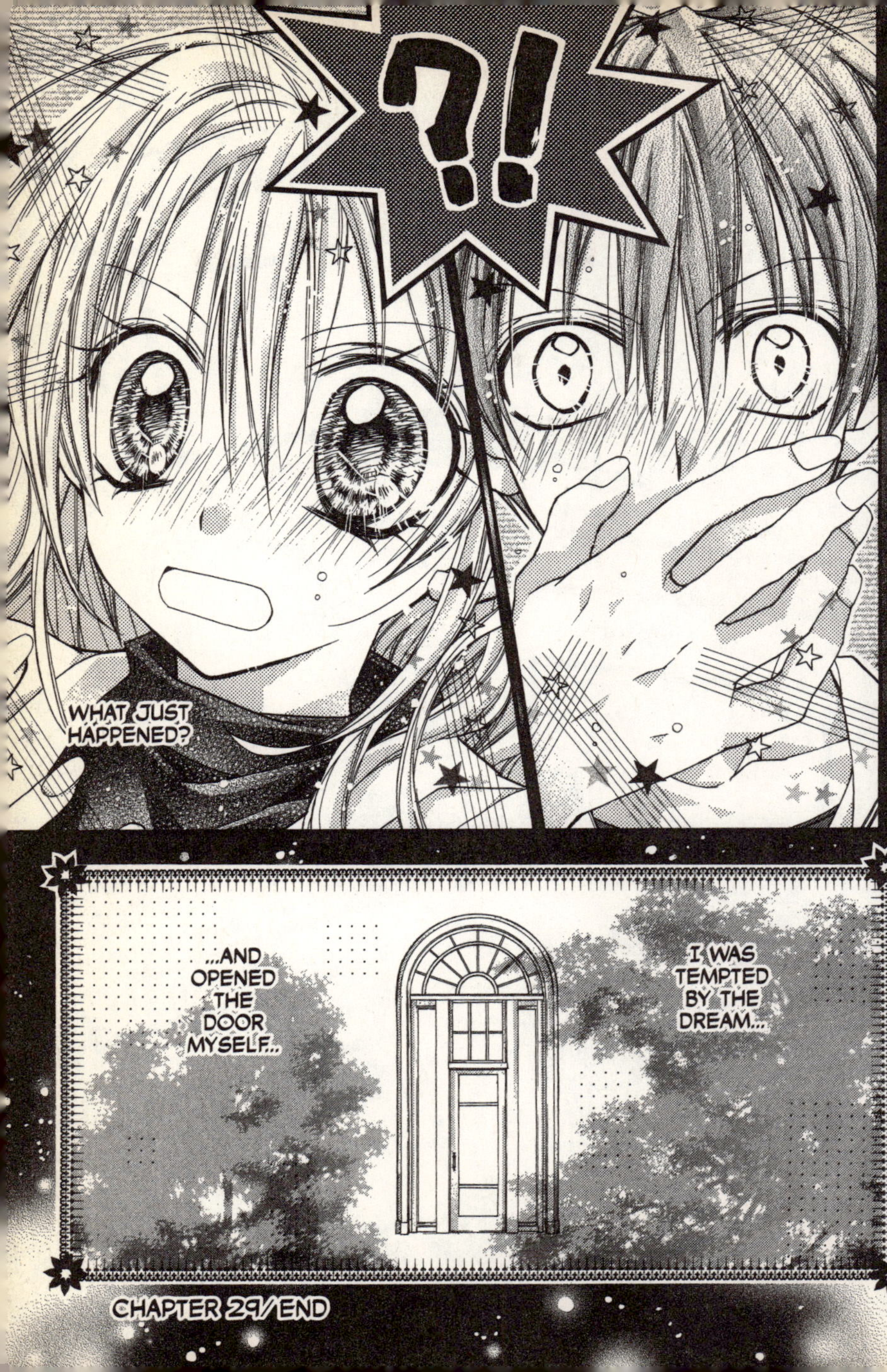
?!
WHAT JUST HAPPENED?
I WAS TEMPTED BY THE DREAM...
...AND OPENED THE DOOR MYSELF...
CHAPTER 29/END

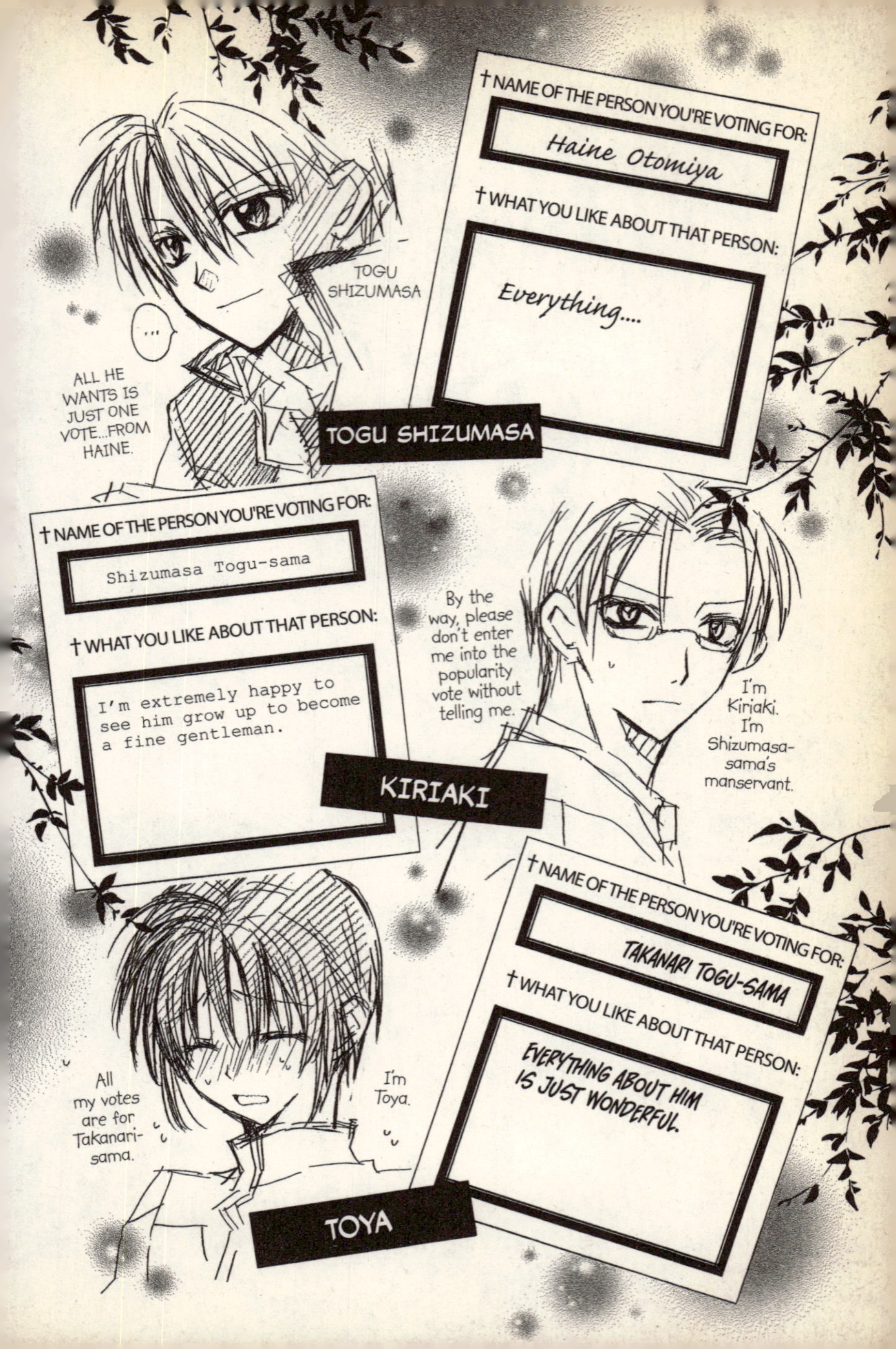
† NAME OF THE PERSON YOU'RE VOTING FOR:
Haine Otomiya
† WHAT YOU LIKE ABOUT THAT PERSON:
Everything....
TOGU SHIZUMASA
TOGU SHIZUMASA
...
ALL HE WANTS IS JUST ONE VOTE...FROM HAINE.
I'm Kiriaki. I'm Shizumasa-sama's manservant.
By the way, please don't enter me into the popularity vote without telling me.
† NAME OF THE PERSON YOU'RE VOTING FOR:
Shizumasa Togu-sama
† WHAT YOU LIKE ABOUT THAT PERSON:
I'm extremely happy to see him grow up to become a fine gentleman.
KIRIAKI
† NAME OF THE PERSON YOU'RE VOTING FOR:
TAKANARI TOGU-SAMA
† WHAT YOU LIKE ABOUT THAT PERSON:
EVERYTHING ABOUT HIM IS JUST WONDERFUL.
TOYA
I'm Toya.
All my votes are for Takanari-sama.

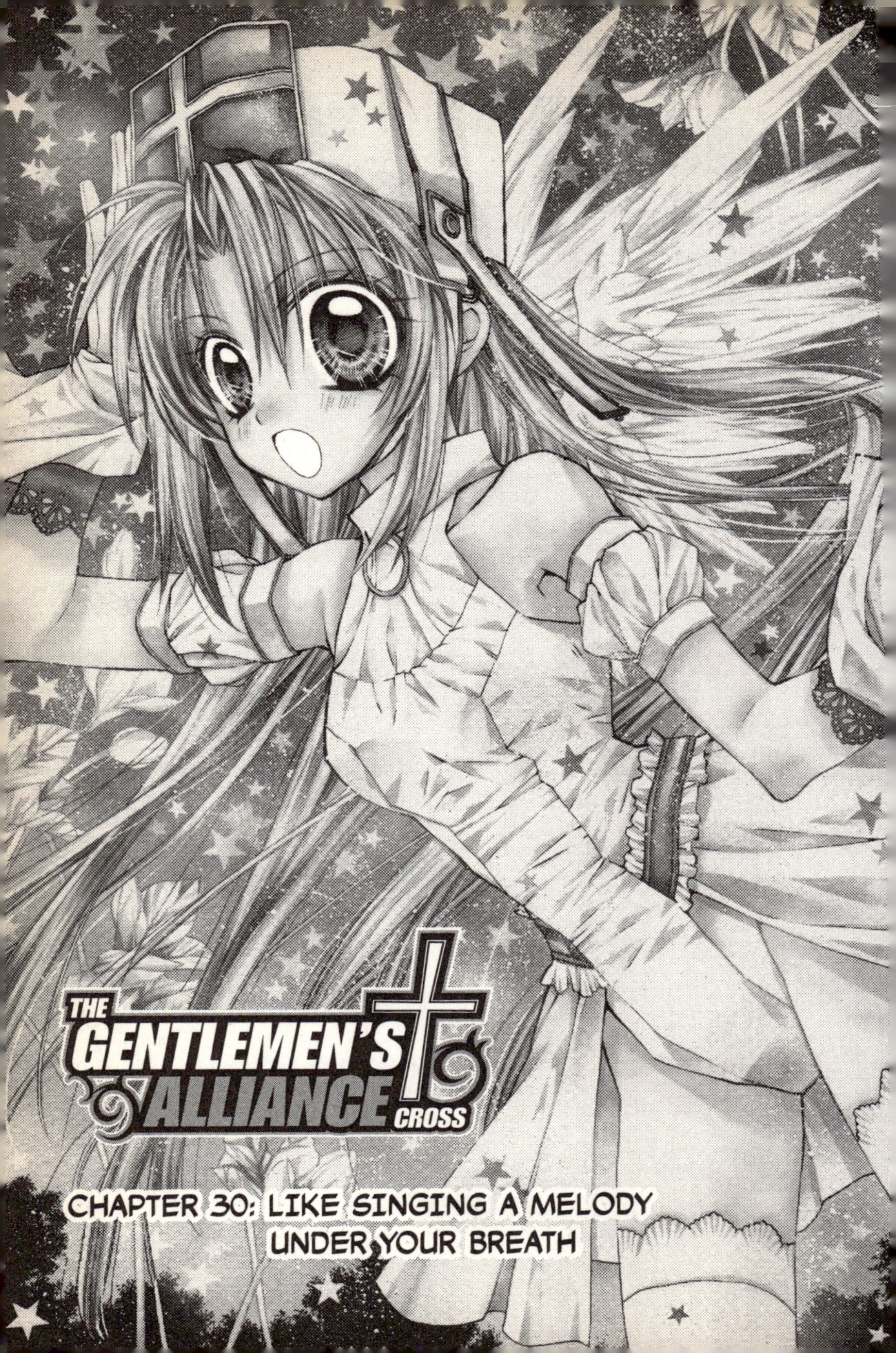
THE GENTLEMEN'S ALLIANCE CROSS
CHAPTER 30: LIKE SINGING A MELODY UNDER YOUR BREATH

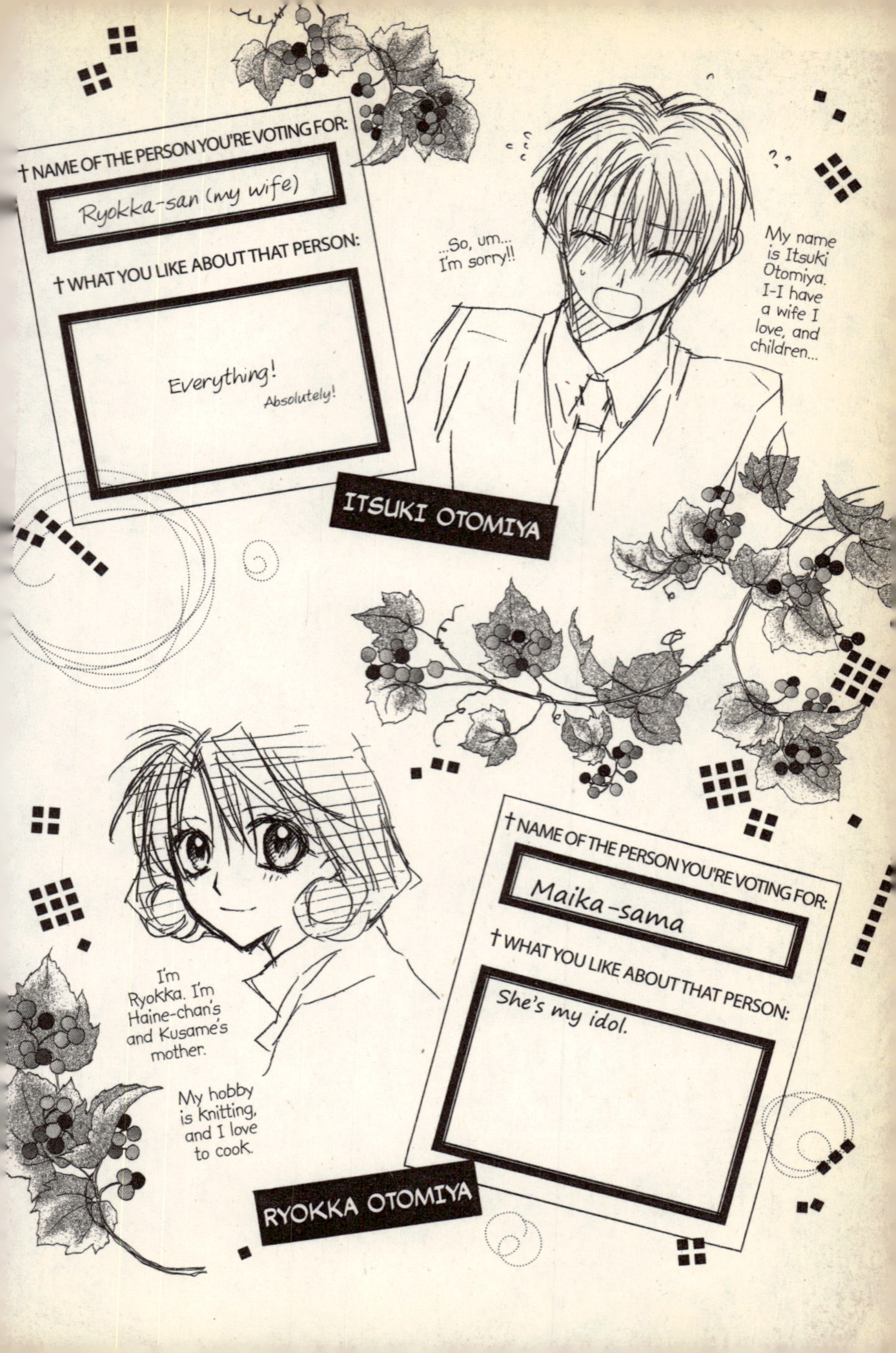

My name is Itsuki Otomiya. I-I have a wife I love, and children...
...So, um... I'm sorry!!
† NAME OF THE PERSON YOU'RE VOTING FOR:
Ryokka-san (my wife)
† WHAT YOU LIKE ABOUT THAT PERSON:
Everything!
Absolutely!
ITSUKI OTOMIYA
† NAME OF THE PERSON YOU'RE VOTING FOR:
Maika-sama
† WHAT YOU LIKE ABOUT THAT PERSON:
She's my idol.
I'm Ryokka. I'm Haine-chan's and Kusame's mother.
My hobby is knitting, and I love to cook.
RYOKKA OTOMIYA

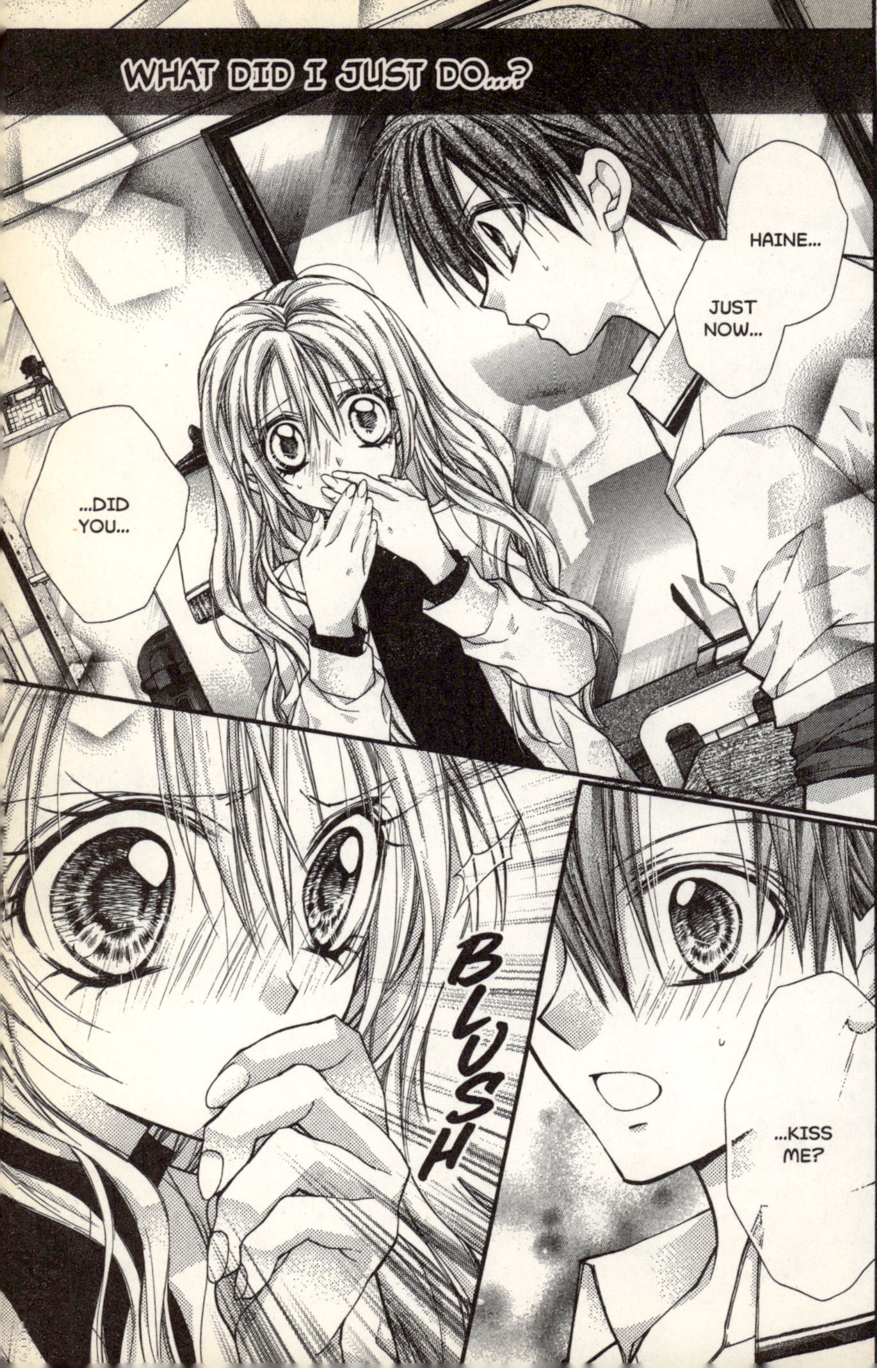
WHAT DID I JUST DO...?
HAINE...
JUST NOW...
...DID YOU...
...KISS ME?
BLUSH

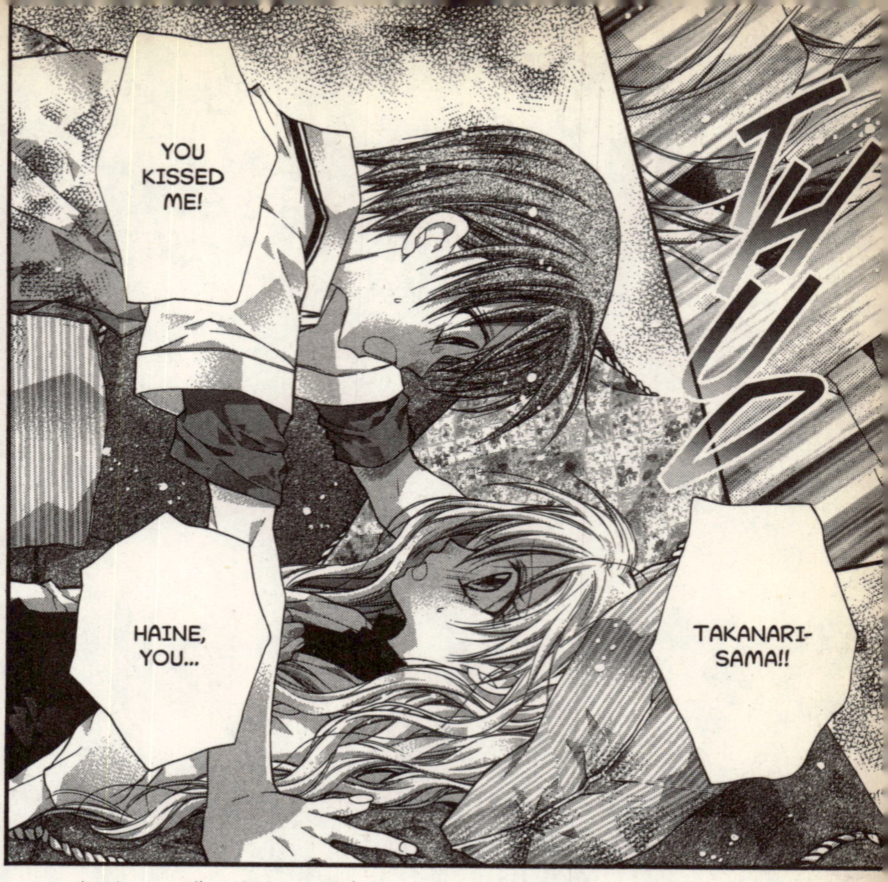
THUD
TAKANARI-SAMA!!
YOU KISSED ME!
HAINE, YOU...

Chapter 30: Like Singing a Melody Under Your Breath

Lead-in: The kiss of a couple in love has the power to make stars rain down upon them...!

I'm giving away the story!

I entrusted the lead-in to my supervisor for this chapter. (It's very spirited and cute.) This chapter is very lovey-dovey, isn't it? I had a question from my readers about Maora's "I wouldn't have stopped" line: Did he mean he wouldn't stop if he was in a situation like that with Maguri, or that he wouldn't stop even if Haine-chan asked him to stop? The answer is the latter, by the way.

He basically meant that even if Haine-chan asked him to stop he wouldn't be able to because she's so cute. (laugh)

And also, just making Komaki appear in a scene really adds color to the page. To tell you the truth, it's pretty tough to paint her hair using a brush, but after the result of the popularity vote (I'll have the details in volume 8), I've become more careful in painting it.

Ushio slept over at Senri-sensei's place. I wonder how far these two have gone...? B-BMP B-BMP I think they don't have much of a relationship yet. I have a feeling that Senri would actually ward her off by saying, "I am the school doctor, you know" or something of that sort.

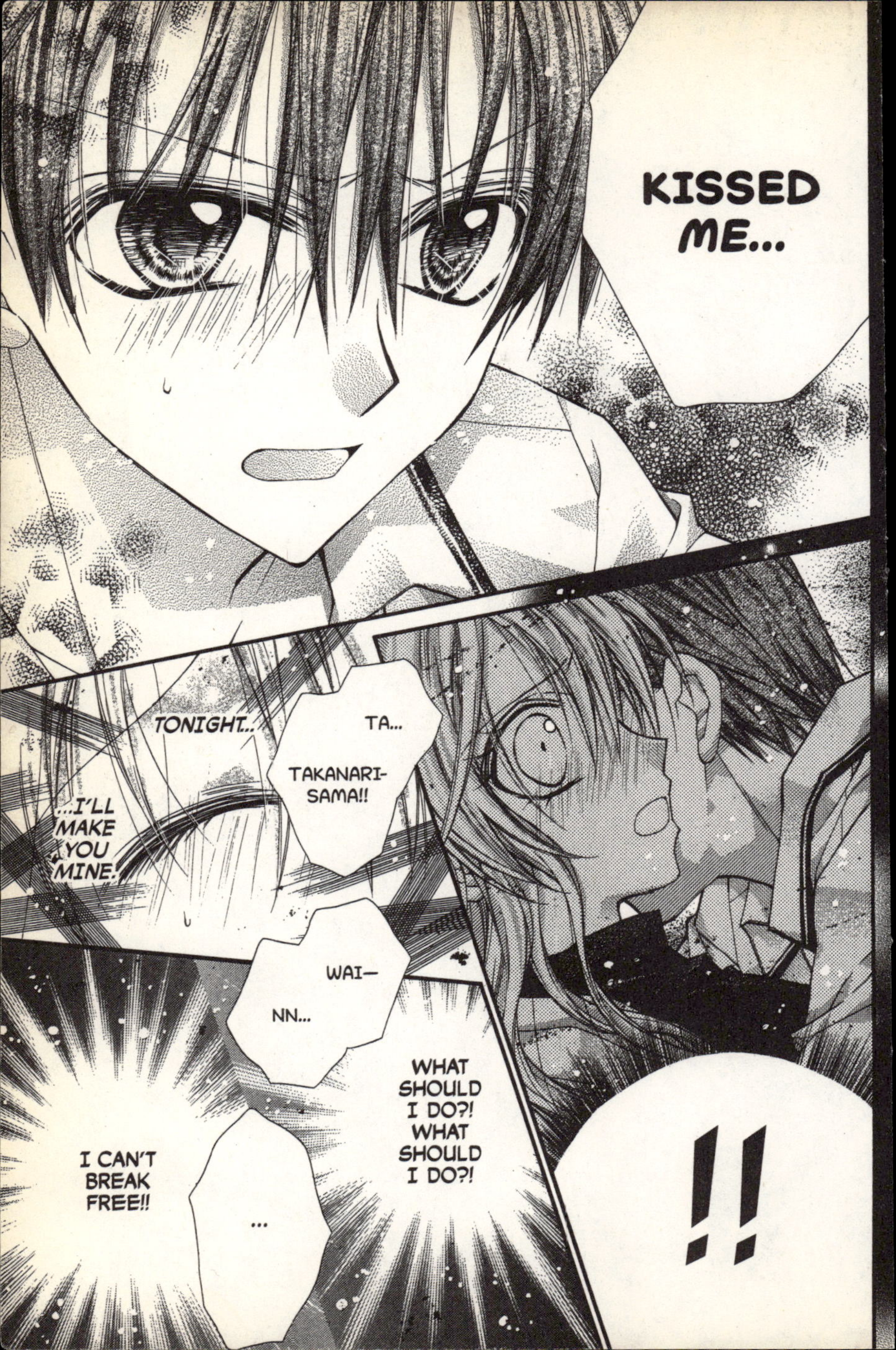
KISSED ME...
TA... TAKANARI-SAMA!!
TONIGHT...
...I'LL MAKE YOU MINE.
WAI— NN...
!!
WHAT SHOULD I DO?! WHAT SHOULD I DO?!
I CAN'T BREAK FREE!!
...

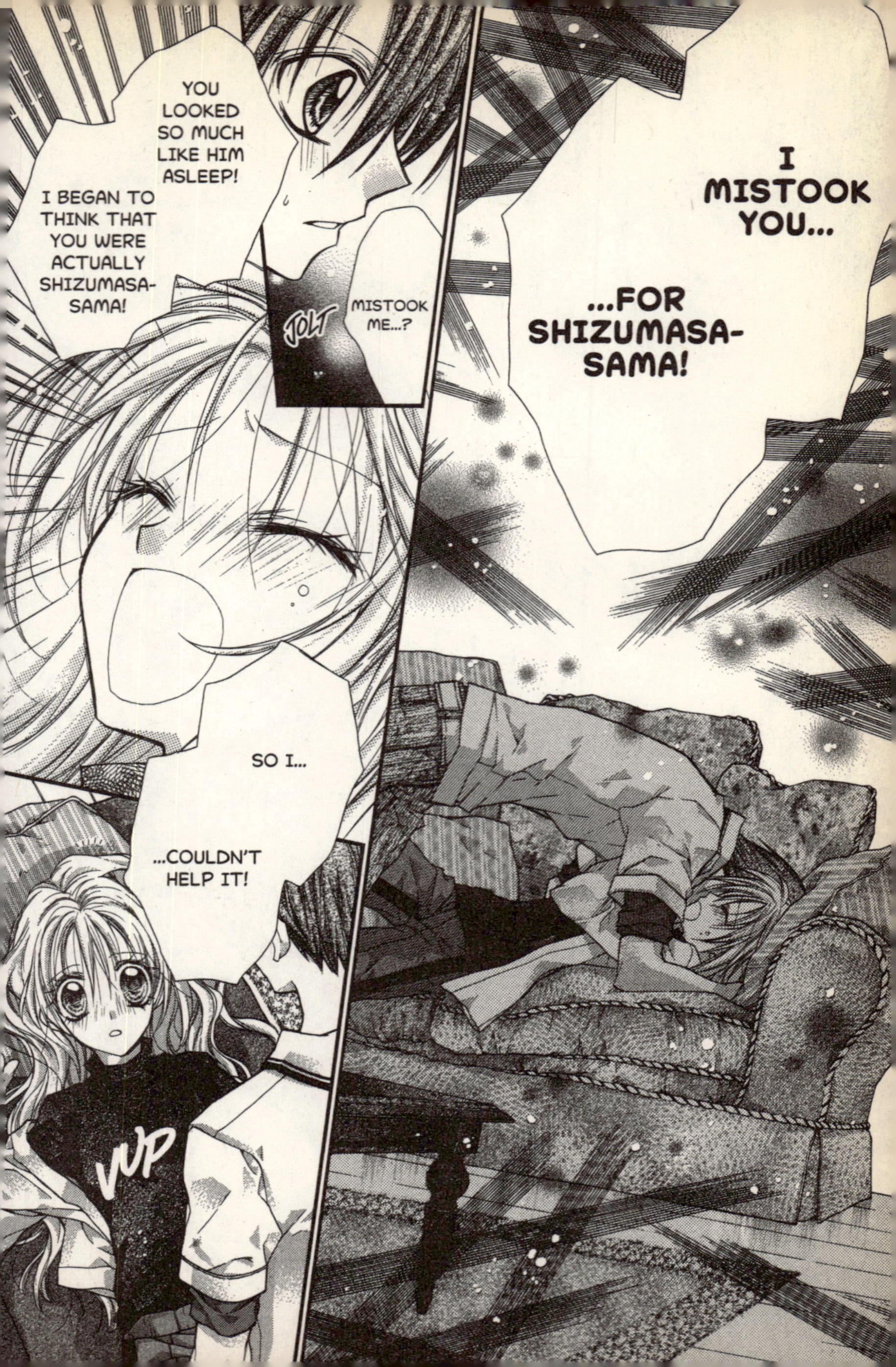
I MISTOOK YOU...
...FOR SHIZUMASA-SAMA!
MISTOOK ME...?
JOLT
YOU LOOKED SO MUCH LIKE HIM ASLEEP!
I BEGAN TO THINK THAT YOU WERE ACTUALLY SHIZUMASA-SAMA!
SO I...
...COULDN'T HELP IT!
VUP

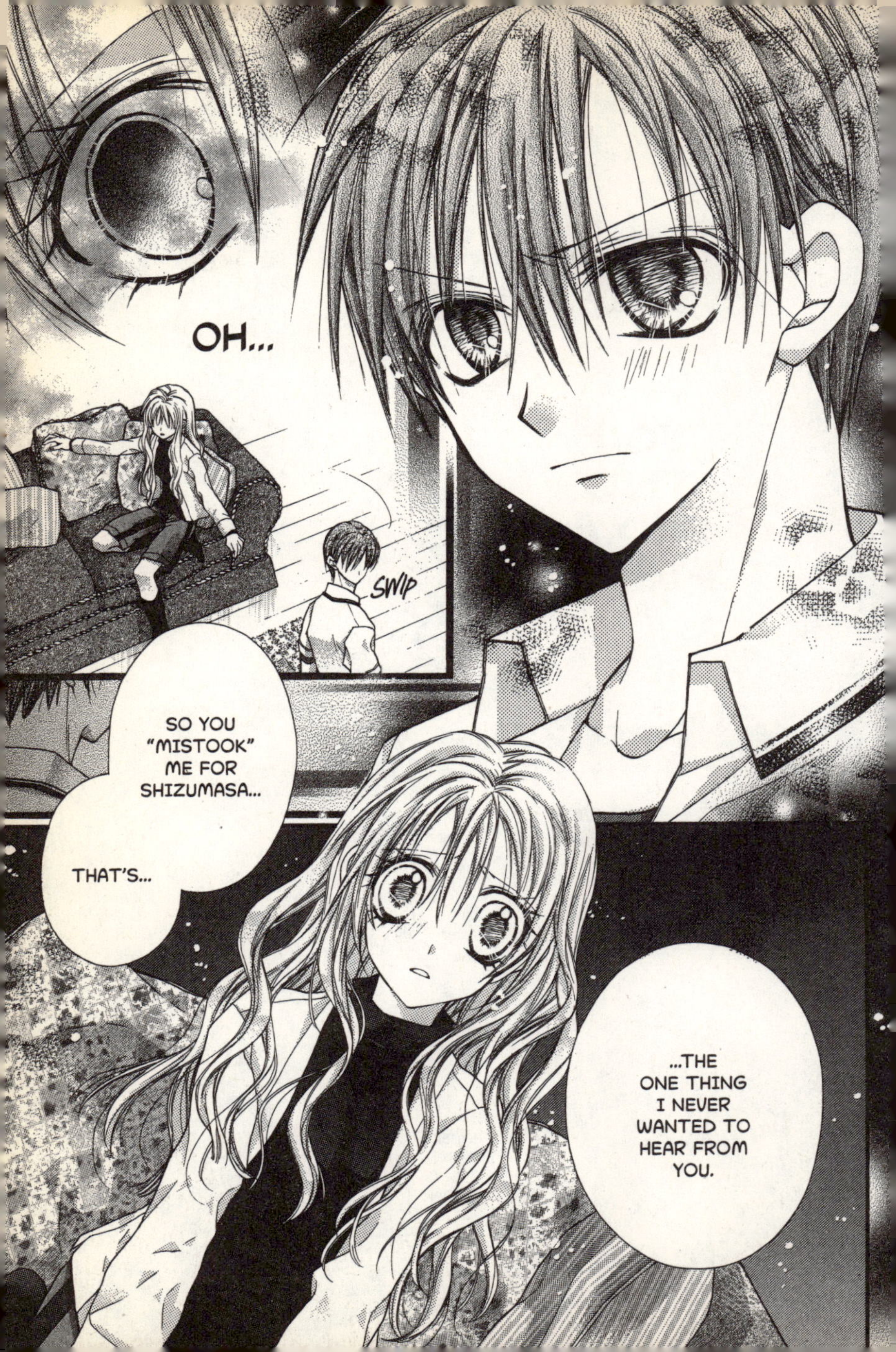
OH...
SWIP
SO YOU "MISTOOK" ME FOR SHIZUMASA...
THAT'S...
...THE ONE THING I NEVER WANTED TO HEAR FROM YOU.

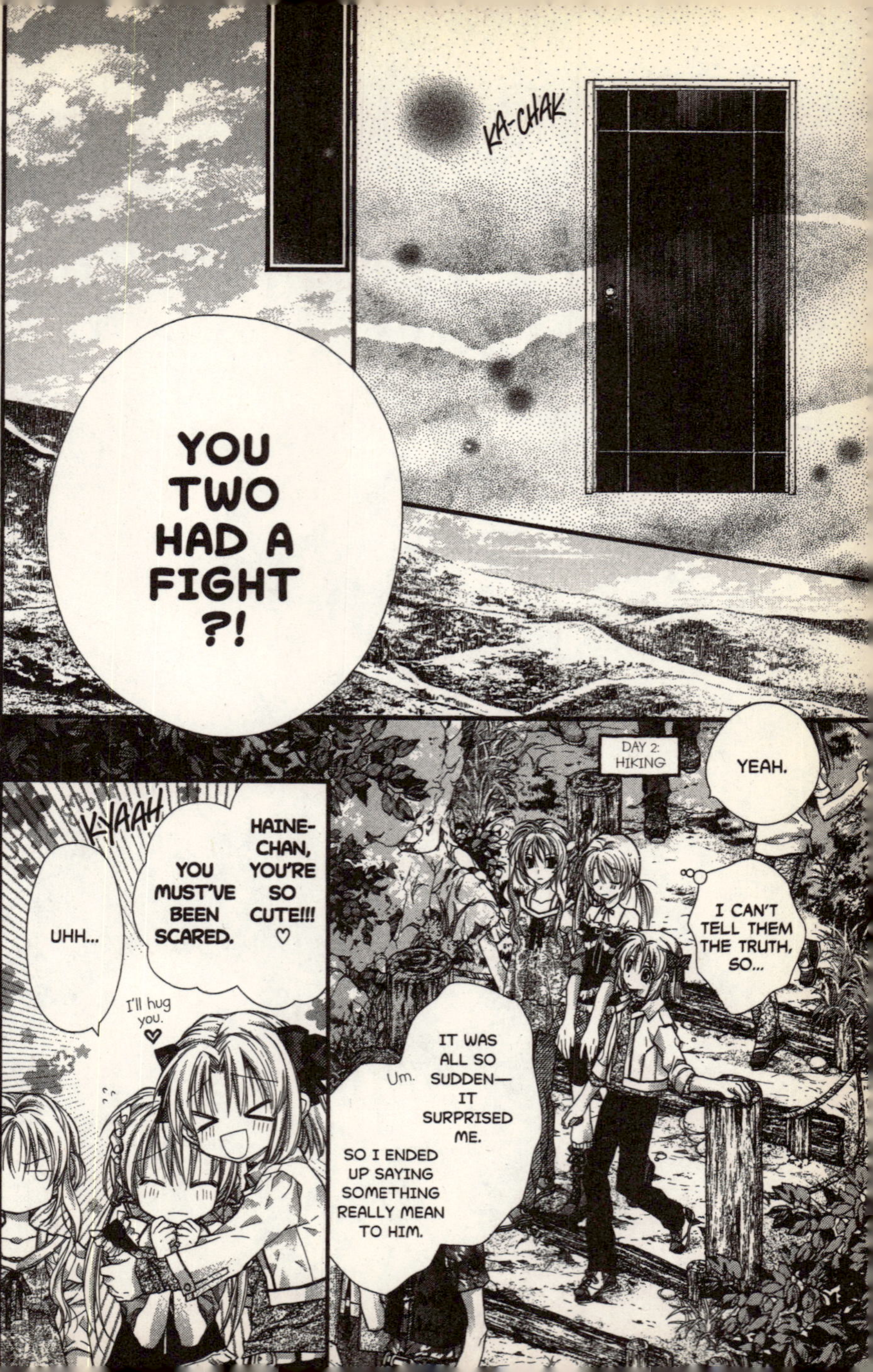
KA-CHAK
YOU TWO HAD A FIGHT?!
DAY 2: HIKING
YEAH.
I CAN'T TELL THEM THE TRUTH, SO...
Um.
IT WAS ALL SO SUDDEN— IT SURPRISED ME.
SO I ENDED UP SAYING SOMETHING REALLY MEAN TO HIM.
KYAAH
HAINE-CHAN, YOU'RE SO CUTE!!! ♡
YOU MUST'VE BEEN SCARED.
UHH...
I'll hug you. ♥

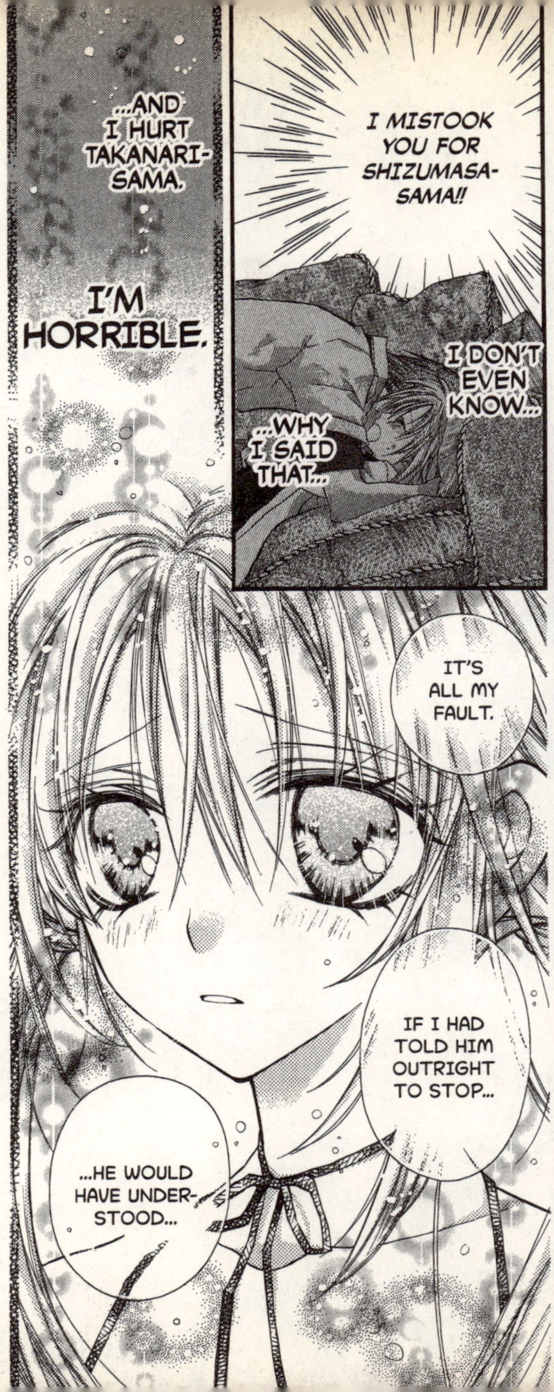
I MISTOOK YOU FOR SHIZUMASA-SAMA!!
I DON'T EVEN KNOW...
...WHY I SAID THAT...
...AND I HURT TAKANARI-SAMA.
I'M HORRIBLE.
IT'S ALL MY FAULT.
IF I HAD TOLD HIM OUTRIGHT TO STOP...
...HE WOULD HAVE UNDER-STOOD...

Hello.

So the cover illustration for the next volume will be of the character who got first place in the popularity vote.

This is to show my gratitude to all the fans who voted. And it's a treat for getting first place. (A treat for that character, that is.)

I can't wait. ❤❤

I'm really busy with both *Jeanne* and *The Gentlemen's Alliance †*, but I'll do my best, so I hope I see you all in the next volume!!

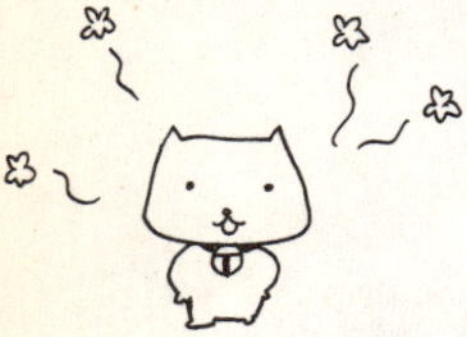

What is this...
Takuto is getting fatter and fatter...
(But the real mystery is that his human form doesn't gain any weight...)

The schedule... was really tight this time, so I'm sorry I couldn't write a lot...

Next time!!
I'll try to include more extra bits and pieces. ❤

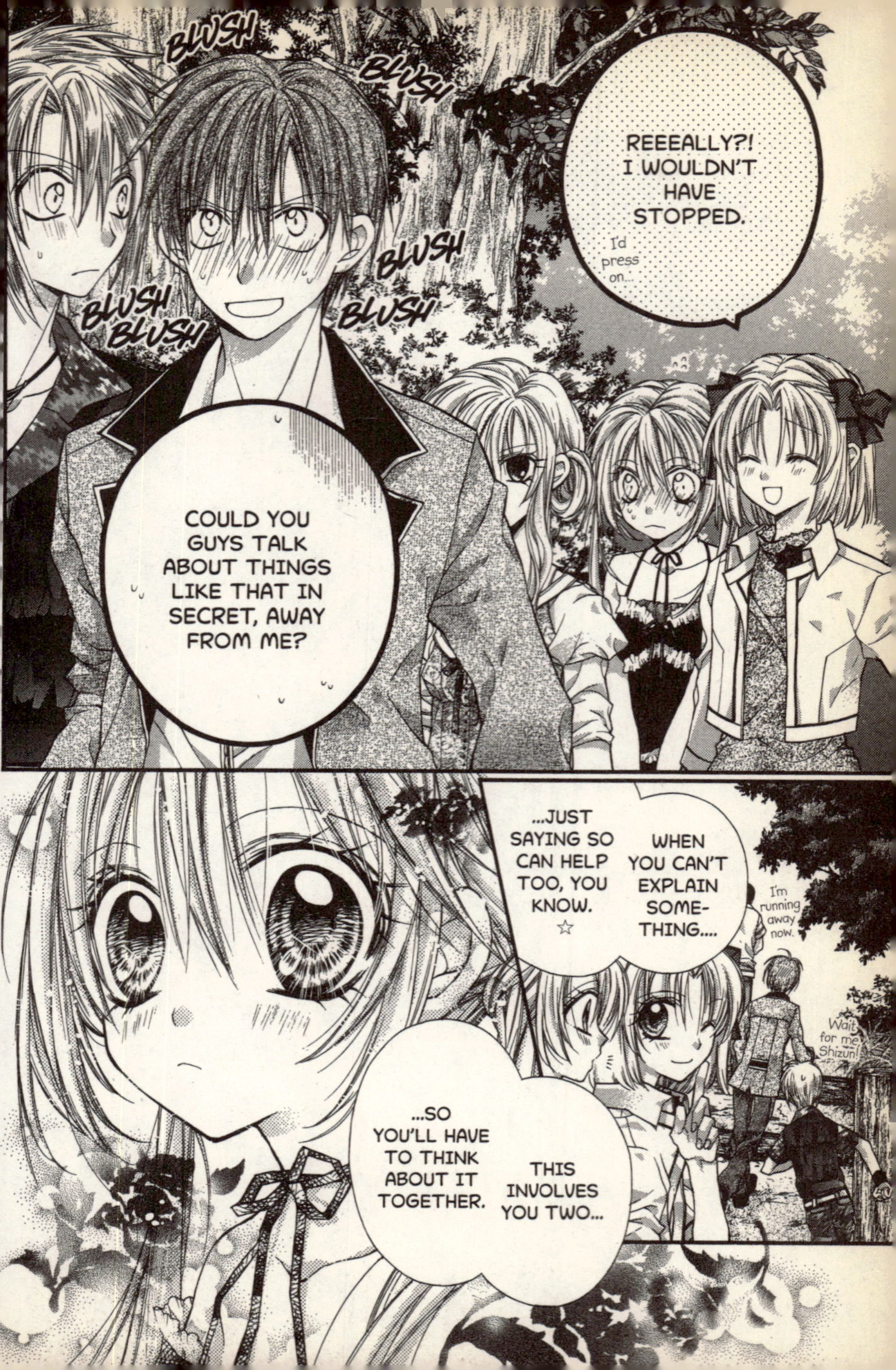
REEEALLY?! I WOULDN'T HAVE STOPPED.
I'd press on...
BLUSH
BLUSH
BLUSH
BLUSH
BLUSH BLUSH
COULD YOU GUYS TALK ABOUT THINGS LIKE THAT IN SECRET, AWAY FROM ME?
I'm running away now.
Wait for me, Shizun!
WHEN YOU CAN'T EXPLAIN SOME-THING....
...JUST SAYING SO CAN HELP TOO, YOU KNOW. ☆
THIS INVOLVES YOU TWO...
...SO YOU'LL HAVE TO THINK ABOUT IT TOGETHER.

I have a blog.

http://rikukai.arina.lolipop.jp/

Arina Nikki

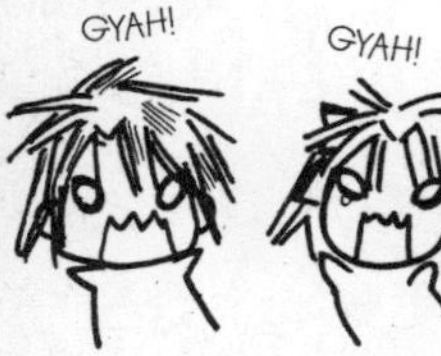

MM Boys

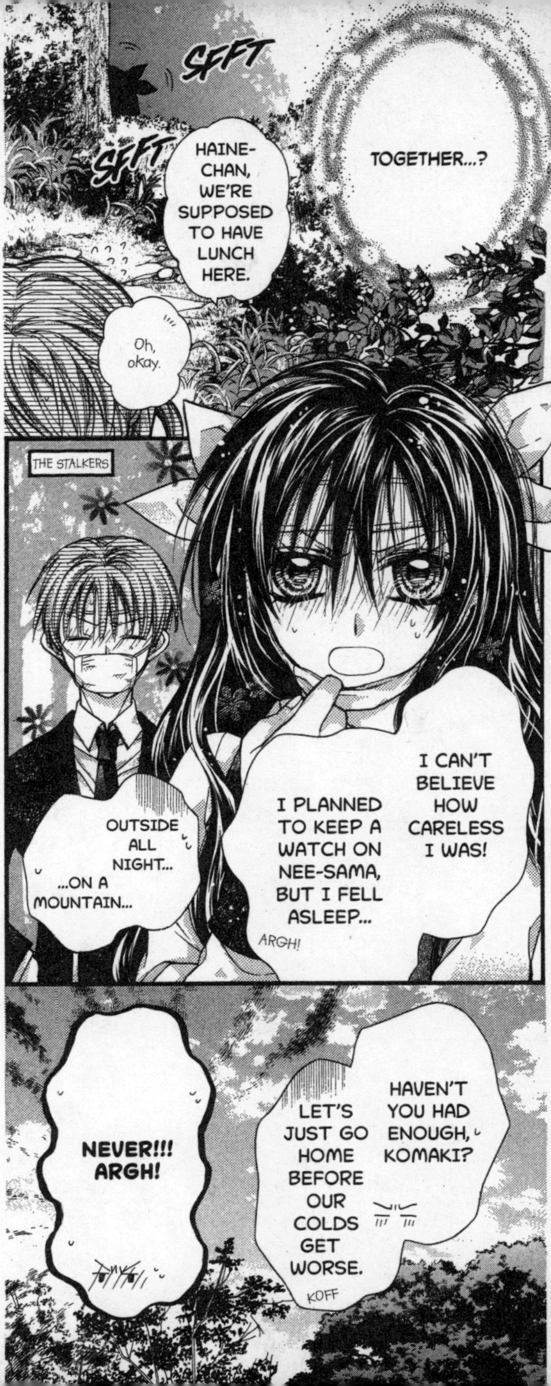

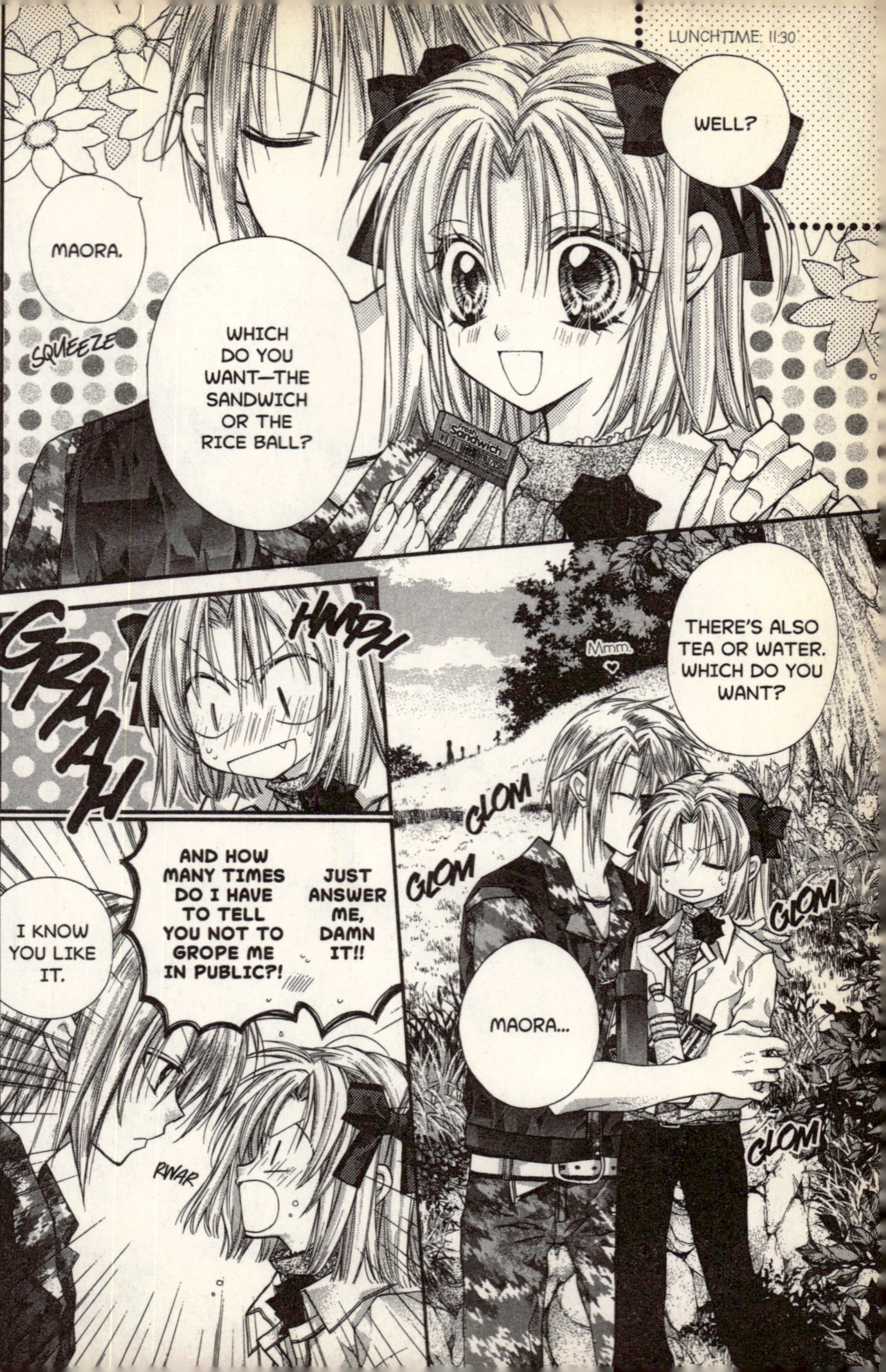
LUNCHTIME: 11:30
WELL?
MAORA.
WHICH DO YOU WANT—THE SANDWICH OR THE RICE BALL?
SQUEEZE
Sandwich
THERE'S ALSO TEA OR WATER. WHICH DO YOU WANT?
Mmm.
GLOM
GLOM
GLOM
GLOM
MAORA...
HMPH
GRAAAH
JUST ANSWER ME, DAMN IT!!
AND HOW MANY TIMES DO I HAVE TO TELL YOU NOT TO GROPE ME IN PUBLIC?!
I KNOW YOU LIKE IT.
RWAR

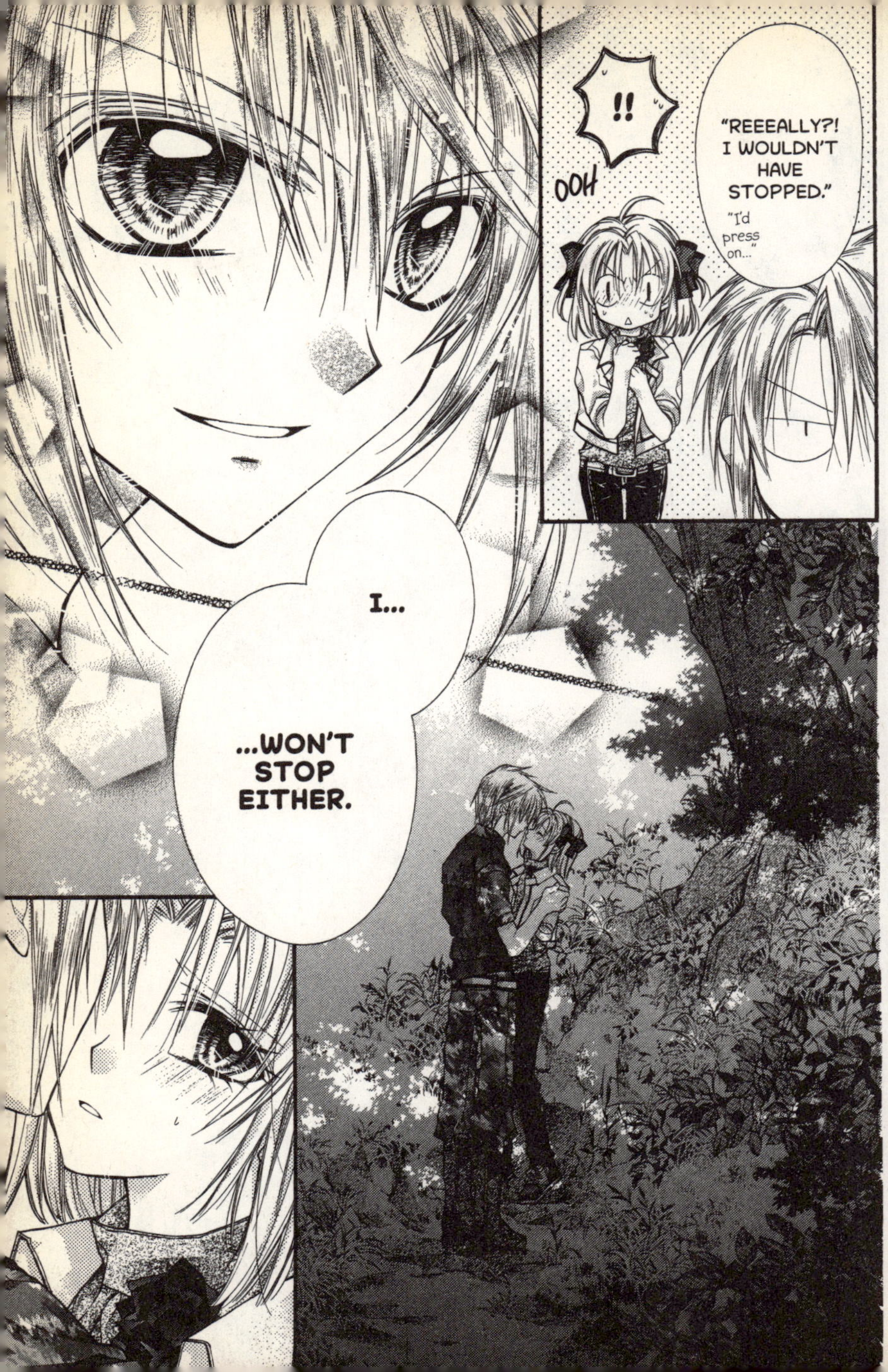
"REEEALLY?! I WOULDN'T HAVE STOPPED."
"I'd press on..."
!!
OOH
I...
...WON'T STOP EITHER.

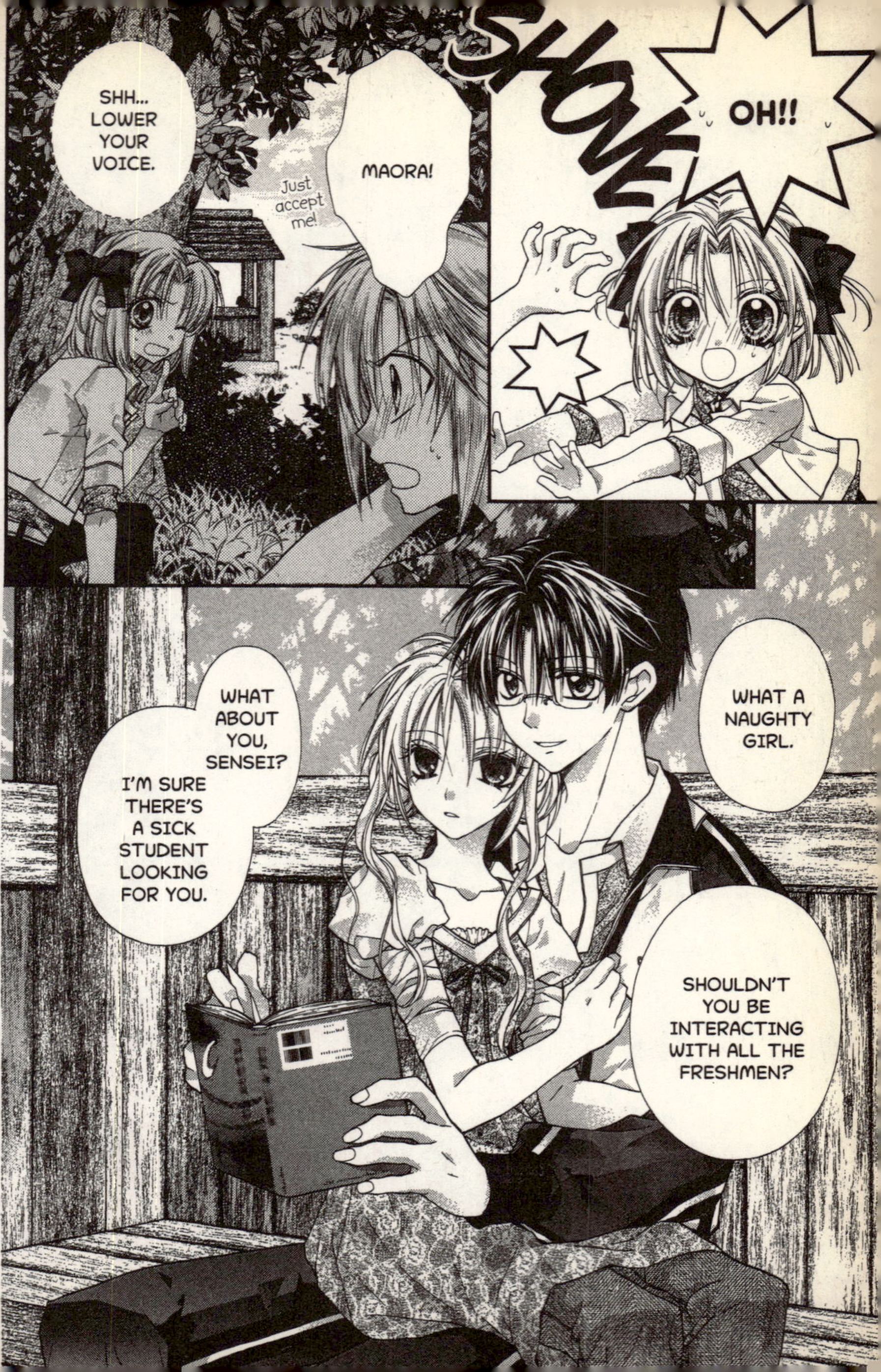
SHOVE
OH!!
MAORA!
Just accept me!
SHH... LOWER YOUR VOICE.
WHAT A NAUGHTY GIRL.
SHOULDN'T YOU BE INTERACTING WITH ALL THE FRESHMEN?
WHAT ABOUT YOU, SENSEI?
I'M SURE THERE'S A SICK STUDENT LOOKING FOR YOU.

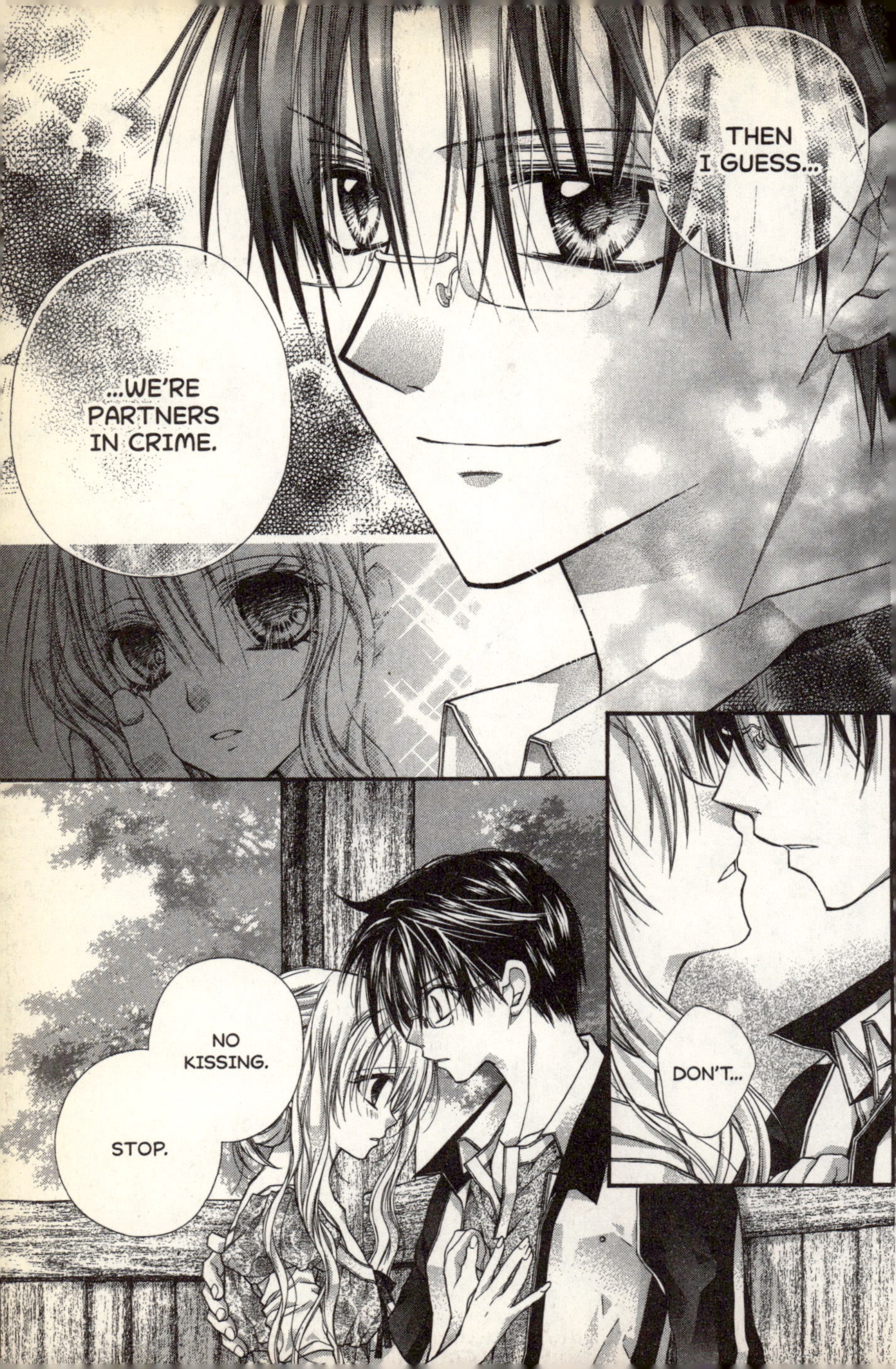
THEN I GUESS...
...WE'RE PARTNERS IN CRIME.
DON'T...
NO KISSING.
STOP.

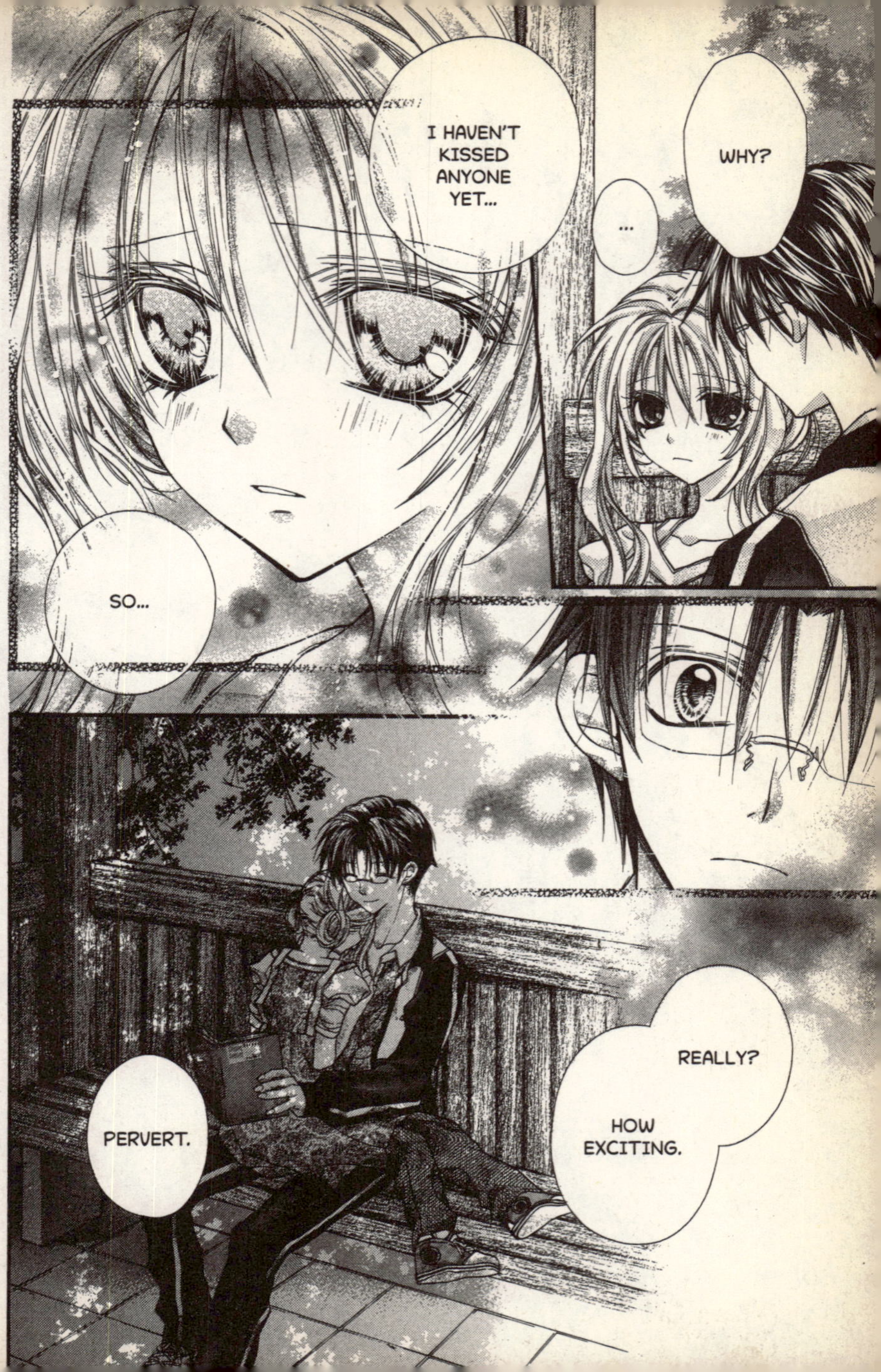
WHY?
...
I HAVEN'T KISSED ANYONE YET...
SO...
REALLY?
HOW EXCITING.
PERVERT.

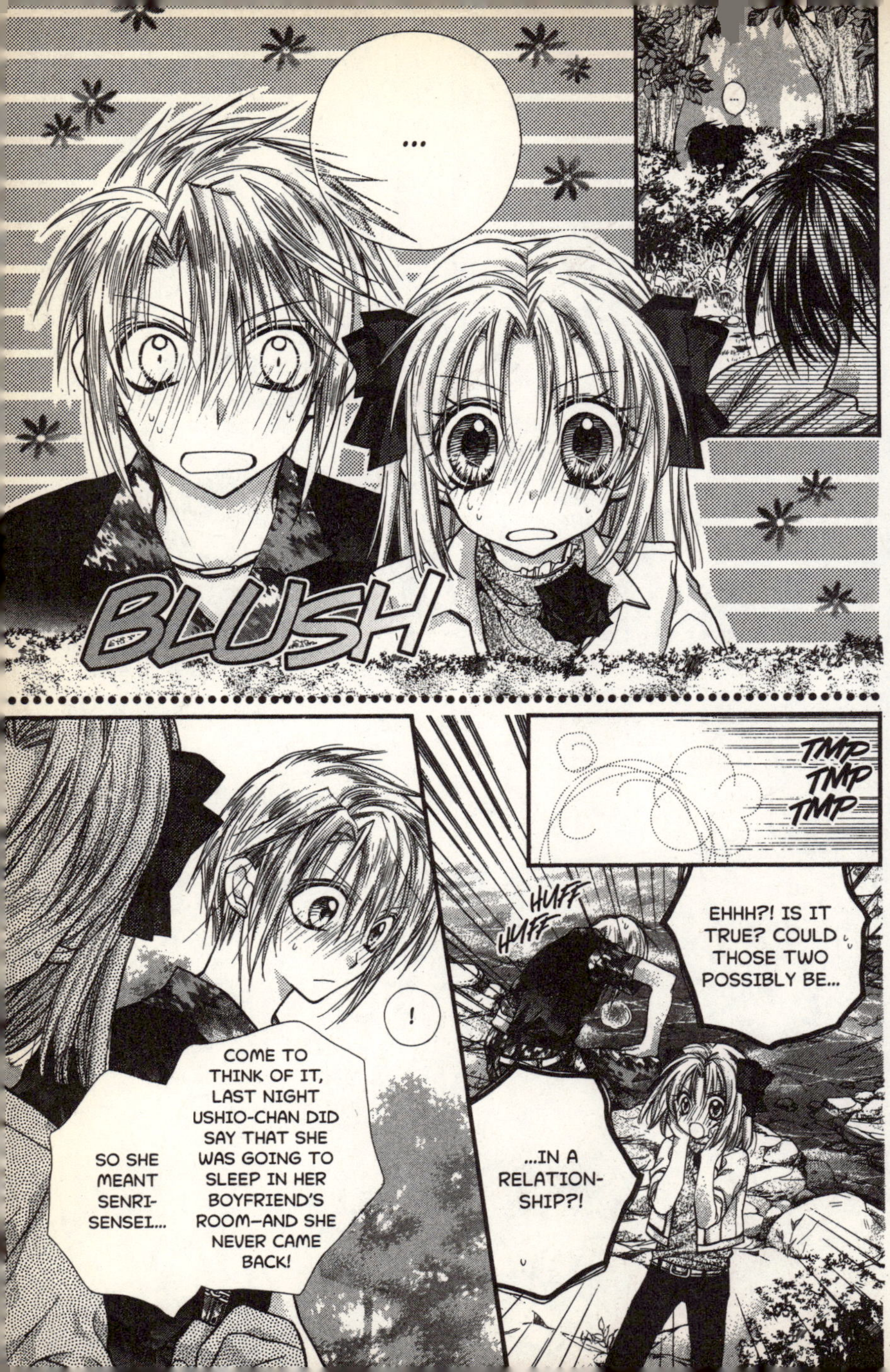
...
...
BLUSH
TMP TMP TMP
HUFF HUFF
EHHH?! IS IT TRUE? COULD THOSE TWO POSSIBLY BE...
...IN A RELATION-SHIP?!
!
COME TO THINK OF IT, LAST NIGHT USHIO-CHAN DID SAY THAT SHE WAS GOING TO SLEEP IN HER BOYFRIEND'S ROOM—AND SHE NEVER CAME BACK!
SO SHE MEANT SENRI-SENSEI...

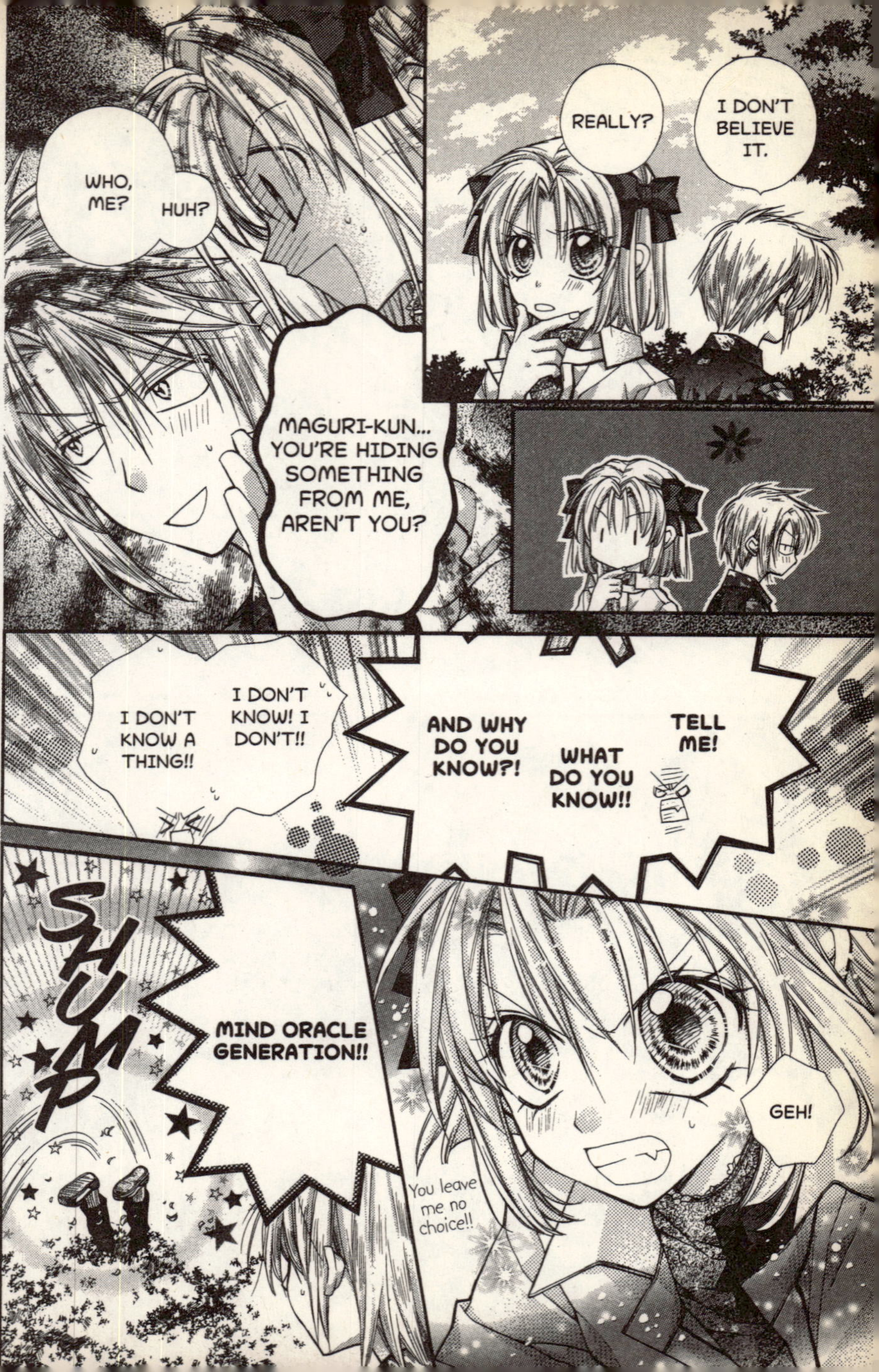
I DON'T BELIEVE IT.
REALLY?
MAGURI-KUN... YOU'RE HIDING SOMETHING FROM ME, AREN'T YOU?
HUH?
WHO, ME?
TELL ME!
WHAT DO YOU KNOW!!
AND WHY DO YOU KNOW?!
I DON'T KNOW! I DON'T!!
I DON'T KNOW A THING!!
GEH!
You leave me no choice!!
MIND ORACLE GENERATION!!
SHUMP

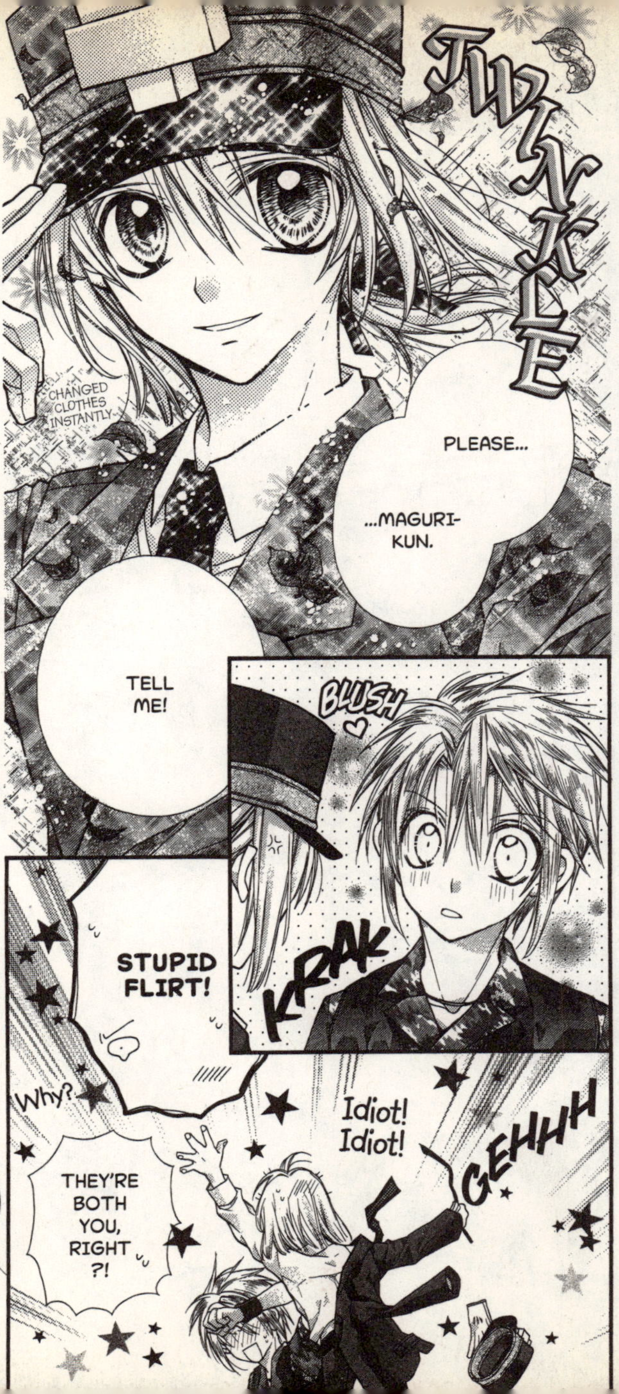
TWINKLE
CHANGED CLOTHES INSTANTLY
PLEASE...
...MAGURI-KUN.
TELL ME!
BLUSH
KRAK
STUPID FLIRT!
GEHHH
Idiot! Idiot!
Why?
THEY'RE BOTH YOU, RIGHT?!

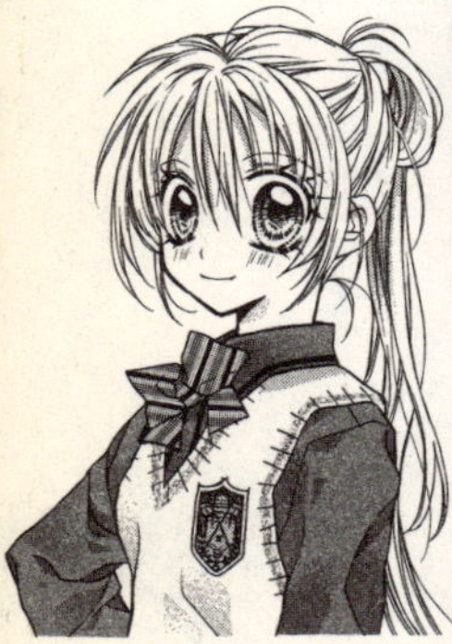

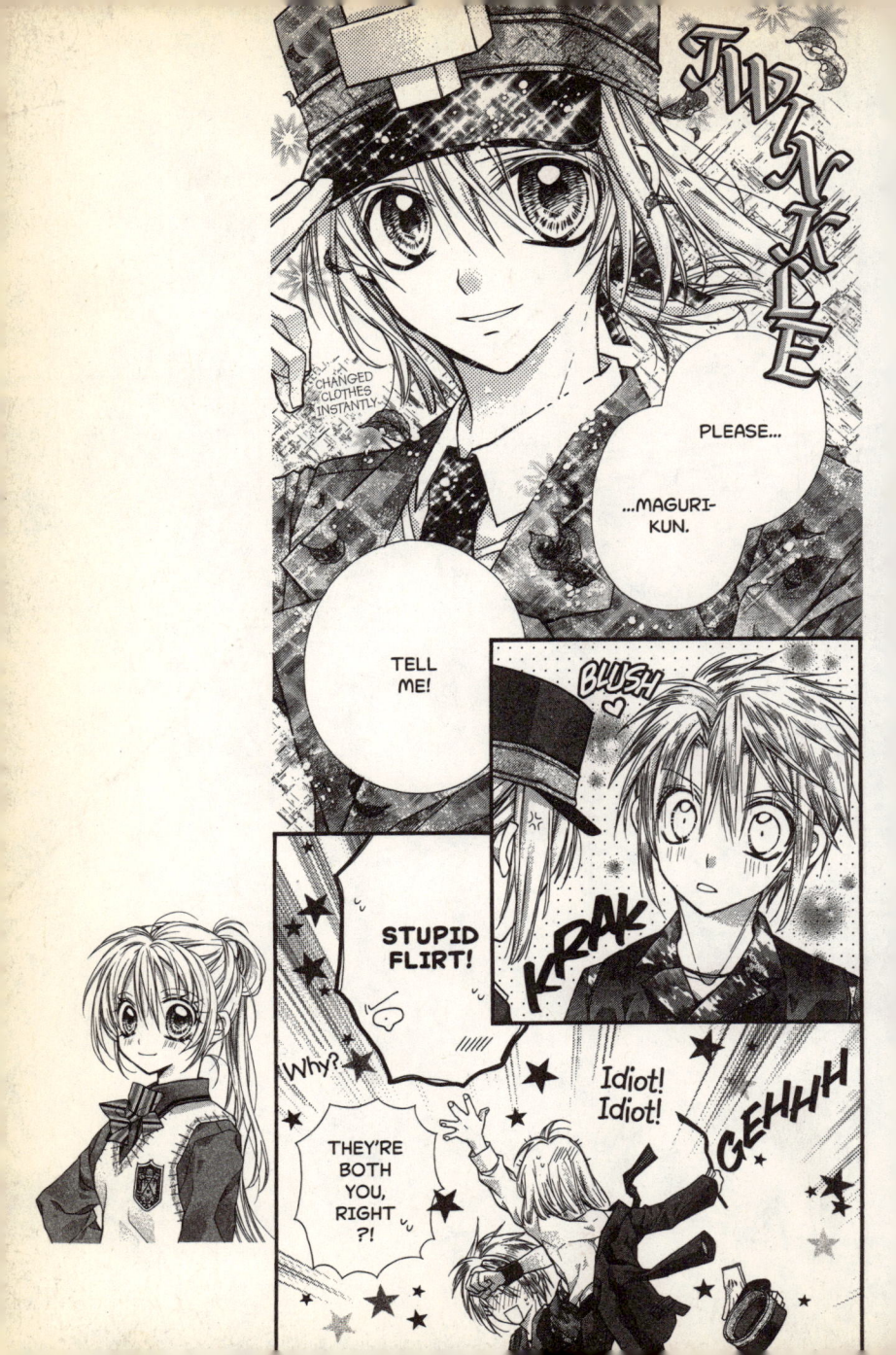

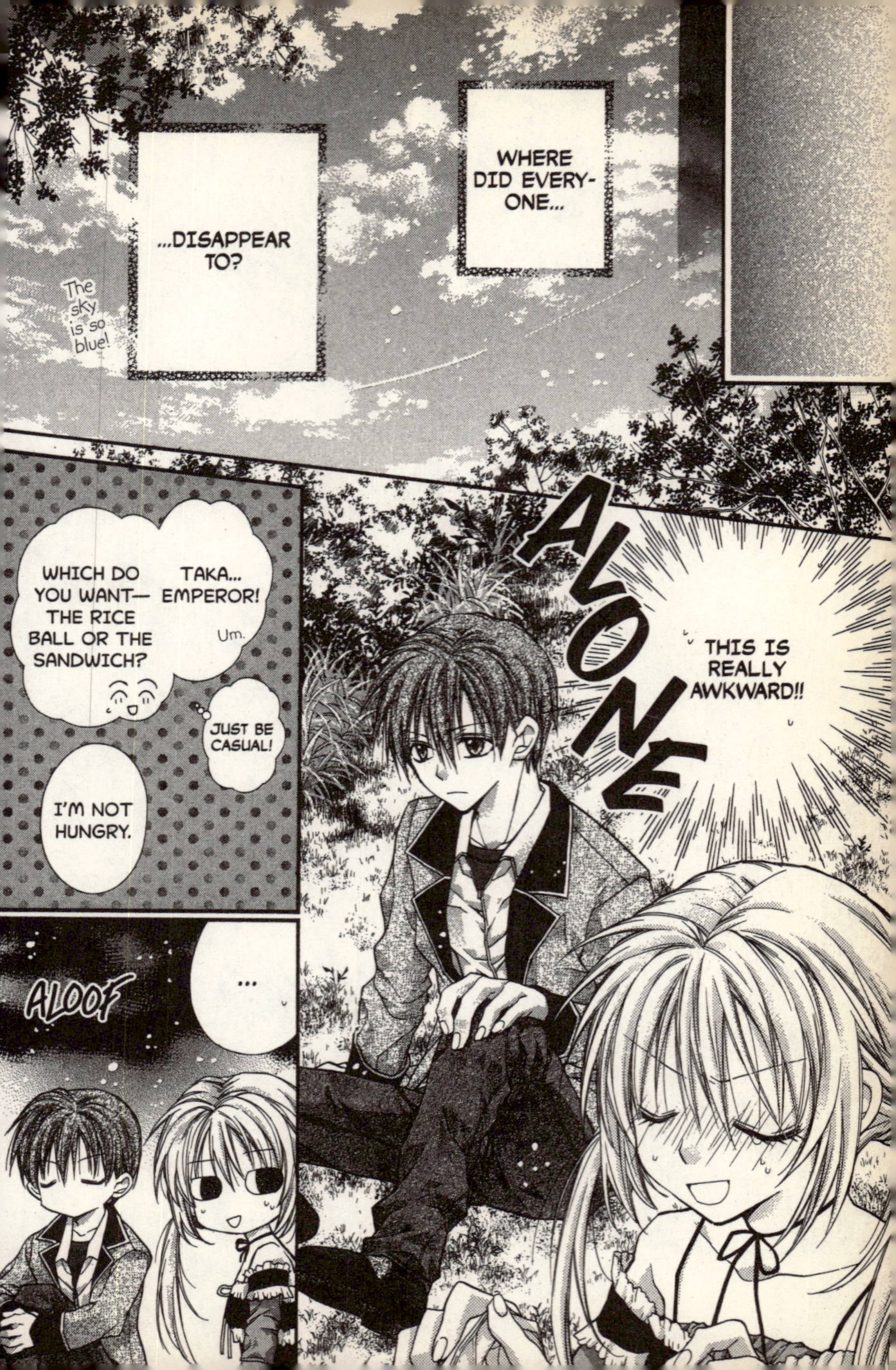
WHERE DID EVERY-ONE...
...DISAPPEAR TO?
The sky is so blue!
ALONE
THIS IS REALLY AWKWARD!!
TAKA... EMPEROR!
Um.
WHICH DO YOU WANT— THE RICE BALL OR THE SANDWICH?
JUST BE CASUAL!
I'M NOT HUNGRY.
...
ALOOF

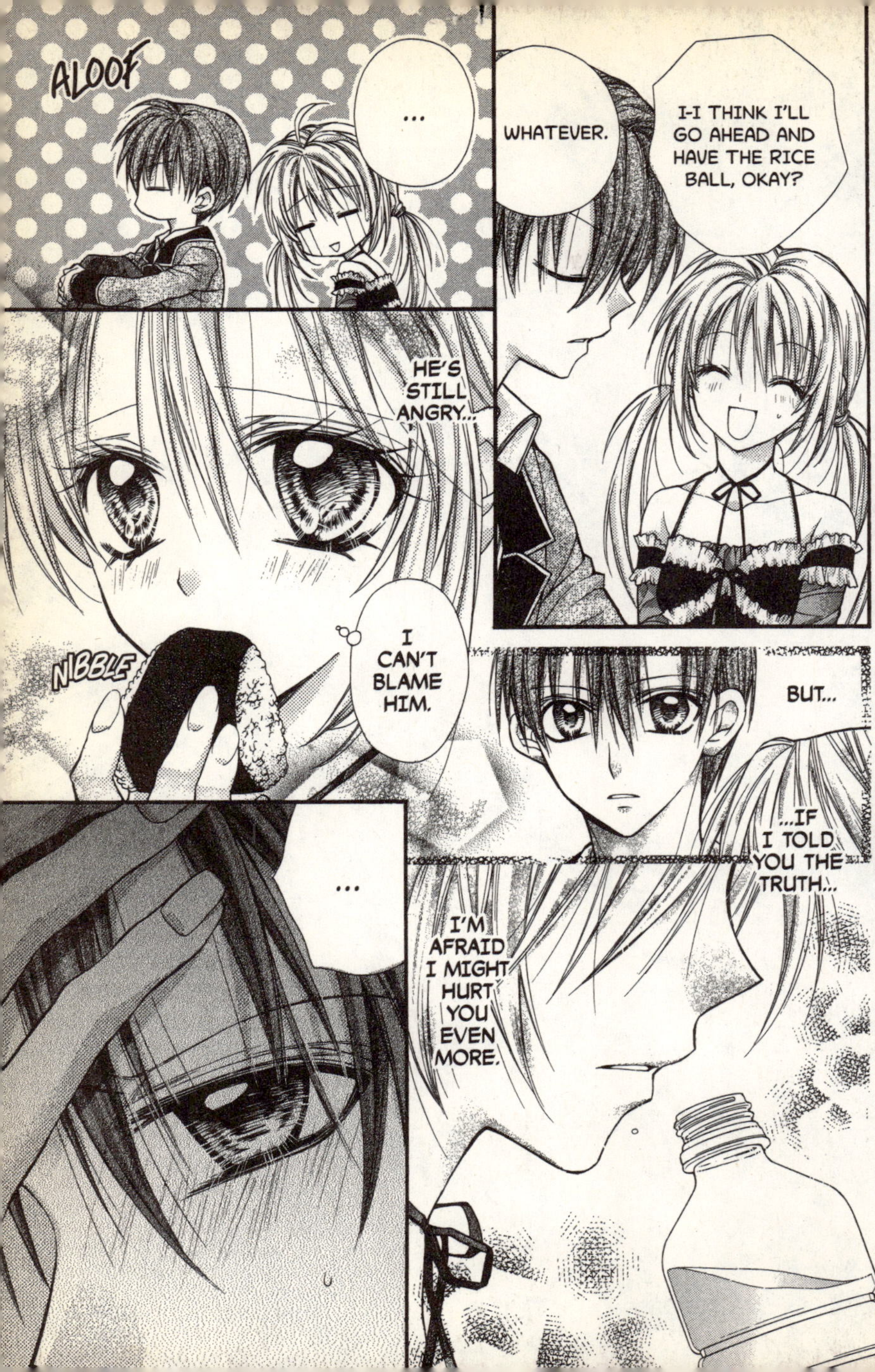
I-I THINK I'LL GO AHEAD AND HAVE THE RICE BALL, OKAY?
WHATEVER.
ALOOF
...
HE'S STILL ANGRY...
NIBBLE
I CAN'T BLAME HIM.
BUT...
...IF I TOLD YOU THE TRUTH...
I'M AFRAID I MIGHT HURT YOU EVEN MORE.
...

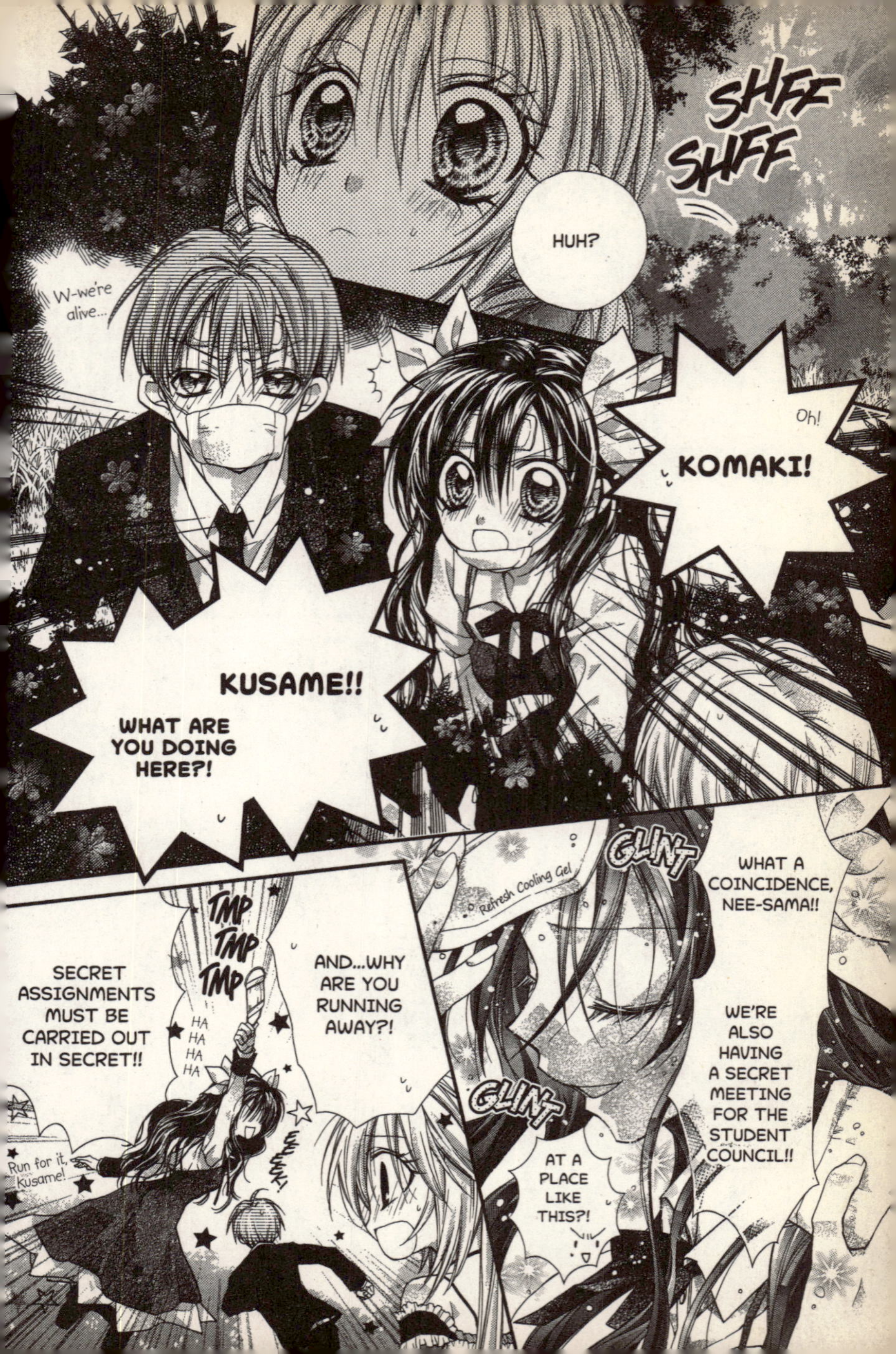
SHFF SHFF
HUH?
W-we're alive...
Oh!
KOMAKI!
KUSAME!!
WHAT ARE YOU DOING HERE?!
GLINT
WHAT A COINCIDENCE, NEE-SAMA!!
WE'RE ALSO HAVING A SECRET MEETING FOR THE STUDENT COUNCIL!!
Refresh Cooling Gel
GLINT
AT A PLACE LIKE THIS?!
AND...WHY ARE YOU RUNNING AWAY?!
TMP TMP TMP
SECRET ASSIGNMENTS MUST BE CARRIED OUT IN SECRET!!
HA HA HA HA
Run for it, Kusame!

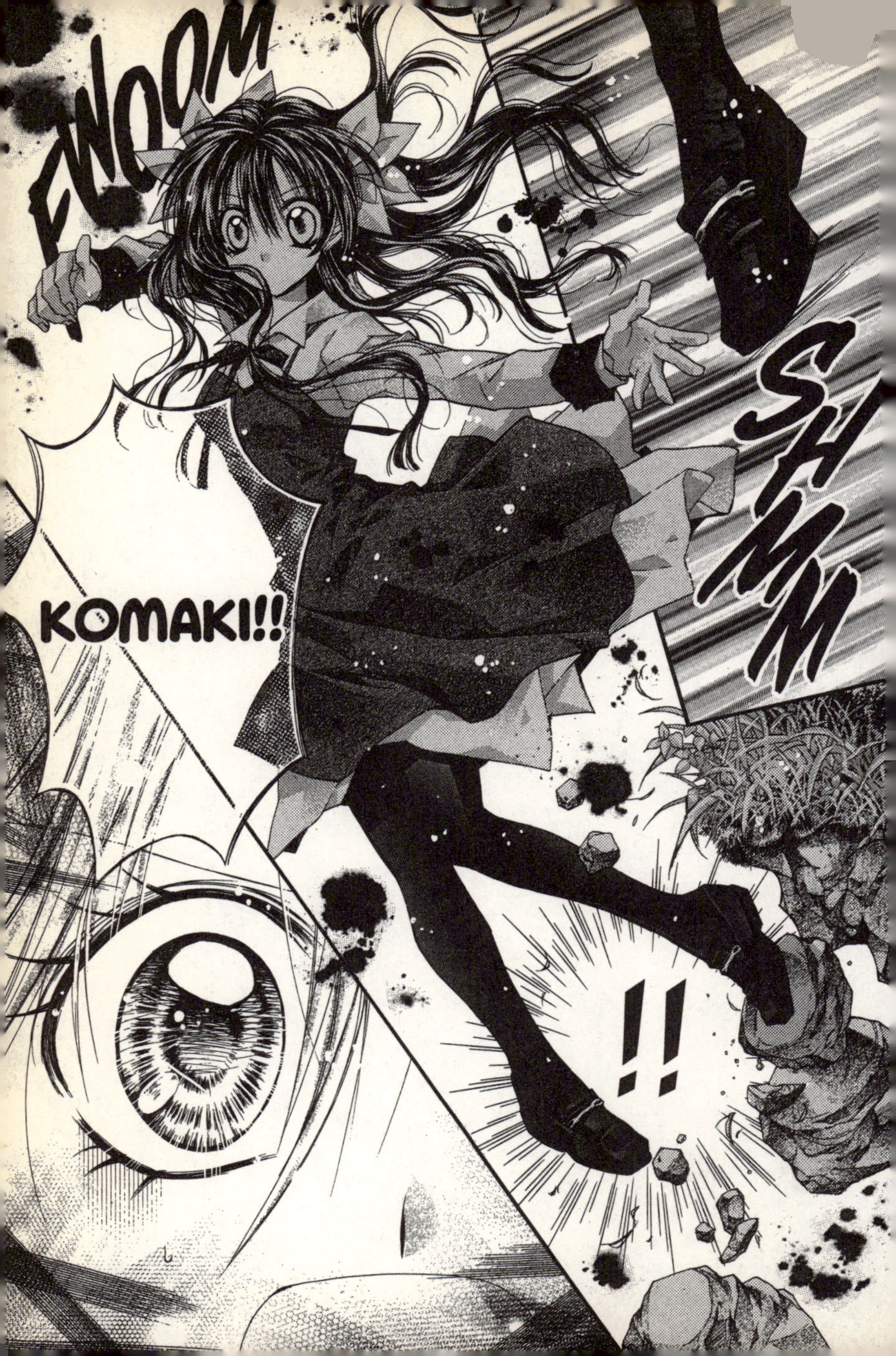
FWOOM
SHMMM
KOMAKI!!
!!

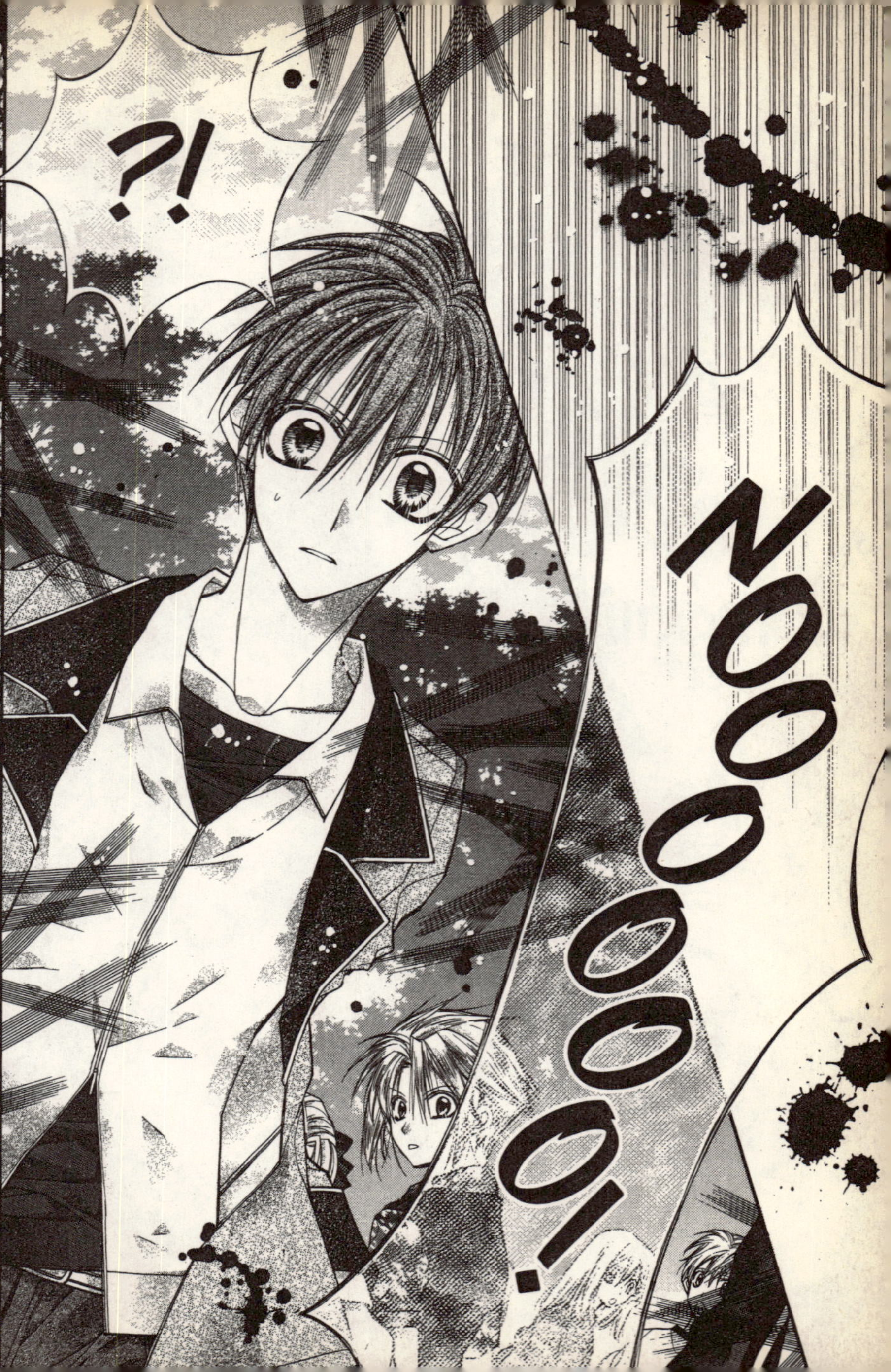

NOOOOOO!
?!

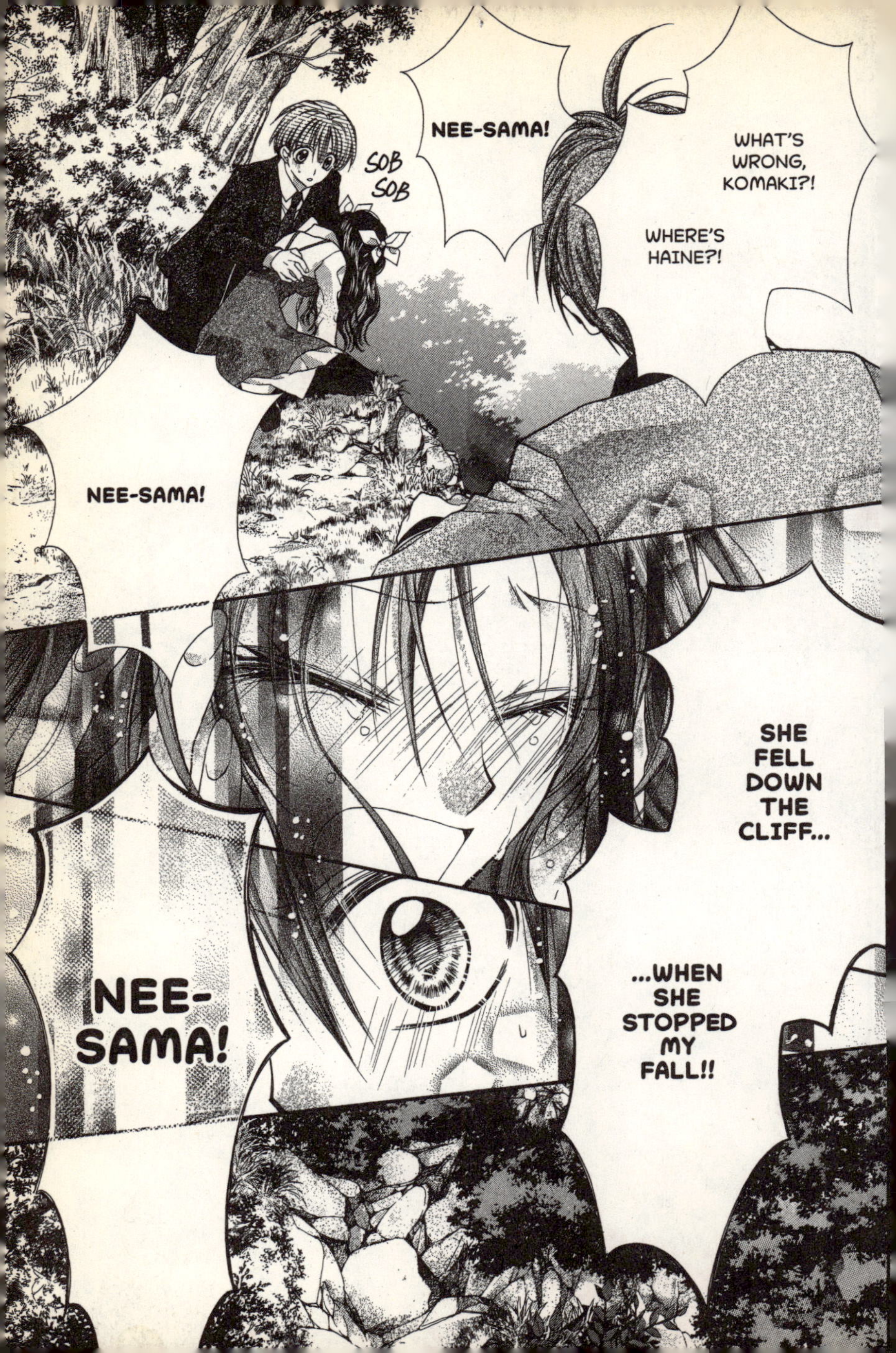
WHAT'S WRONG, KOMAKI?!
WHERE'S HAINE?!
NEE-SAMA!
SOB SOB
NEE-SAMA!
SHE FELL DOWN THE CLIFF...
...WHEN SHE STOPPED MY FALL!!
NEE-SAMA!

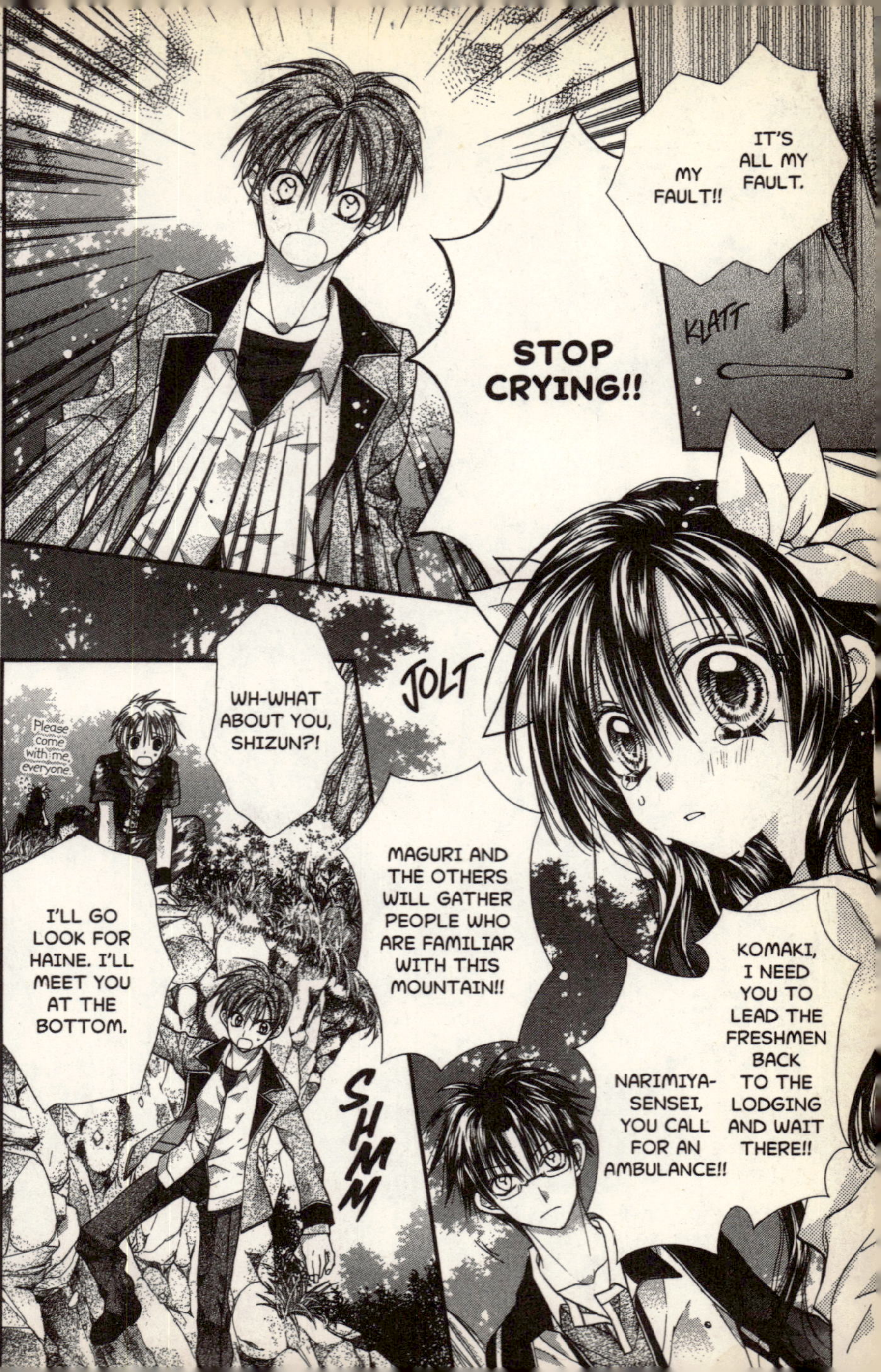
IT'S ALL MY FAULT.
MY FAULT!!
KLATT
STOP CRYING!!
JOLT
KOMAKI, I NEED YOU TO LEAD THE FRESHMEN BACK TO THE LODGING AND WAIT THERE!!
NARIMIYA-SENSEI, YOU CALL FOR AN AMBULANCE!!
MAGURI AND THE OTHERS WILL GATHER PEOPLE WHO ARE FAMILIAR WITH THIS MOUNTAIN!!
WH-WHAT ABOUT YOU, SHIZUN?!
SHMM
I'LL GO LOOK FOR HAINE. I'LL MEET YOU AT THE BOTTOM.
Please come with me, everyone.

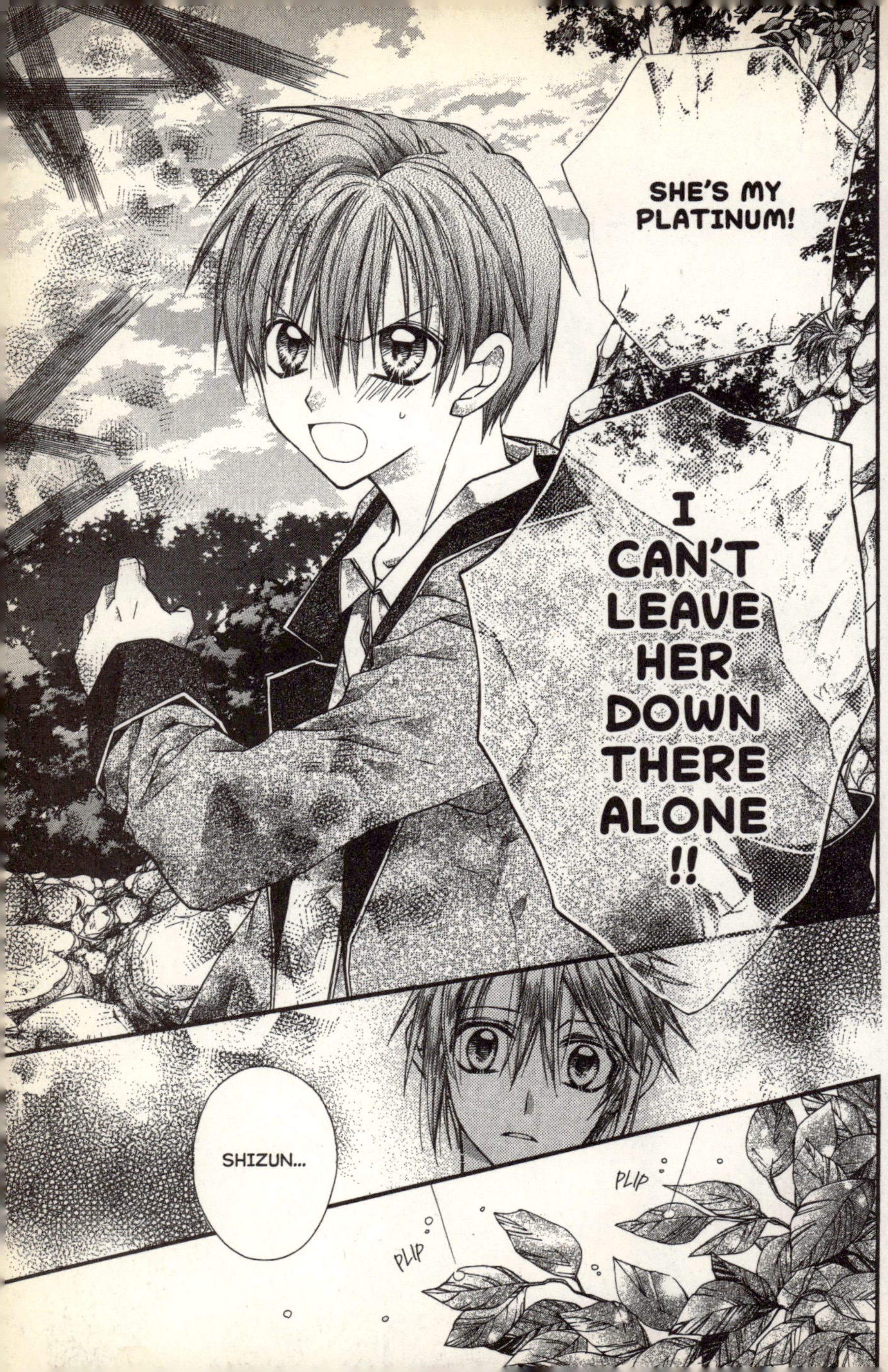
SHE'S MY PLATINUM!
I CAN'T LEAVE HER DOWN THERE ALONE !!
SHIZUN...
PLIP
PLIP

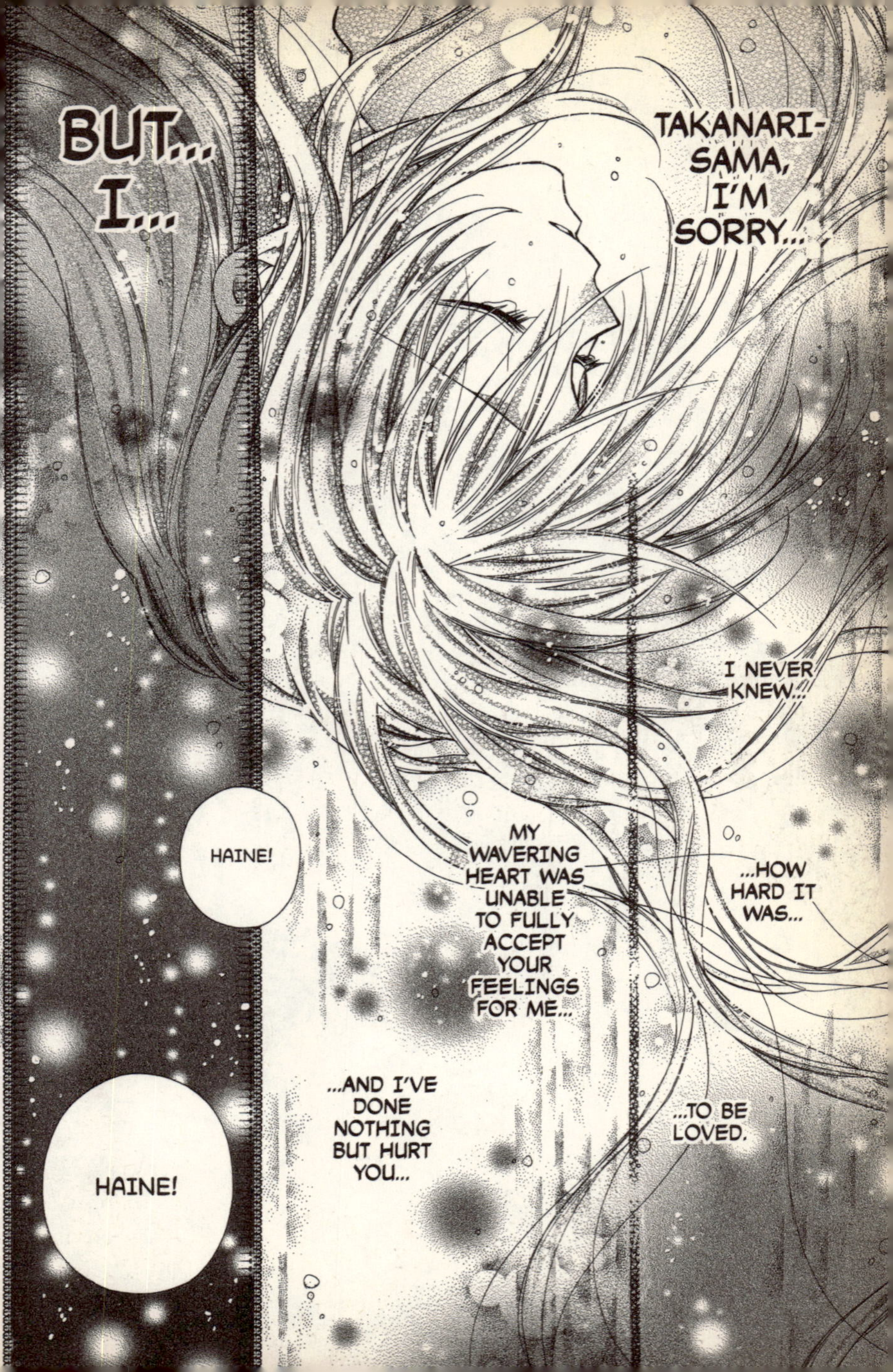
TAKANARI-SAMA, I'M SORRY...
I NEVER KNEW...
...HOW HARD IT WAS...
...TO BE LOVED.
MY WAVERING HEART WAS UNABLE TO FULLY ACCEPT YOUR FEELINGS FOR ME...
...AND I'VE DONE NOTHING BUT HURT YOU...
BUT... I...
HAINE!
HAINE!

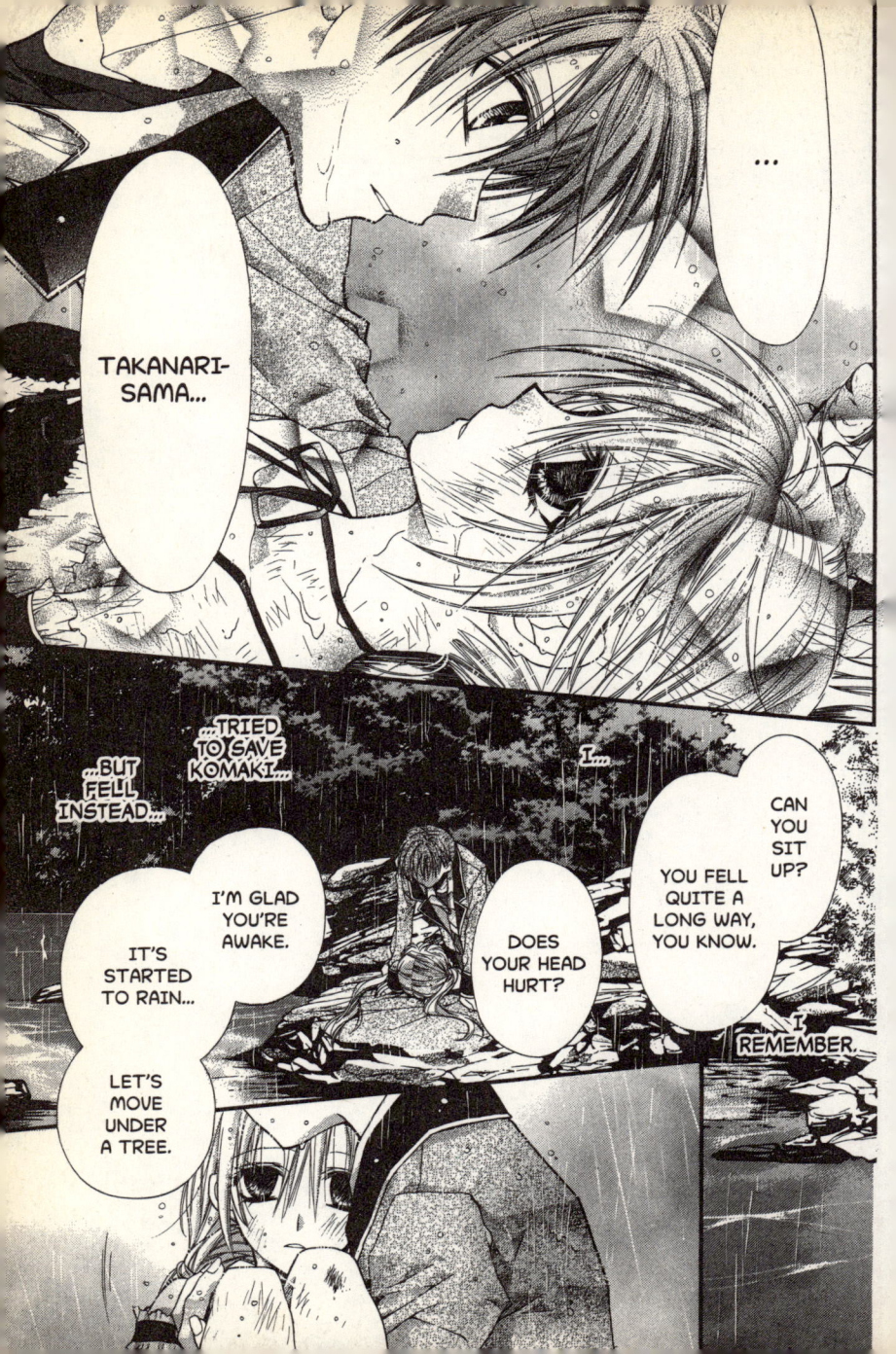

...

TAKANARI-SAMA...

...TRIED TO SAVE KOMAKI...

...BUT FELL INSTEAD...

I....

CAN YOU SIT UP?

YOU FELL QUITE A LONG WAY, YOU KNOW.

DOES YOUR HEAD HURT?

I'M GLAD YOU'RE AWAKE.

IT'S STARTED TO RAIN...

LET'S MOVE UNDER A TREE.

I REMEMBER.

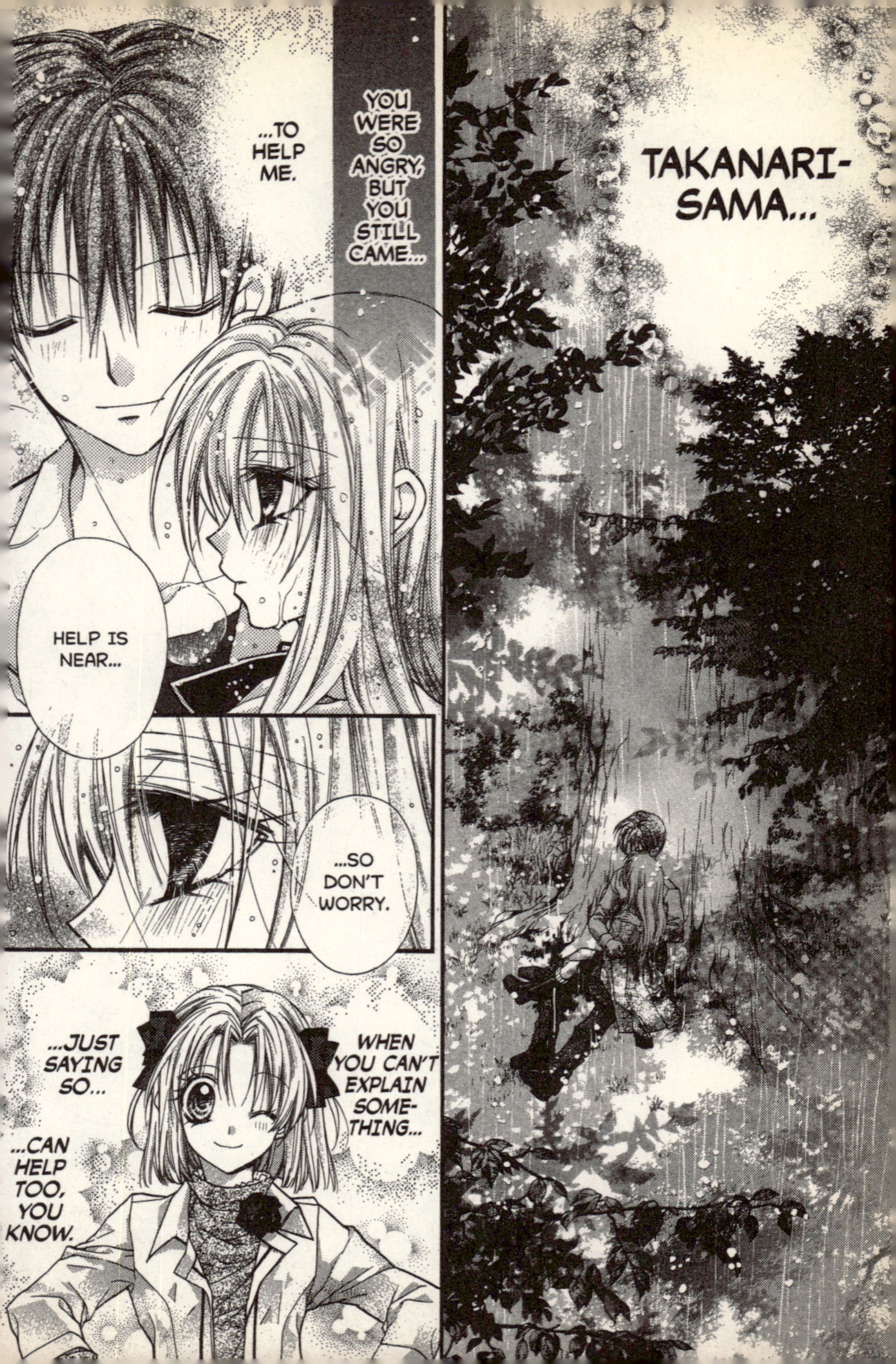
TAKANARI-SAMA...
YOU WERE SO ANGRY, BUT YOU STILL CAME...
...TO HELP ME.
HELP IS NEAR...
...SO DON'T WORRY.
WHEN YOU CAN'T EXPLAIN SOMETHING...
...JUST SAYING SO...
...CAN HELP TOO, YOU KNOW.

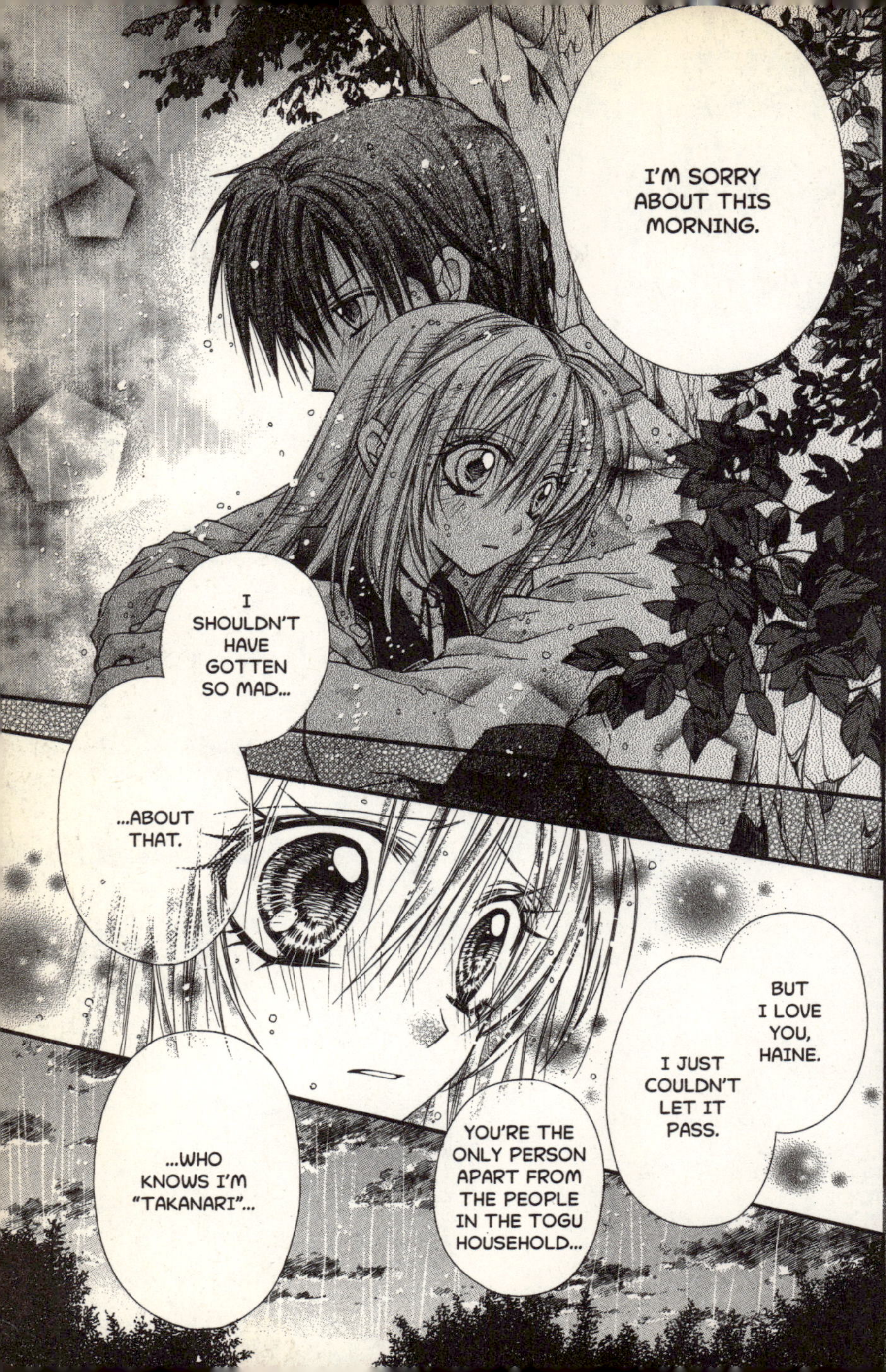
I'M SORRY ABOUT THIS MORNING.
I SHOULDN'T HAVE GOTTEN SO MAD...
...ABOUT THAT.
BUT I LOVE YOU, HAINE.
I JUST COULDN'T LET IT PASS.
YOU'RE THE ONLY PERSON APART FROM THE PEOPLE IN THE TOGU HOUSEHOLD...
...WHO KNOWS I'M "TAKANARI"...

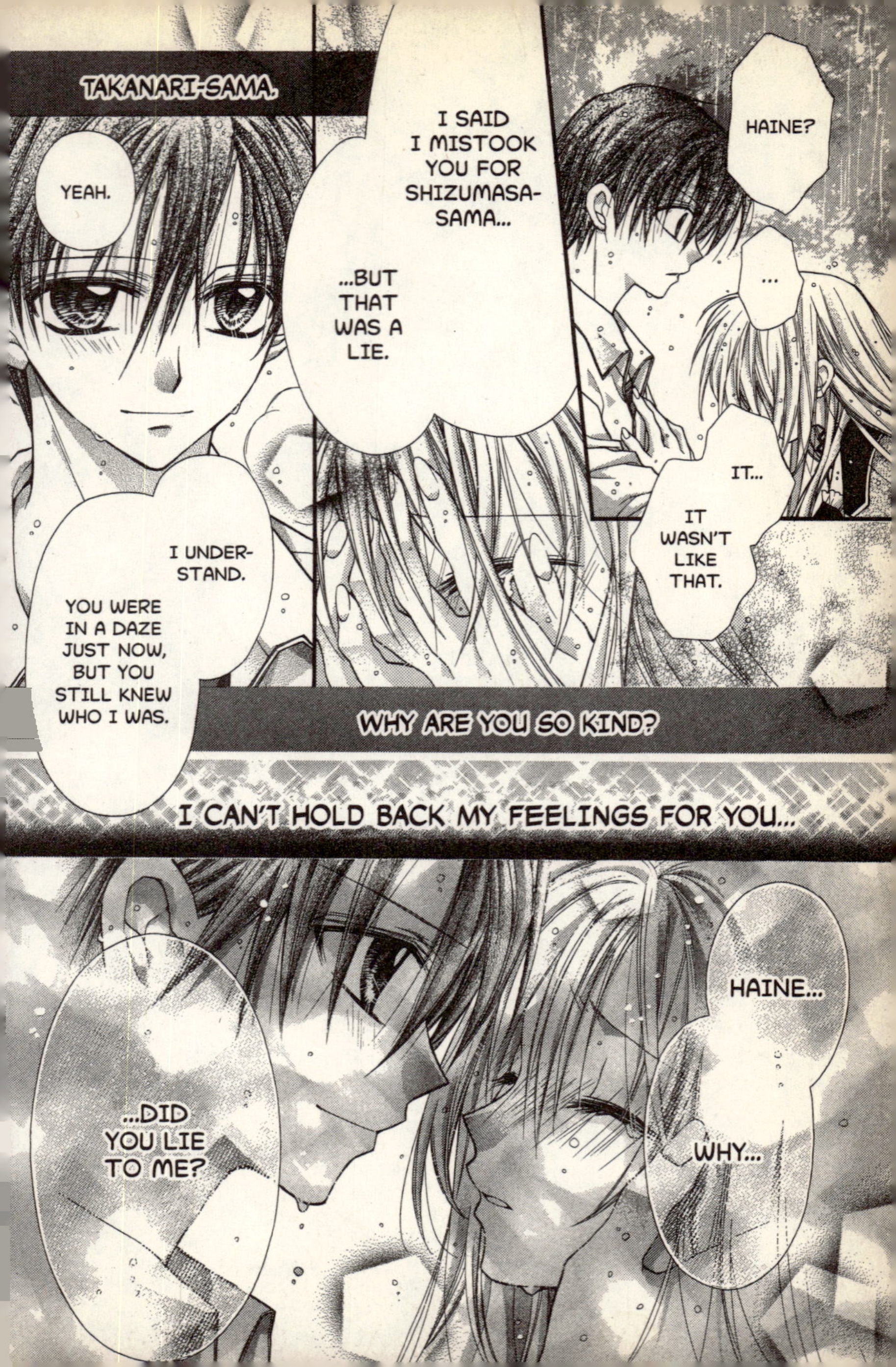
HAINE?
...
IT...
IT WASN'T LIKE THAT.
I SAID I MISTOOK YOU FOR SHIZUMASA-SAMA...
...BUT THAT WAS A LIE.
TAKANARI-SAMA.
YEAH.
I UNDERSTAND.
YOU WERE IN A DAZE JUST NOW, BUT YOU STILL KNEW WHO I WAS.
WHY ARE YOU SO KIND?
I CAN'T HOLD BACK MY FEELINGS FOR YOU...
HAINE...
WHY...
...DID YOU LIE TO ME?

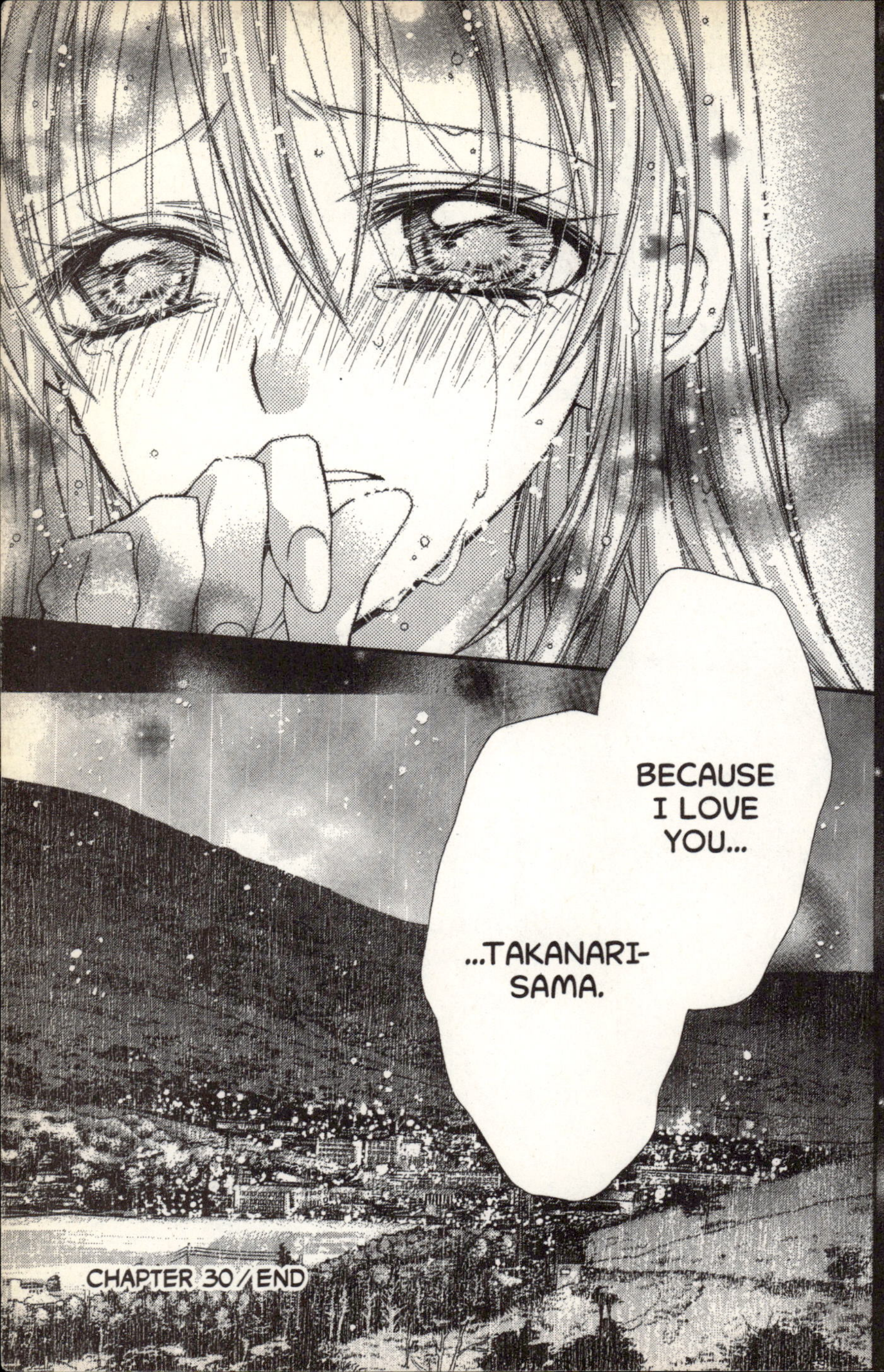
BECAUSE I LOVE YOU...
...TAKANARI-SAMA.
CHAPTER 30/END

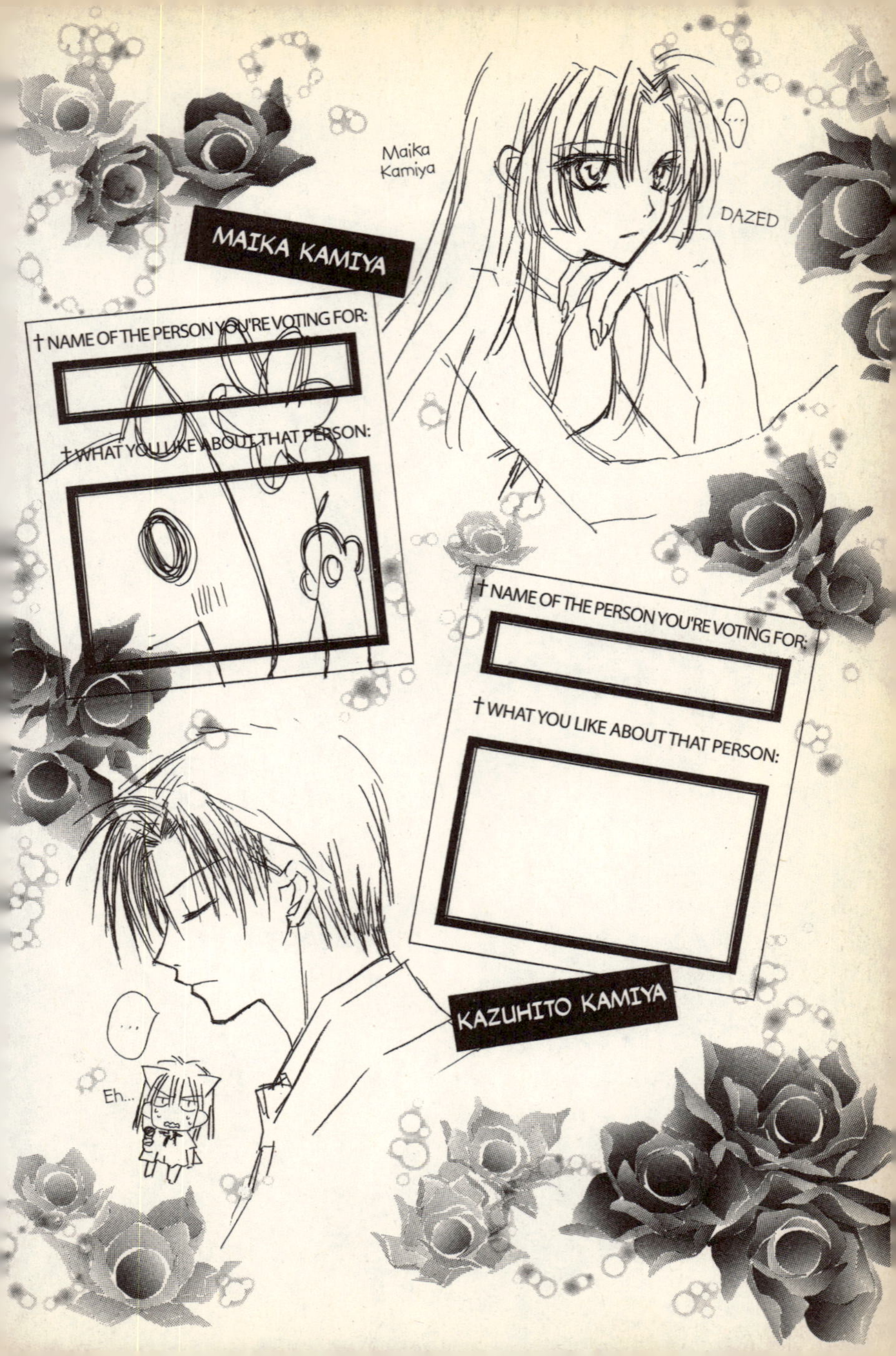
...
Maika Kamiya
DAZED
MAIKA KAMIYA
† NAME OF THE PERSON YOU'RE VOTING FOR:
† WHAT YOU LIKE ABOUT THAT PERSON:
† NAME OF THE PERSON YOU'RE VOTING FOR:
† WHAT YOU LIKE ABOUT THAT PERSON:
KAZUHITO KAMIYA
...
Eh...

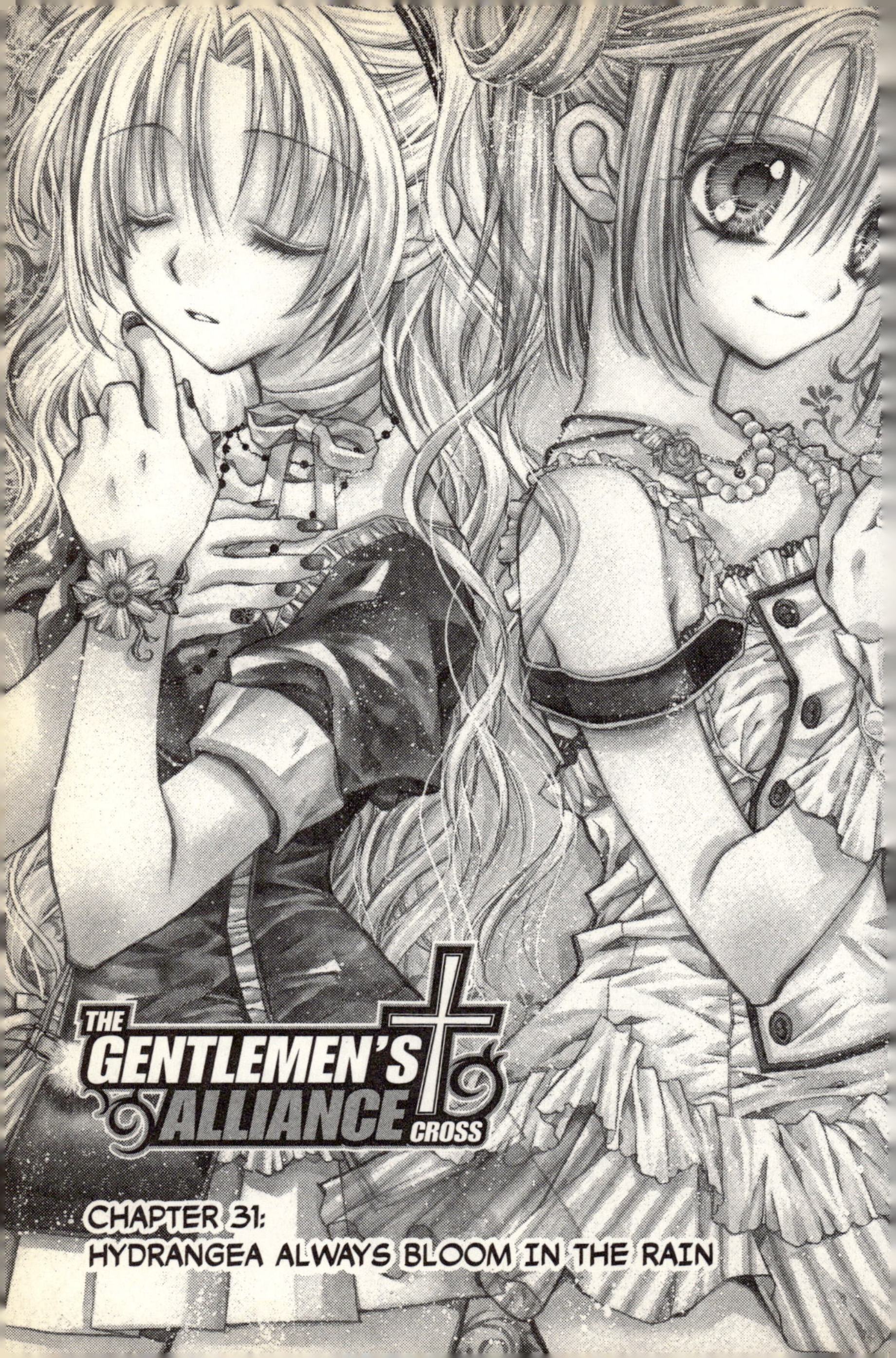
THE GENTLEMEN'S ALLIANCE CROSS
CHAPTER 31:
HYDRANGEA ALWAYS BLOOM IN THE RAIN

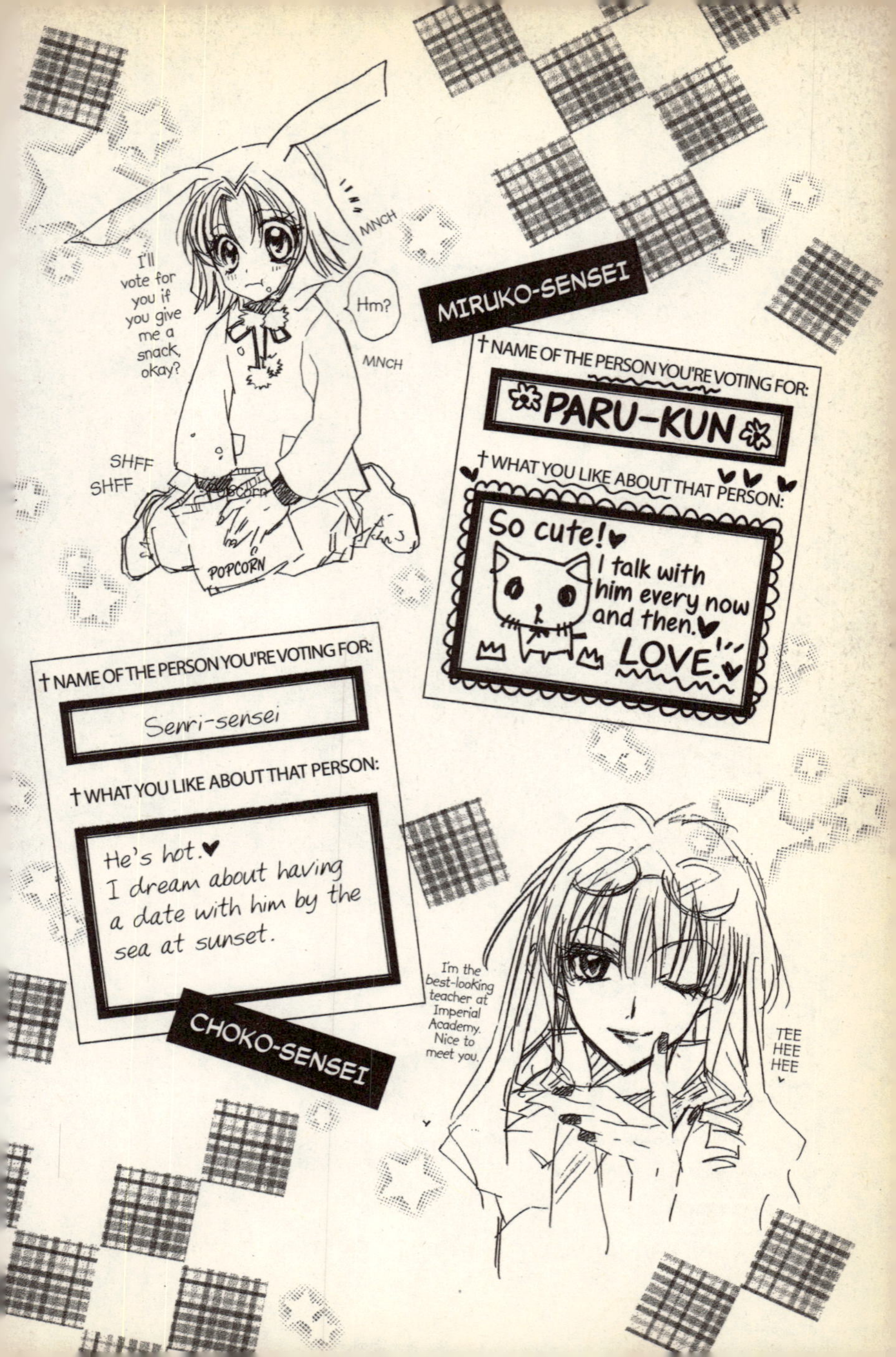
MIRUKO-SENSEI
† NAME OF THE PERSON YOU'RE VOTING FOR:
PARU-KUN
† WHAT YOU LIKE ABOUT THAT PERSON:
So cute!♥
I talk with him every now and then.♥
LOVE.♥
MNCH
Hm?
MNCH
I'll vote for you if you give me a snack, okay?
SHFF SHFF
POPCORN
I'm the best-looking teacher at Imperial Academy. Nice to meet you.
TEE HEE HEE ♥
† NAME OF THE PERSON YOU'RE VOTING FOR:
Senri-sensei
† WHAT YOU LIKE ABOUT THAT PERSON:
He's hot.♥
I dream about having a date with him by the sea at sunset.
CHOKO-SENSEI

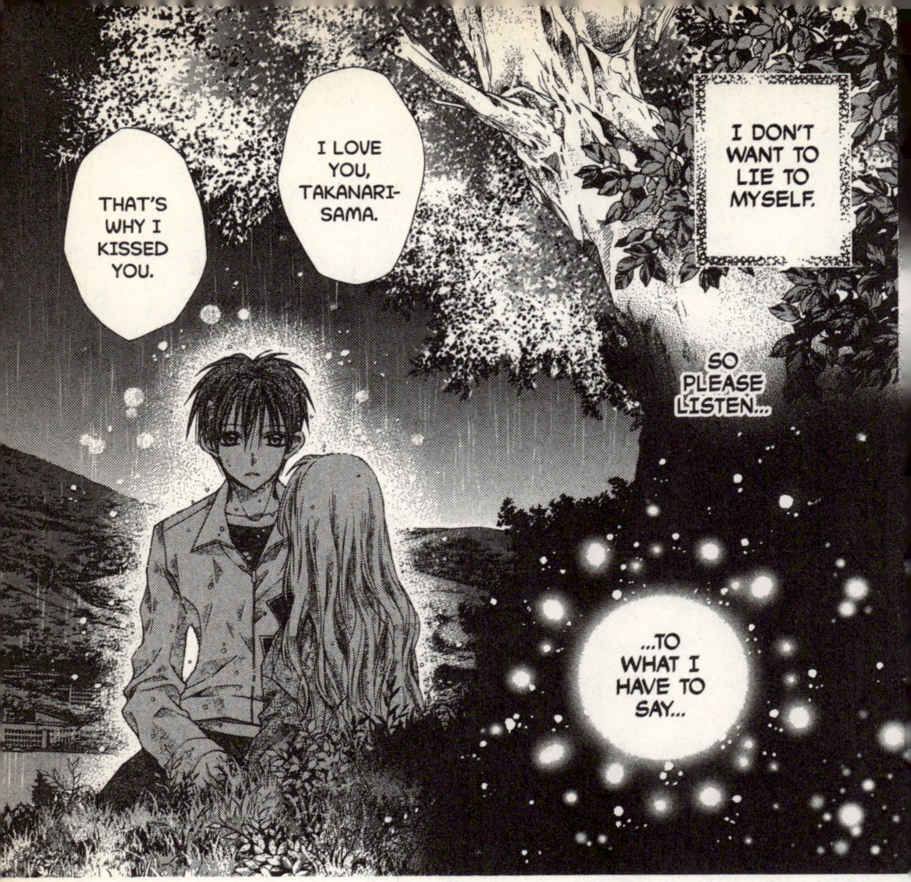
I DON'T WANT TO LIE TO MYSELF.
I LOVE YOU, TAKANARI-SAMA.
THAT'S WHY I KISSED YOU.
SO PLEASE LISTEN...
...TO WHAT I HAVE TO SAY...

Chapter 31: Hydrangea Always Bloom in the Rain

Lead-in

Haine's wish. Ushio's feelings.
Two hearts melt together as one...

I'm giving away the story!

This is the chapter of the enraged Ushio! (I really like the lead-in my supervisor came up with.) I put the most effort into the scene with Maora and Ushio. Mao-chan is pretending to be tough, but he's actually pretty shocked. He's easygoing, but he's also very delicate...

The scene with Haine and Senri is an important scene too. When you see the close-up of Senri's eyes—that's clearly a look of jealousy toward Haine. You know, jealousy. He must have been a little irritated with her. It's a "why don't you think for yourself" look. But he's not going to take responsibility for Ushio... What a terrible guy!

Yuki-chan is in an interesting position so I'd like to try and have him appear again in later chapters.

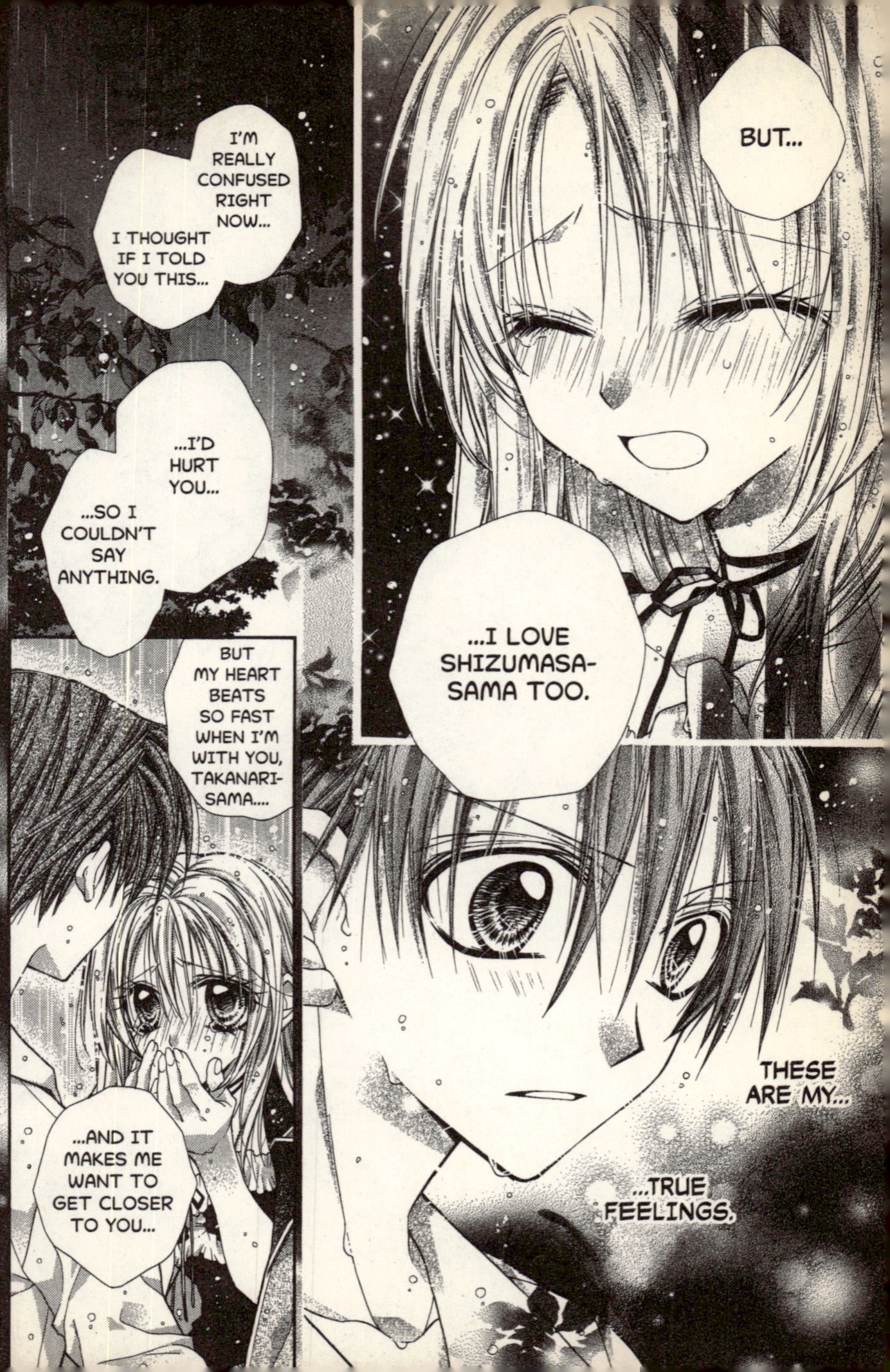
BUT...
...I LOVE SHIZUMASA-SAMA TOO.
I'M REALLY CONFUSED RIGHT NOW...
I THOUGHT IF I TOLD YOU THIS...
...I'D HURT YOU...
...SO I COULDN'T SAY ANYTHING.
THESE ARE MY...
...TRUE FEELINGS.
BUT MY HEART BEATS SO FAST WHEN I'M WITH YOU, TAKANARI-SAMA....
...AND IT MAKES ME WANT TO GET CLOSER TO YOU...

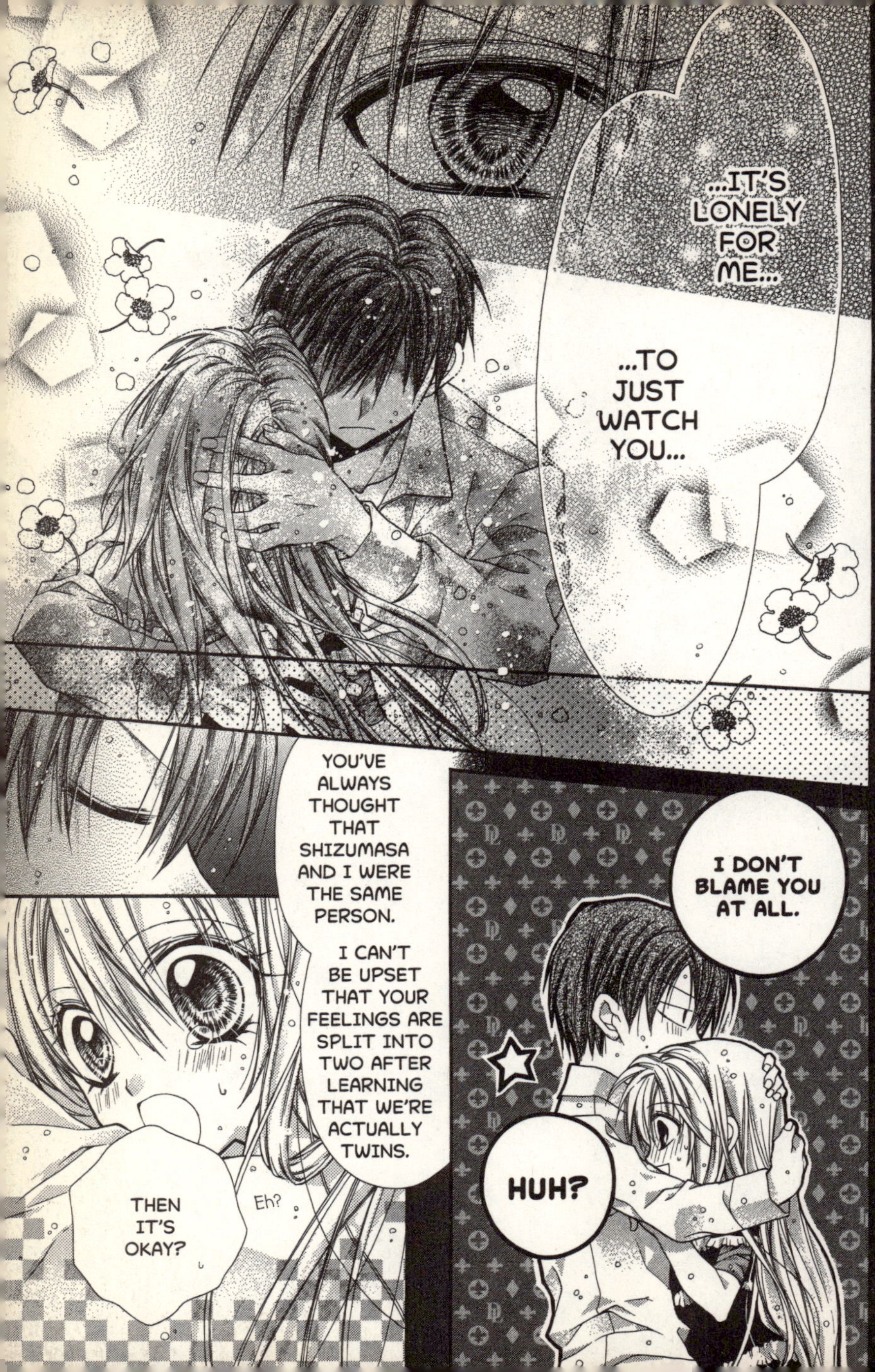
...IT'S LONELY FOR ME...
...TO JUST WATCH YOU...
YOU'VE ALWAYS THOUGHT THAT SHIZUMASA AND I WERE THE SAME PERSON.
I CAN'T BE UPSET THAT YOUR FEELINGS ARE SPLIT INTO TWO AFTER LEARNING THAT WE'RE ACTUALLY TWINS.
I DON'T BLAME YOU AT ALL.
HUH?
THEN IT'S OKAY?
Eh?

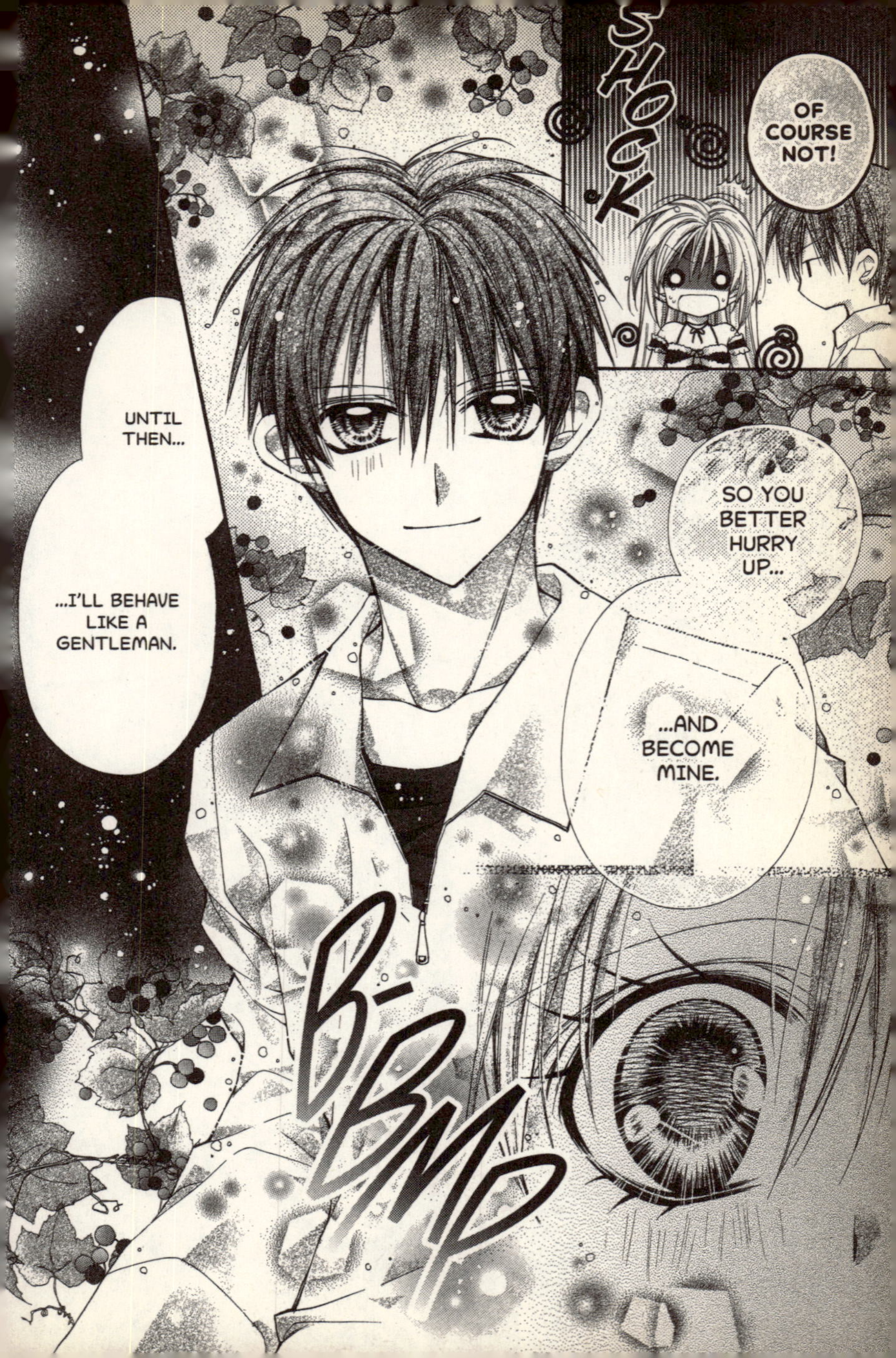
SHOCK
OF COURSE NOT!
SO YOU BETTER HURRY UP...
...AND BECOME MINE.
UNTIL THEN...
...I'LL BEHAVE LIKE A GENTLEMAN.
B-BMP

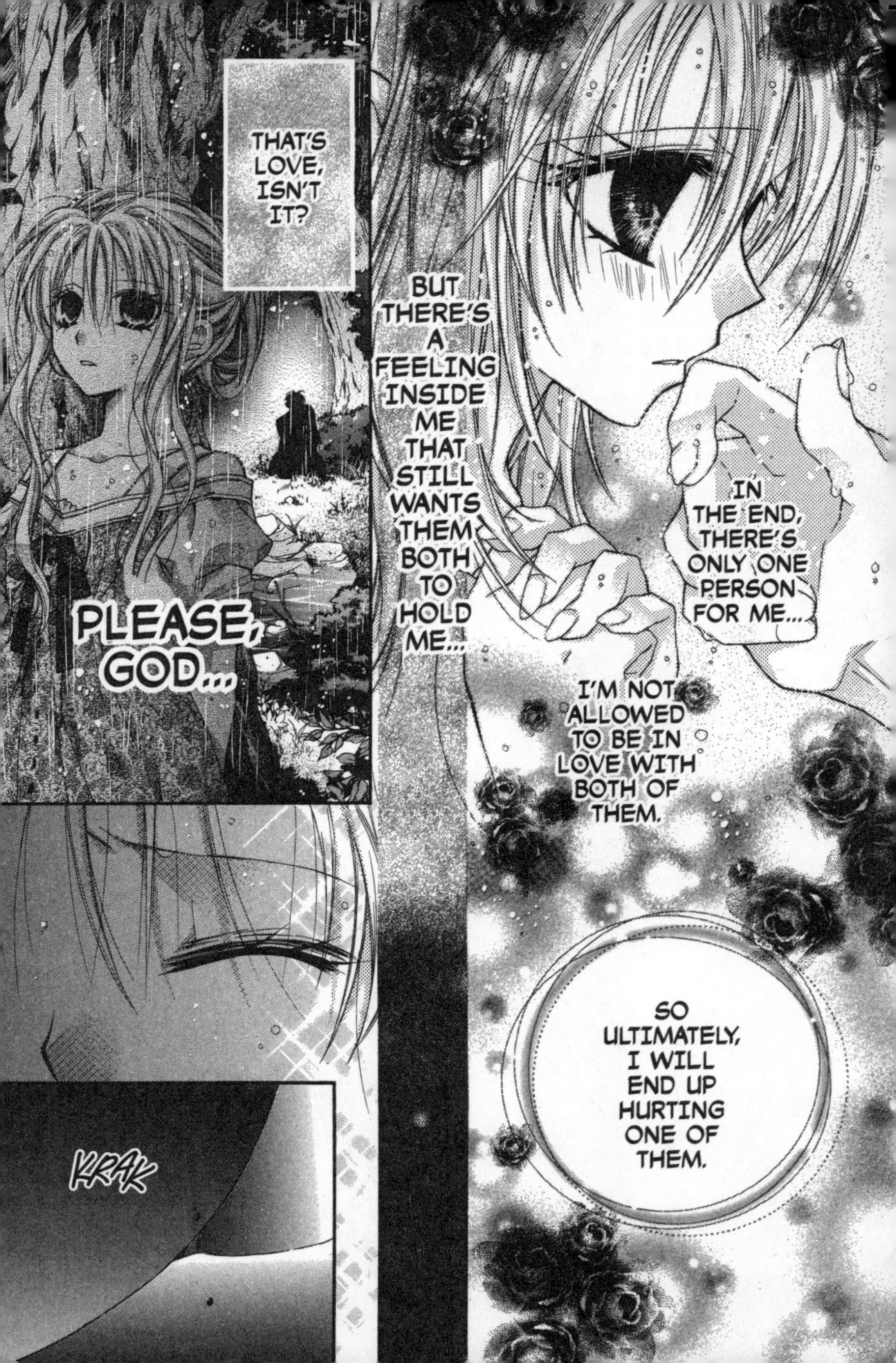
IN THE END, THERE'S ONLY ONE PERSON FOR ME...
I'M NOT ALLOWED TO BE IN LOVE WITH BOTH OF THEM.
SO ULTIMATELY, I WILL END UP HURTING ONE OF THEM.
THAT'S LOVE, ISN'T IT?
BUT THERE'S A FEELING INSIDE ME THAT STILL WANTS THEM BOTH TO HOLD ME...
PLEASE, GOD...
KRAK

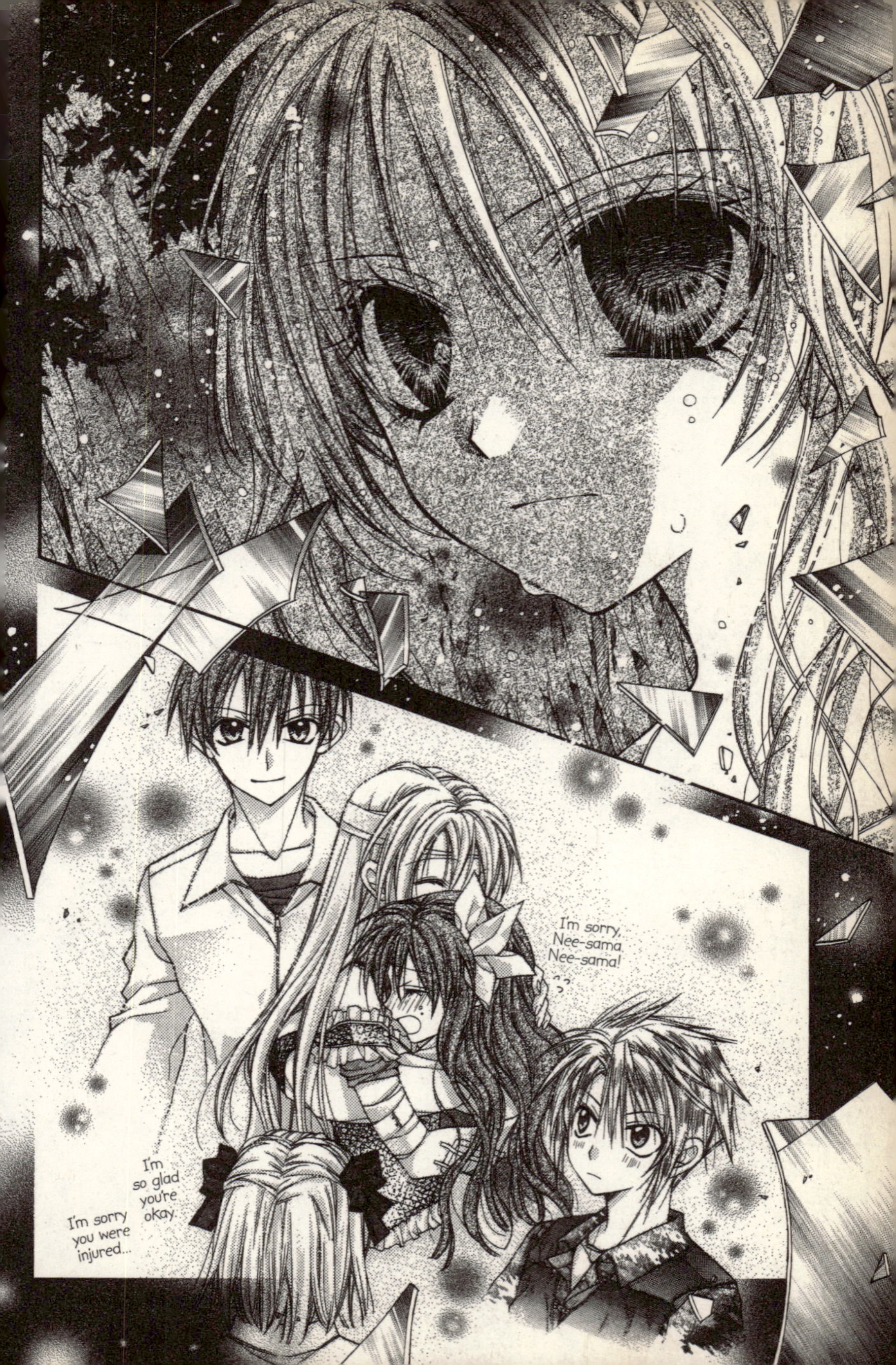
I'm sorry, Nee-sama. Nee-sama!
I'm so glad you're okay.
I'm sorry you were injured...

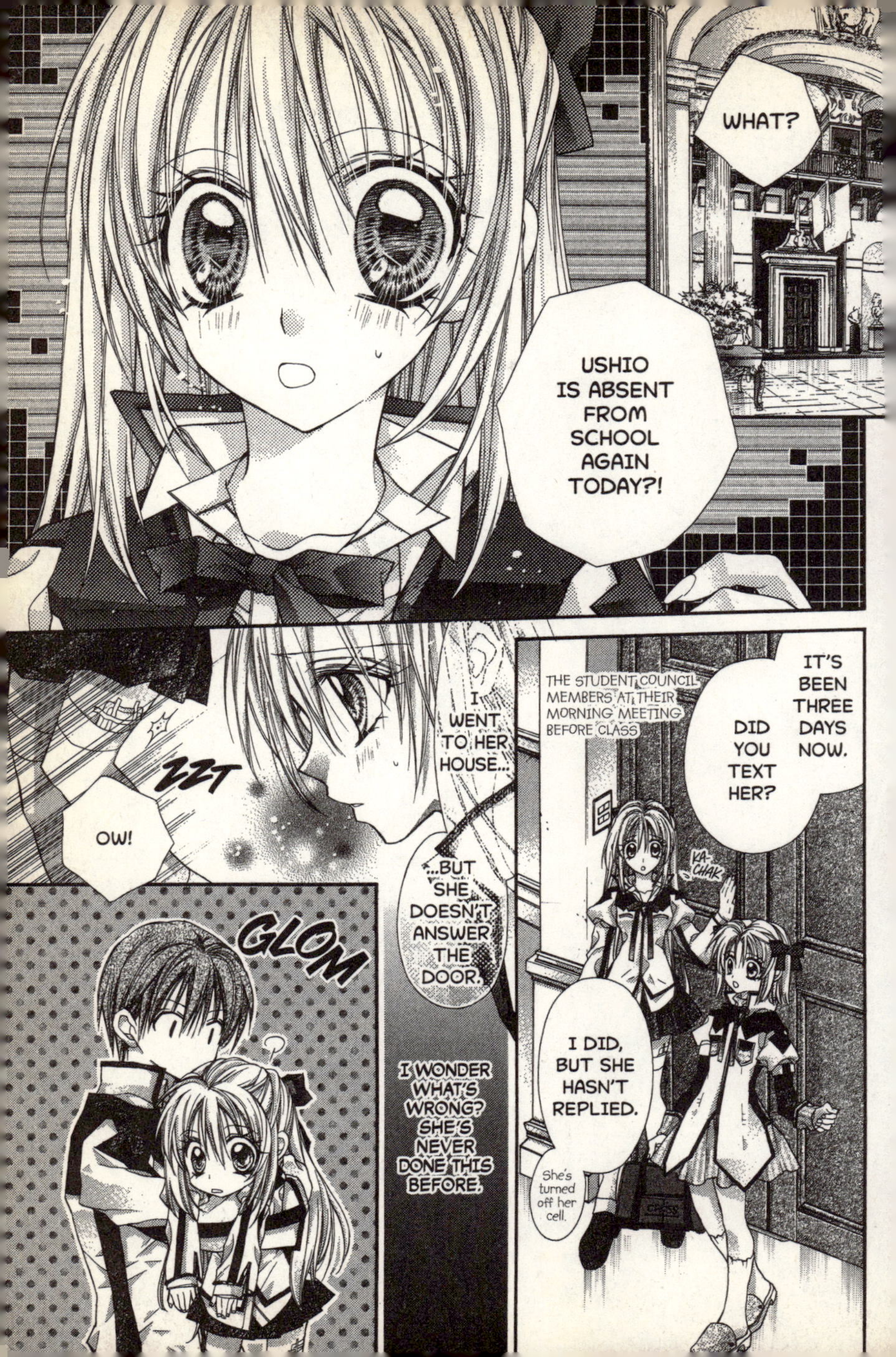
WHAT?
USHIO IS ABSENT FROM SCHOOL AGAIN TODAY?!
THE STUDENT COUNCIL MEMBERS AT THEIR MORNING MEETING BEFORE CLASS
IT'S BEEN THREE DAYS NOW.
DID YOU TEXT HER?
KA-CHAK
I DID, BUT SHE HASN'T REPLIED.
She's turned off her cell.
I WENT TO HER HOUSE...
...BUT SHE DOESN'T ANSWER THE DOOR.
ZZZT
OW!
GLOM
I WONDER WHAT'S WRONG? SHE'S NEVER DONE THIS BEFORE.

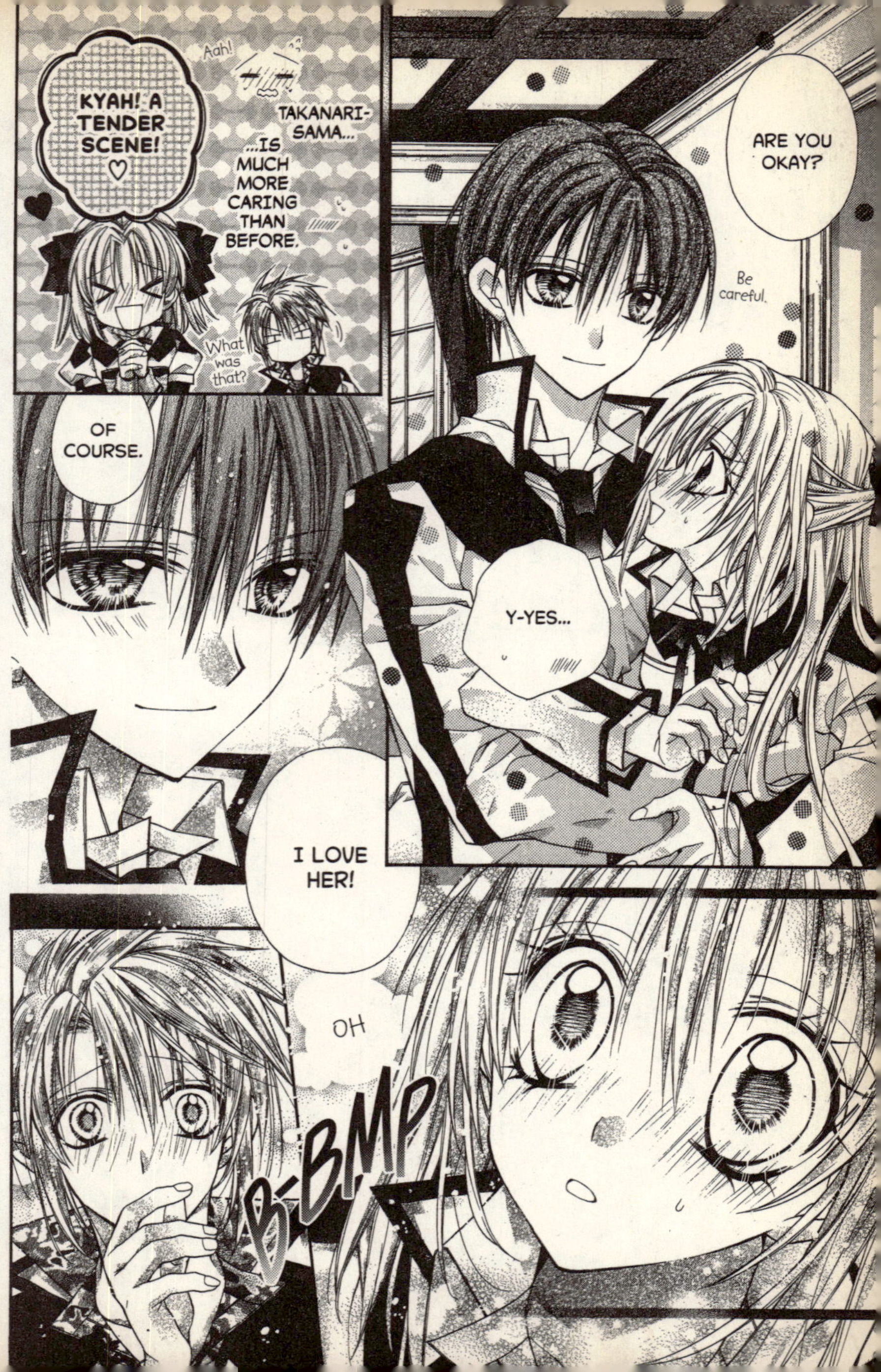
ARE YOU OKAY?
Be careful.
Y-YES...
Aah!
TAKANARI-SAMA...
...IS MUCH MORE CARING THAN BEFORE.
KYAH! A TENDER SCENE! ♡
What was that?
OF COURSE.
I LOVE HER!
OH
B-BMP

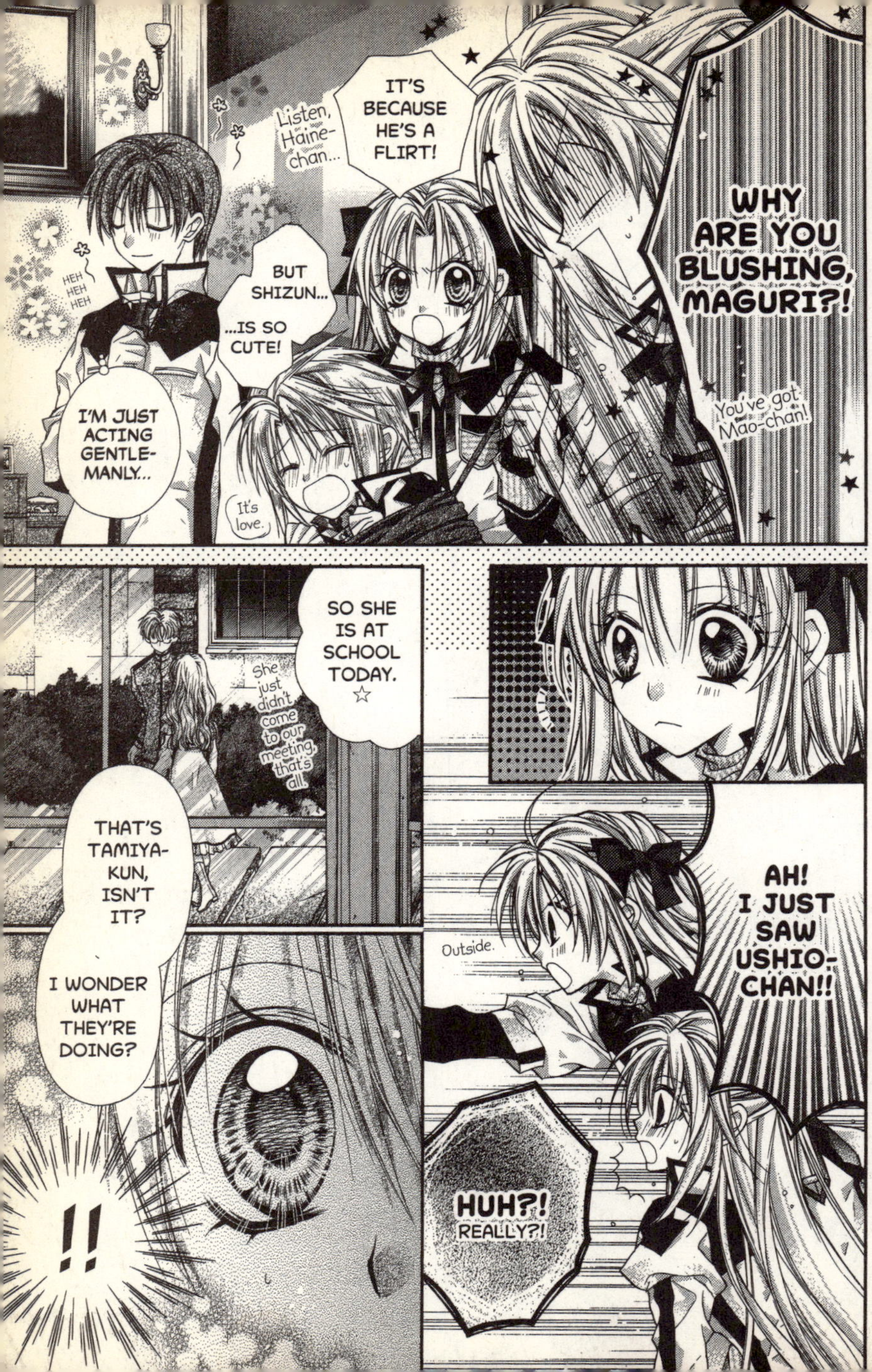
WHY ARE YOU BLUSHING, MAGURI?!
You've got Mao-chan!
IT'S BECAUSE HE'S A FLIRT!
Listen, Haine-chan...
BUT SHIZUN...
...IS SO CUTE!
It's love.
HEH HEH HEH
I'M JUST ACTING GENTLE-MANLY...
SO SHE IS AT SCHOOL TODAY. ☆
She just didn't come to our meeting, that's all.
AH! I JUST SAW USHIO-CHAN!!
Outside.
HUH?! REALLY?!
THAT'S TAMIYA-KUN, ISN'T IT?
I WONDER WHAT THEY'RE DOING?
!!

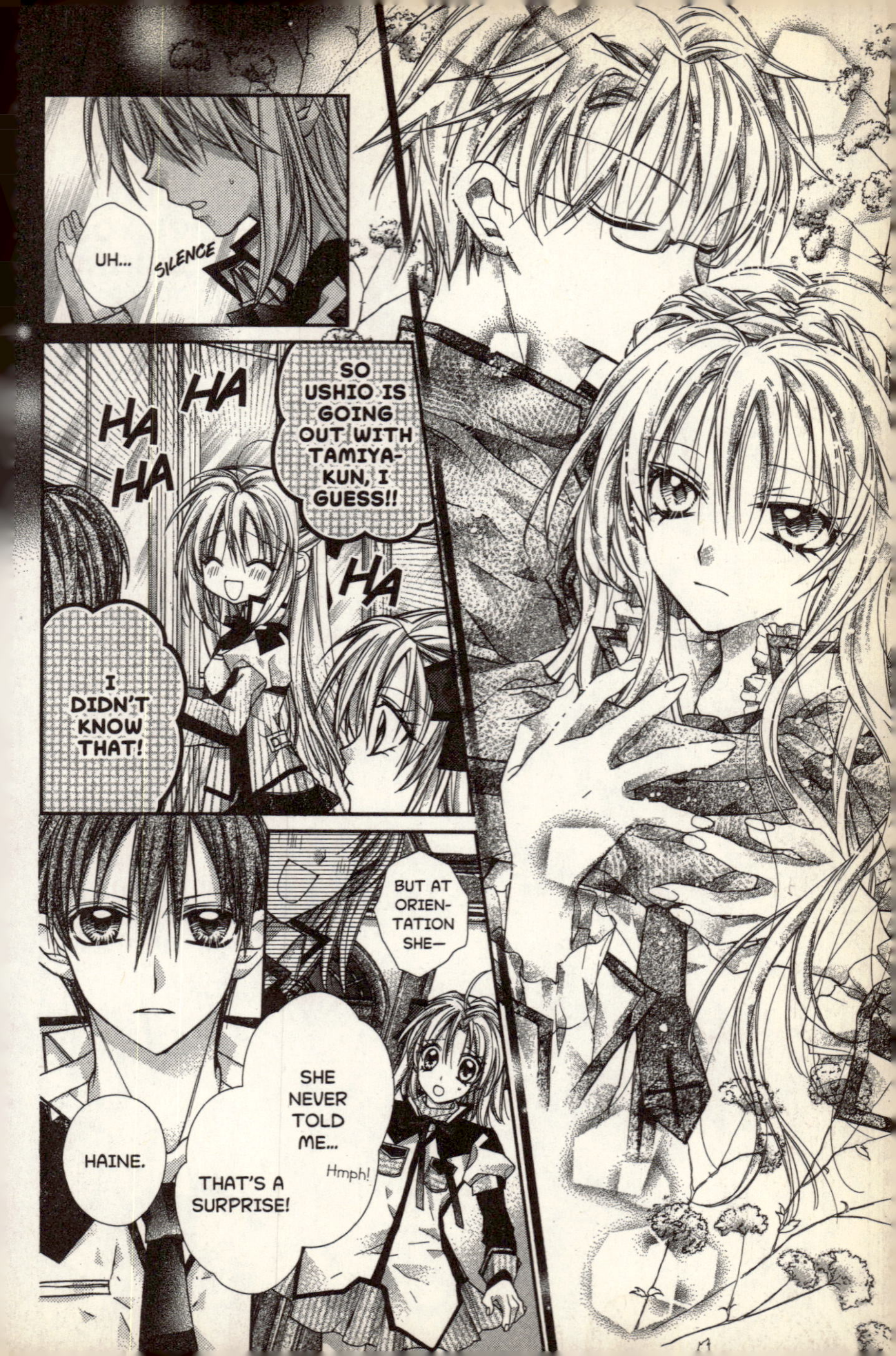
UH...
SILENCE
SO USHIO IS GOING OUT WITH TAMIYA-KUN, I GUESS!!
HA
HA
HA
HA
I DIDN'T KNOW THAT!
BUT AT ORIENTATION SHE—
SHE NEVER TOLD ME...
Hmph!
THAT'S A SURPRISE!
HAINE.

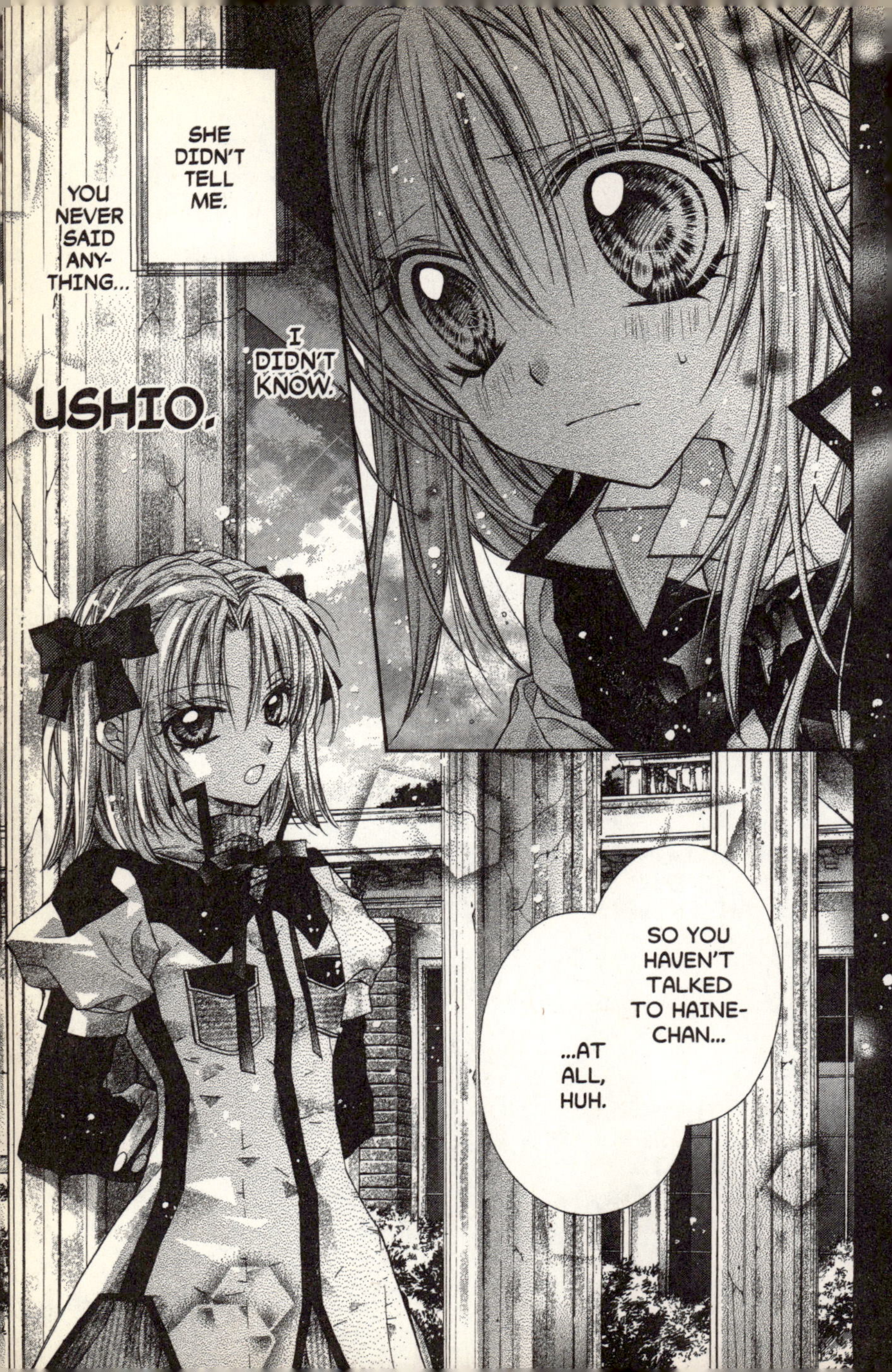
I DIDN'T KNOW.
SHE DIDN'T TELL ME.
YOU NEVER SAID ANY-THING...
USHIO.
SO YOU HAVEN'T TALKED TO HAINE-CHAN...
...AT ALL, HUH.

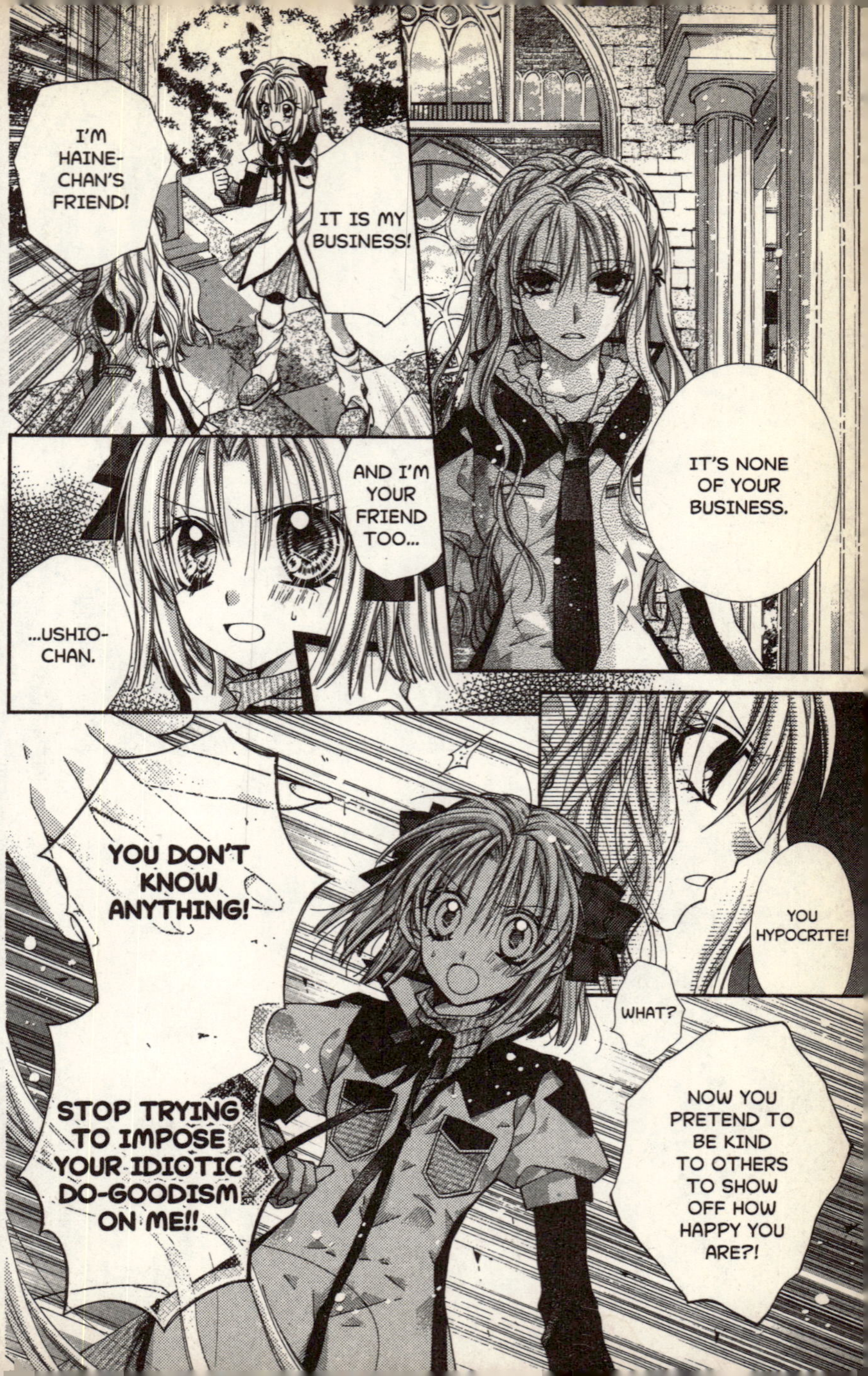
IT'S NONE OF YOUR BUSINESS.
IT IS MY BUSINESS!
I'M HAINE-CHAN'S FRIEND!
AND I'M YOUR FRIEND TOO...
...USHIO-CHAN.
YOU HYPOCRITE!
WHAT?
NOW YOU PRETEND TO BE KIND TO OTHERS TO SHOW OFF HOW HAPPY YOU ARE?!
YOU DON'T KNOW ANYTHING!
STOP TRYING TO IMPOSE YOUR IDIOTIC DO-GOODISM ON ME!!

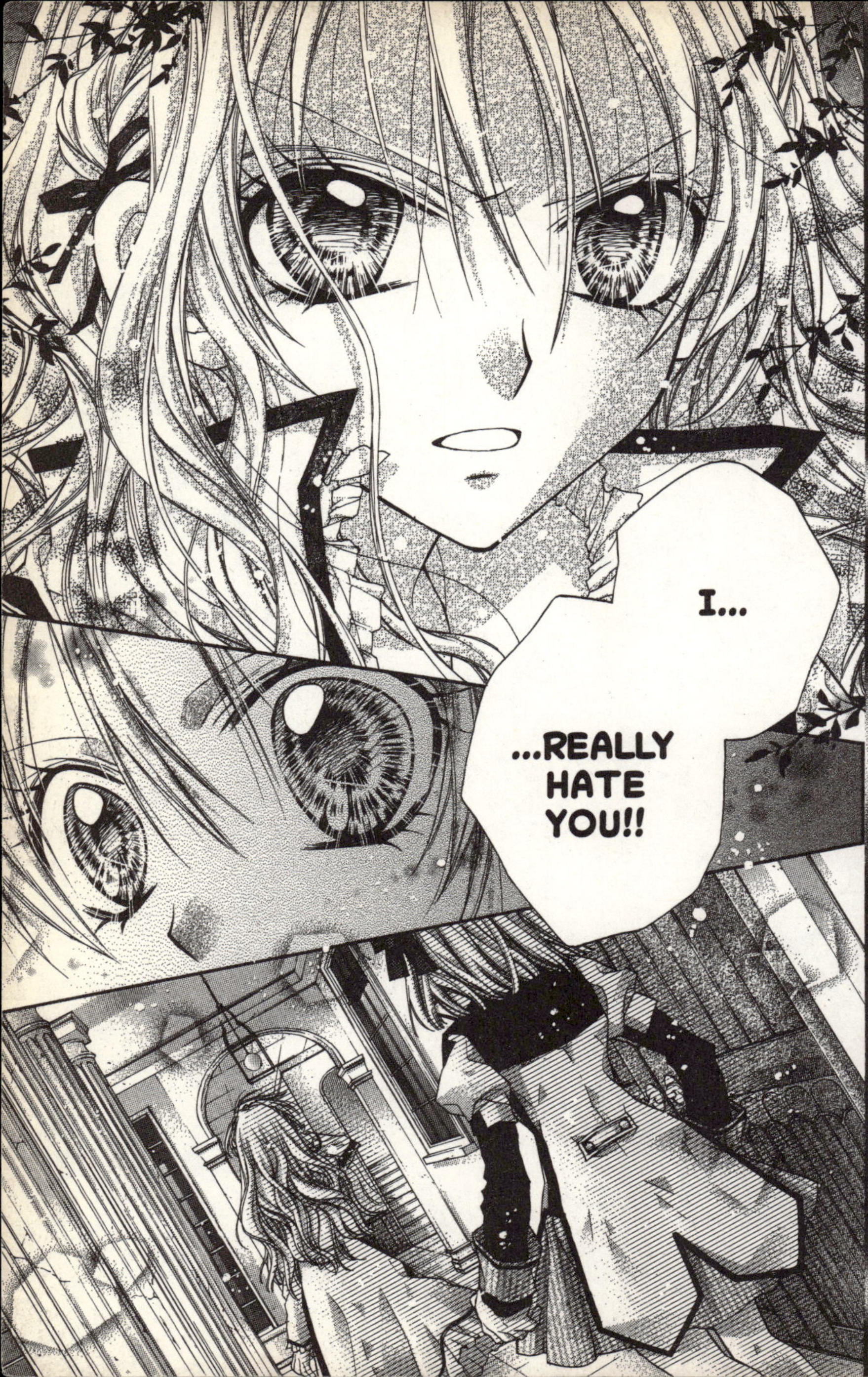
I...
...REALLY HATE YOU!!

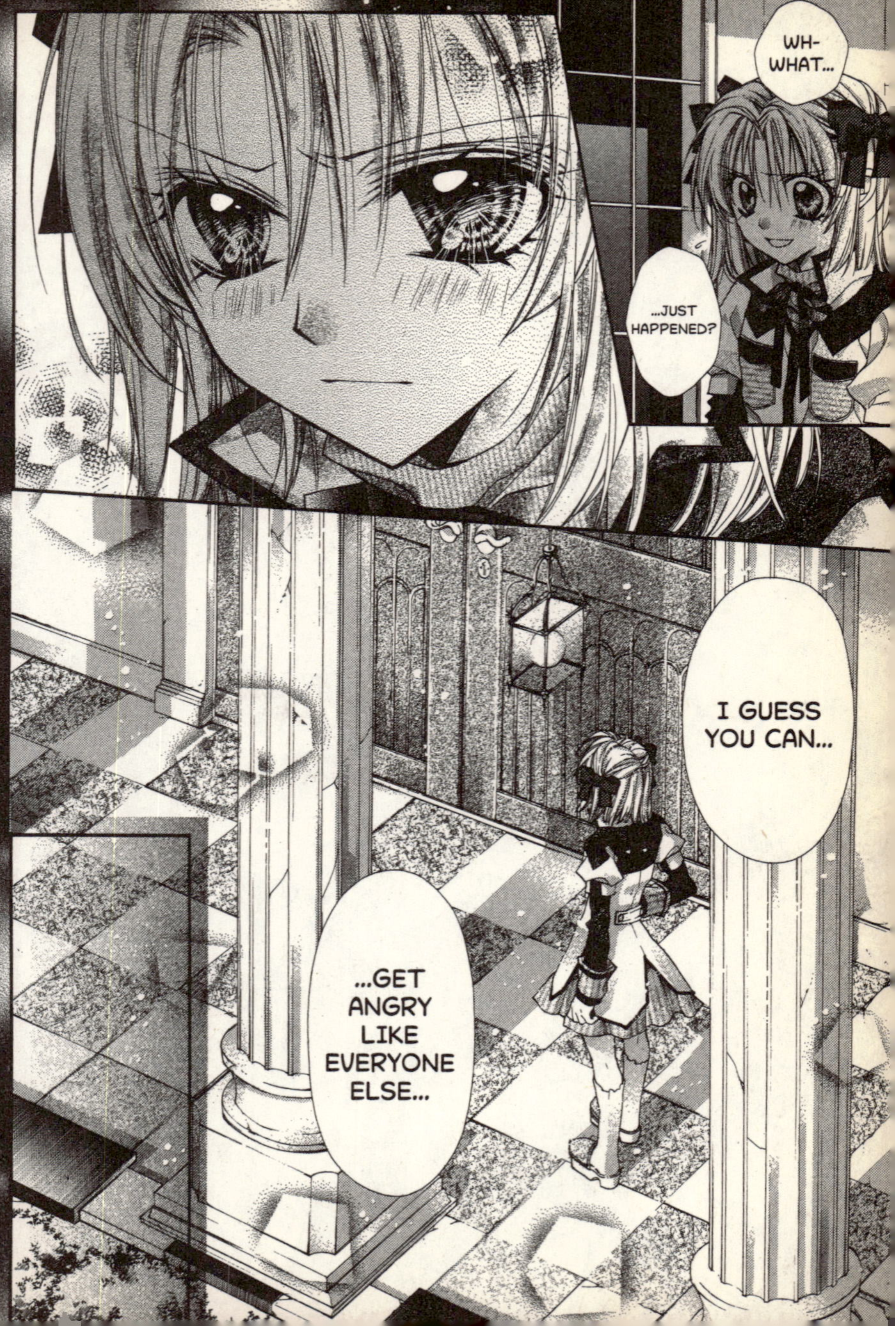
WH-
WHAT...
...JUST HAPPENED?
I GUESS YOU CAN...
...GET ANGRY LIKE EVERYONE ELSE...

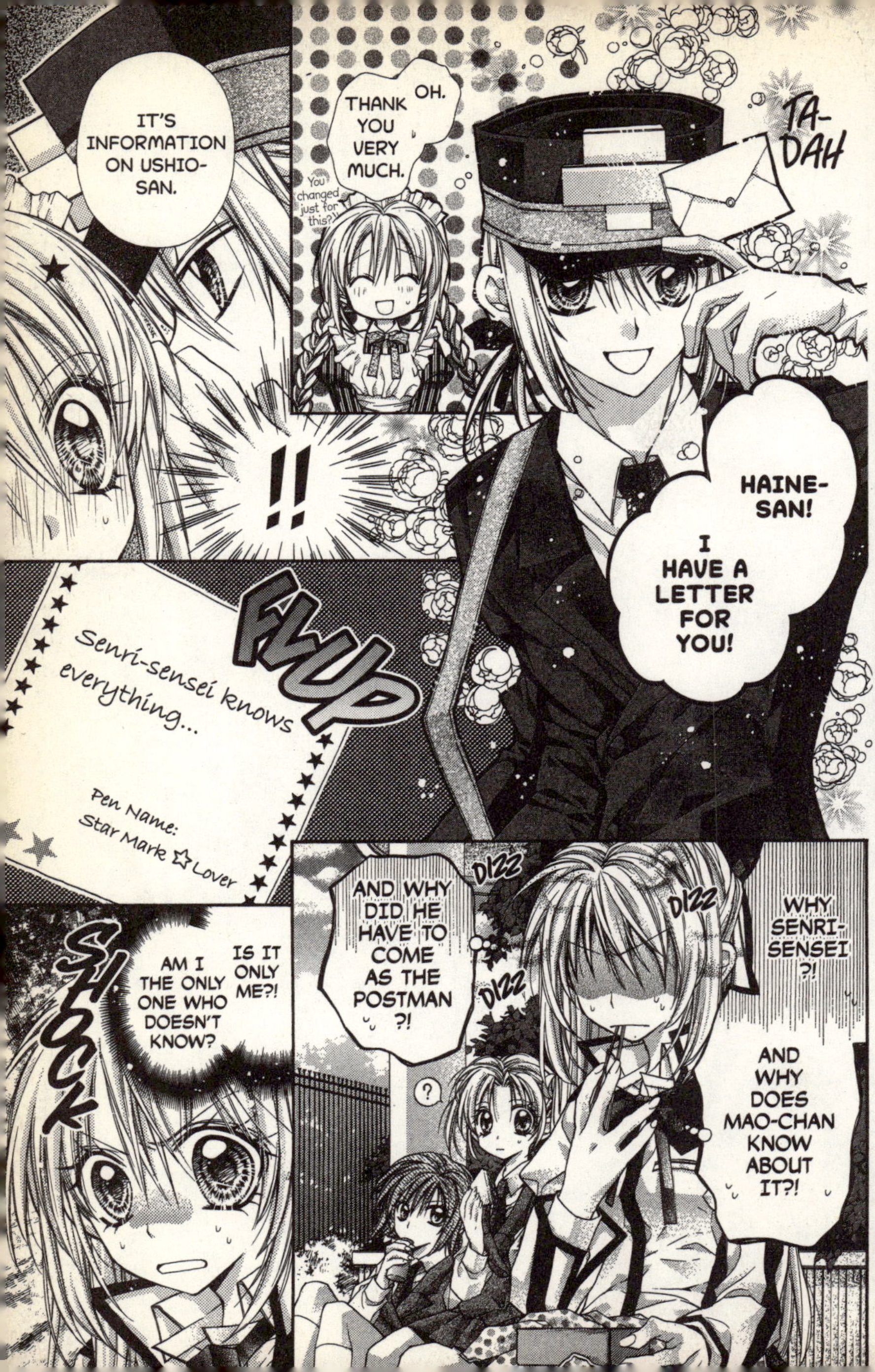
TA-DAH
HAINE-SAN!
I HAVE A LETTER FOR YOU!
OH.
THANK YOU VERY MUCH.
You changed just for this?
IT'S INFORMATION ON USHIO-SAN.
!!
FWUP
Senri-sensei knows everything...
Pen Name: Star Mark ☆ Lover
WHY SENRI-SENSEI?!
DIZZ
DIZZ
AND WHY DID HE HAVE TO COME AS THE POSTMAN?!
DIZZ
AND WHY DOES MAO-CHAN KNOW ABOUT IT?!
?
SHOCK
IS IT ONLY ME?!
AM I THE ONLY ONE WHO DOESN'T KNOW?

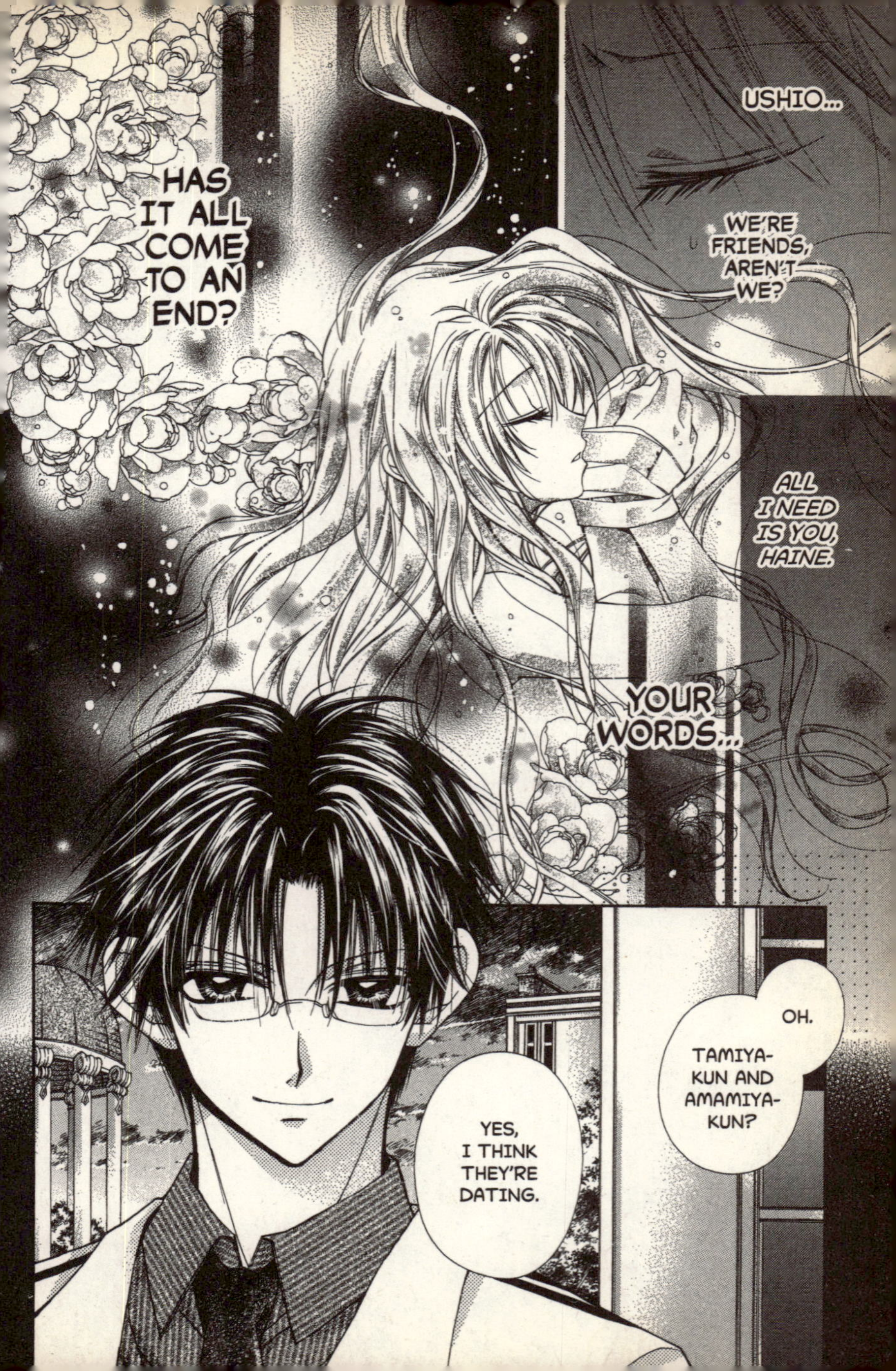
USHIO...
WE'RE FRIENDS, AREN'T WE?
HAS IT ALL COME TO AN END?
ALL I NEED IS YOU, HAINE.
YOUR WORDS...
OH.
TAMIYA-KUN AND AMAMIYA-KUN?
YES, I THINK THEY'RE DATING.

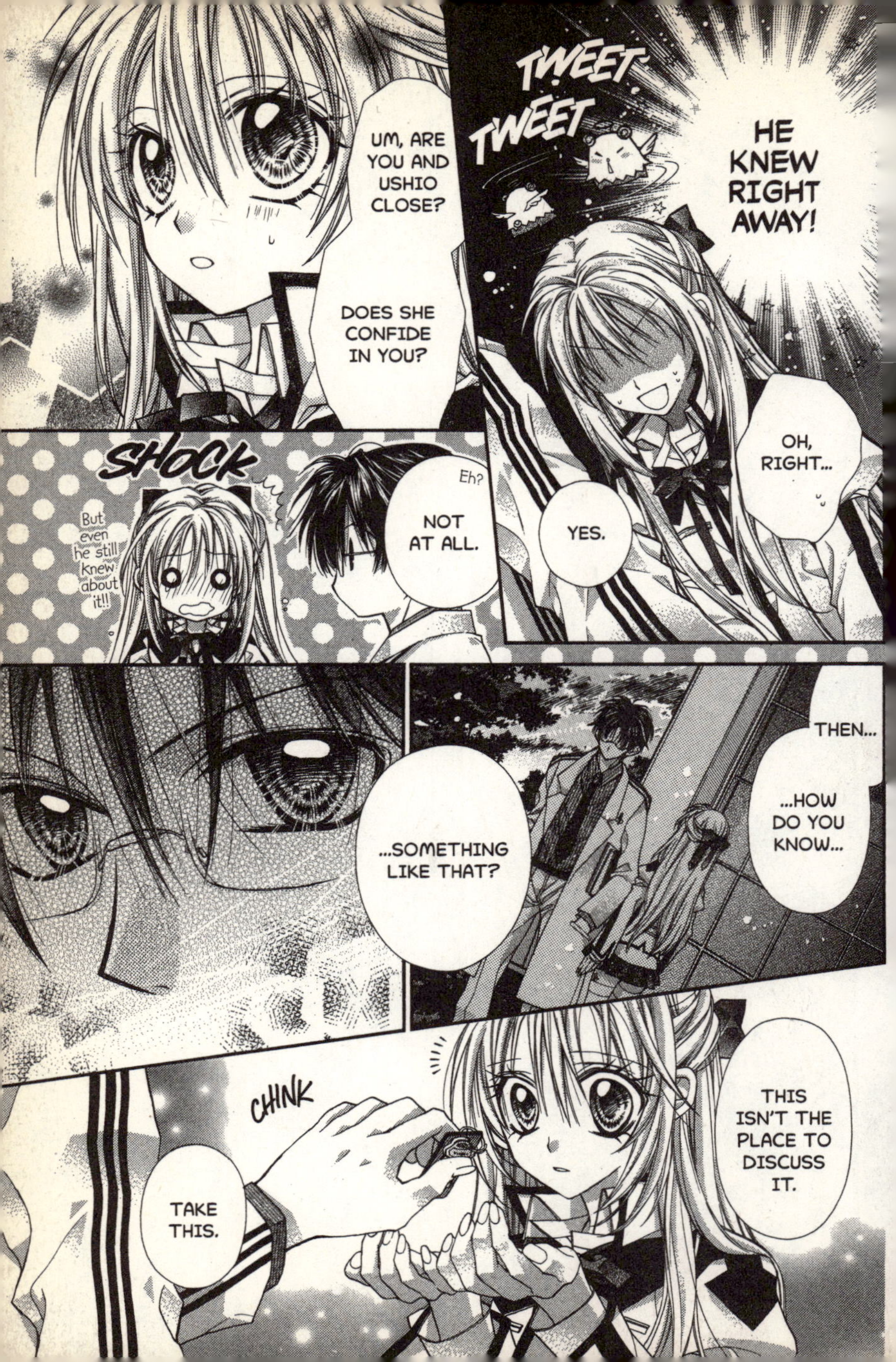
TWEET
TWEET
HE KNEW RIGHT AWAY!
OH, RIGHT...
YES.
UM, ARE YOU AND USHIO CLOSE?
DOES SHE CONFIDE IN YOU?
Eh?
NOT AT ALL.
SHOCK
But even he still knew about it!!
THEN...
...HOW DO YOU KNOW...
...SOMETHING LIKE THAT?
THIS ISN'T THE PLACE TO DISCUSS IT.
CHINK
TAKE THIS.

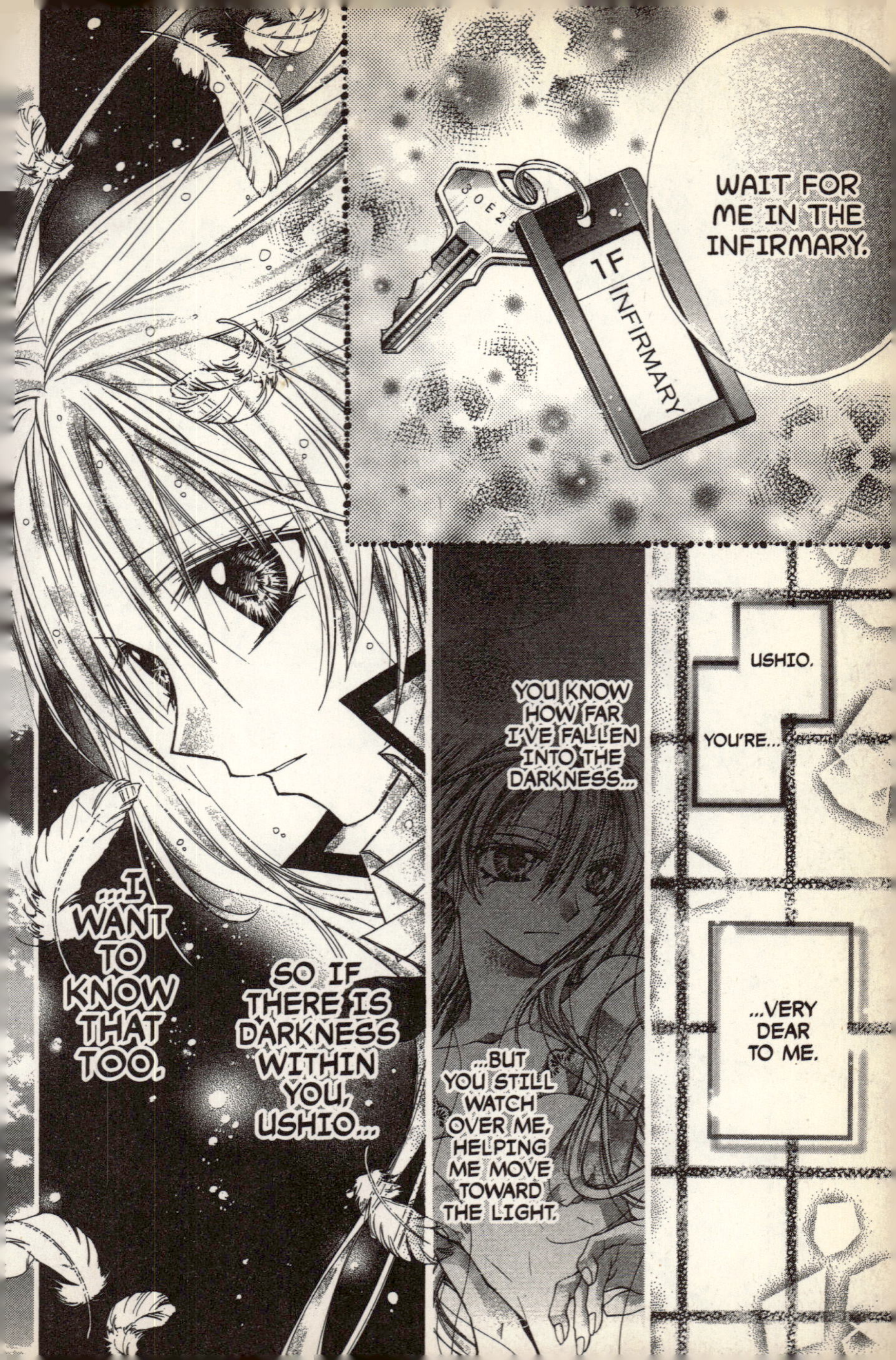
WAIT FOR ME IN THE INFIRMARY.
1F INFIRMARY
USHIO.
YOU'RE...
...VERY DEAR TO ME.
YOU KNOW HOW FAR I'VE FALLEN INTO THE DARKNESS...
...BUT YOU STILL WATCH OVER ME, HELPING ME MOVE TOWARD THE LIGHT.
SO IF THERE IS DARKNESS WITHIN YOU, USHIO...
...I WANT TO KNOW THAT TOO.

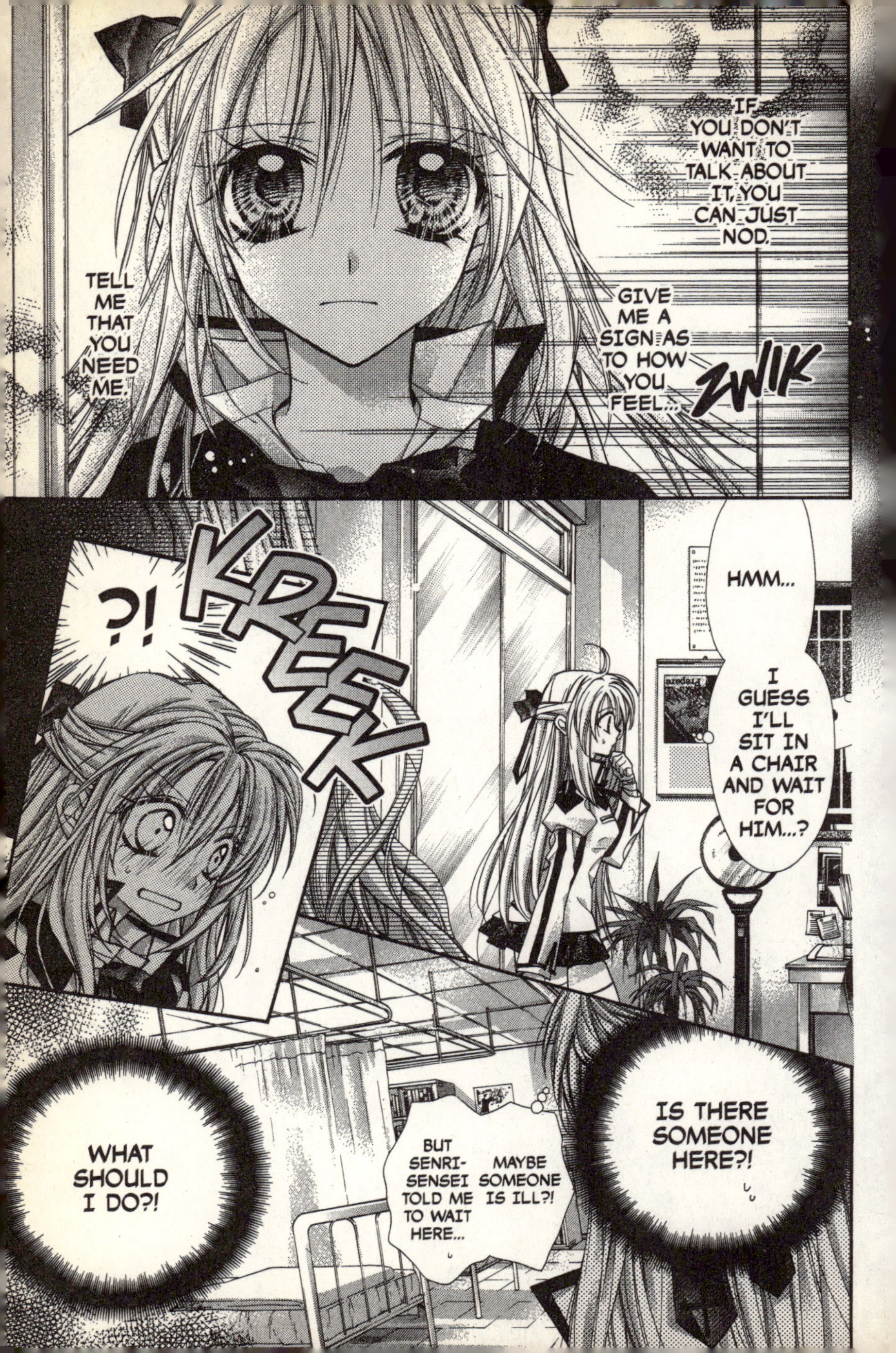
IF YOU DON'T WANT TO TALK ABOUT IT, YOU CAN JUST NOD.
GIVE ME A SIGN AS TO HOW YOU FEEL...
TELL ME THAT YOU NEED ME.
ZWIK
HMM...
I GUESS I'LL SIT IN A CHAIR AND WAIT FOR HIM...?
KREEK
?!
IS THERE SOMEONE HERE?!
MAYBE SOMEONE IS ILL?!
BUT SENRI-SENSEI TOLD ME TO WAIT HERE...
WHAT SHOULD I DO?!

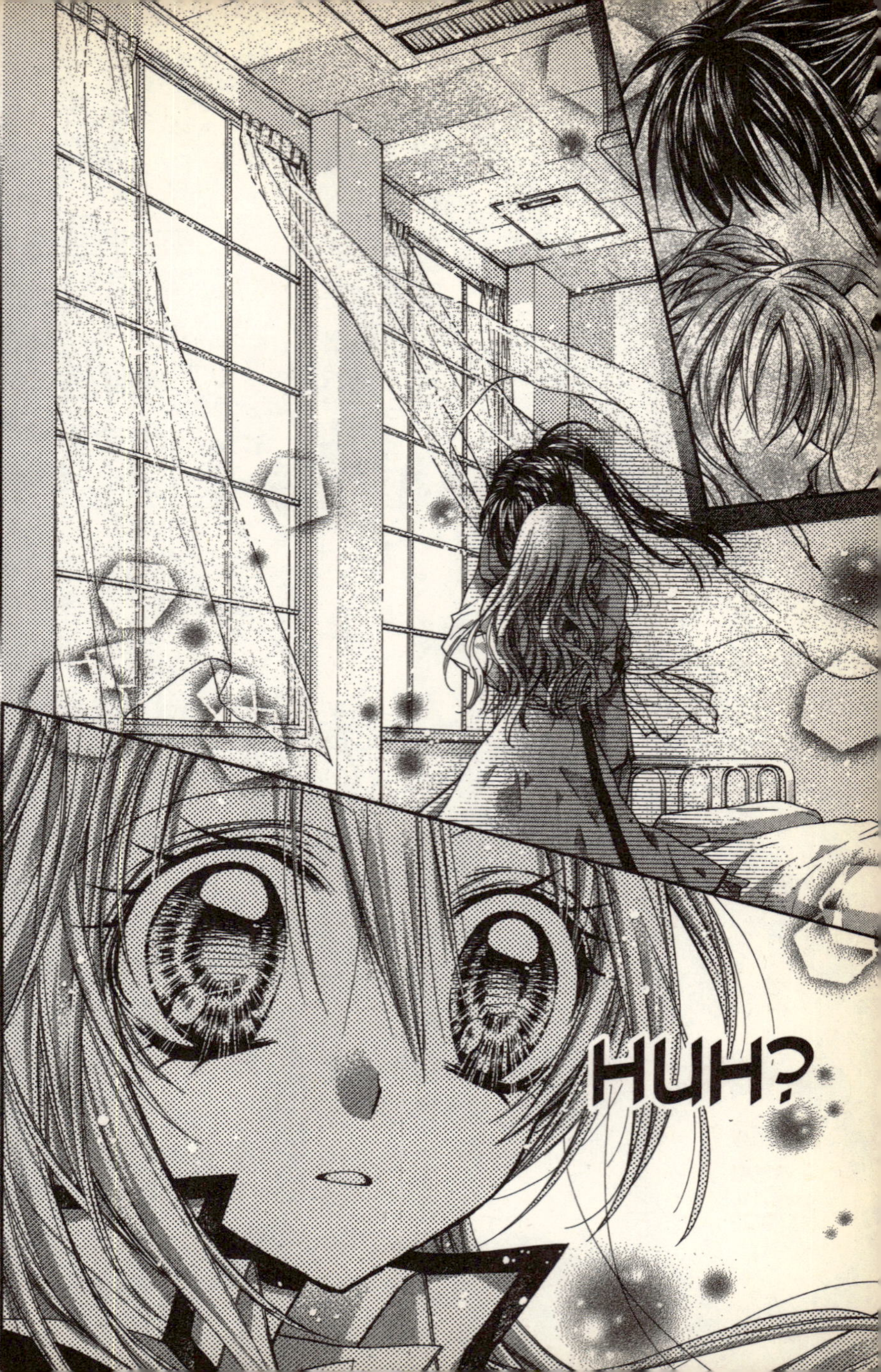
HUH?

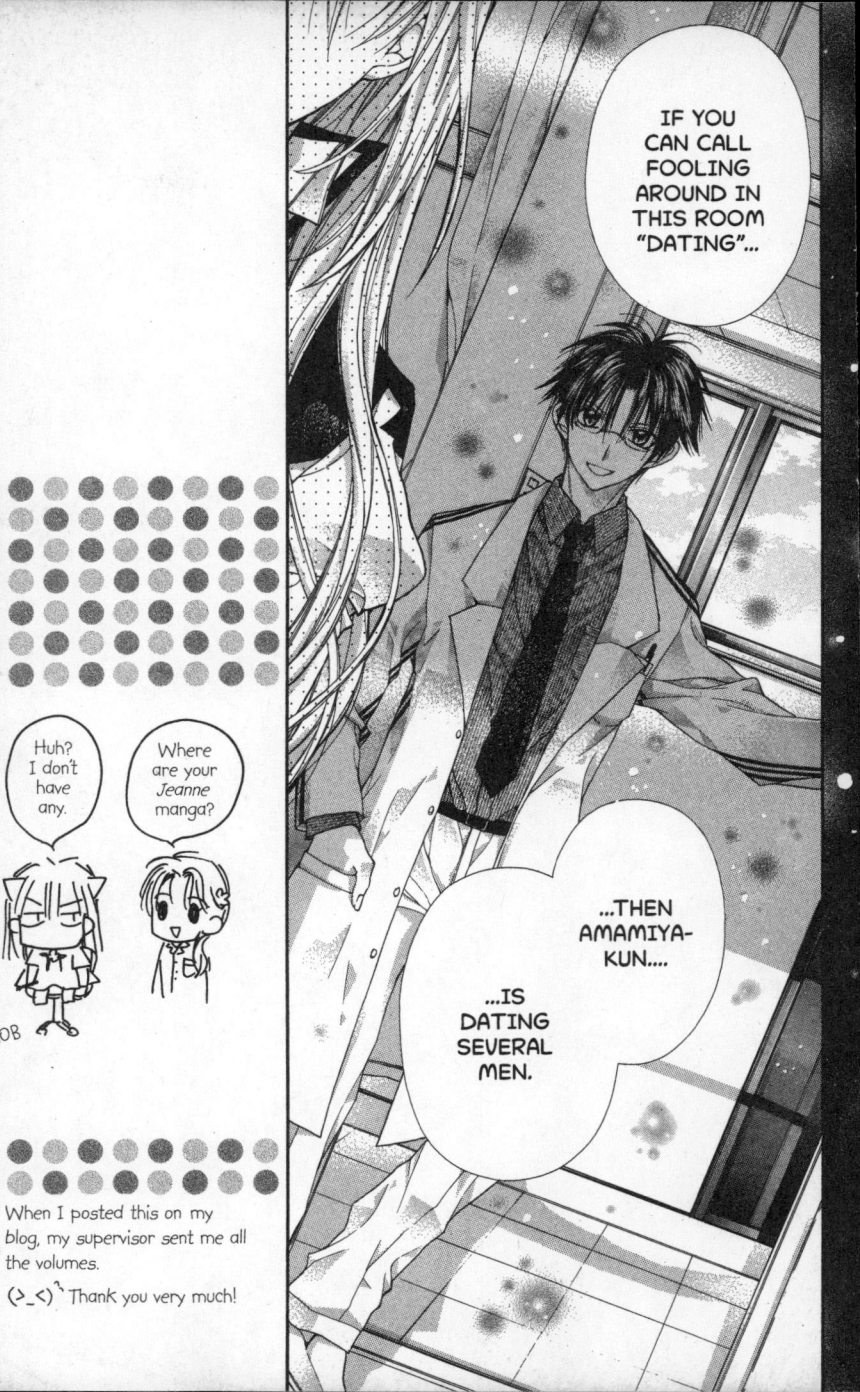

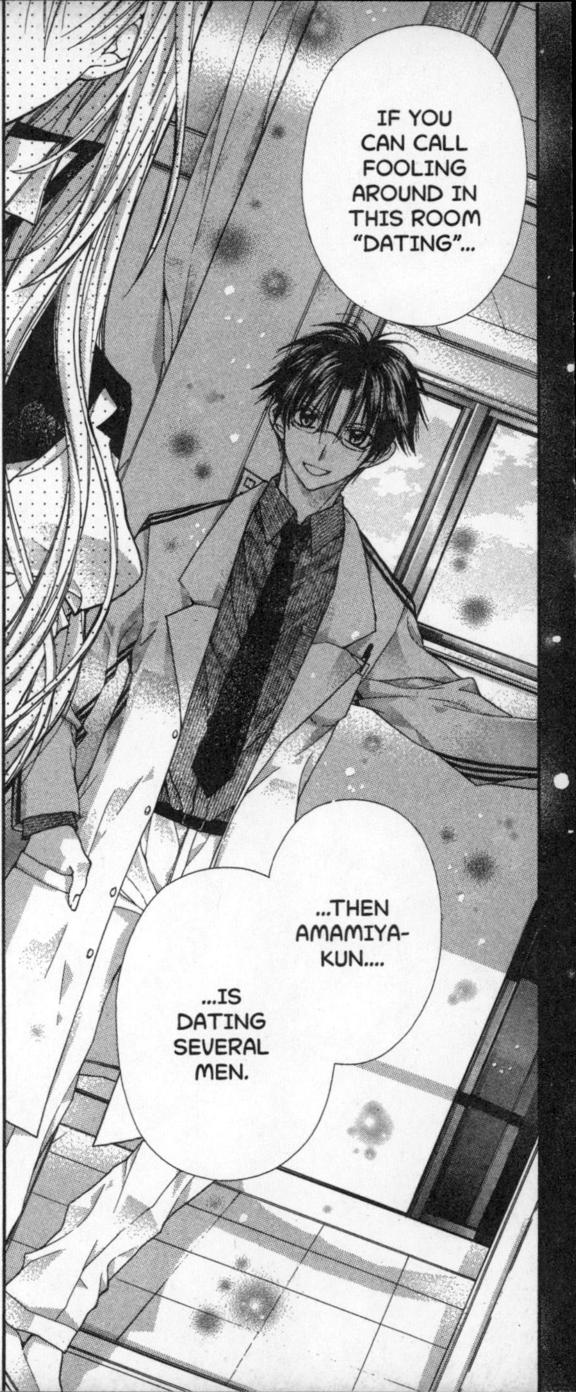
IF YOU CAN CALL FOOLING AROUND IN THIS ROOM "DATING"...
...THEN AMAMIYA-KUN....
...IS DATING SEVERAL MEN.

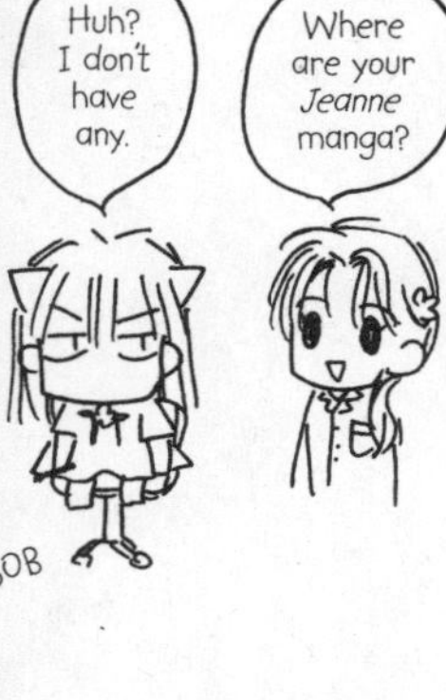
Where are your *Jeanne* manga?
Huh? I don't have any.
SOB

When I posted this on my blog, my supervisor sent me all the volumes.

(>_<)ʾ Thank you very much!

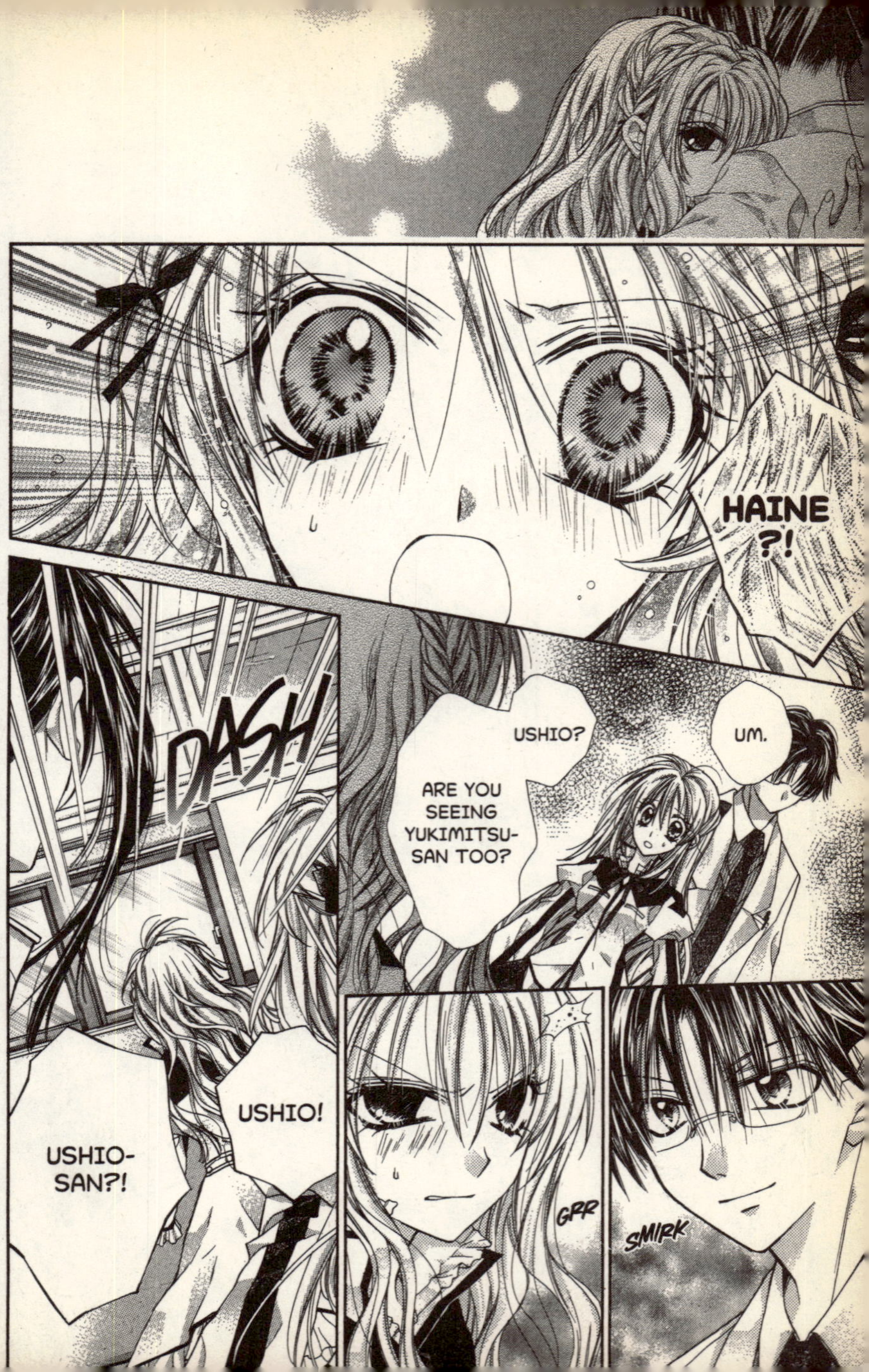
HAINE ?!
UM.
USHIO?
ARE YOU SEEING YUKIMITSU-SAN TOO?
SMIRK
GRR
DASH
USHIO!
USHIO-SAN?!

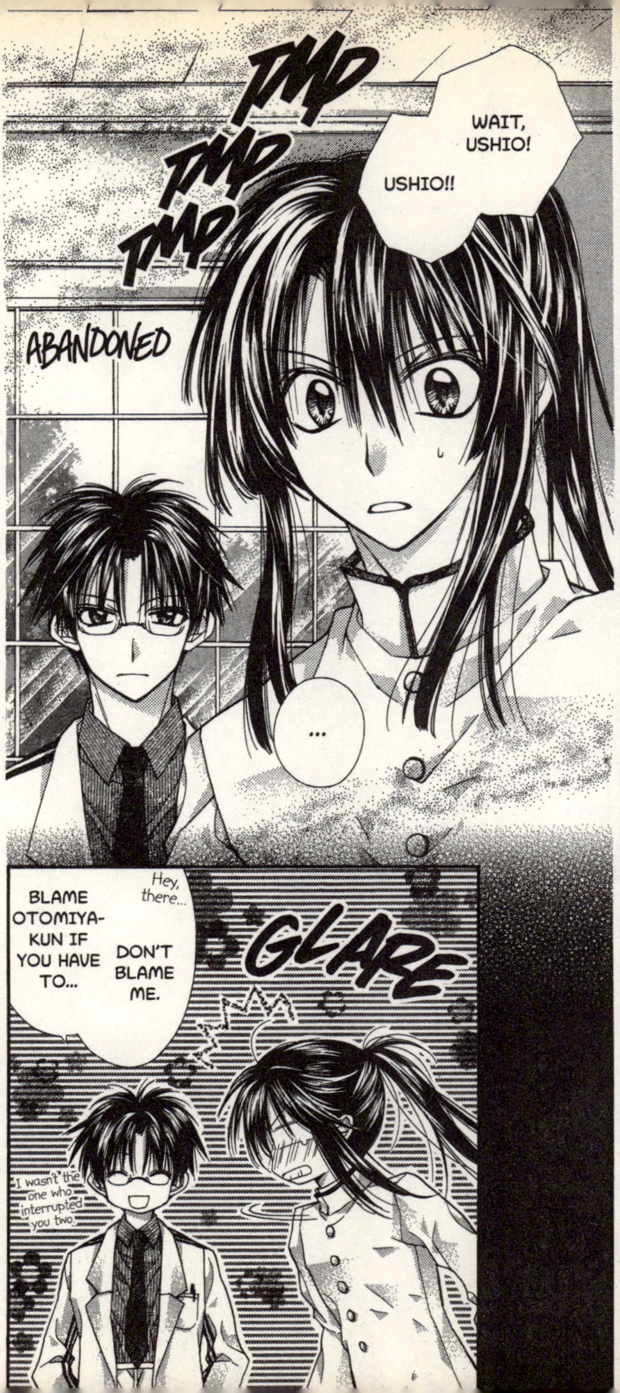
WAIT, USHIO!
USHIO!!
TMP TMP TMP
ABANDONED
...
Hey, there...
DON'T BLAME ME.
BLAME OTOMIYA-KUN IF YOU HAVE TO...
GLARE
I wasn't the one who interrupted you two.

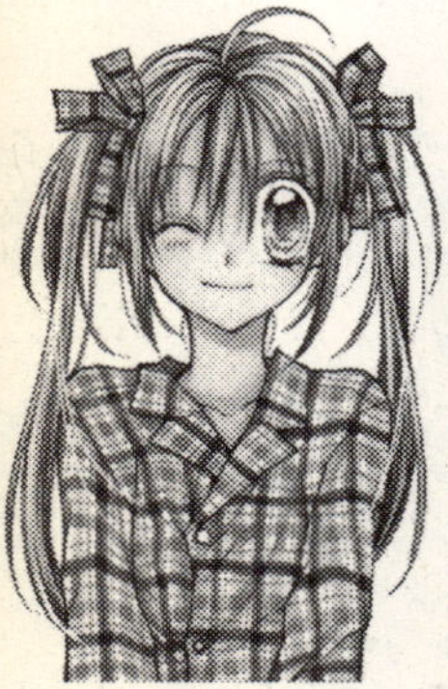

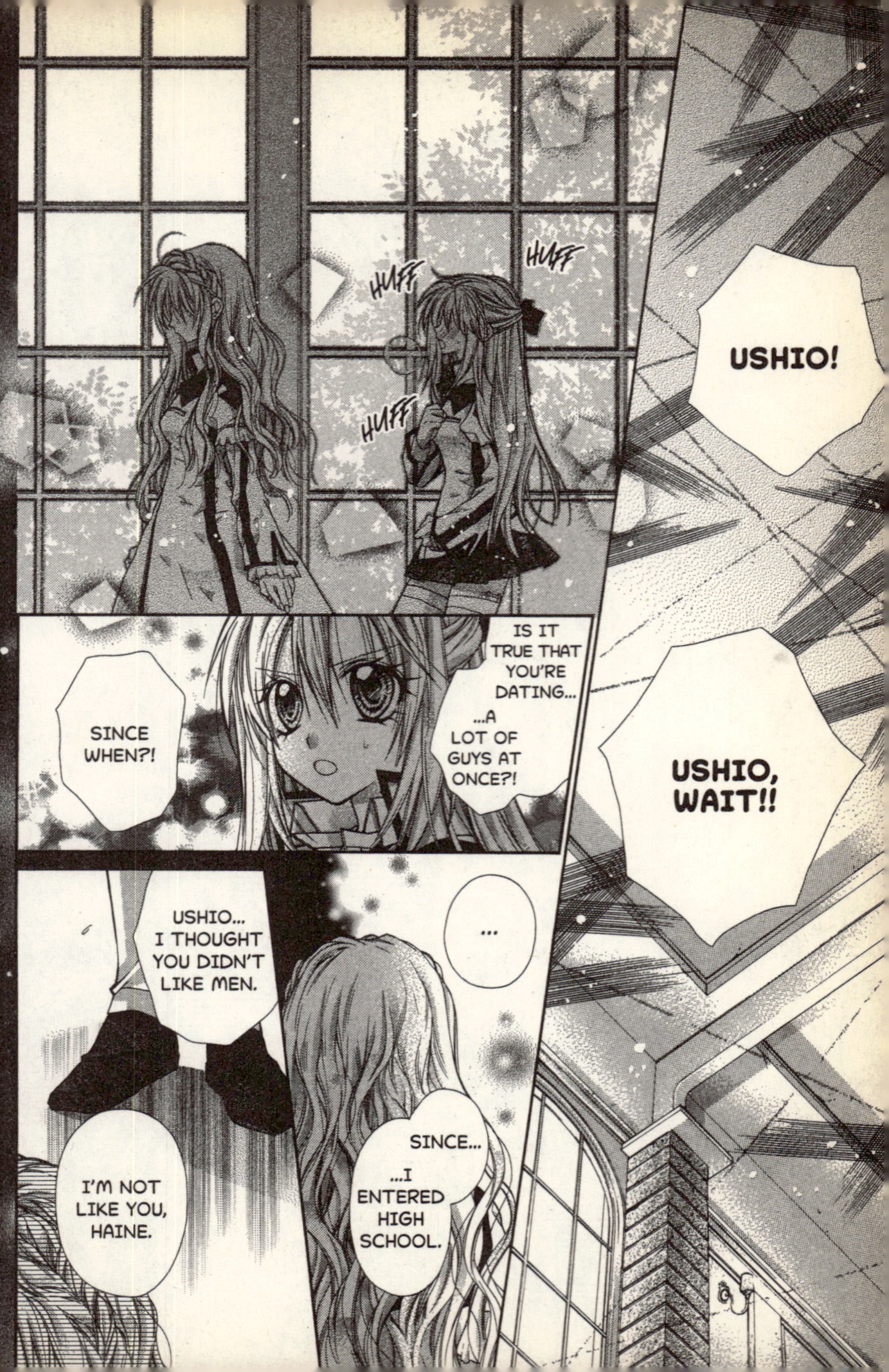
USHIO!
USHIO, WAIT!!
HUFF
HUFF
HUFF
IS IT TRUE THAT YOU'RE DATING...
...A LOT OF GUYS AT ONCE?!
SINCE WHEN?!
...
SINCE...
...I ENTERED HIGH SCHOOL.
USHIO... I THOUGHT YOU DIDN'T LIKE MEN.
I'M NOT LIKE YOU, HAINE.

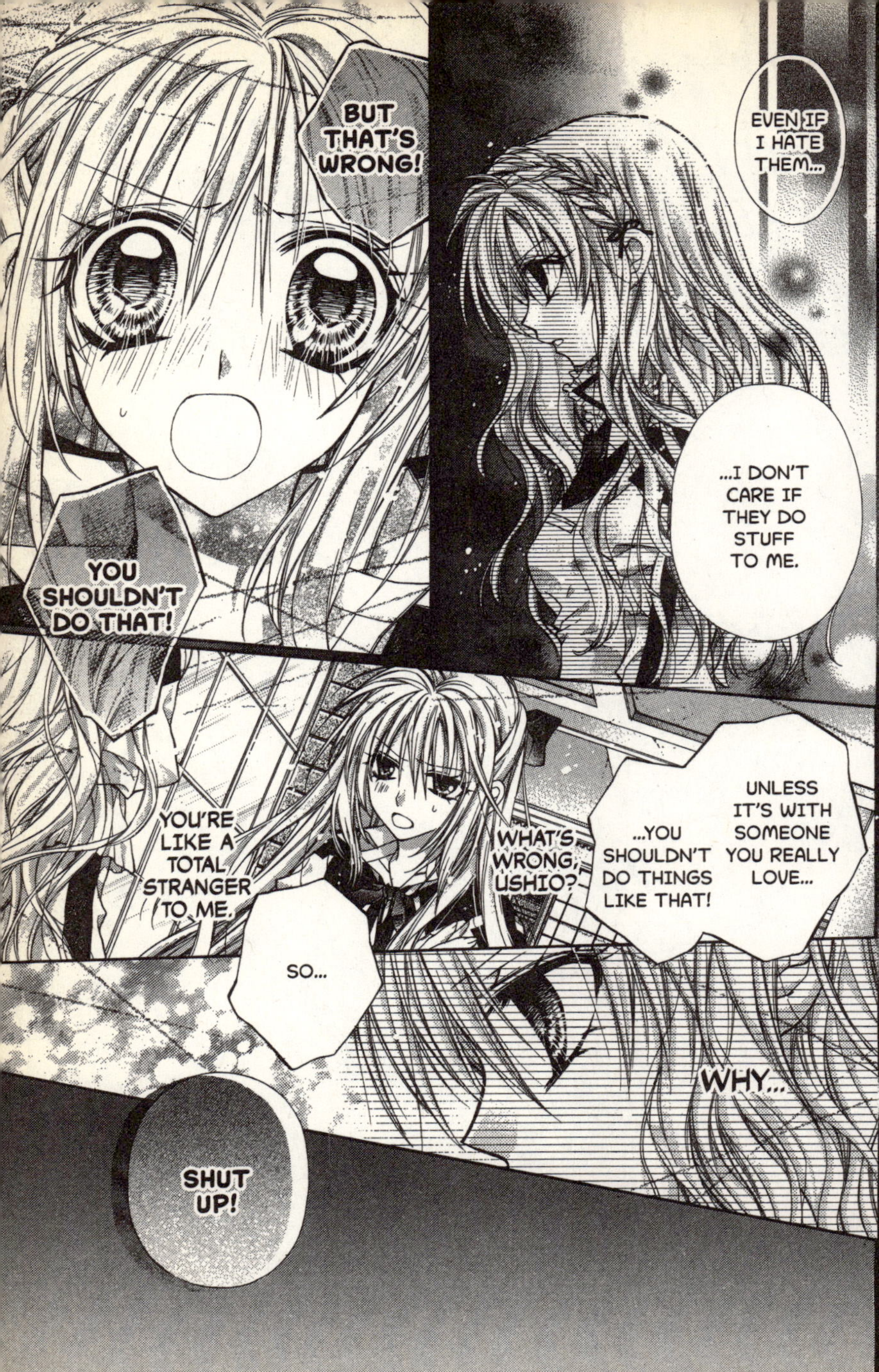
EVEN IF I HATE THEM...
...I DON'T CARE IF THEY DO STUFF TO ME.
BUT THAT'S WRONG!
YOU SHOULDN'T DO THAT!
UNLESS IT'S WITH SOMEONE YOU REALLY LOVE...
...YOU SHOULDN'T DO THINGS LIKE THAT!
WHAT'S WRONG, USHIO?
YOU'RE LIKE A TOTAL STRANGER TO ME.
SO...
WHY...
SHUT UP!

IF I STOPPED...

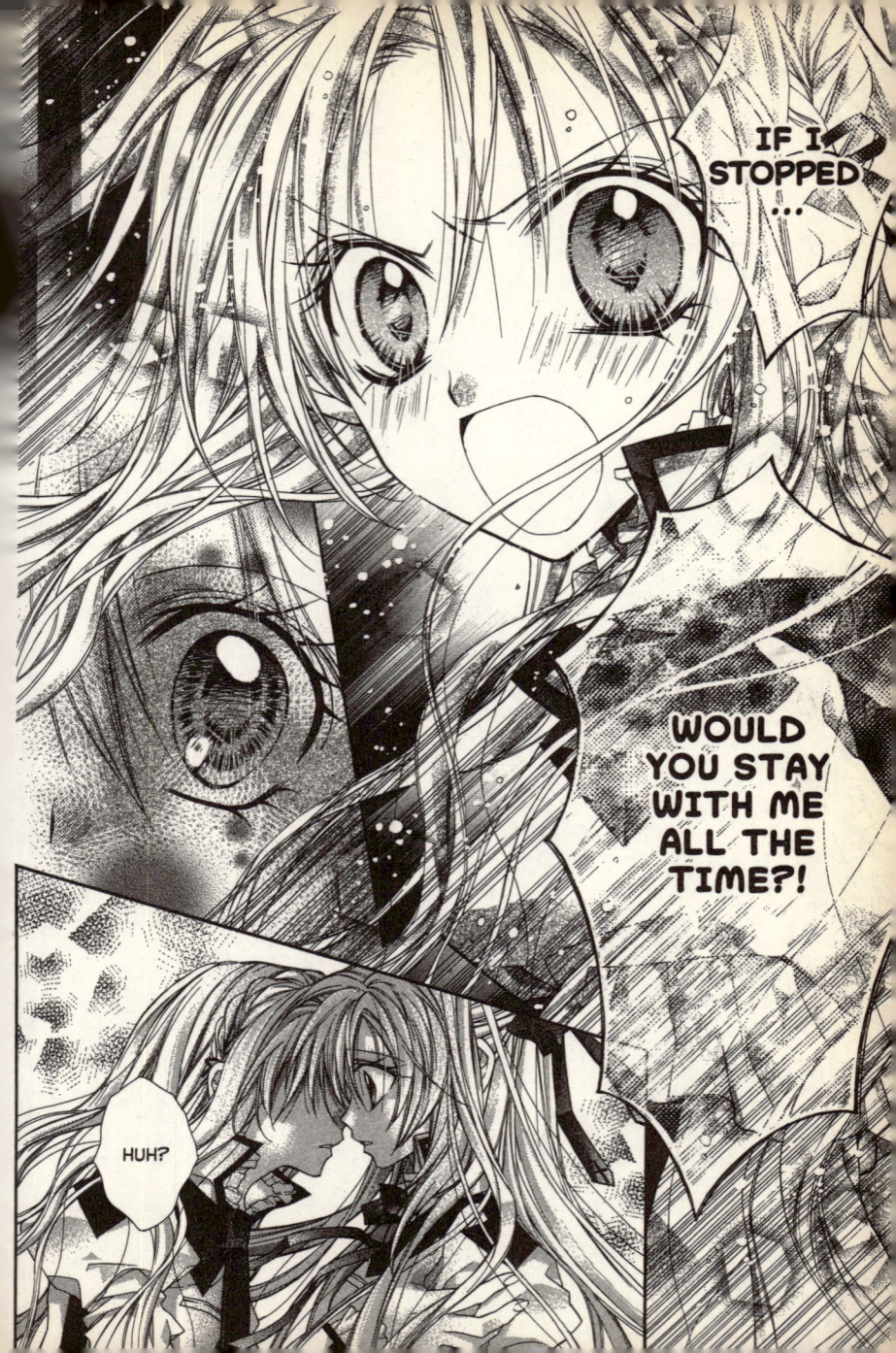

WOULD YOU STAY WITH ME ALL THE TIME?!

HUH?

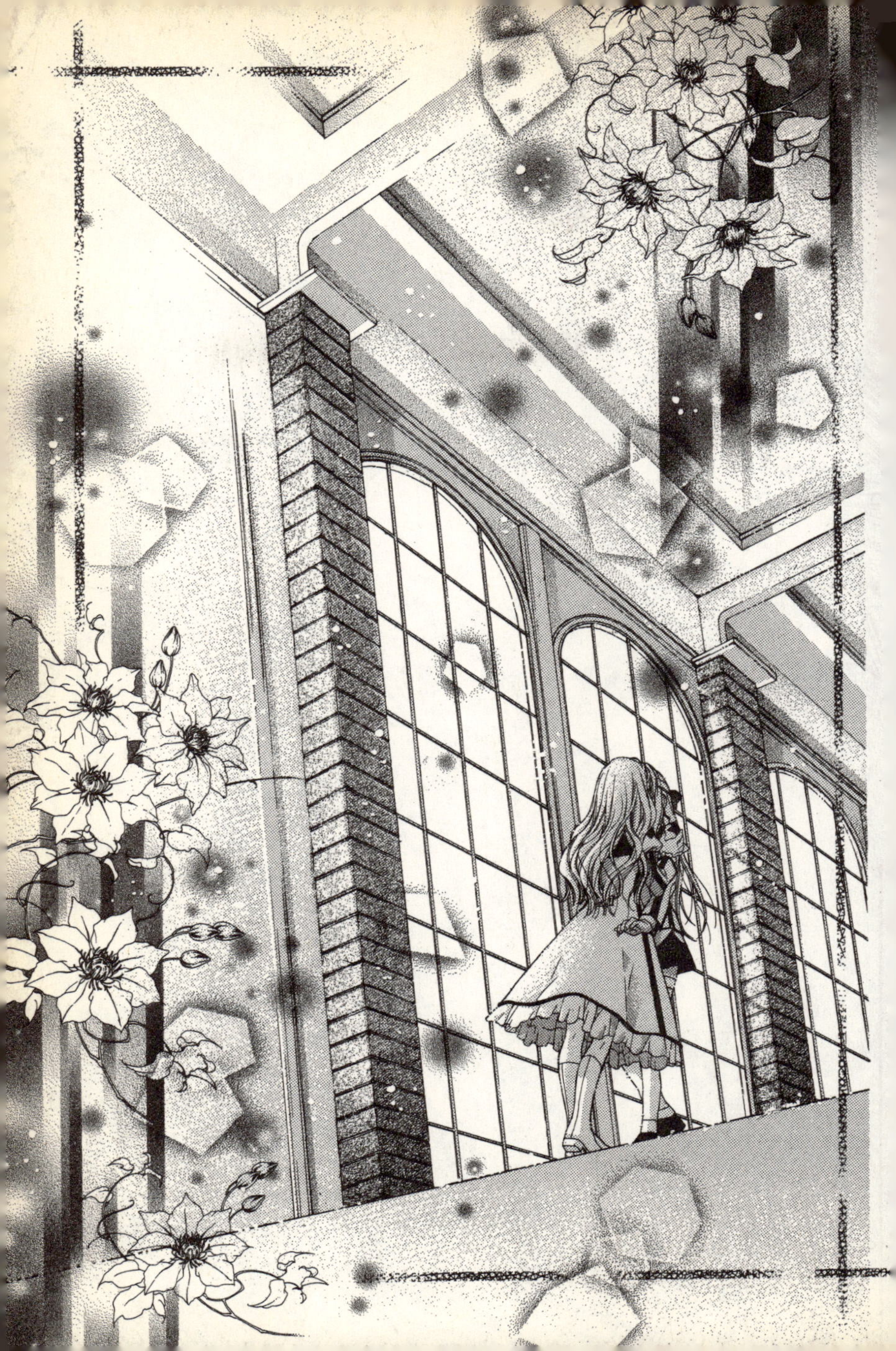

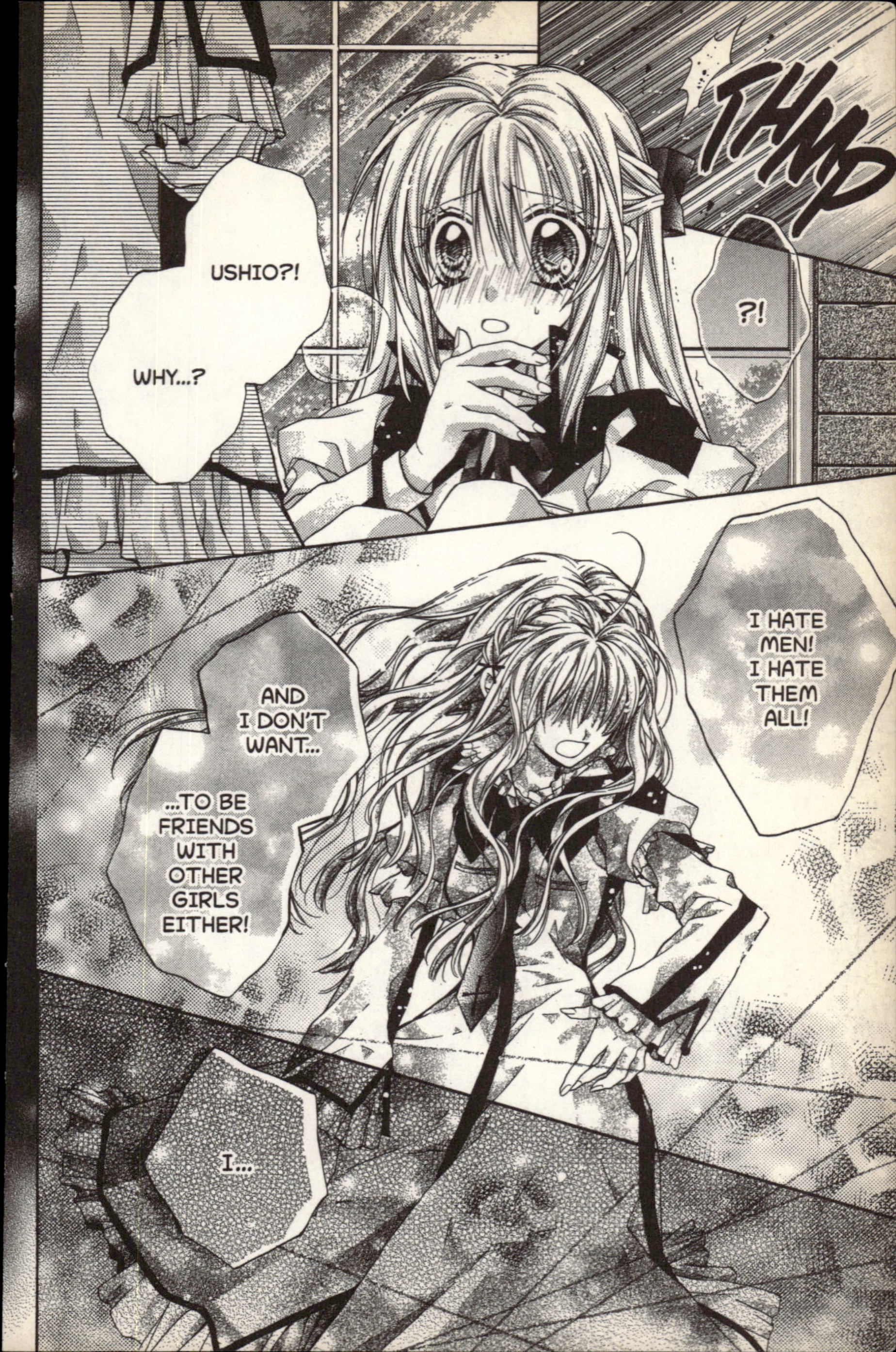
THMP
?!
USHIO?!
WHY...?
I HATE MEN! I HATE THEM ALL!
AND I DON'T WANT...
...TO BE FRIENDS WITH OTHER GIRLS EITHER!
I...

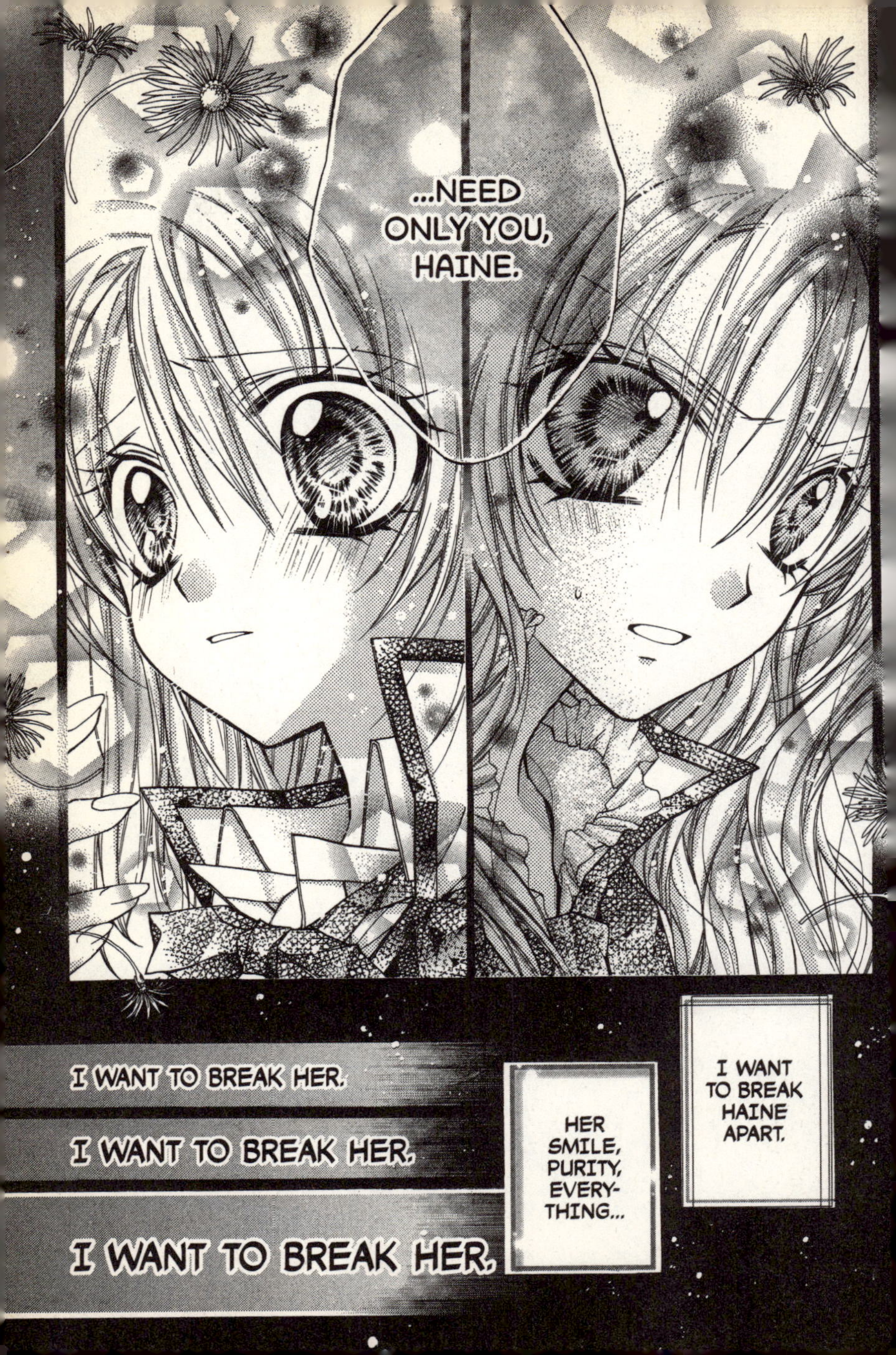
...NEED ONLY YOU, HAINE.
I WANT TO BREAK HAINE APART.
HER SMILE, PURITY, EVERY-THING...
I WANT TO BREAK HER.
I WANT TO BREAK HER.
I WANT TO BREAK HER.

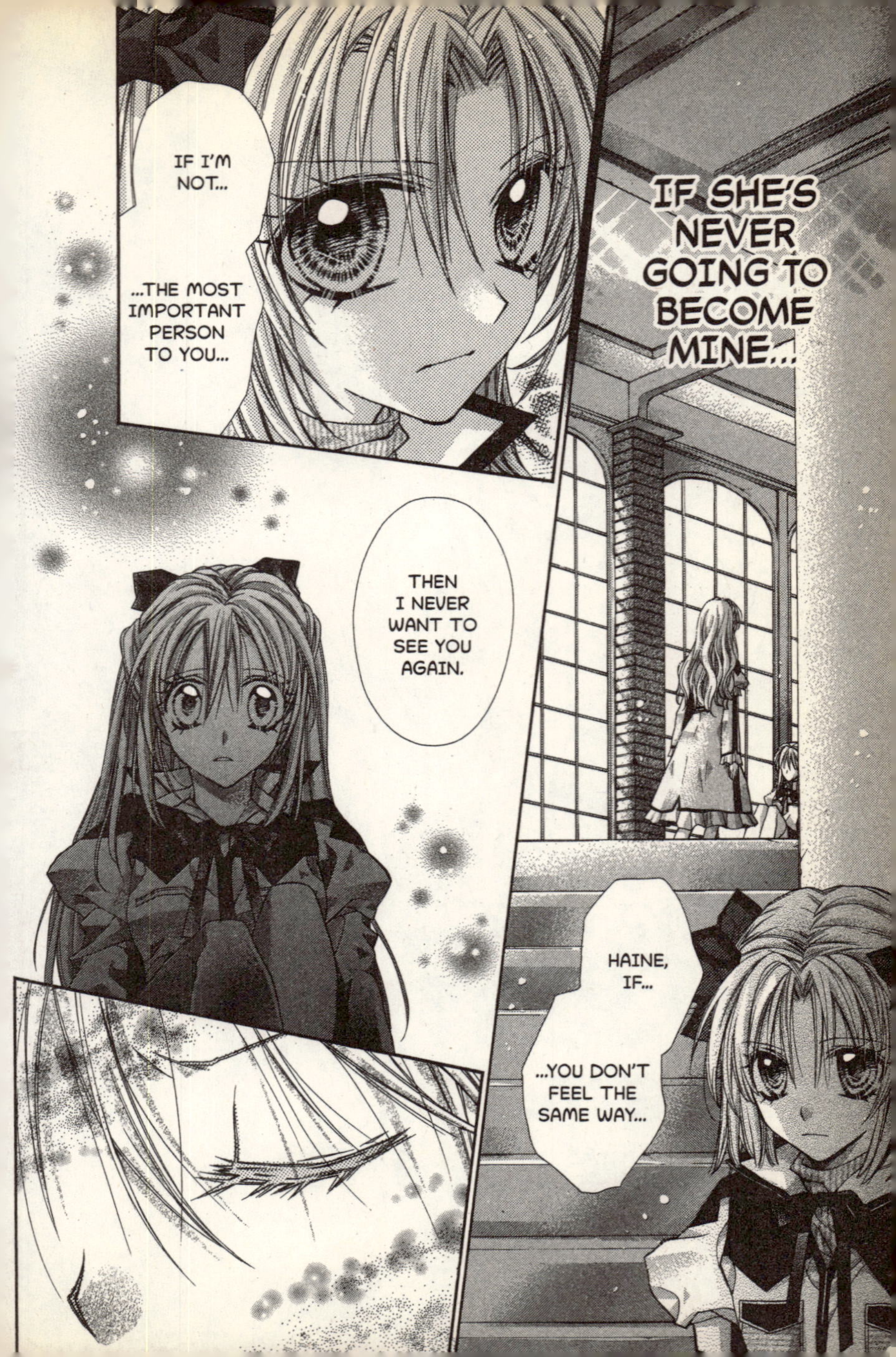
IF SHE'S NEVER GOING TO BECOME MINE...
IF I'M NOT...
...THE MOST IMPORTANT PERSON TO YOU...
THEN I NEVER WANT TO SEE YOU AGAIN.
HAINE, IF...
...YOU DON'T FEEL THE SAME WAY...

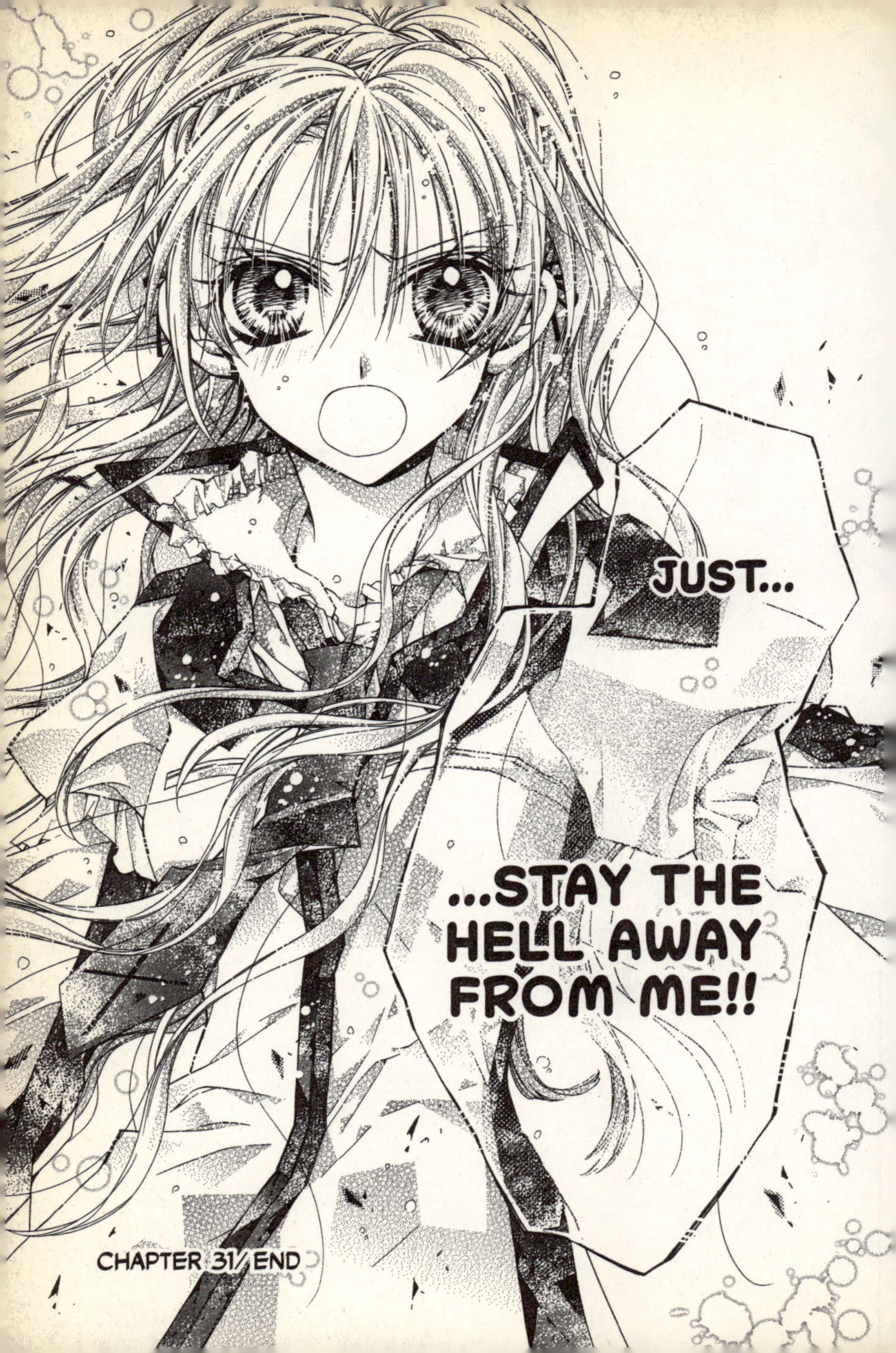
JUST...
...STAY THE HELL AWAY FROM ME!!
CHAPTER 31/END

† NAME OF THE PERSON YOU'RE VOTING FOR:

Komaki, of course!!

† WHAT YOU LIKE ABOUT THAT PERSON:

I just suddenly realized how much I like her.

Really...!!

ARINA TANEMURA

Hmph.

...anything to appeal.

I don't have...

Hi, it's me, Arina.

PHFF PHFF

Senri here.

Je t'aime.

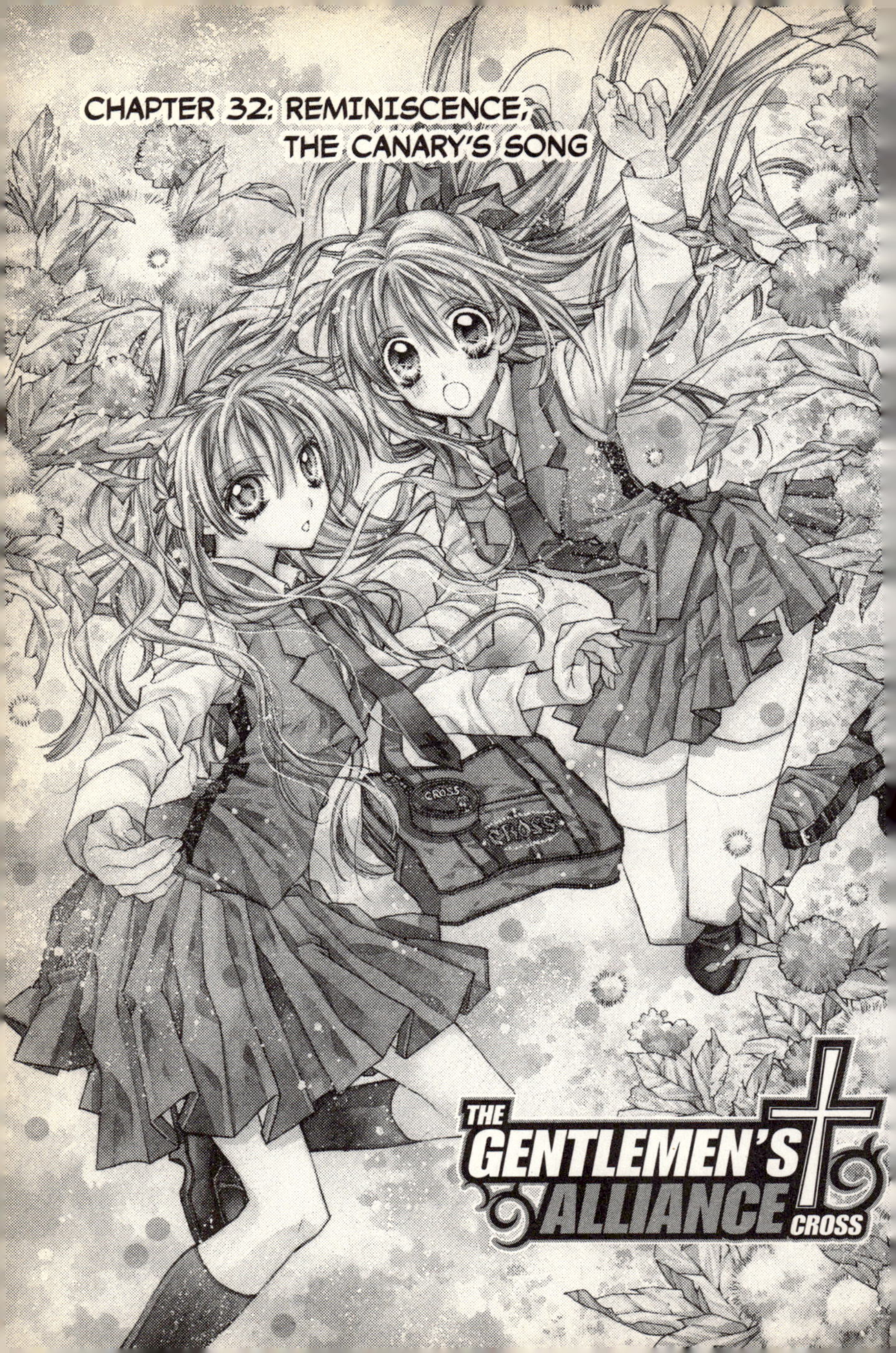
CHAPTER 32: REMINISCENCE, THE CANARY'S SONG
THE GENTLEMEN'S ALLIANCE CROSS

It's absolutely intolerable for a mere butler like you to appear in the poll twice...!

HA HA HA
HA HA HA

You should draw Nee-sama! Nee-sama, I say!

Komaki

I agree...

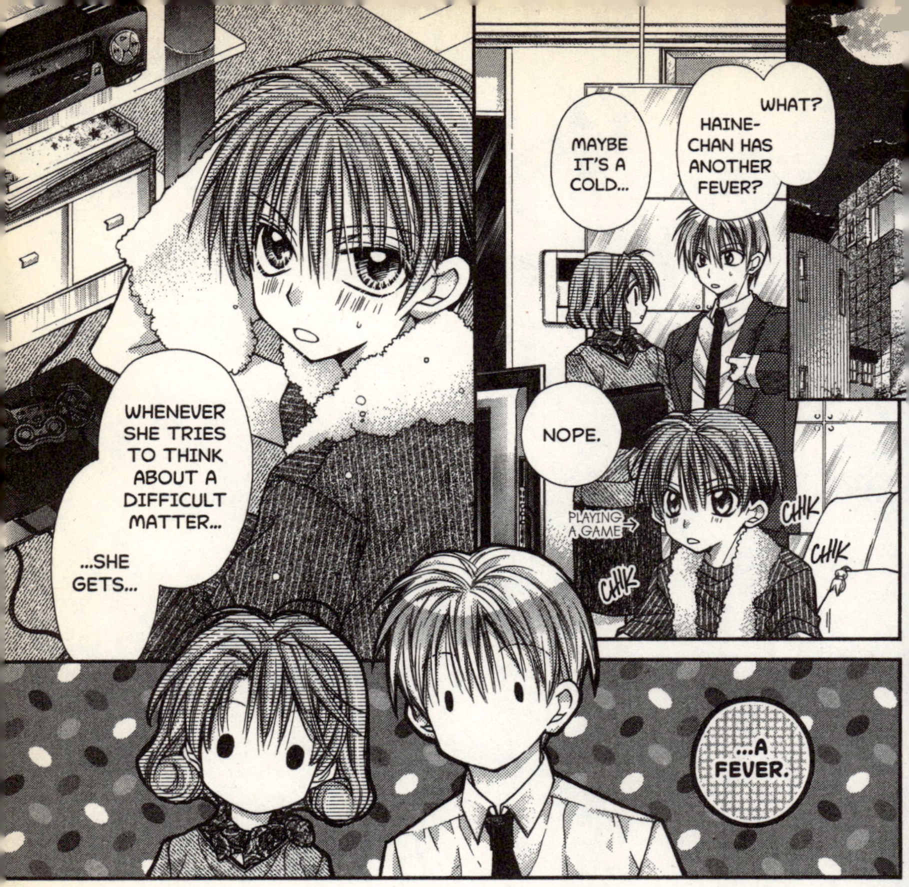
WHAT? HAINE-CHAN HAS ANOTHER FEVER?
MAYBE IT'S A COLD...
NOPE.
PLAYING A GAME
CHK
CHK
CHK
WHENEVER SHE TRIES TO THINK ABOUT A DIFFICULT MATTER...
...SHE GETS...
...A FEVER.

Chapter 32: Reminiscence, the Canary's Song

Lead-in: Will there ever be a day when we can smile again...?

I'm giving away the story!

I've finally been able to throw in the Heretics again...but there's one thing I noticed... Haine tends to become rather menacing when I have her interact with the Heretic members... Maybe the Yanki inside awakens?! Well, it's funny, so I enjoy it a lot. (laugh)

A friend of mine asked, "Who got the notebook ready for the exchange diary?!" I'd like to answer that here! Yuki-chan went to buy it himself. (The Heretics tailed him and watched over him from afar.)

I put a lot of effort into the scene with Haine and Mao-chan. Maybe I favor Mao-chan? (Or it could be that he's easy to draw and include in the story?)

The phrase, "If Ushio is to have a new friend..." is a very complex one for Haine. When she said it, about 80 percent of her feelings were against it. Basically, Haine-chan's feelings for Ushio are as strong as Ushio's for her, and she really wants to be Ushio's one and only friend. But she knows that it wouldn't be good for Ushio, so she's forcing herself to say so. Mao-chan understands this. Ah, friendship... By the way, it's also taboo for the main character to get a haircut during the series, but I've broken that rule too. Haine-chan seems like the docile type, but she can be rather reckless at times...

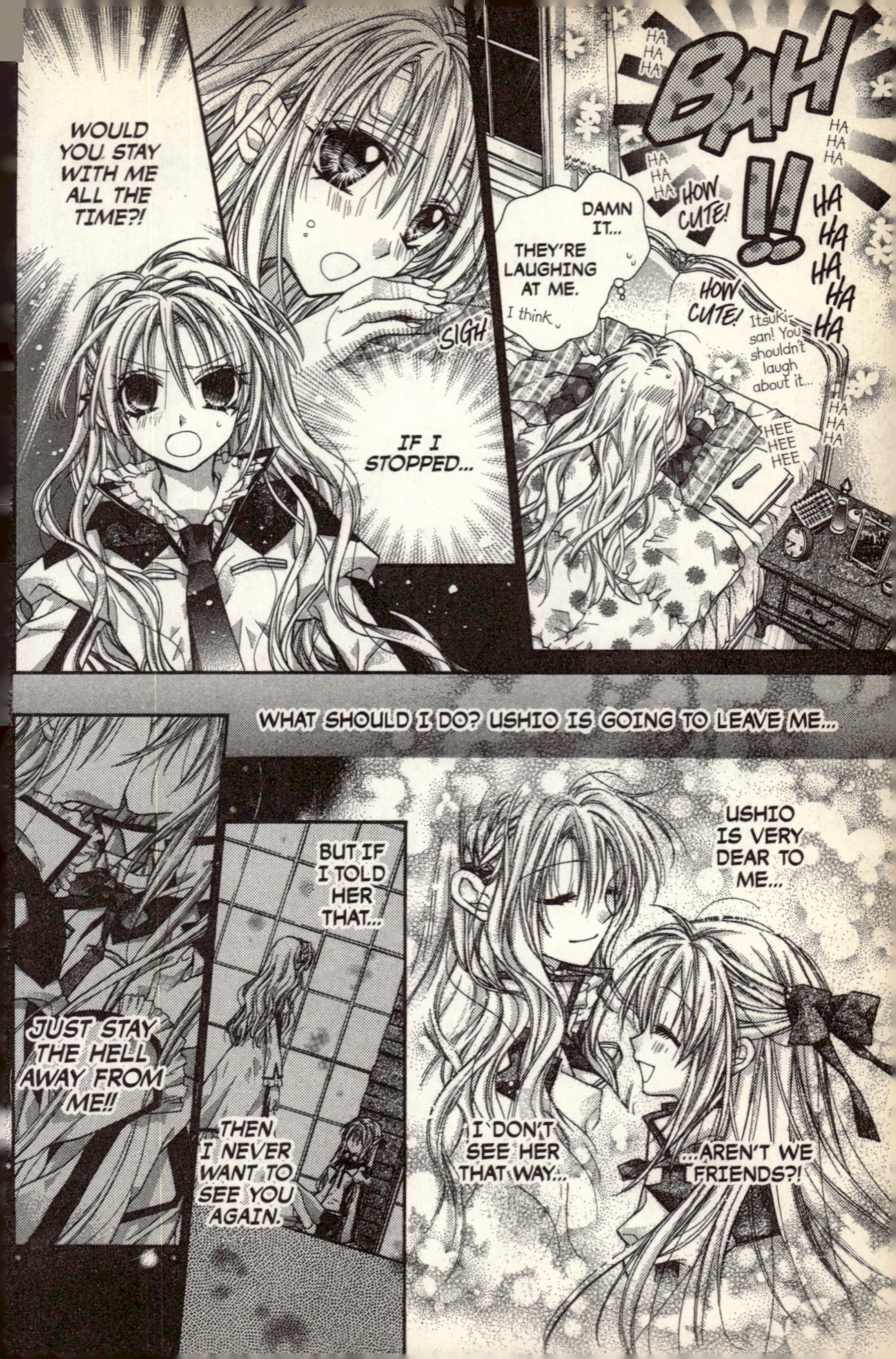

HA HA HA
BAH!!
HA HA HA
HA HA HA
HOW CUTE!
HA HA HA HA HA HA
HOW CUTE!
Itsuki-san! You shouldn't laugh about it...
HA HA HA
HEE HEE HEE
DAMN IT... THEY'RE LAUGHING AT ME.
I think.
SIGH
IF I STOPPED...
WOULD YOU STAY WITH ME ALL THE TIME?!
WHAT SHOULD I DO? USHIO IS GOING TO LEAVE ME...
USHIO IS VERY DEAR TO ME...
...AREN'T WE FRIENDS?!
I DON'T SEE HER THAT WAY...
BUT IF I TOLD HER THAT...
THEN I NEVER WANT TO SEE YOU AGAIN.
JUST STAY THE HELL AWAY FROM ME!!

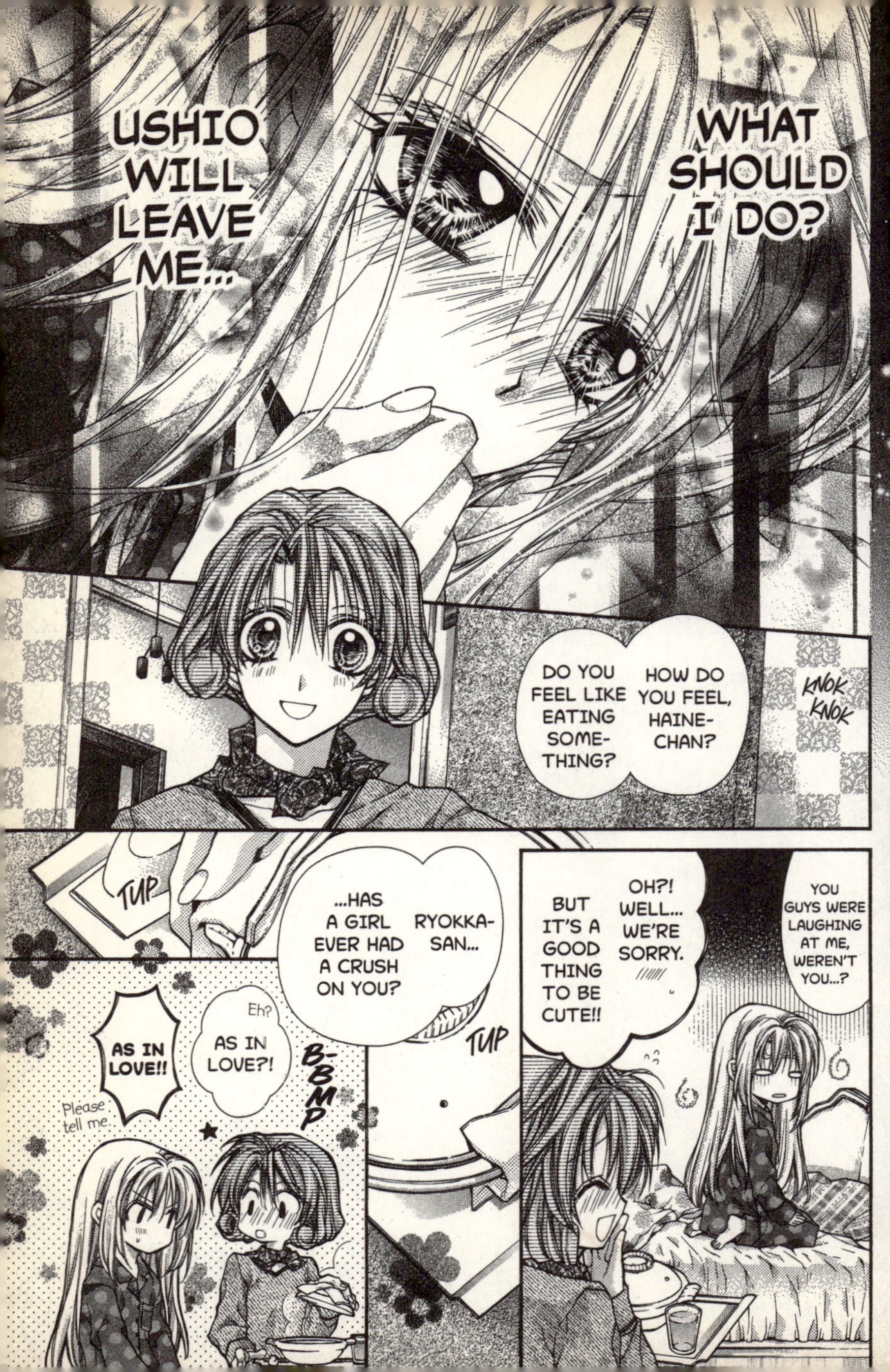
WHAT SHOULD I DO?
USHIO WILL LEAVE ME...
KNOK KNOK
HOW DO YOU FEEL, HAINE-CHAN?
DO YOU FEEL LIKE EATING SOME-THING?
YOU GUYS WERE LAUGHING AT ME, WEREN'T YOU...?
OH?! WELL... WE'RE SORRY.
BUT IT'S A GOOD THING TO BE CUTE!!
TUP
RYOKKA-SAN...
...HAS A GIRL EVER HAD A CRUSH ON YOU?
TUP
Eh?
AS IN LOVE?!
B-BMP
AS IN LOVE!!
Please tell me.

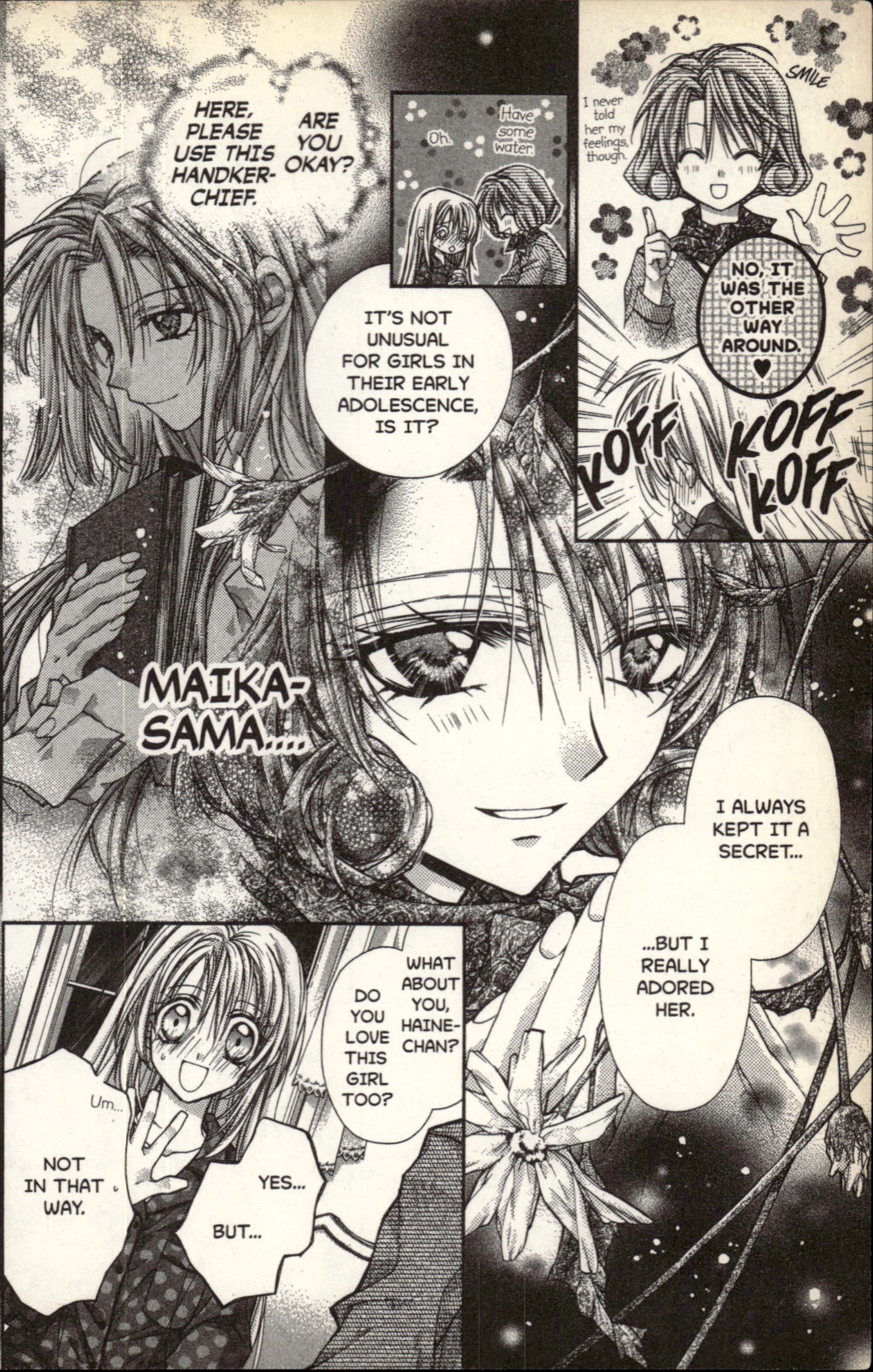
SMILE
I never told her my feelings, though.
NO, IT WAS THE OTHER WAY AROUND. ♥
KOFF KOFF KOFF
Have some water.
Oh.
ARE YOU OKAY?
HERE, PLEASE USE THIS HANDKER-CHIEF.
IT'S NOT UNUSUAL FOR GIRLS IN THEIR EARLY ADOLESCENCE, IS IT?
MAIKA-SAMA....
I ALWAYS KEPT IT A SECRET...
...BUT I REALLY ADORED HER.
WHAT ABOUT YOU, HAINE-CHAN?
DO YOU LOVE THIS GIRL TOO?
Um...
YES...
BUT...
NOT IN THAT WAY.

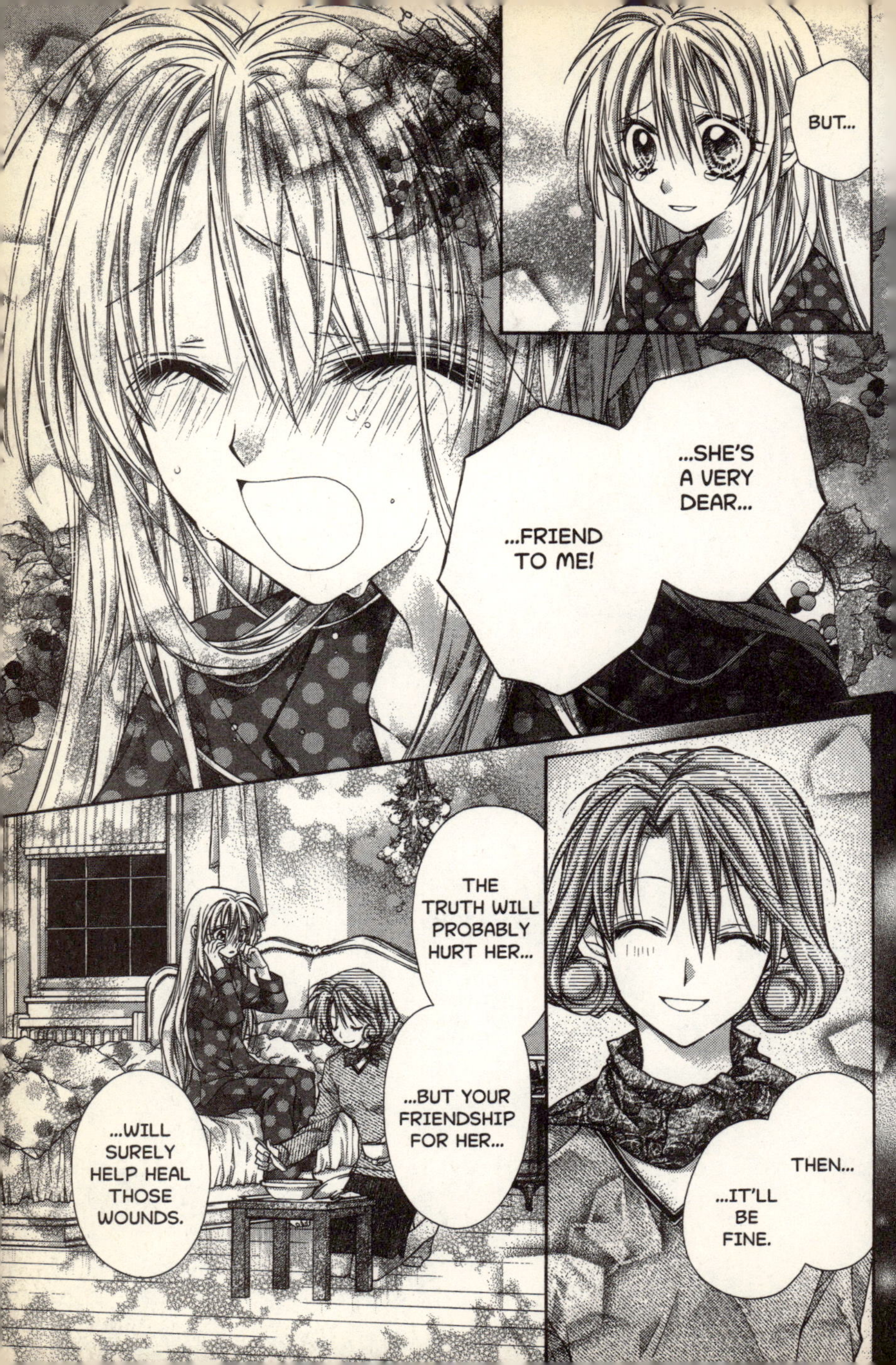
BUT...
...SHE'S A VERY DEAR...
...FRIEND TO ME!
THEN...
...IT'LL BE FINE.
THE TRUTH WILL PROBABLY HURT HER...
...BUT YOUR FRIENDSHIP FOR HER...
...WILL SURELY HELP HEAL THOSE WOUNDS.

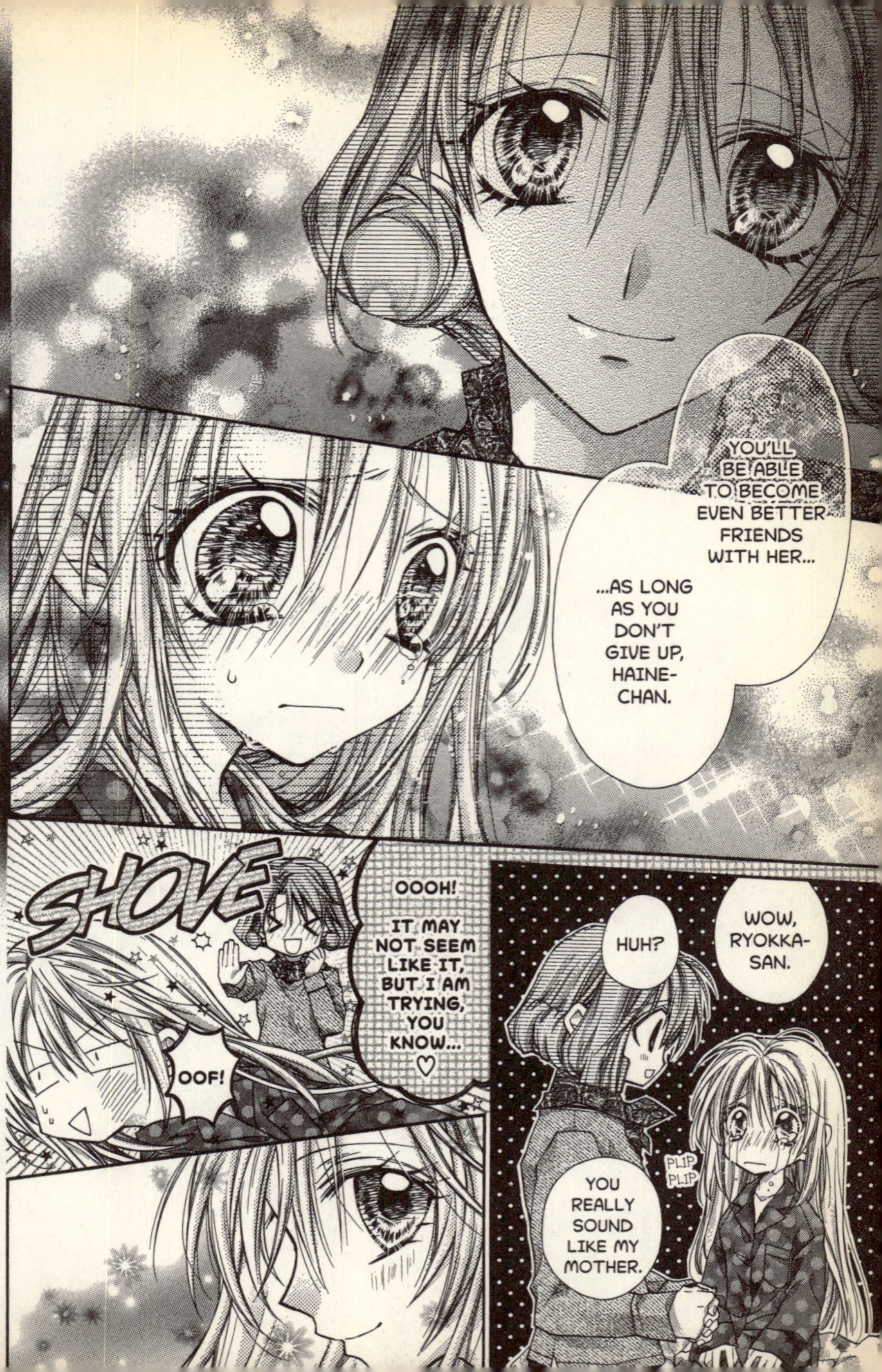
YOU'LL BE ABLE TO BECOME EVEN BETTER FRIENDS WITH HER...
...AS LONG AS YOU DON'T GIVE UP, HAINE-CHAN.
WOW, RYOKKA-SAN.
HUH?
PLIP PLIP
YOU REALLY SOUND LIKE MY MOTHER.
OOOH!
IT MAY NOT SEEM LIKE IT, BUT I AM TRYING, YOU KNOW... ♡
SHOVE
OOF!

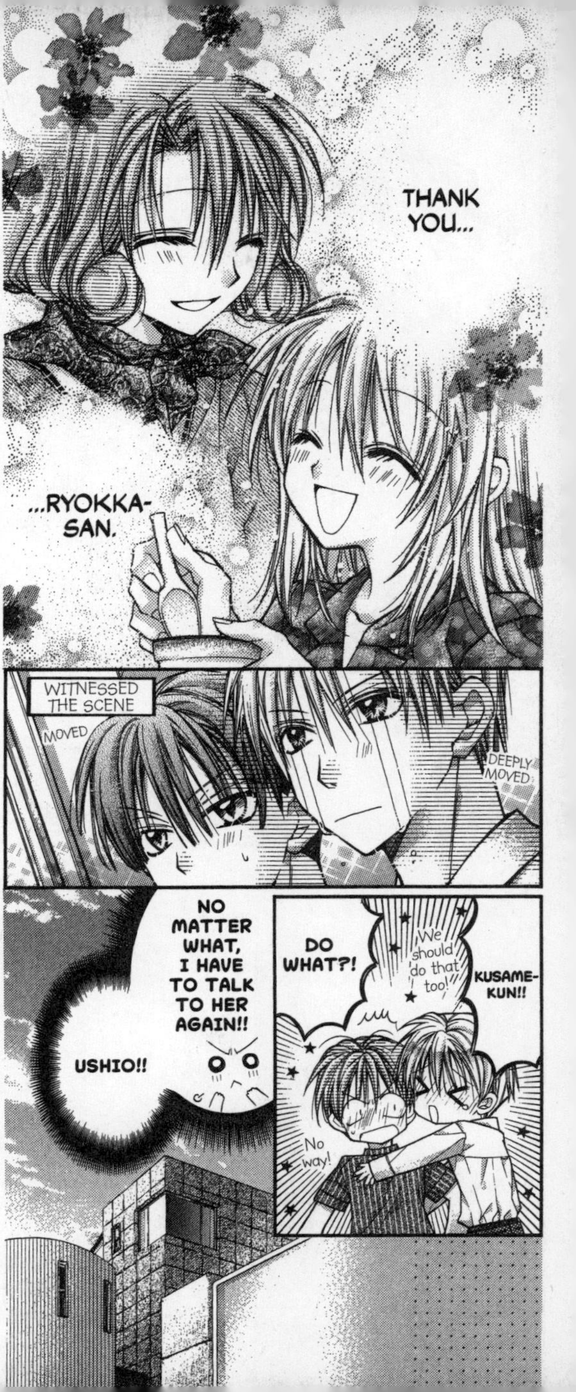
THANK YOU...
...RYOKKA-SAN.
WITNESSED THE SCENE
DEEPLY MOVED
MOVED
KUSAME-KUN!!
We should do that too!
DO WHAT?!
No way!
NO MATTER WHAT, I HAVE TO TALK TO HER AGAIN!!
USHIO!!

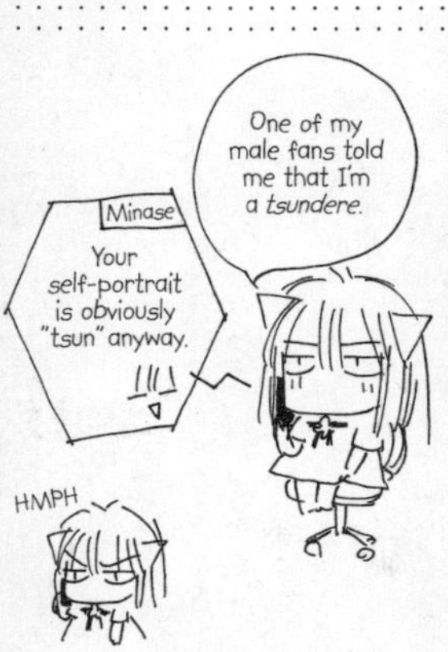
One of my male fans told me that I'm a *tsundere*.
Minase
Your self-portrait is obviously "tsun" anyway.
HMPH

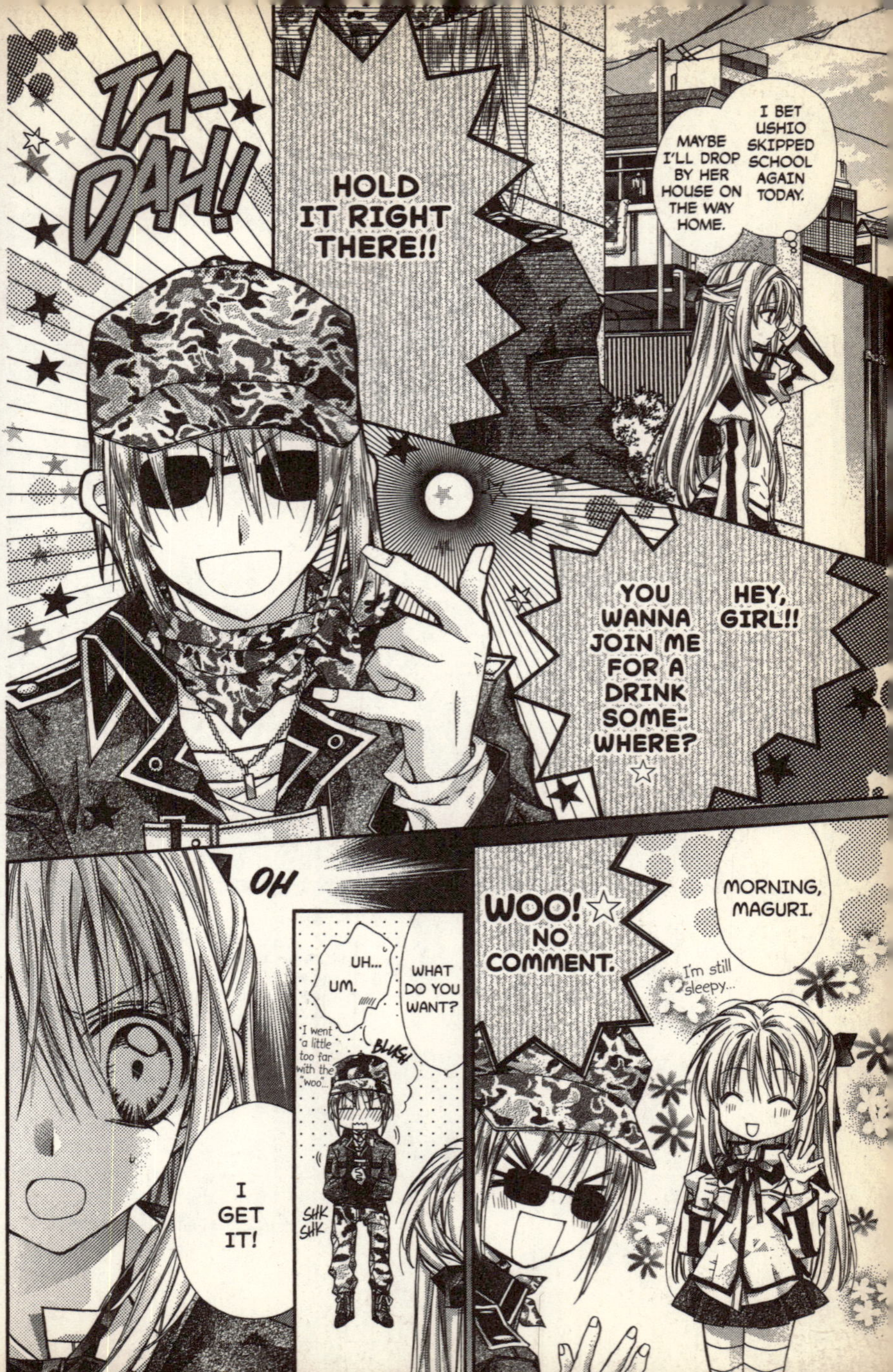
I BET USHIO SKIPPED SCHOOL AGAIN TODAY.
MAYBE I'LL DROP BY HER HOUSE ON THE WAY HOME.
HOLD IT RIGHT THERE!!
TA-DAH!!
HEY, GIRL!!
YOU WANNA JOIN ME FOR A DRINK SOME-WHERE?
MORNING, MAGURI.
I'm still sleepy...
WOO! NO COMMENT.
WHAT DO YOU WANT?
UH... UM.
BLUSH
I went a little too far with the "woo"...
SHK SHK
OH
I GET IT!

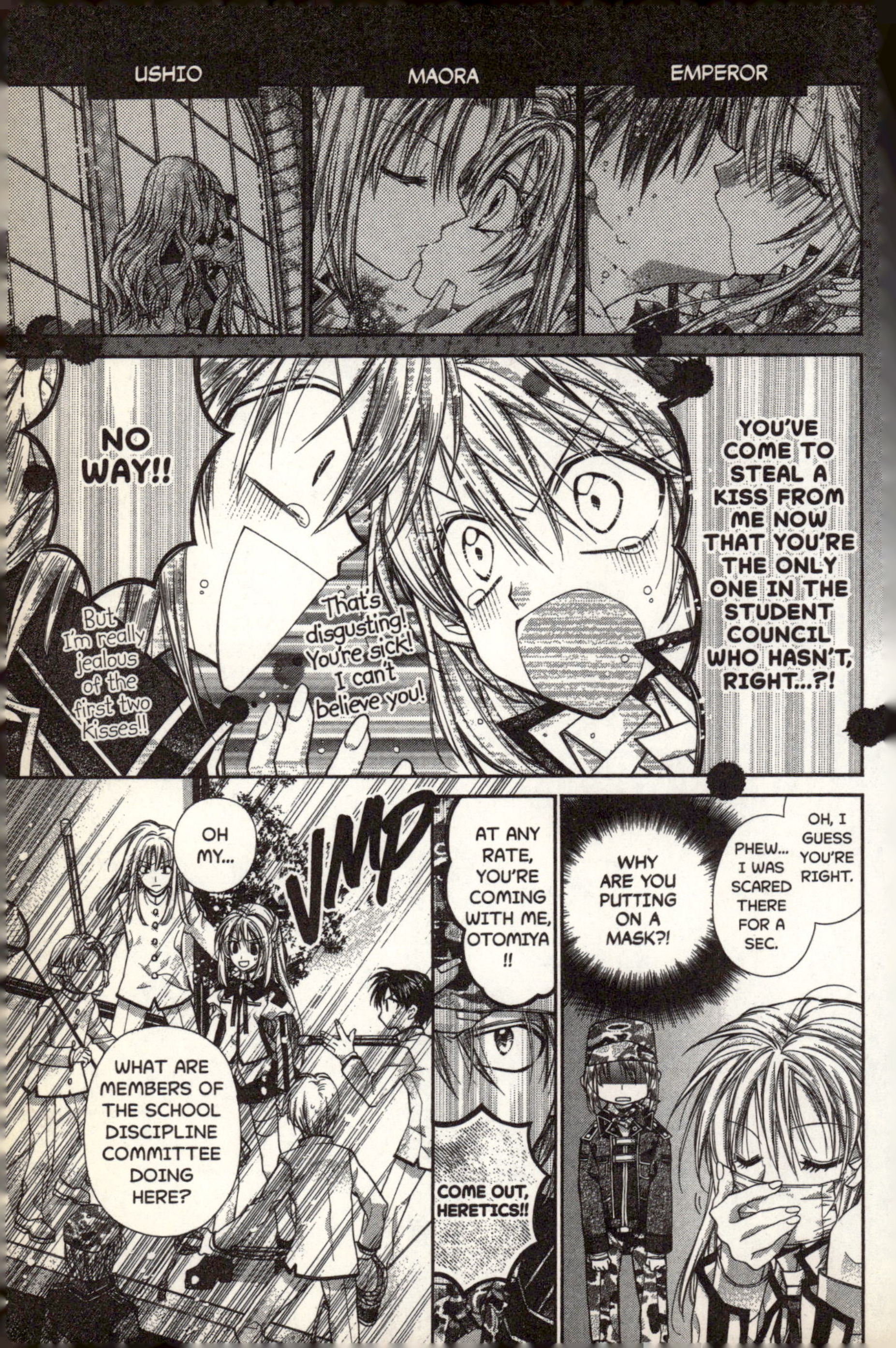
EMPEROR
MAORA
USHIO
YOU'VE COME TO STEAL A KISS FROM ME NOW THAT YOU'RE THE ONLY ONE IN THE STUDENT COUNCIL WHO HASN'T, RIGHT...?!
NO WAY!!
That's disgusting! You're sick! I can't believe you!
But I'm really jealous of the first two kisses!!
OH, I GUESS YOU'RE RIGHT.
PHEW... I WAS SCARED THERE FOR A SEC.
WHY ARE YOU PUTTING ON A MASK?!
AT ANY RATE, YOU'RE COMING WITH ME, OTOMIYA!!
COME OUT, HERETICS!!
VMP
OH MY...
WHAT ARE MEMBERS OF THE SCHOOL DISCIPLINE COMMITTEE DOING HERE?

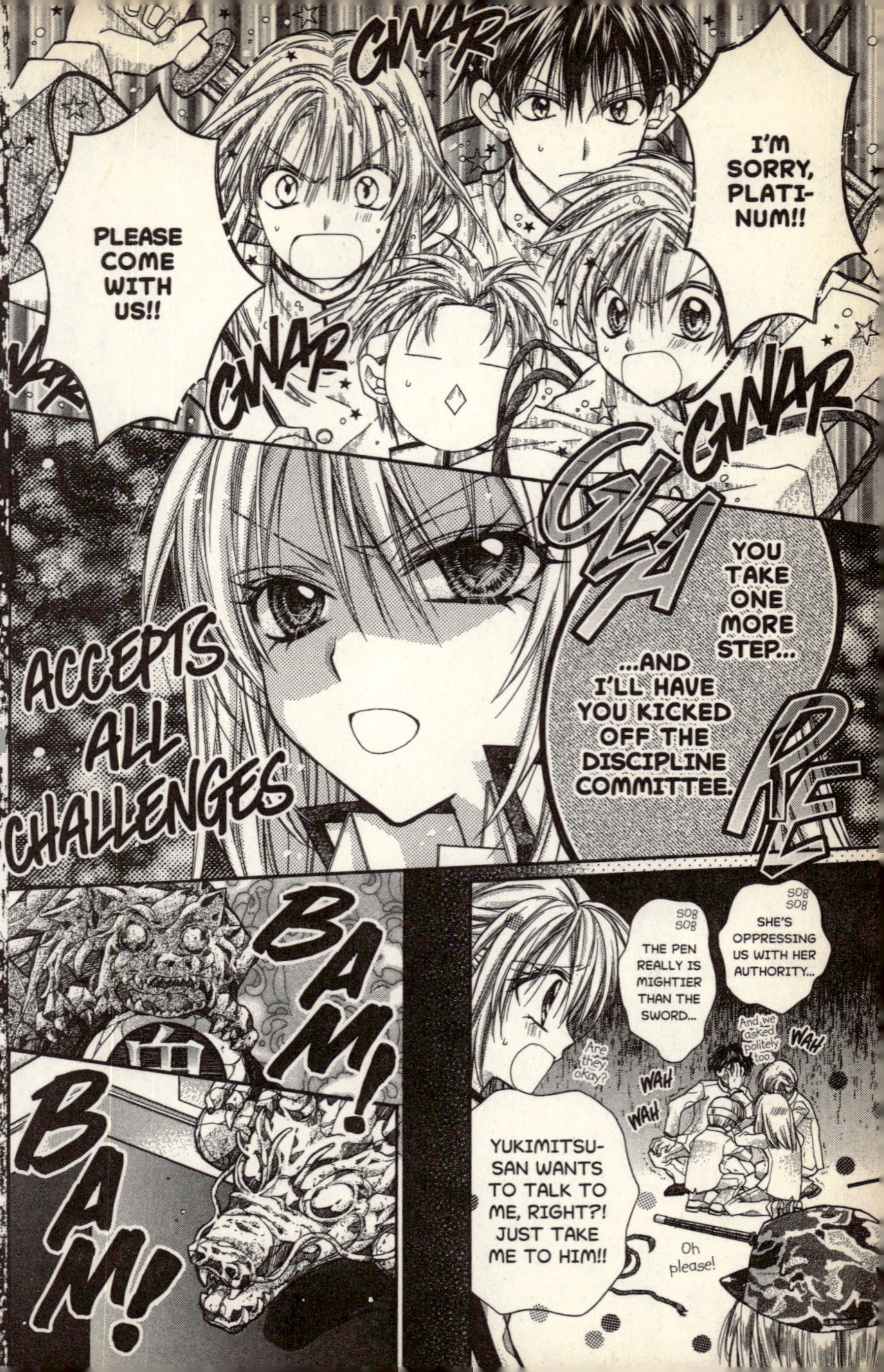
GWAR
I'M SORRY, PLATINUM!!
PLEASE COME WITH US!!
GWAR
GWAR
GLARE
YOU TAKE ONE MORE STEP...
...AND I'LL HAVE YOU KICKED OFF THE DISCIPLINE COMMITTEE.
ACCEPTS ALL CHALLENGES
SOB SOB
SHE'S OPPRESSING US WITH HER AUTHORITY...
SOB SOB
THE PEN REALLY IS MIGHTIER THAN THE SWORD...
And we asked politely too.
WAH
Are they okay?
WAH
WAH
YUKIMITSU-SAN WANTS TO TALK TO ME, RIGHT?! JUST TAKE ME TO HIM!!
Oh please!
BAM!
BAM!

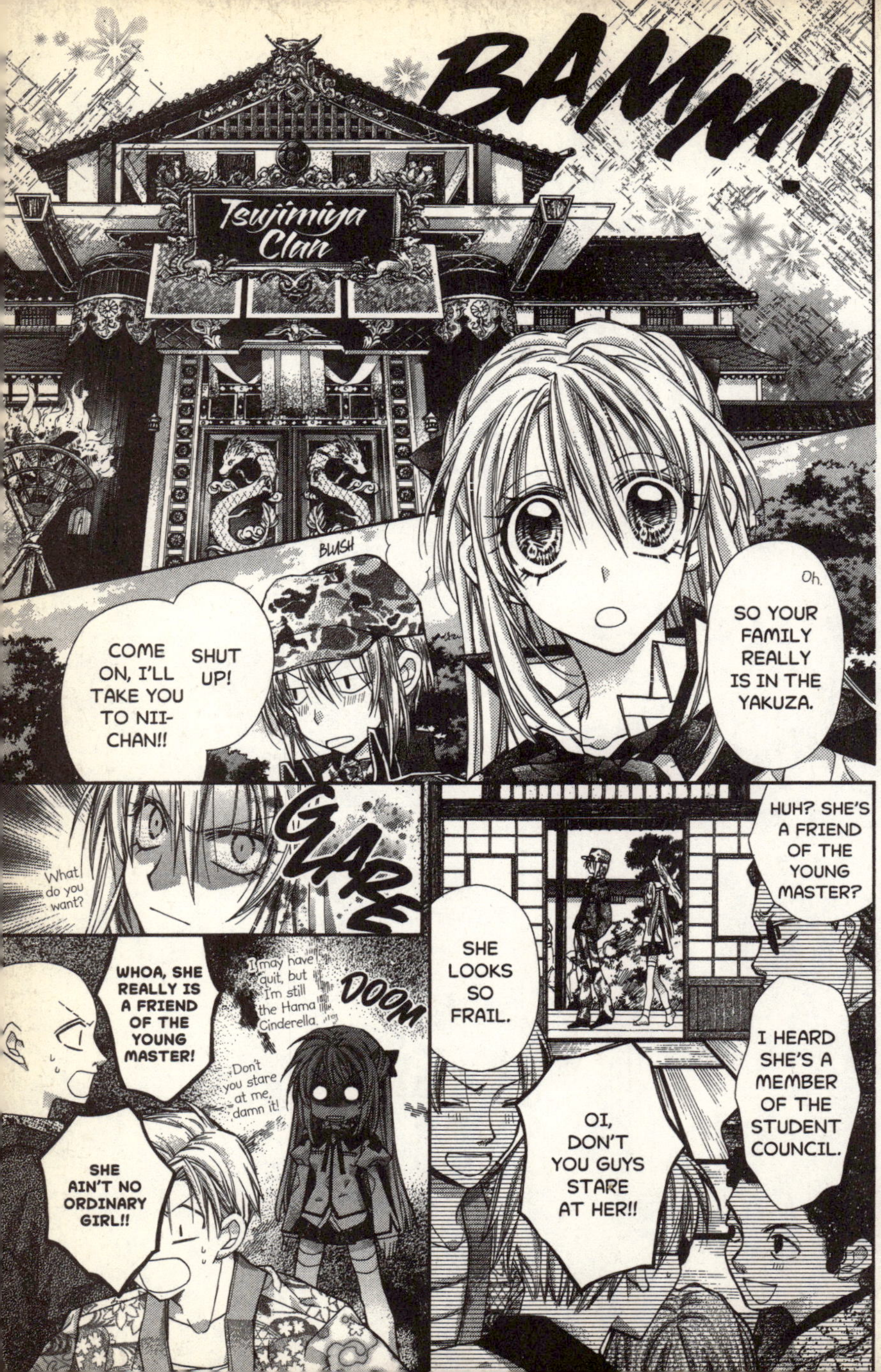
BAMM!
Tsujimiya Clan
Oh.
SO YOUR FAMILY REALLY IS IN THE YAKUZA.
BLUSH
SHUT UP!
COME ON, I'LL TAKE YOU TO NII-CHAN!!
HUH? SHE'S A FRIEND OF THE YOUNG MASTER?
GLARE
What do you want?
SHE LOOKS SO FRAIL.
I HEARD SHE'S A MEMBER OF THE STUDENT COUNCIL.
OI, DON'T YOU GUYS STARE AT HER!!
DOOM
I may have quit, but I'm still the Hama Cinderella.
WHOA, SHE REALLY IS A FRIEND OF THE YOUNG MASTER!
Don't you stare at me, damn it!
SHE AIN'T NO ORDINARY GIRL!!

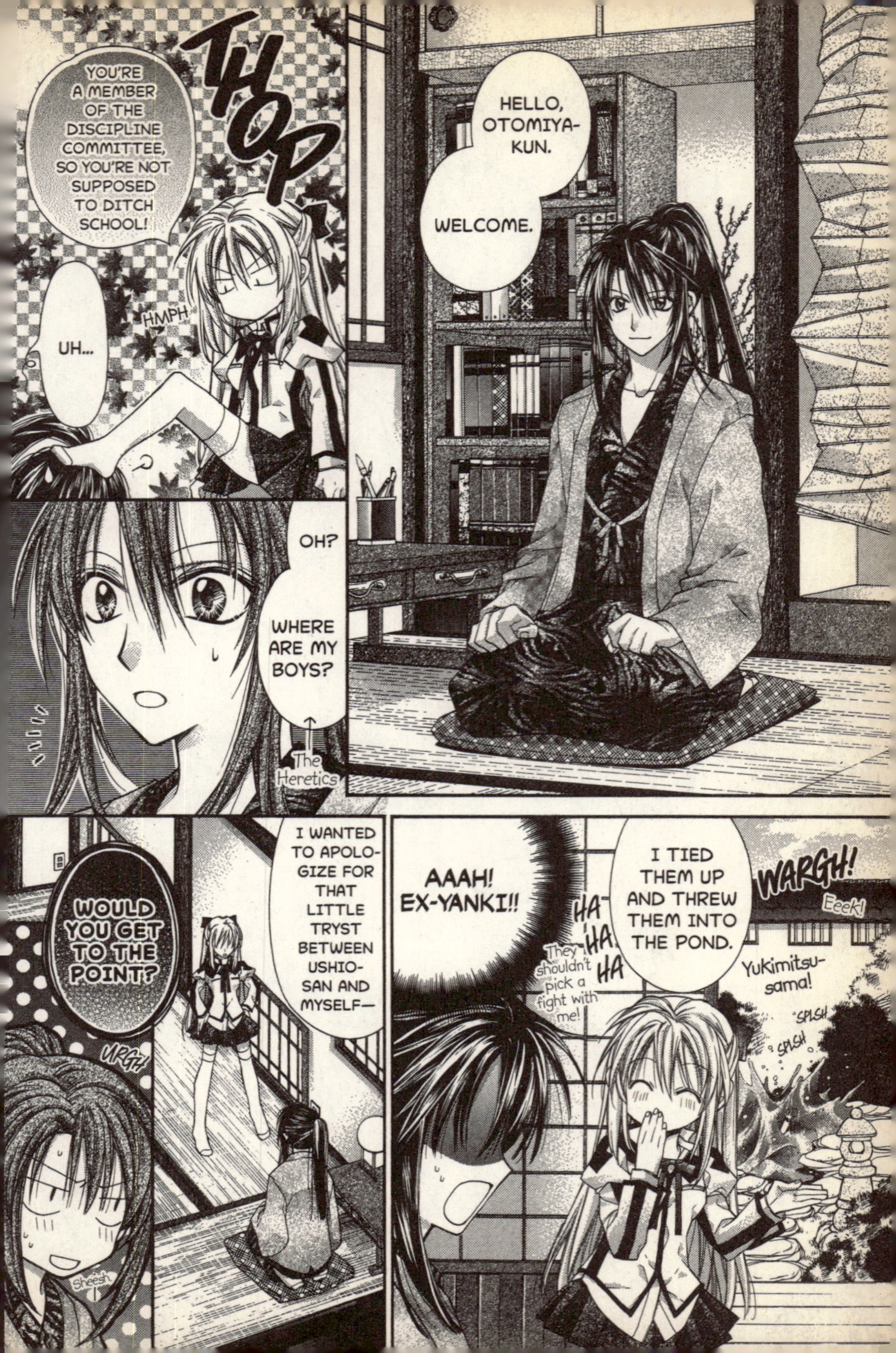
HELLO, OTOMIYA-KUN.
WELCOME.
THOP
YOU'RE A MEMBER OF THE DISCIPLINE COMMITTEE, SO YOU'RE NOT SUPPOSED TO DITCH SCHOOL!
HMPH
UH...
OH?
WHERE ARE MY BOYS?
The Heretics
I TIED THEM UP AND THREW THEM INTO THE POND.
WARGH!
Eeek!
Yukimitsu-sama!
SPLSH
SPLSH
AAAH! EX-YANKI!!
HA HA HA
They shouldn't pick a fight with me!
I WANTED TO APOLOGIZE FOR THAT LITTLE TRYST BETWEEN USHIO-SAN AND MYSELF—
WOULD YOU GET TO THE POINT?
URGH
Sheesh

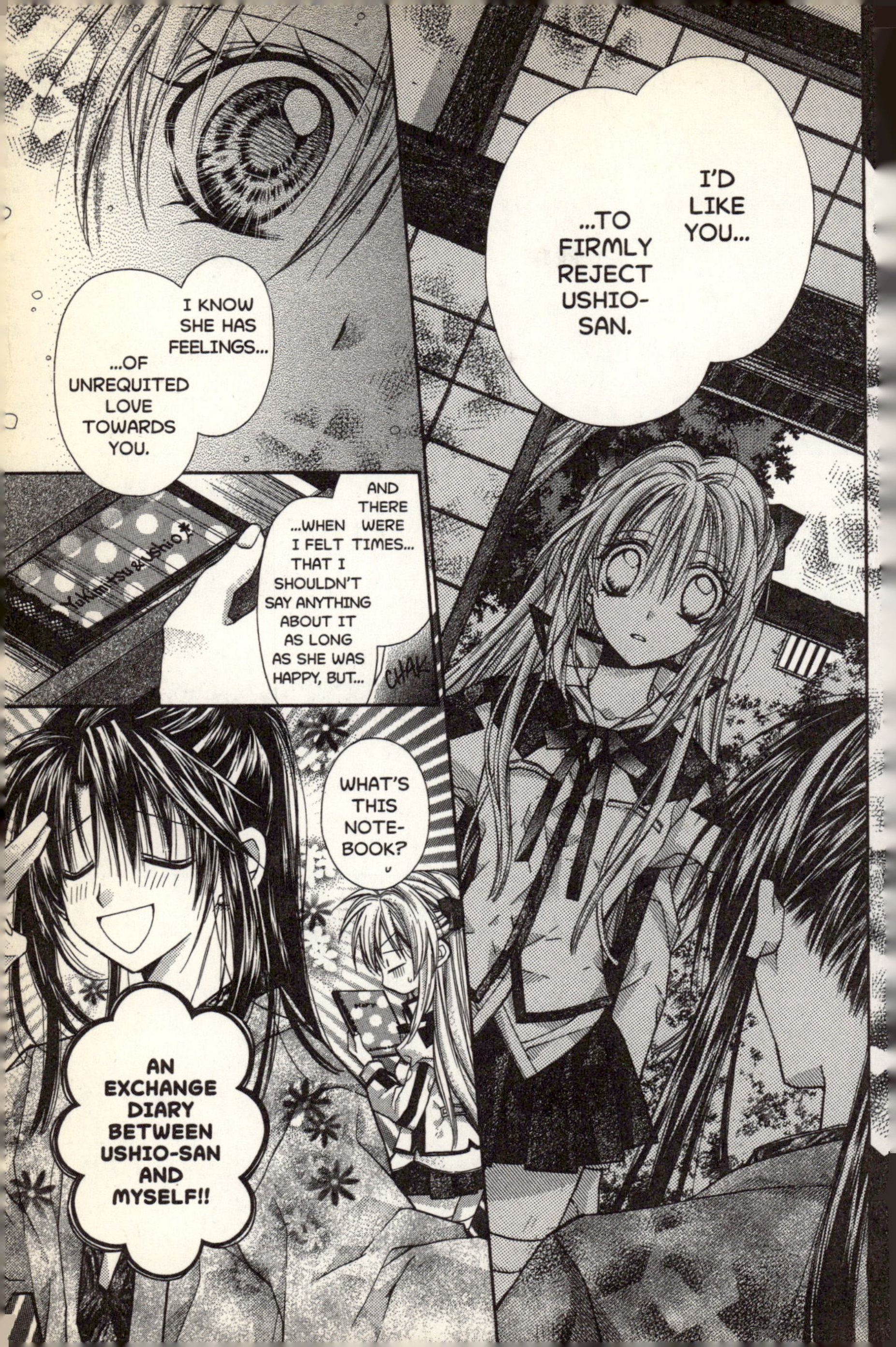
I'D LIKE YOU...
...TO FIRMLY REJECT USHIO-SAN.
I KNOW SHE HAS FEELINGS...
...OF UNREQUITED LOVE TOWARDS YOU.
AND THERE WERE TIMES...
...WHEN I FELT THAT I SHOULDN'T SAY ANYTHING ABOUT IT AS LONG AS SHE WAS HAPPY, BUT...
Yukimitsu & Ushio
CHAK
WHAT'S THIS NOTE-BOOK?
AN EXCHANGE DIARY BETWEEN USHIO-SAN AND MYSELF!!

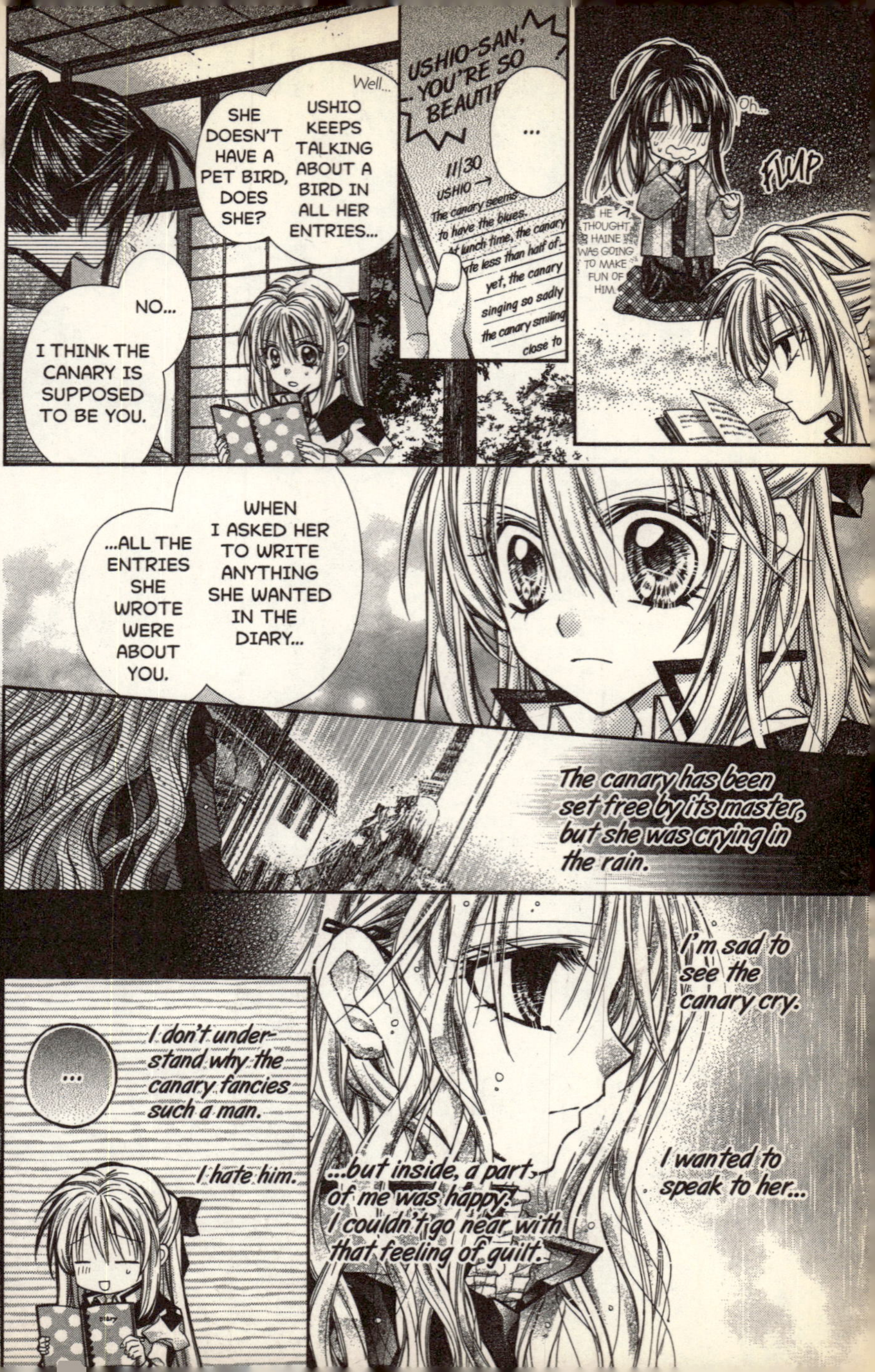

Oh...
FLUP
HE THOUGHT HAINE WAS GOING TO MAKE FUN OF HIM.
USHIO-SAN, YOU'RE SO BEAUTI
11/30
USHIO →
The canary seems
to have the blues.
t lunch time, the canary
te less than half of...
yet, the canary
singing so sadly
the canary smiling
close to
Well...
...
USHIO KEEPS TALKING ABOUT A BIRD IN ALL HER ENTRIES...
SHE DOESN'T HAVE A PET BIRD, DOES SHE?
NO...
I THINK THE CANARY IS SUPPOSED TO BE YOU.
WHEN I ASKED HER TO WRITE ANYTHING SHE WANTED IN THE DIARY...
...ALL THE ENTRIES SHE WROTE WERE ABOUT YOU.
The canary has been set free by its master, but she was crying in the rain.
I'm sad to see the canary cry.
I wanted to speak to her...
...but inside, a part of me was happy. I couldn't go near with that feeling of guilt.
...
I don't understand why the canary fancies such a man.
I hate him.

But it's fine.

As long as the canary doesn't have her feelings returned...

...I can listen to her songs with a peaceful mind.

FLIP

The canary is kind to everyone.

The canary shares her smiles with everyone.

And at times like that, I feel a strong hatred inside me, making me want to capture the canary.

But...

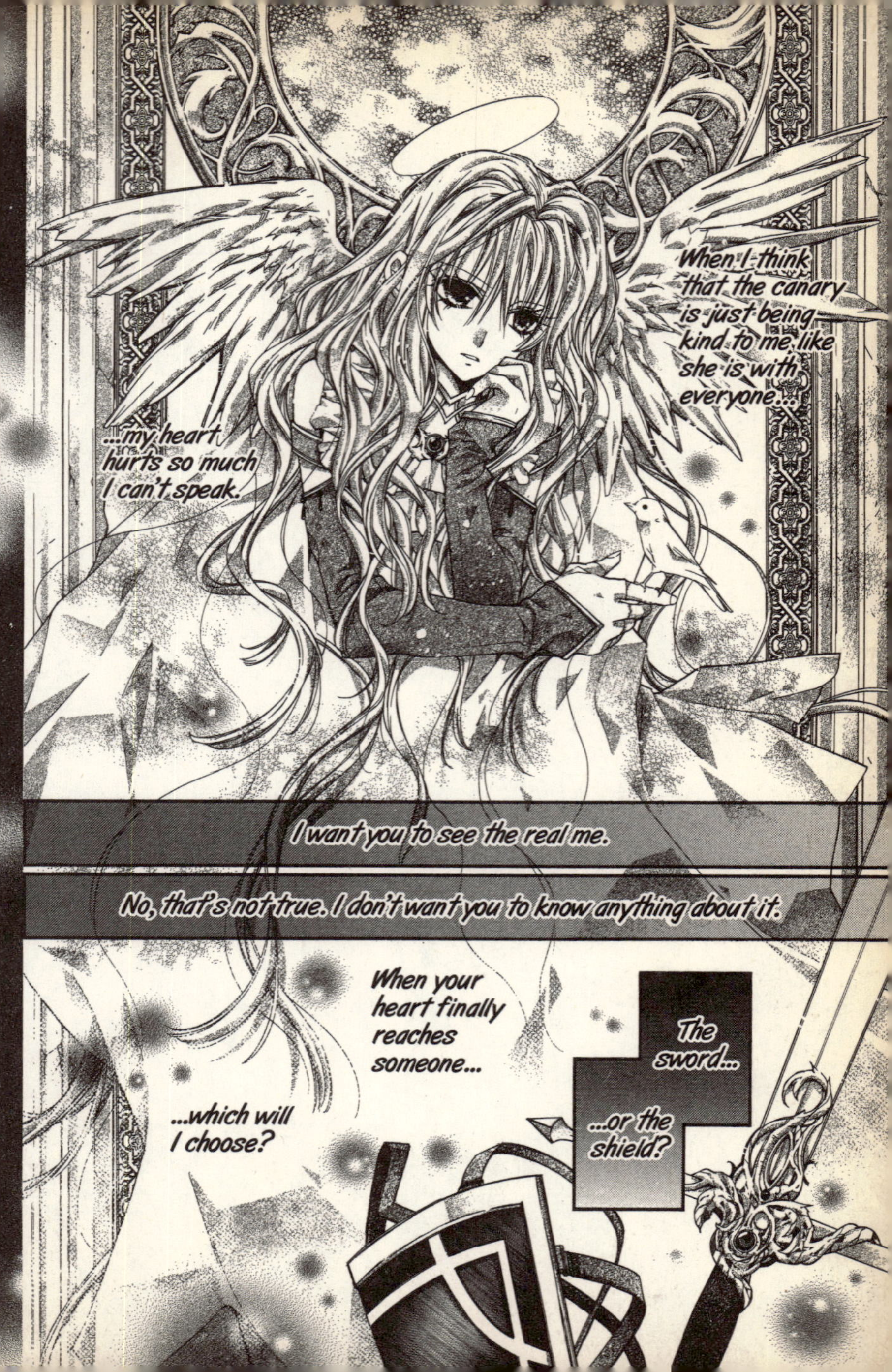
When I think that the canary is just being kind to me like she is with everyone...
...my heart hurts so much I can't speak.
I want you to see the real me.
No, that's not true. I don't want you to know anything about it.
The sword...
...or the shield?
When your heart finally reaches someone...
...which will I choose?

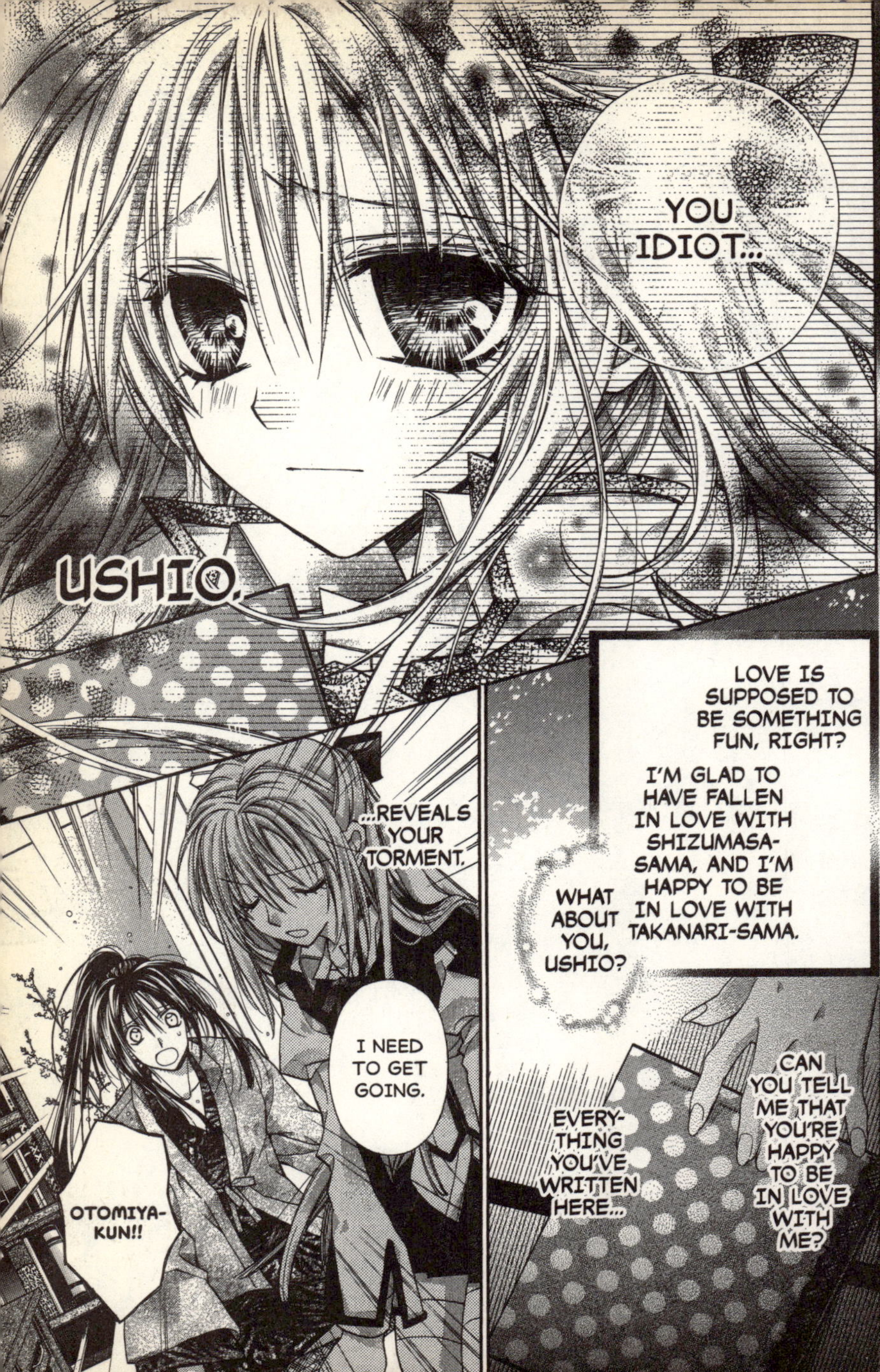
YOU IDIOT...
USHIO.
LOVE IS SUPPOSED TO BE SOMETHING FUN, RIGHT?
I'M GLAD TO HAVE FALLEN IN LOVE WITH SHIZUMASA-SAMA, AND I'M HAPPY TO BE IN LOVE WITH TAKANARI-SAMA.
WHAT ABOUT YOU, USHIO?
CAN YOU TELL ME THAT YOU'RE HAPPY TO BE IN LOVE WITH ME?
EVERY-THING YOU'VE WRITTEN HERE...
...REVEALS YOUR TORMENT.
I NEED TO GET GOING.
OTOMIYA-KUN!!

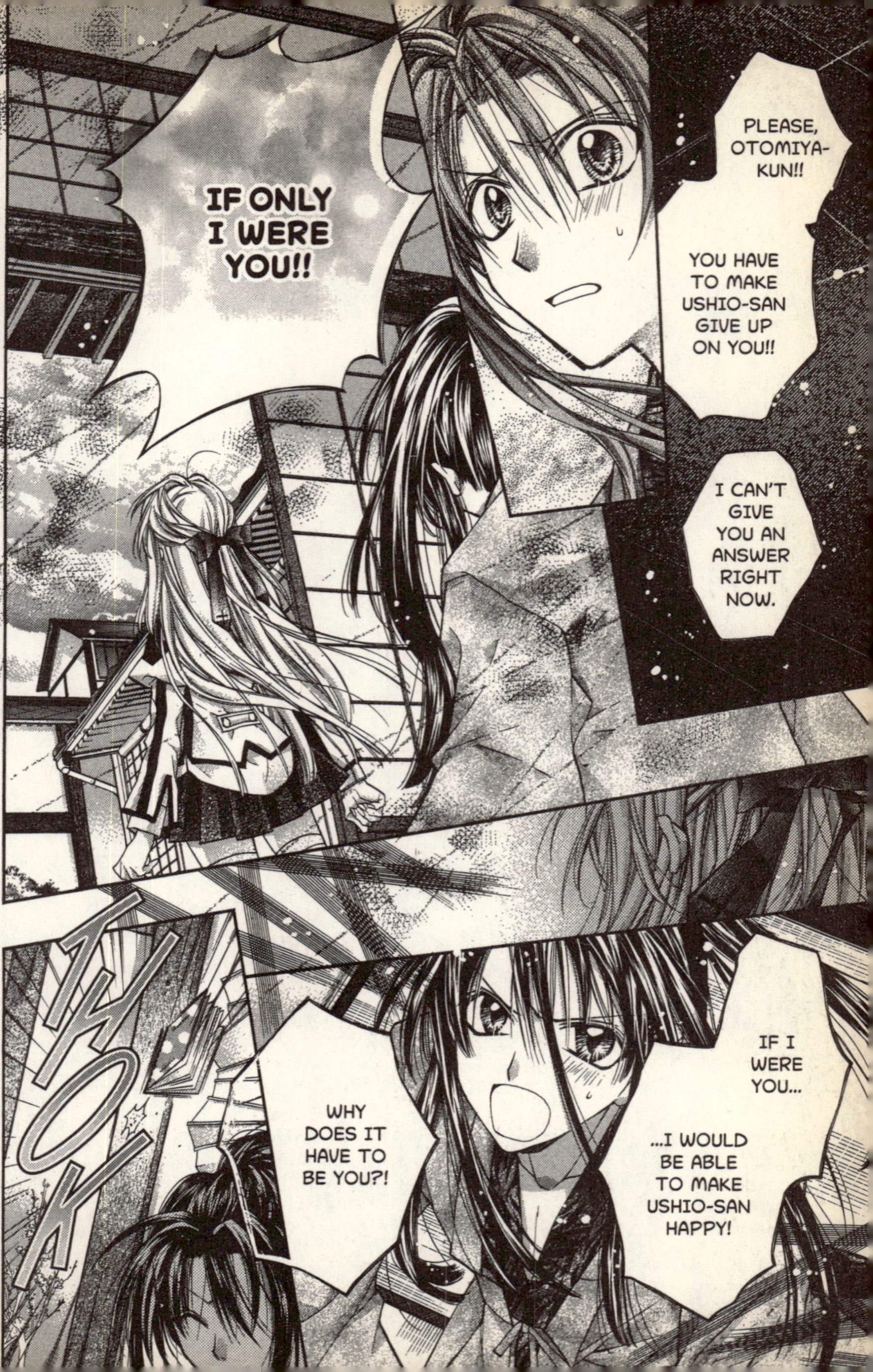
PLEASE, OTOMIYA-KUN!!
YOU HAVE TO MAKE USHIO-SAN GIVE UP ON YOU!!
I CAN'T GIVE YOU AN ANSWER RIGHT NOW.
IF ONLY I WERE YOU!!
IF I WERE YOU...
...I WOULD BE ABLE TO MAKE USHIO-SAN HAPPY!
WHY DOES IT HAVE TO BE YOU?!
TWOK

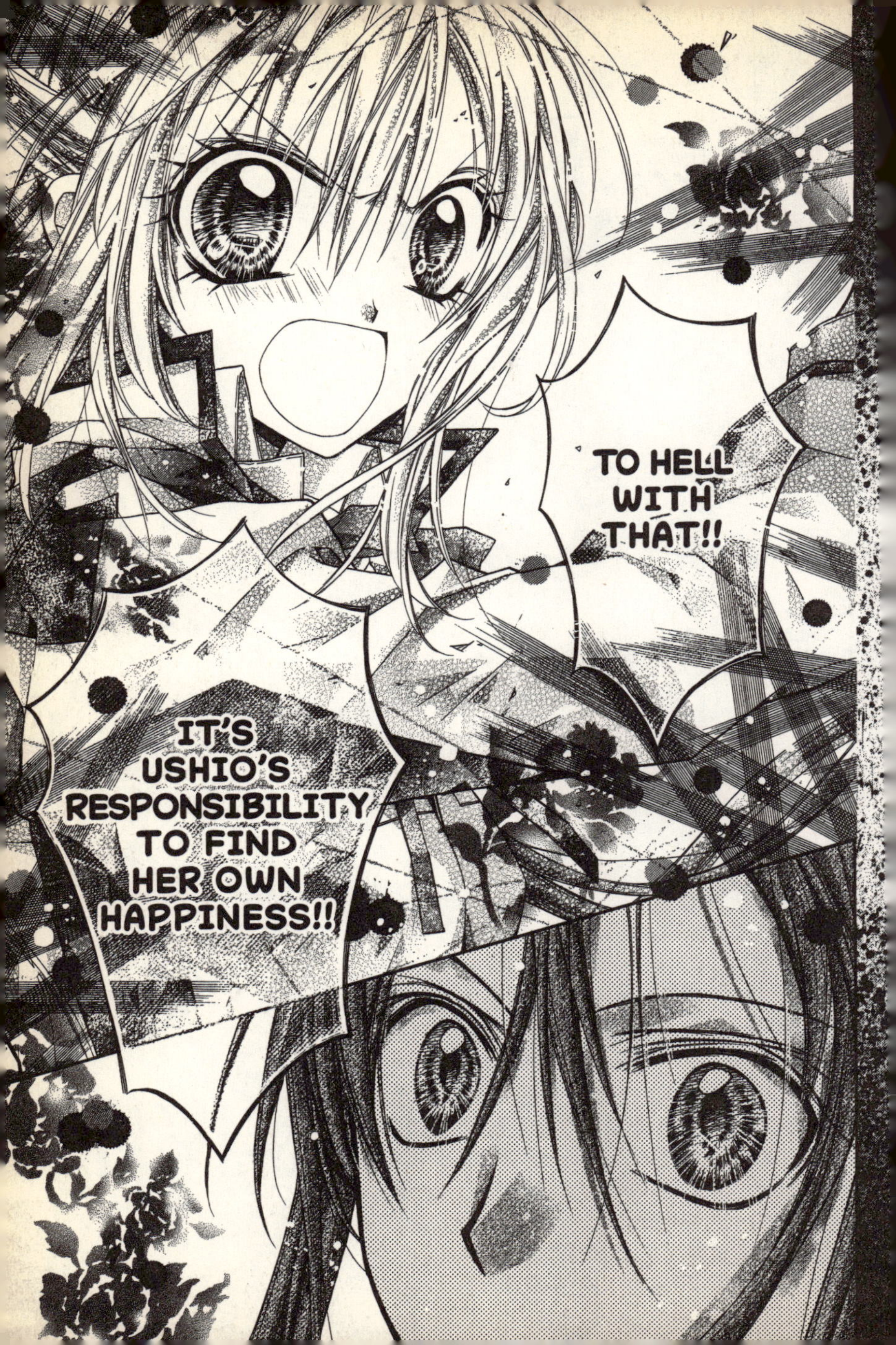
TO HELL WITH THAT!!
IT'S USHIO'S RESPONSIBILITY TO FIND HER OWN HAPPINESS!!

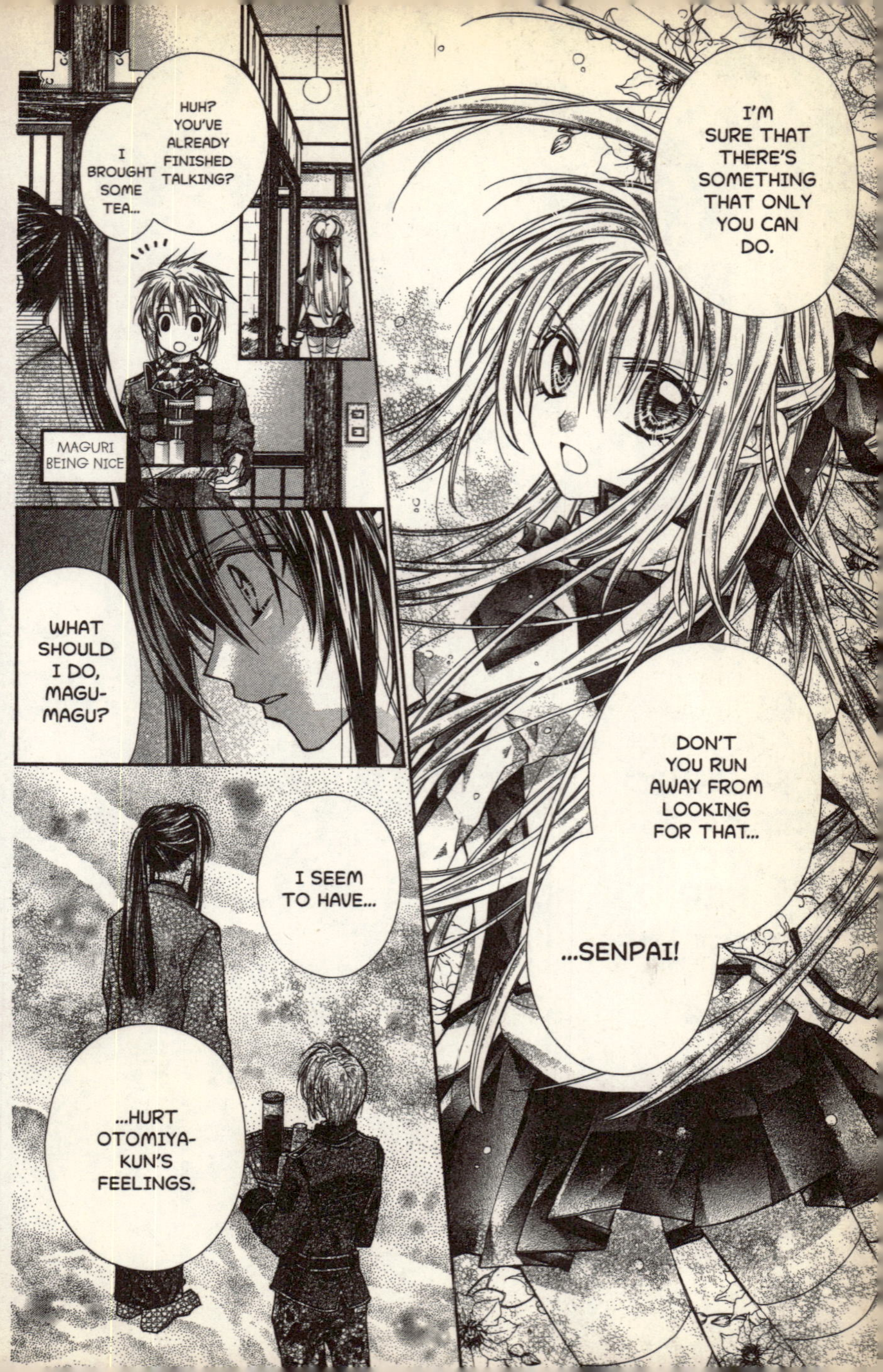
I'M SURE THAT THERE'S SOMETHING THAT ONLY YOU CAN DO.
DON'T YOU RUN AWAY FROM LOOKING FOR THAT...
...SENPAI!
HUH? YOU'VE ALREADY FINISHED TALKING?
I BROUGHT SOME TEA...
MAGURI BEING NICE
WHAT SHOULD I DO, MAGU-MAGU?
I SEEM TO HAVE...
...HURT OTOMIYA-KUN'S FEELINGS.

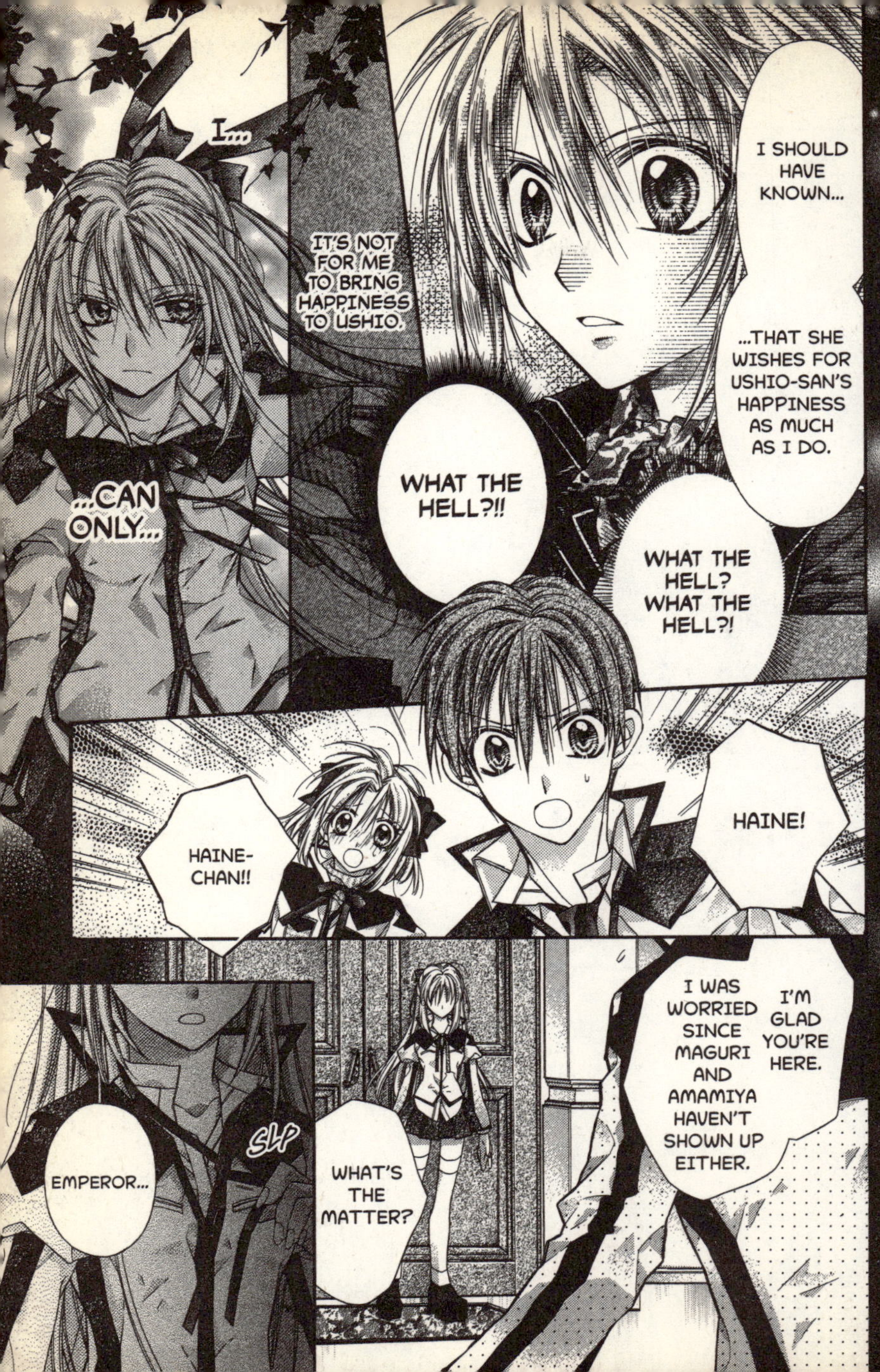
I SHOULD HAVE KNOWN...
...THAT SHE WISHES FOR USHIO-SAN'S HAPPINESS AS MUCH AS I DO.
WHAT THE HELL? WHAT THE HELL?!
WHAT THE HELL?!!
HAINE!
HAINE-CHAN!!
I...
IT'S NOT FOR ME TO BRING HAPPINESS TO USHIO.
...CAN ONLY...
I'M GLAD YOU'RE HERE.
I WAS WORRIED SINCE MAGURI AND AMAMIYA HAVEN'T SHOWN UP EITHER.
WHAT'S THE MATTER?
SLIP
EMPEROR...

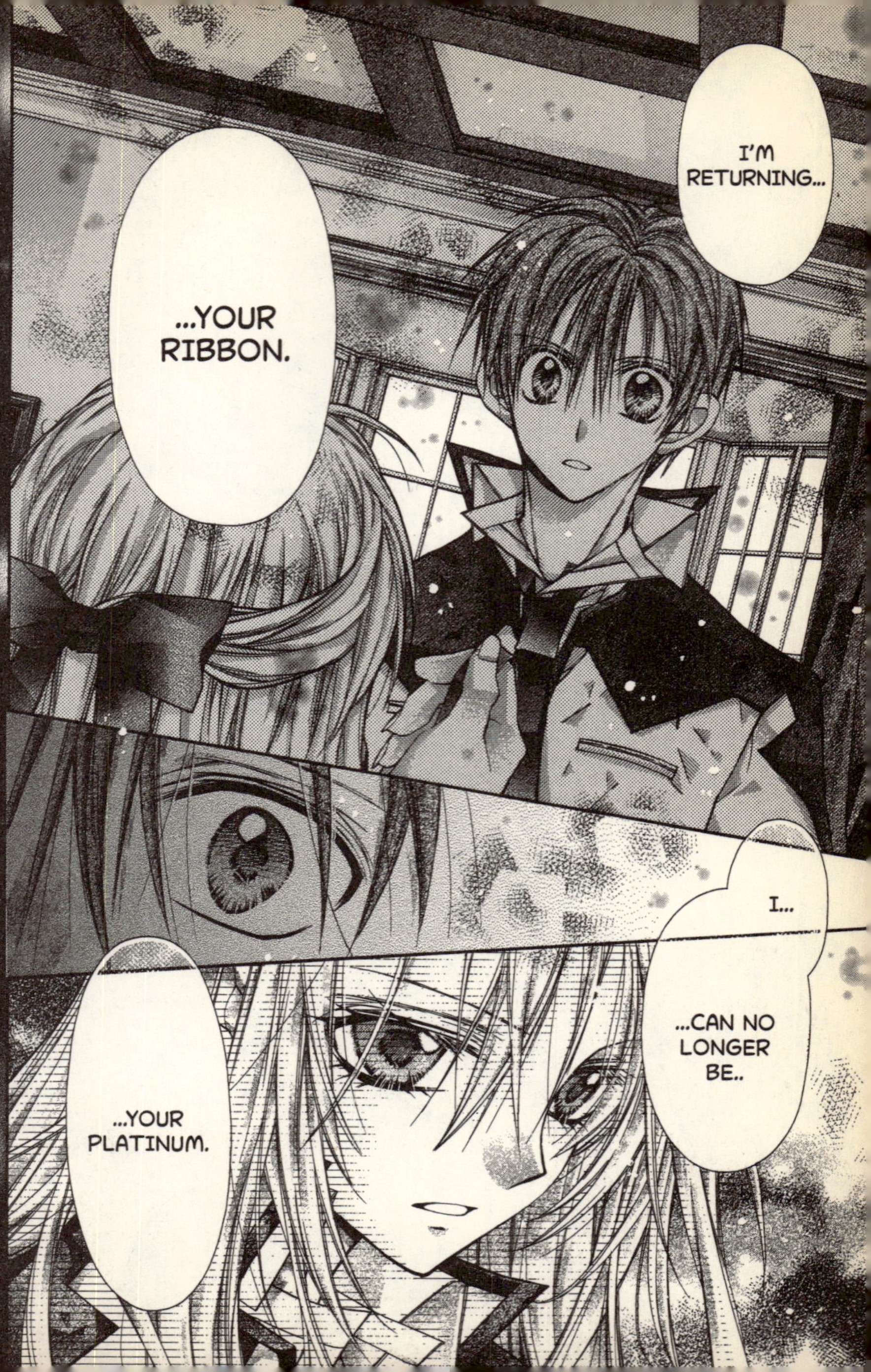
I'M RETURNING...
...YOUR RIBBON.
I...
...CAN NO LONGER BE..
...YOUR PLATINUM.

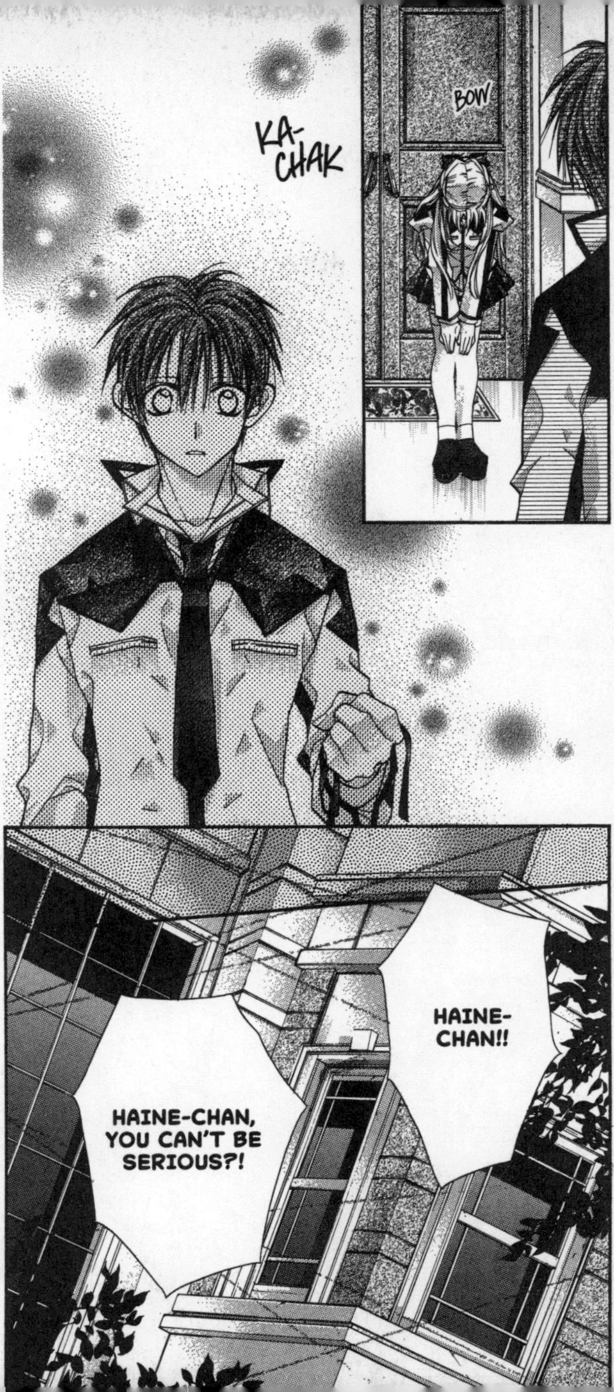
BOW
KA-
CHAK
HAINE-
CHAN!!
HAINE-CHAN,
YOU CAN'T BE
SERIOUS?!
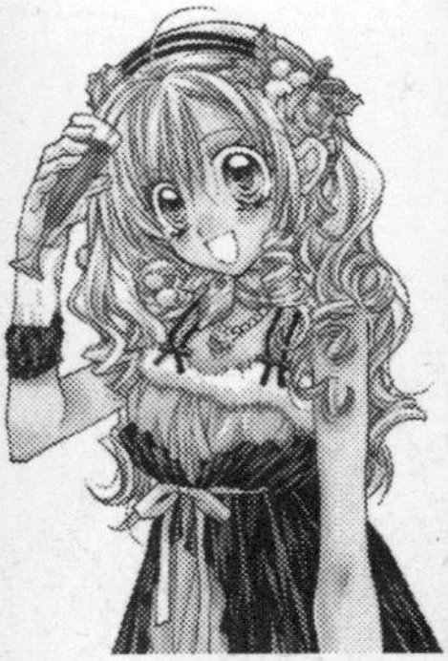

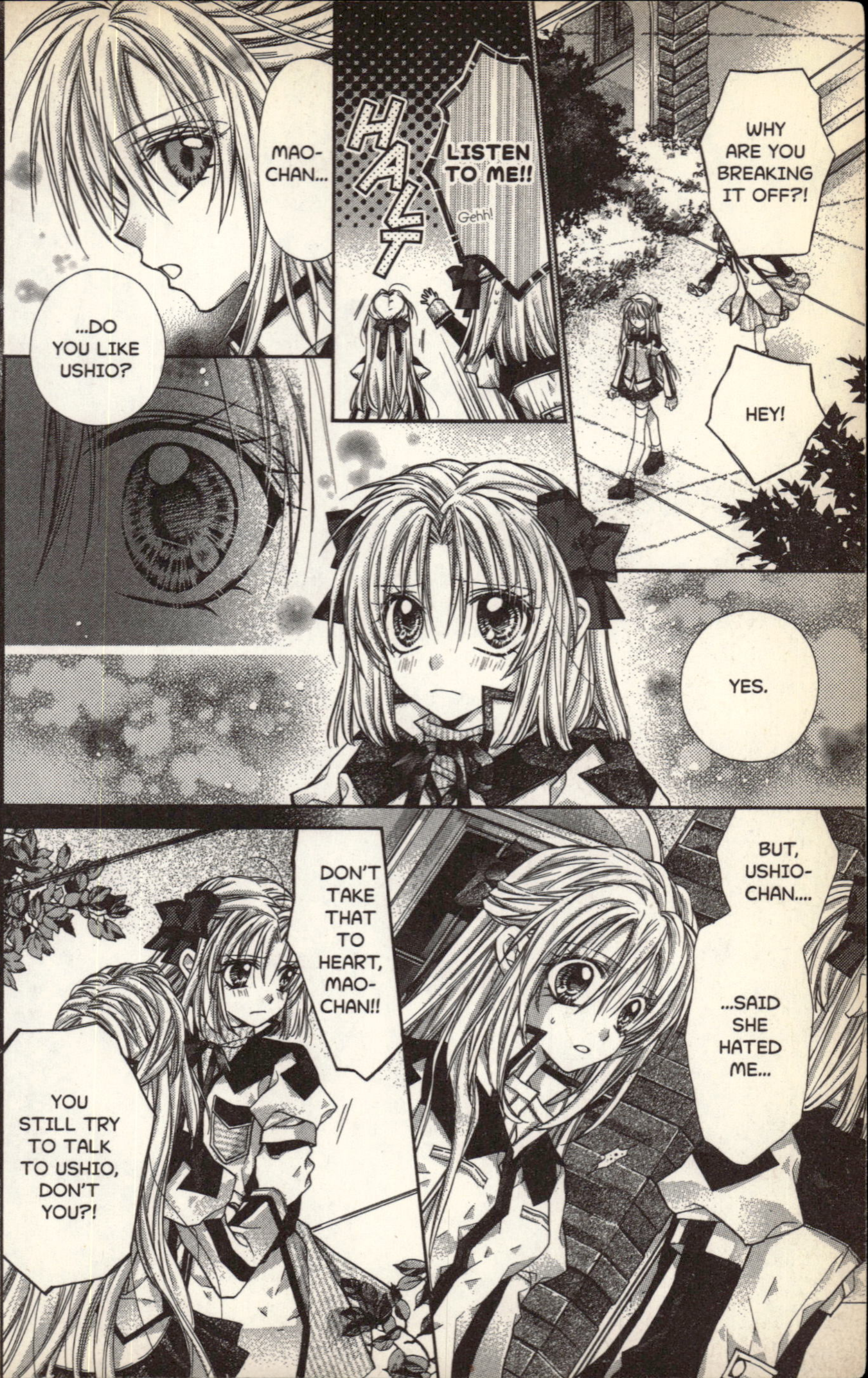
WHY ARE YOU BREAKING IT OFF?!
HEY!
HALT
LISTEN TO ME!!
Gehh!
MAO-CHAN...
...DO YOU LIKE USHIO?
YES.
BUT, USHIO-CHAN....
...SAID SHE HATED ME...
DON'T TAKE THAT TO HEART, MAO-CHAN!!
YOU STILL TRY TO TALK TO USHIO, DON'T YOU?!

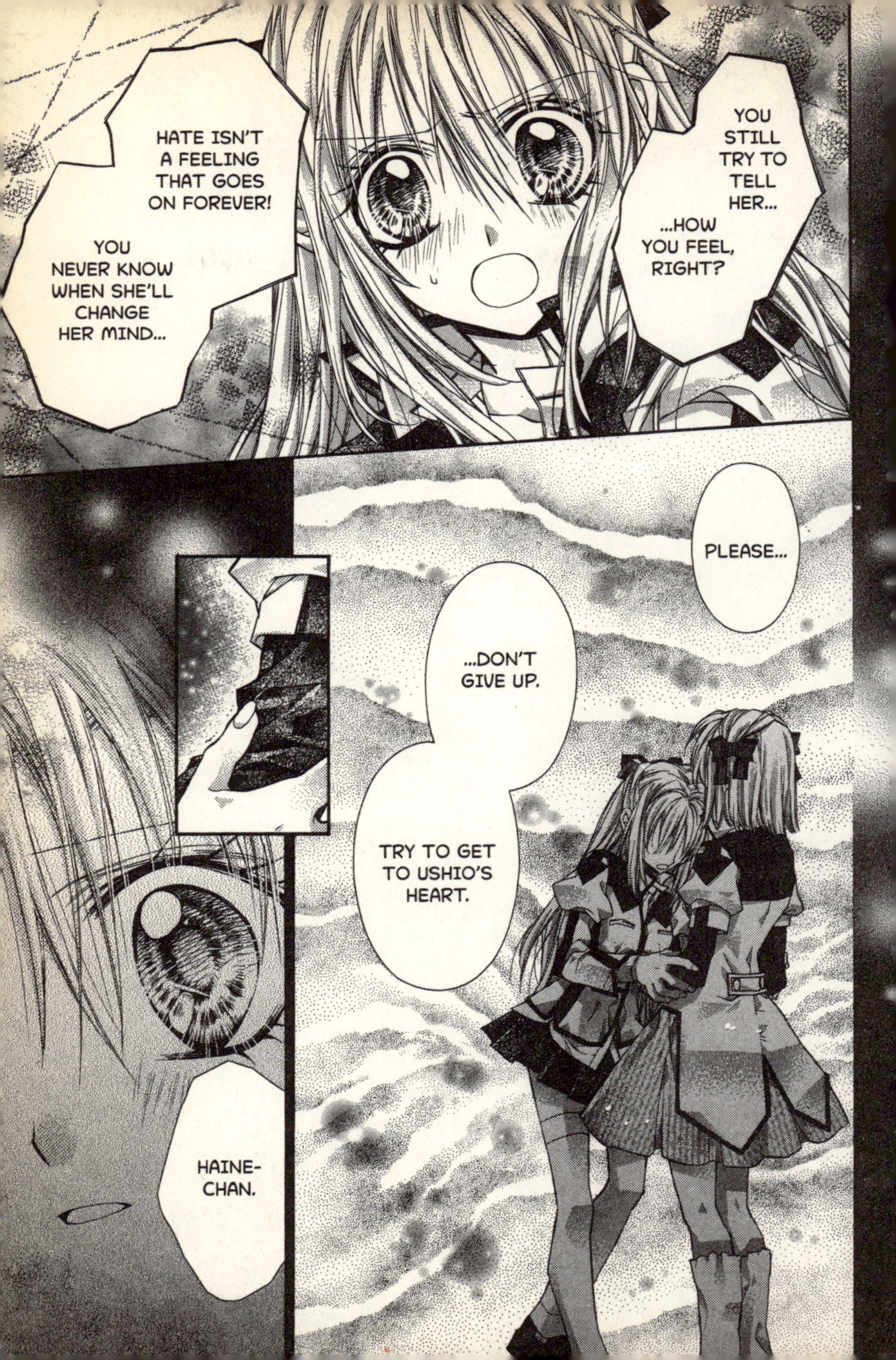
YOU STILL TRY TO TELL HER...
...HOW YOU FEEL, RIGHT?
HATE ISN'T A FEELING THAT GOES ON FOREVER!
YOU NEVER KNOW WHEN SHE'LL CHANGE HER MIND...
PLEASE...
...DON'T GIVE UP.
TRY TO GET TO USHIO'S HEART.
HAINE-CHAN.

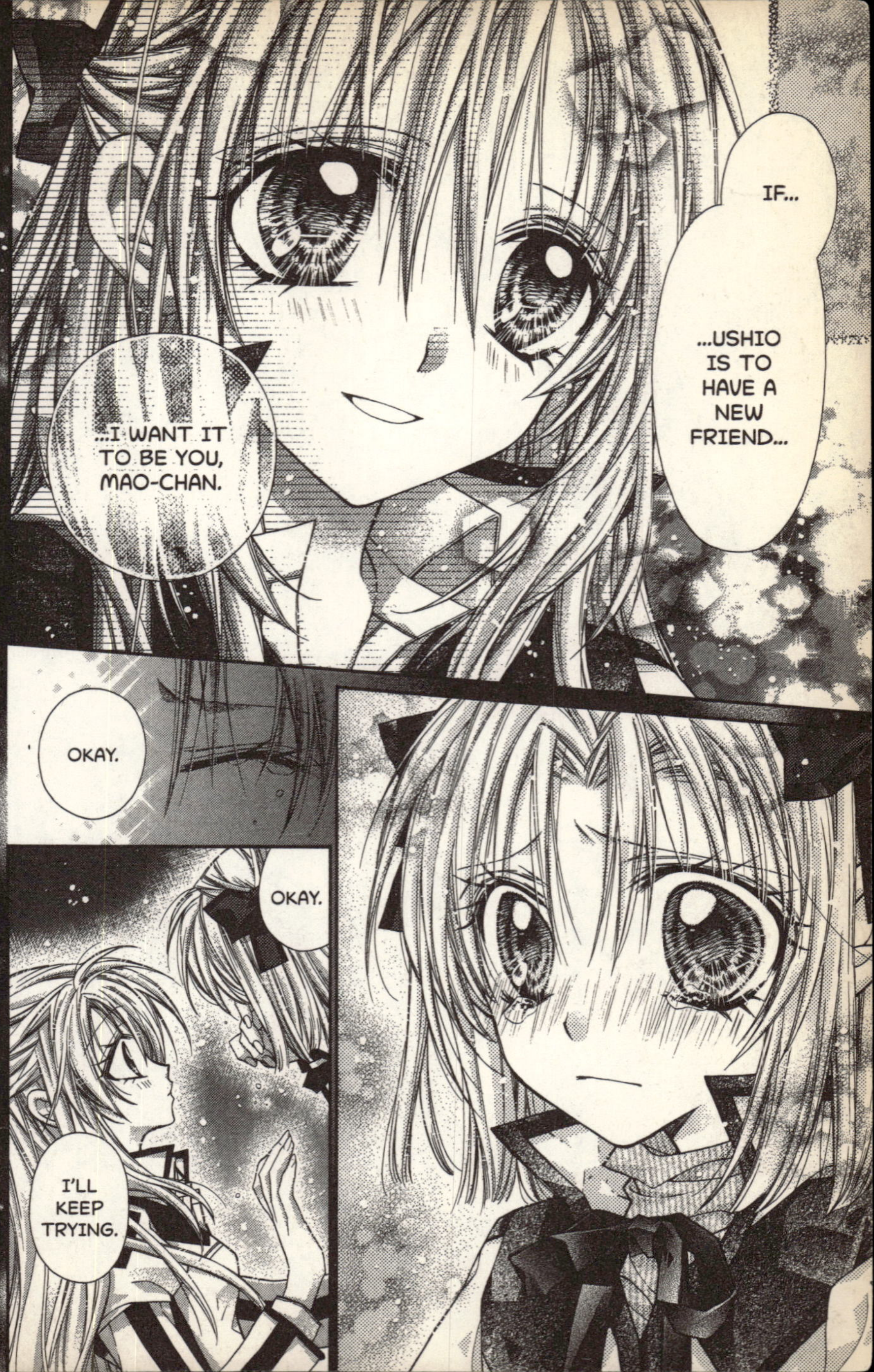
IF...
...USHIO IS TO HAVE A NEW FRIEND...
...I WANT IT TO BE YOU, MAO-CHAN.
OKAY.
OKAY.
I'LL KEEP TRYING.

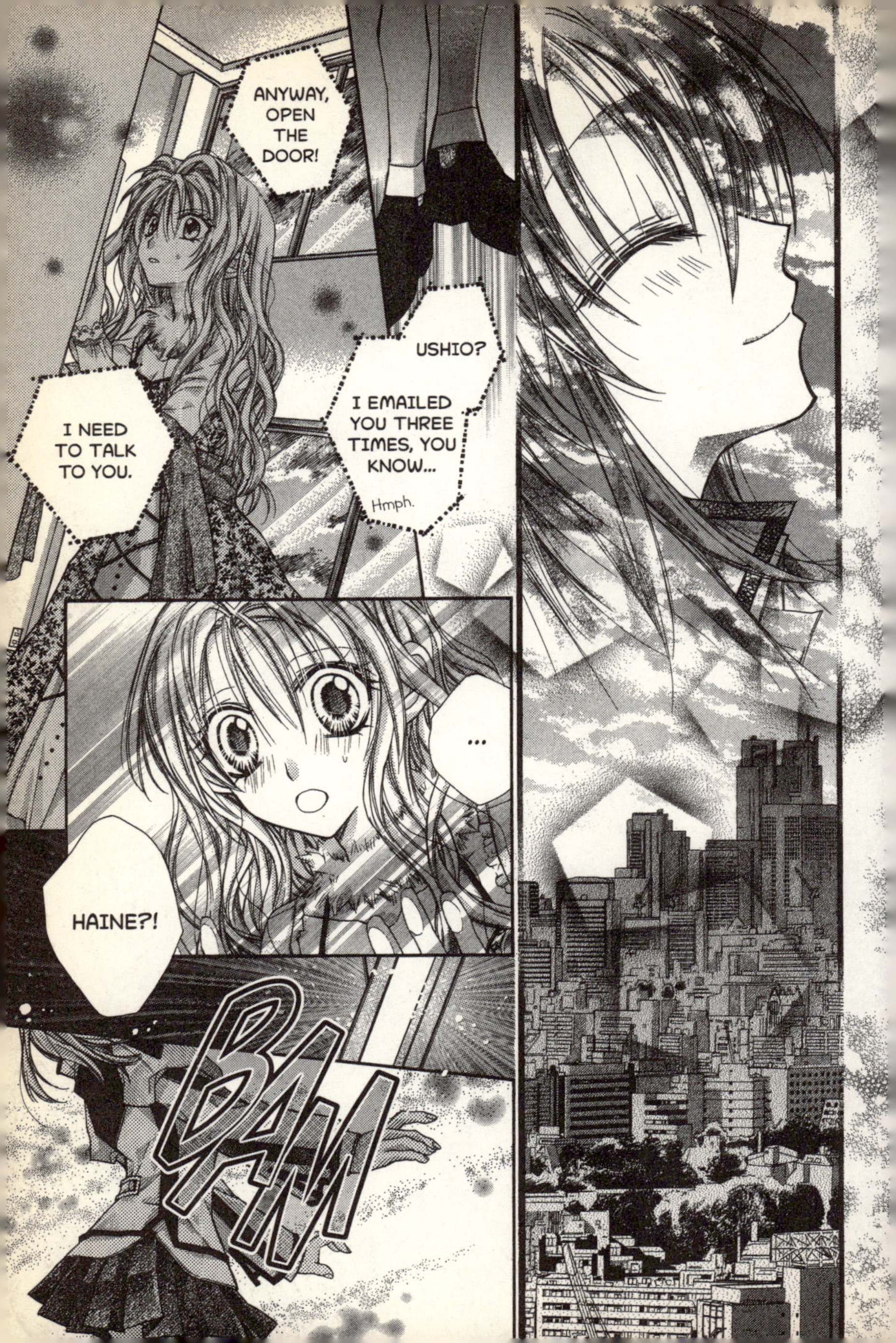

ANYWAY, OPEN THE DOOR!
USHIO?
I EMAILED YOU THREE TIMES, YOU KNOW...
Hmph.
I NEED TO TALK TO YOU.
...
HAINE?!
BAM

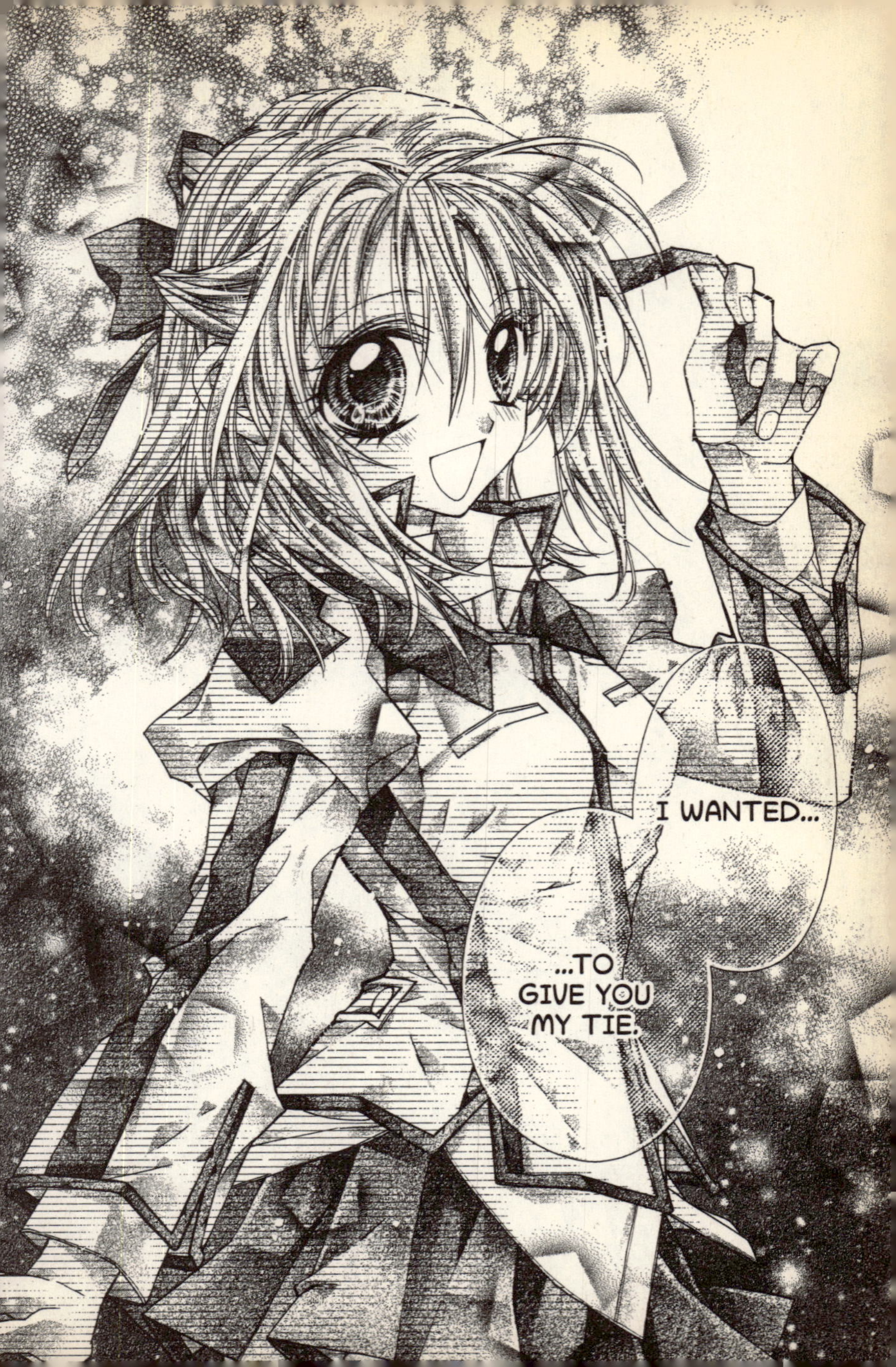
I WANTED...
...TO GIVE YOU MY TIE.

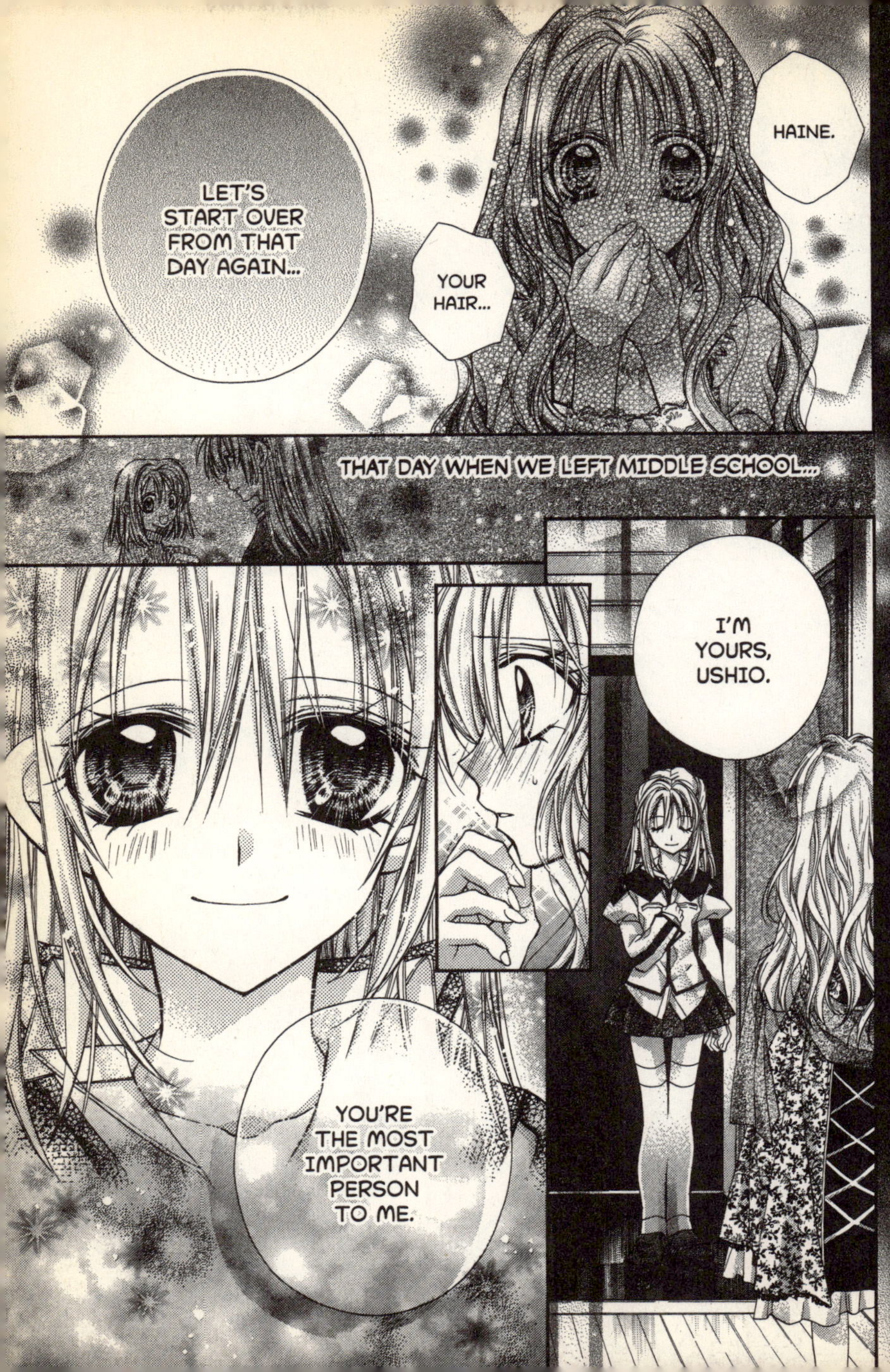
HAINE.
YOUR HAIR...
LET'S START OVER FROM THAT DAY AGAIN...
THAT DAY WHEN WE LEFT MIDDLE SCHOOL...
I'M YOURS, USHIO.
YOU'RE THE MOST IMPORTANT PERSON TO ME.

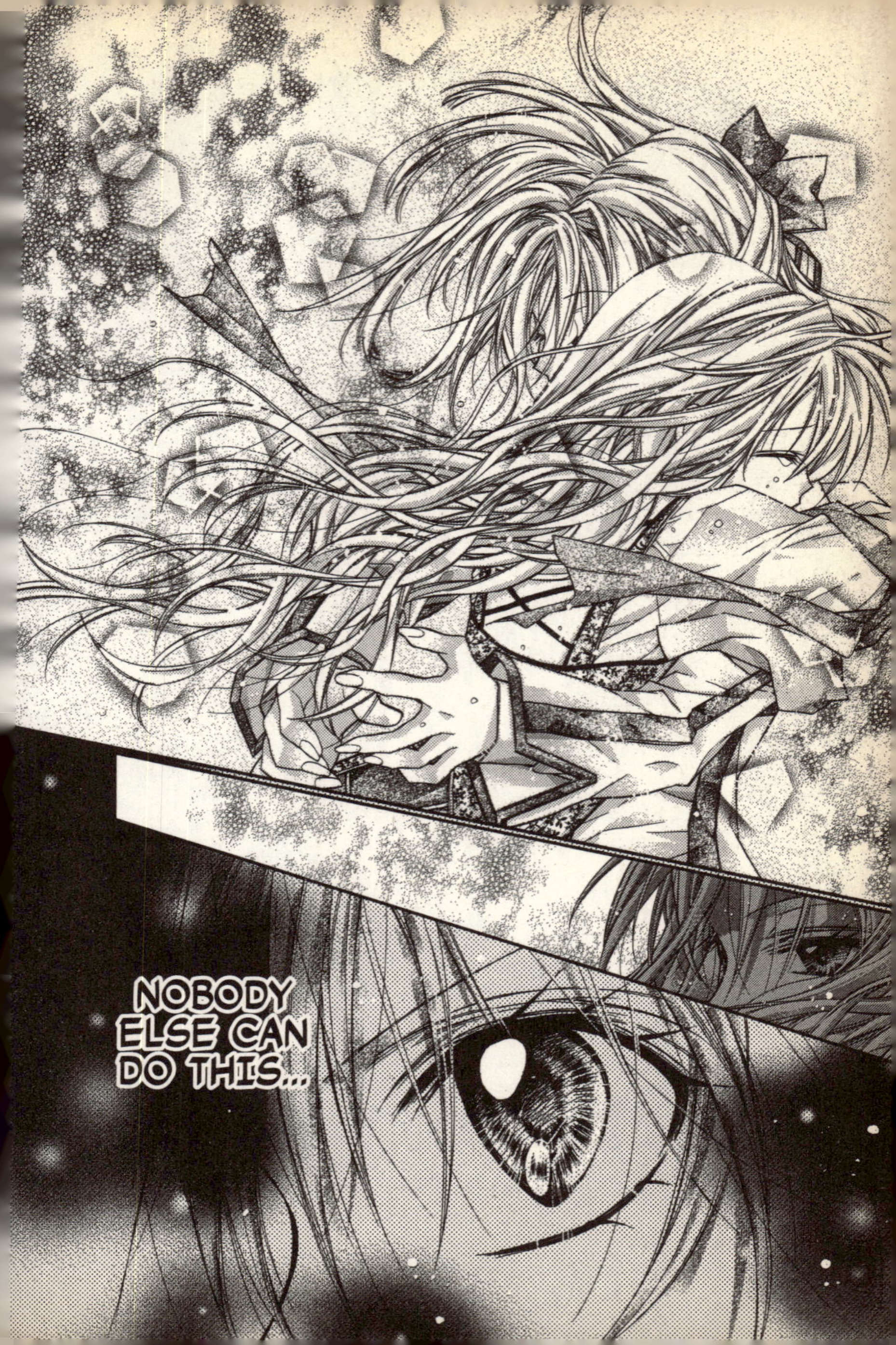
NOBODY ELSE CAN DO THIS...

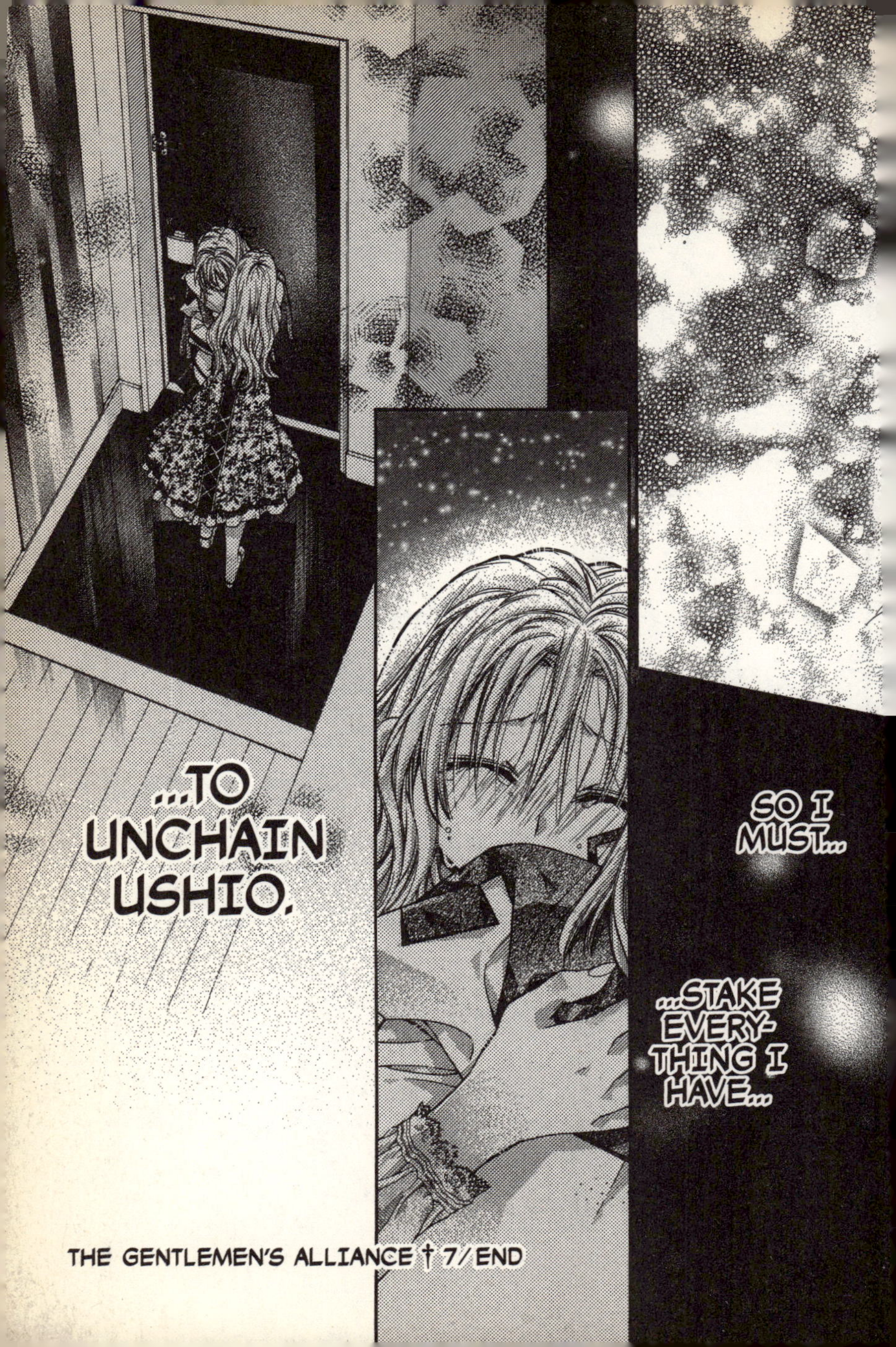
SO I MUST...
...STAKE EVERY-THING I HAVE...
...TO UNCHAIN USHIO.
THE GENTLEMEN'S ALLIANCE † 7/END

THE GENTLEMEN'S ALLIANCE CROSS

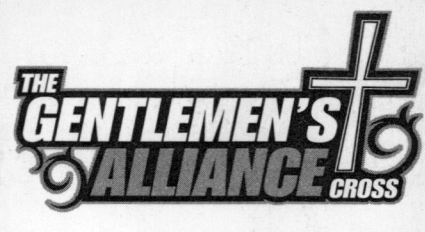

BONUS FUNNIES

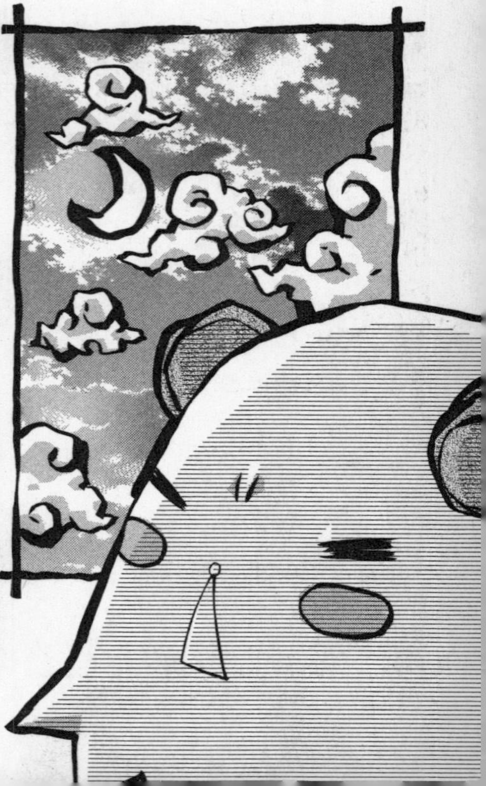

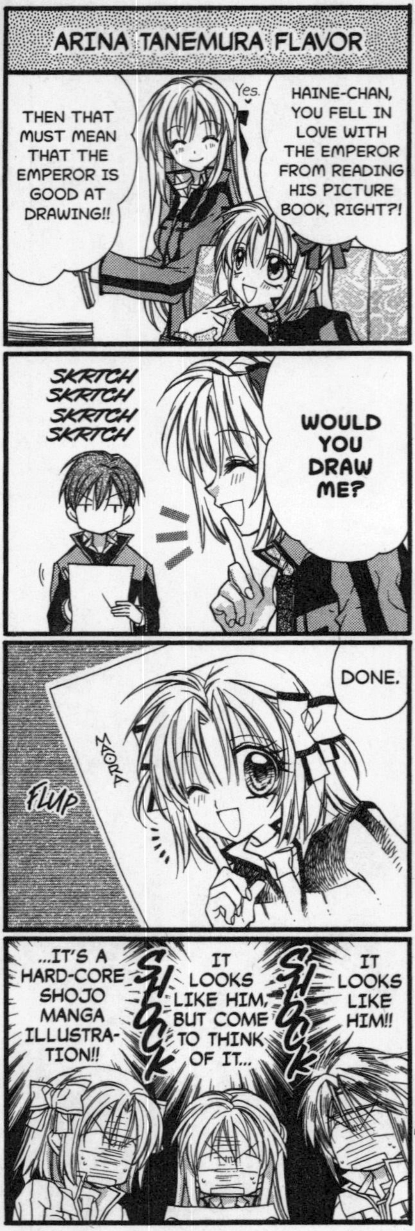
ARINA TANEMURA FLAVOR
HAINE-CHAN, YOU FELL IN LOVE WITH THE EMPEROR FROM READING HIS PICTURE BOOK, RIGHT?!
Yes.
THEN THAT MUST MEAN THAT THE EMPEROR IS GOOD AT DRAWING!!
WOULD YOU DRAW ME?
SKRTCH SKRTCH SKRTCH SKRTCH
DONE.
FLUP
IT LOOKS LIKE HIM!!
SHOCK
IT LOOKS LIKE HIM, BUT COME TO THINK OF IT...
SHOCK
...IT'S A HARD-CORE SHOJO MANGA ILLUSTRATION!!

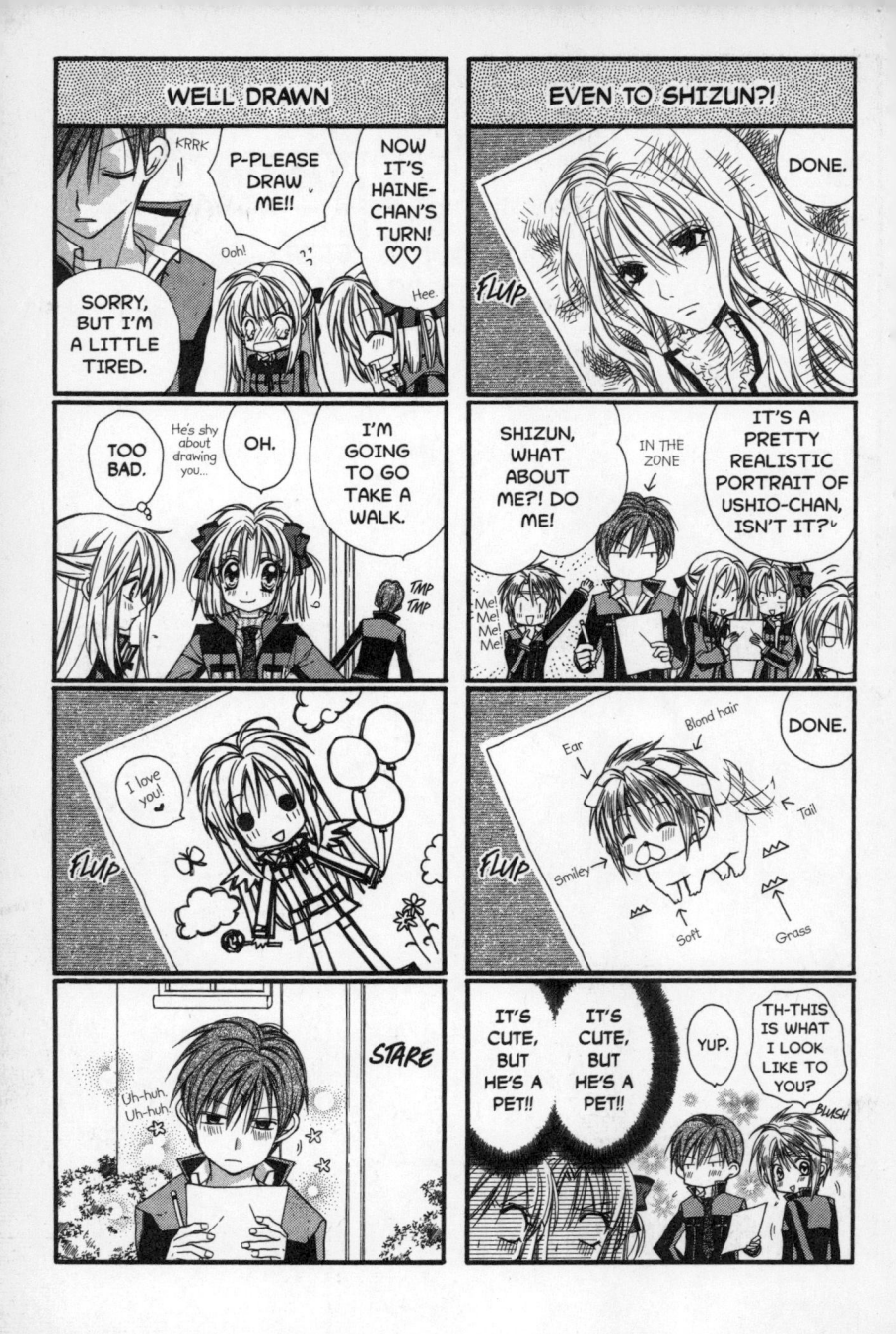
EVEN TO SHIZUN?!
DONE.
FLUP
IT'S A PRETTY REALISTIC PORTRAIT OF USHIO-CHAN, ISN'T IT?
IN THE ZONE
SHIZUN, WHAT ABOUT ME?! DO ME!
Me! Me! Me! Me!
DONE.
Blond hair
Ear
Tail
FLUP
Smiley
Soft
Grass
TH-THIS IS WHAT I LOOK LIKE TO YOU?
BLUSH
YUP.
IT'S CUTE, BUT HE'S A PET!!
IT'S CUTE, BUT HE'S A PET!!
WELL DRAWN
NOW IT'S HAINE-CHAN'S TURN! ♡♡
Hee.
P-PLEASE DRAW ME!!
Ooh!
KRRK
SORRY, BUT I'M A LITTLE TIRED.
I'M GOING TO GO TAKE A WALK.
TMP TMP
OH.
He's shy about drawing you...
TOO BAD.
I love you!
FLUP
STARE
Uh-huh. Uh-huh.

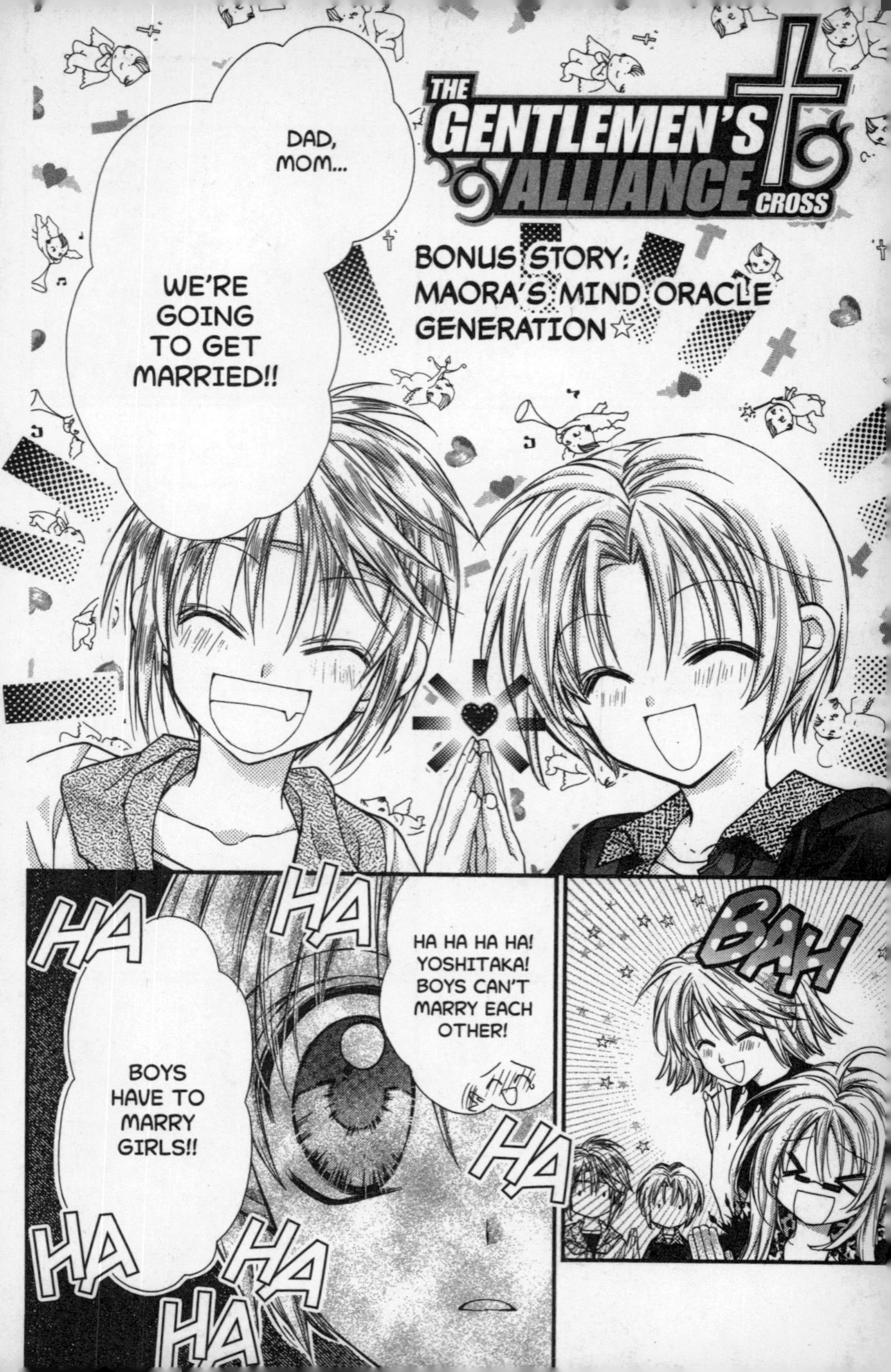
THE GENTLEMEN'S ALLIANCE CROSS
BONUS STORY: MAORA'S MIND ORACLE GENERATION☆
DAD, MOM...
WE'RE GOING TO GET MARRIED!!
BAH
HA HA HA HA! YOSHITAKA! BOYS CAN'T MARRY EACH OTHER!
BOYS HAVE TO MARRY GIRLS!!
HA HA HA HA HA HA

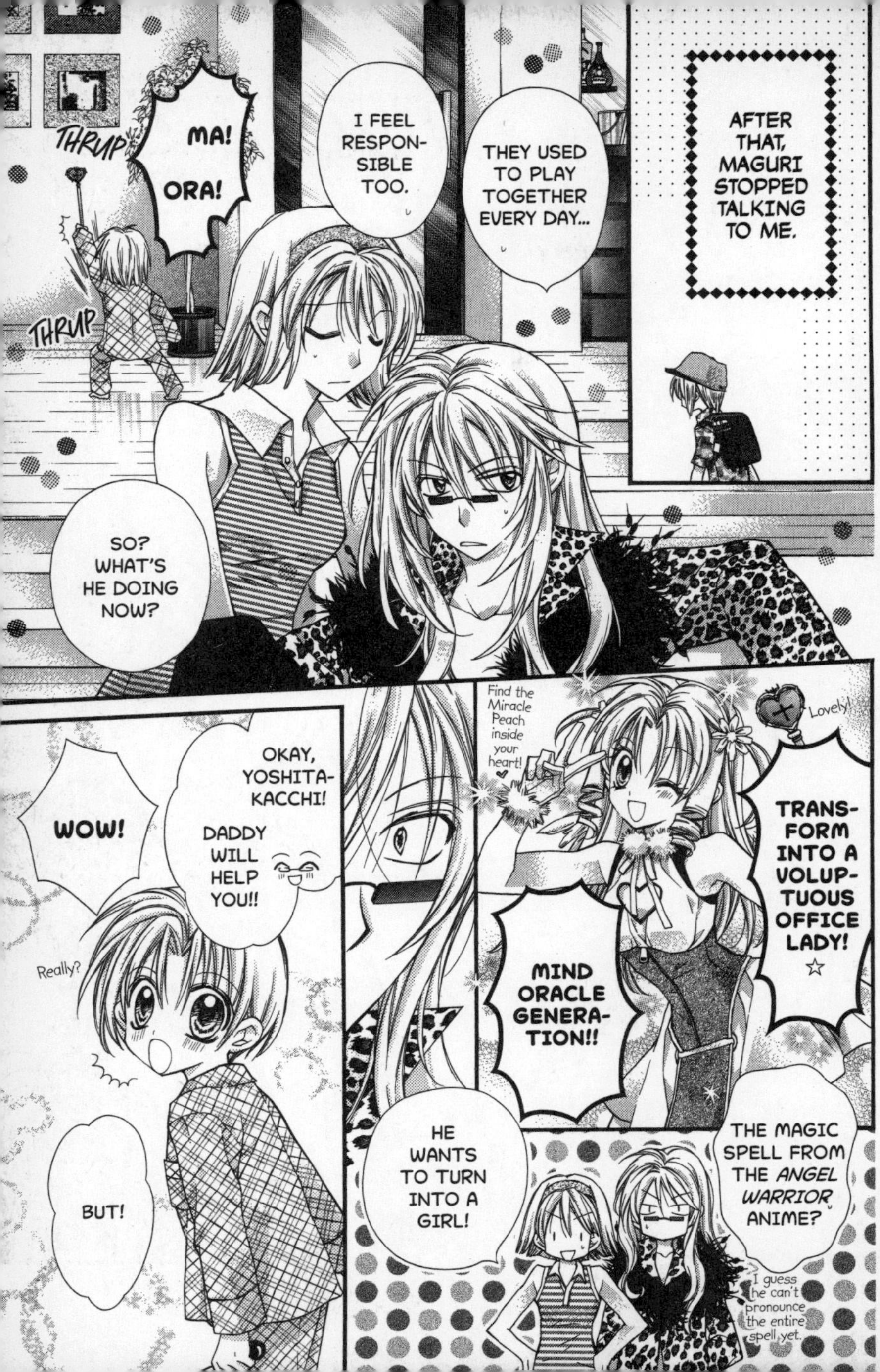

AFTER THAT, MAGURI STOPPED TALKING TO ME.
THEY USED TO PLAY TOGETHER EVERY DAY...
I FEEL RESPON-SIBLE TOO.
MA! ORA!
THRUP
THRUP
SO? WHAT'S HE DOING NOW?
Lovely!
TRANS-FORM INTO A VOLUP-TUOUS OFFICE LADY! ☆
Find the Miracle Peach inside your heart! ♥
MIND ORACLE GENERA-TION!!
THE MAGIC SPELL FROM THE ANGEL WARRIOR ANIME?
HE WANTS TO TURN INTO A GIRL!
I guess he can't pronounce the entire spell yet.
OKAY, YOSHITA-KACCHI!
DADDY WILL HELP YOU!!
WOW!
Really?
BUT!

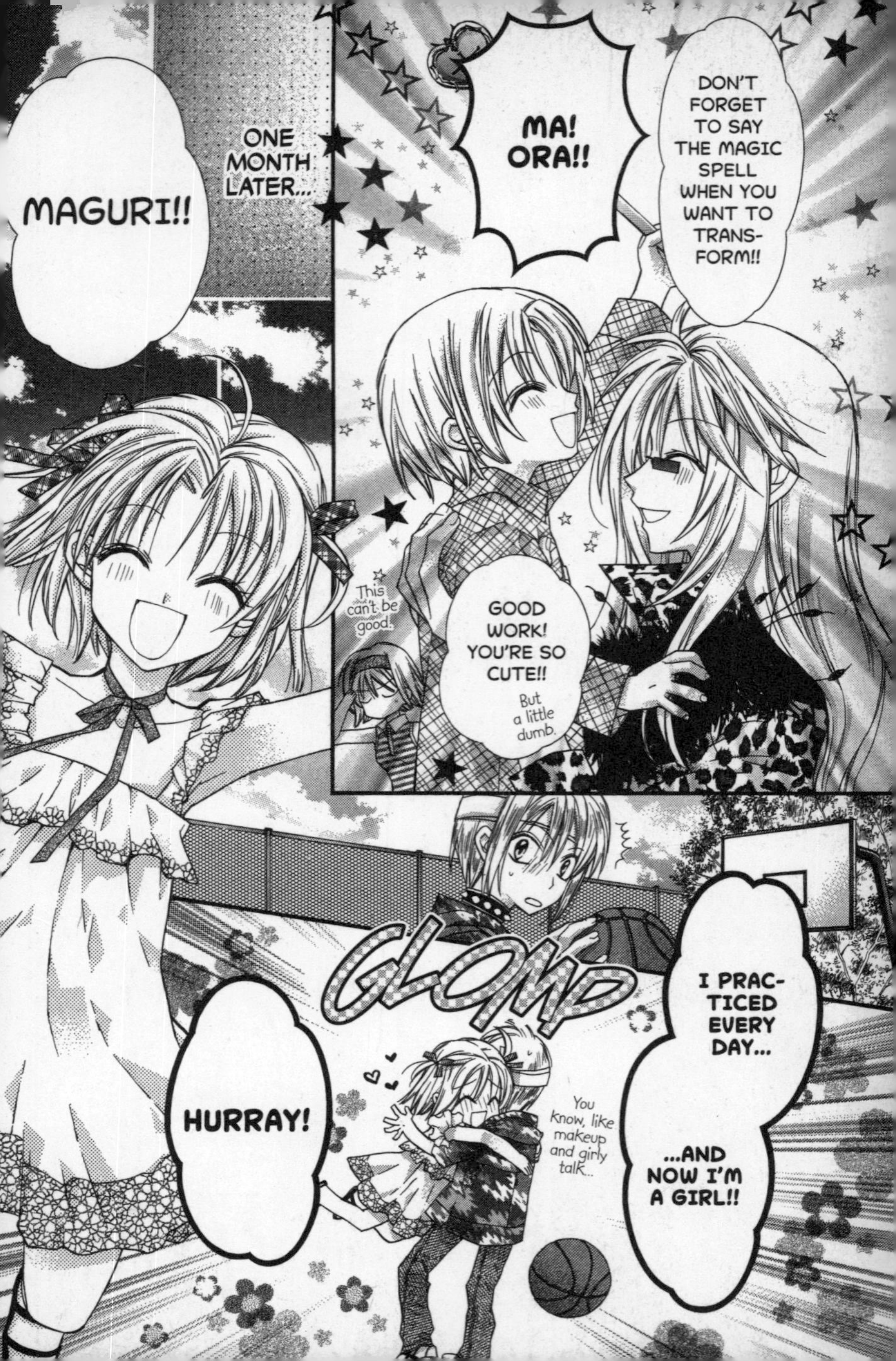

DON'T FORGET TO SAY THE MAGIC SPELL WHEN YOU WANT TO TRANS-FORM!!
MA! ORA!!
GOOD WORK! YOU'RE SO CUTE!!
But a little dumb.
This can't be good.
ONE MONTH LATER...
MAGURI!!
GLOMP
I PRAC-TICED EVERY DAY...
...AND NOW I'M A GIRL!!
You know, like makeup and girly talk...
HURRAY!

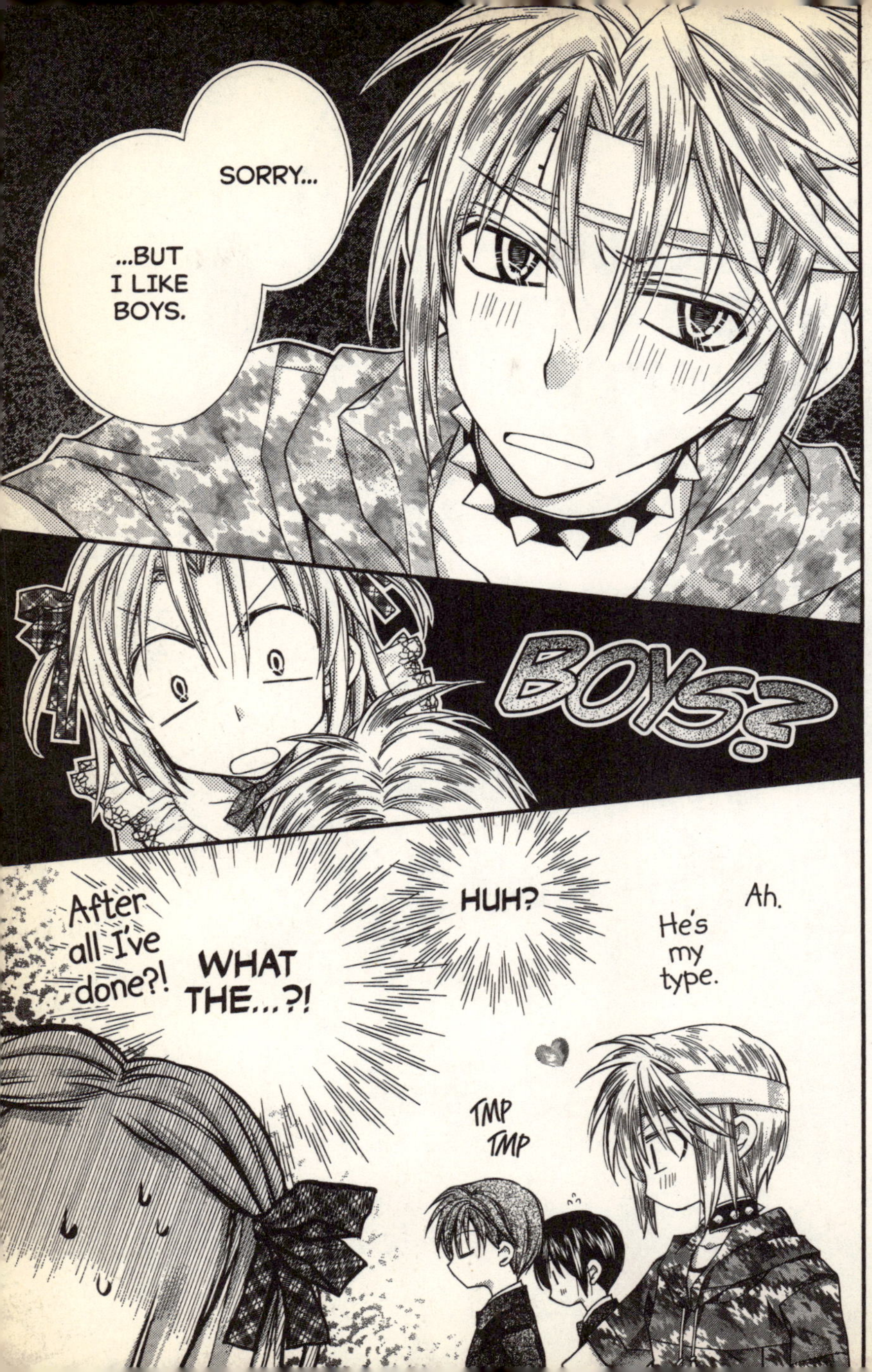
SORRY...
...BUT I LIKE BOYS.
BOYS?
Ah.
He's my type.
HUH?
WHAT THE...?!
After all I've done?!
TMP TMP

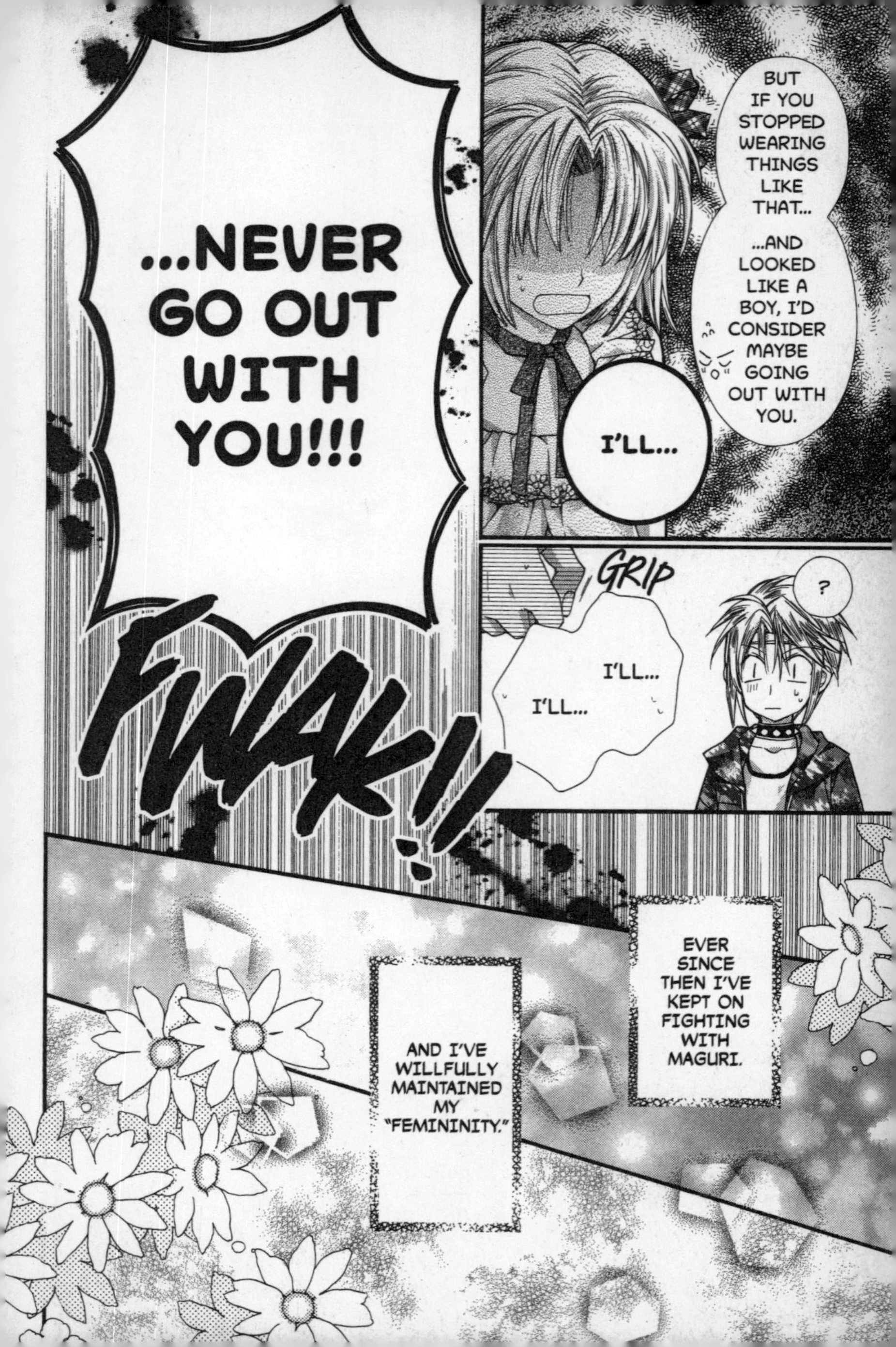
BUT IF YOU STOPPED WEARING THINGS LIKE THAT...
...AND LOOKED LIKE A BOY, I'D CONSIDER MAYBE GOING OUT WITH YOU.
I'LL...
GRIP
?
I'LL...
I'LL...
...NEVER GO OUT WITH YOU!!!
FWAK!!
EVER SINCE THEN I'VE KEPT ON FIGHTING WITH MAGURI.
AND I'VE WILLFULLY MAINTAINED MY "FEMININITY."

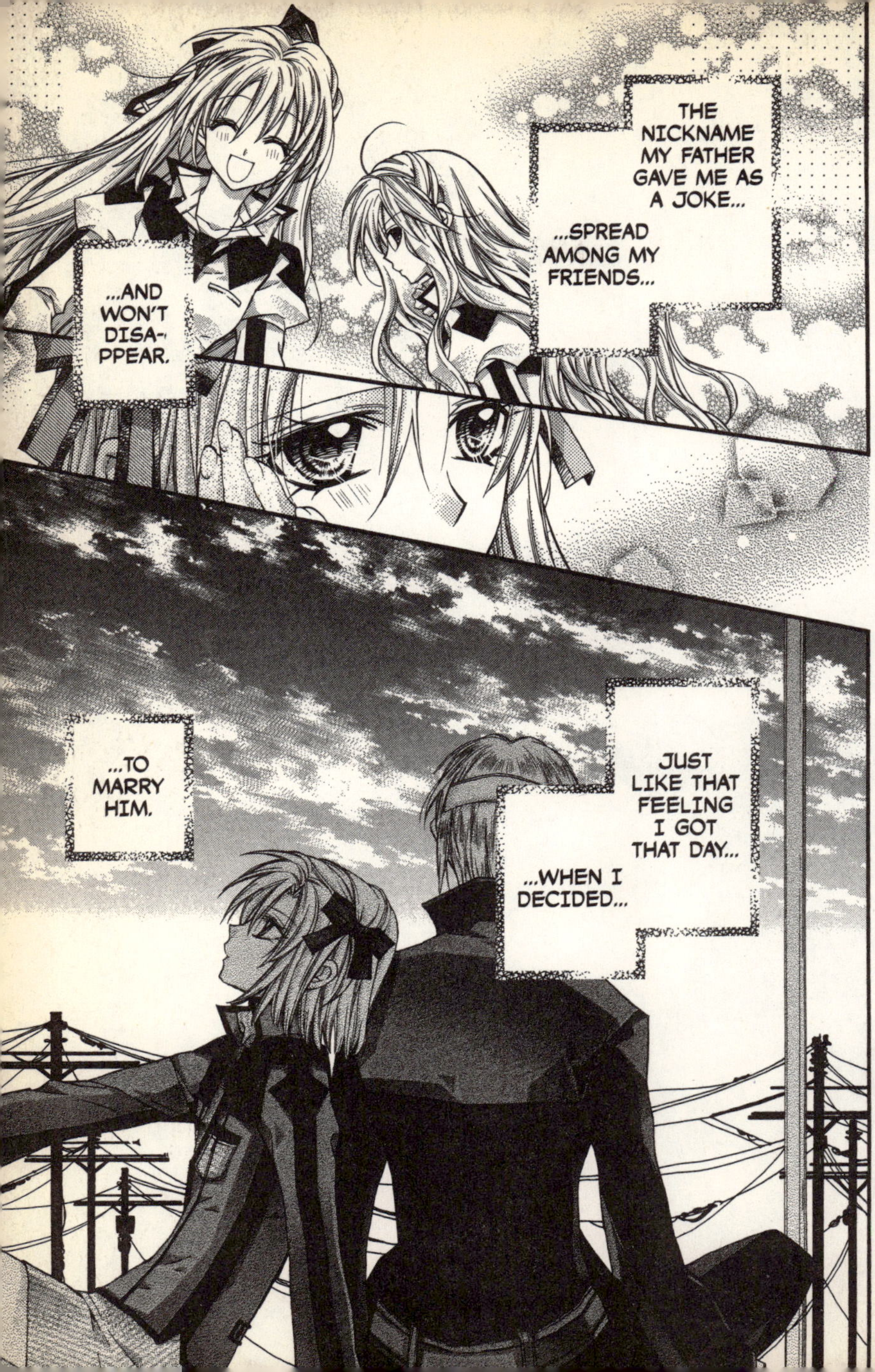
THE NICKNAME MY FATHER GAVE ME AS A JOKE...
...SPREAD AMONG MY FRIENDS...
...AND WON'T DISA-PPEAR.
JUST LIKE THAT FEELING I GOT THAT DAY...
...WHEN I DECIDED...
...TO MARRY HIM.

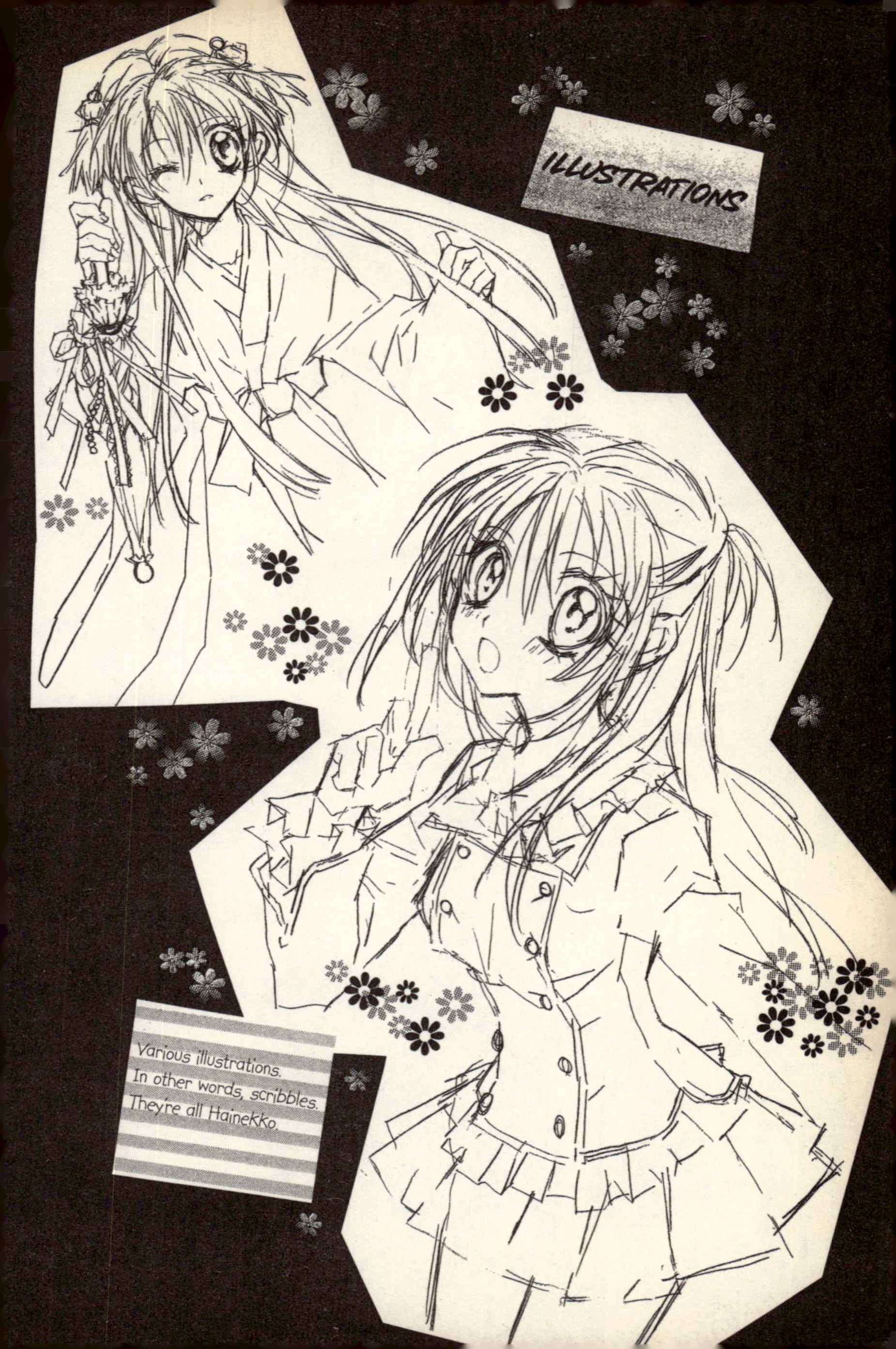
ILLUSTRATIONS
Various illustrations.
In other words, scribbles.
They're all Hainekko.

NOTES ON THE TEXT

PAGE 6:
"This is a one-shot, which is rare for *The Gentleman's Alliance †*."
A "one-shot" is a story that starts and concludes in one chapter. The literal term is *ichiwa kanketsu*, which means "one episode conclusive style."

"I tried drawing her in a mini form…"
Tanemura-sensei is talking about a *mini-kyara*, or "mini character."

PAGE 11:
Animal Crossing
Animal Crossing, or *Doubutsu no Mori*, is an interactive game in which the player leads a virtual life in "real time." Your friends can also visit you in the game. You can go fishing, shopping, grow vegetables, etc.

PAGE 12:
"A stray cat with a fish in his mouth…"
Osakana kuwaeta doraneko seems to be a classical theme in Japan. Since the Japanese consume a lot of fish, in the old days stray cats were known for stealing fish from the fishmongers.

PAGE 43:
Moe
Moe is an otaku term meaning a strong love or fetish for something or someone—usually manga, anime, or game characters.

PAGE 51:
Karuta Tournament
Karuta is a Japanese card game. The name itself is from the Portuguese word *carta*, or "card". There are several versions of the game, but usually the cards are split into "reading cards" and "illustration cards." Each illustration card has a letter written on it from the Japanese alphabet (in hiragana). Someone will read out the contents of the reading card, and the goal of the players is to find the matching illustration card. There is a letter in the corner of the illustration card that coincides with the first letter of the sentence being read out, so the players are able to look for the right card from the moment the reading card is read out loud. The aim of the game is to collect as many illustration cards as possible and to have the highest number of cards at the end. Karuta cards are extremely large (as you can see from Ushio carrying them).

Shinji and Natsuki
Shinji and Natsuki are characters from *Kamikaze Kaito Jeanne*. Shinji is the rebirth of Access, and he is Miyako and Yamato's son. Natsuki is the rebirth of Fin, and she is the daughter of Maron and Chiaki.

Maroyan
"Maroyan" is Tanemura-sensei's nickname for Maron—the main character in *Jeanne*.

PAGE 53:
Bamboo Group roll call...
Although some schools in Japan have classroom name designations rather than number, this is probably just a group name for the orientation and not an actual classroom name.

PAGE 81:
Arina Nikki
Arina Nikki is the name of the blog.

MM Boys
This is an abbreviation for "Maguri Maora Boys."

PAGE 141:
Exchange Diary
An exchange diary is a diary or notebook shared between friends who write entries and comments. Exchange diaries were pretty popular among girls in elementary and middle schools in the 1990s.

PAGE 143:
"Do you feel like eating something?"
Ryokka-san made Haine *zousui*, which is soupy rice.

PAGE 147:
Tsundere
Tsundere is an otaku term for girls who tend to be rather unfriendly or prickly at first, but are gentle, loving, and kind once you get to know them. The word is a combination of *tsunsun*, or "prickly, morose" and *dere dere*, or "lovestruck."

PAGE 151:
Nii-chan
Nii-chan means "older brother."

"Don't you stare at me, damn it!"
Literally this is *menchi o kiru*, a yanki term meaning "to give someone the eye."

PAGE 160:
Senpai
Senpai means "senior." It refers to someone older than the speaker. Many students call students who are older than they are "Senpai." In this case, Haine is using it to reprimand Yukimitsu—normally she refers to him as "Yukimitsu-san."

PAGE 175:
"Transform into a voluptuous office lady!"
In the Japanese, she also says *bon kyu bon*, which is "bam, squeeze, bam!" It is slang used to talk about women with big boobs, small waists, and large hips.

"Find the Miracle Peach inside your heart!"
This is a play on the Japanese tongue-twister *sumomo mo momo mo momo no uchi*, meaning "the word *momo* can be found in both *sumomo* (plum) and *momo* (peach)."

The student council members started to get along gradually, so recently it's been a joy to draw them. A while ago, they tended to be very individualistic, but now they have become closer friends and naturally interfere with each other. I feel like a headmaster watching over them (I don't exactly feel like a parent to them). Anyway, the Ushio arc has begun, and another big wave is heading toward them!

—Arina Tanemura

Arina Tanemura was born in Aichi, Japan. She got her start in 1996, publishing *Nibanme no Koi no Katachi* (The Style of the Second Love) in *Ribon Original* magazine. Her early work includes a collection of short stories called *Kanshaku Dama no Yuutsu* (Short-Tempered Melancholic). Two of her titles, *Kamikaze Kaito Jeanne* and *Full Moon*, were made into popular TV series. Tanemura enjoys karaoke and is a huge *Lord of the Rings* fan.

THE GENTLEMEN'S ALLIANCE † vol. 7
The Shojo Beat Manga Edition

STORY & ART BY
ARINA TANEMURA

English Translation & Adaptation/Tetsuichiro Miyaki
Touch-up Art & Lettering/George Caltsoudas
Design/Amy Martin
Editor/Nancy Thistlethwaite

Editor in Chief, Books/Alvin Lu
Editor in Chief, Magazines/Marc Weidenbaum
VP of Publishing Licensing/Rika Inouye
VP of Sales/Gonzalo Ferreyra
Sr. VP of Marketing/Liza Coppola
Publisher/Hyoe Narita

THE GENTLEMEN ALLIANCE -CROSS- © 2004 by Arina Tanemura. All rights reserved. First published in Japan in 2004 by SHUEISHA Inc., Tokyo. English translation rights arranged by SHUEISHA Inc. The stories, characters and incidents mentioned in this publication are entirely fictional.

No portion of this book may be reproduced or transmitted in any form or by any means without written permission from the copyright holders.

The rights of the author(s) of the work(s) in this publication to be so identified have been asserted in accordance with the Copyright, Designs and Patents Act 1988. A CIP catalogue record for this book is available from the British Library.

Printed in Canada

Published by VIZ Media, LLC
P.O. Box 77010
San Francisco, CA 94107

Shojo Beat Manga Edition
10 9 8 7 6 5 4 3 2 1
First printing, September 2008

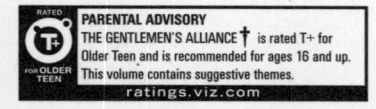

PARENTAL ADVISORY
THE GENTLEMEN'S ALLIANCE † is rated T+ for Older Teen and is recommended for ages 16 and up. This volume contains suggestive themes.
ratings.viz.com

Arina Tanemura Series

The Gentlemen's Alliance †
Haine Otomiya joins Imperial Academy in pursuit of the boy she's loved since she was a child, unaware that he has many secrets of his own.

I·O·N
Chanting the letters of her first name has always brought Ion Tsuburagi good luck—but her good-luck charm is really the result of psychic powers!

Full Moon
Mitsuki Koyama dreams of becoming a pop star, but she is dying of throat cancer. Can she live out a lifetime of dreams in just one year?

Short-Tempered Melancholic
A collection of short stories including Arina Tanemura's debut manga, "In the Style of the Second Love"!

Time Stranger Kyoko
Kyoko Suomi must find 12 holy stones and 12 telepaths to awaken her sister who has been trapped in time since birth.

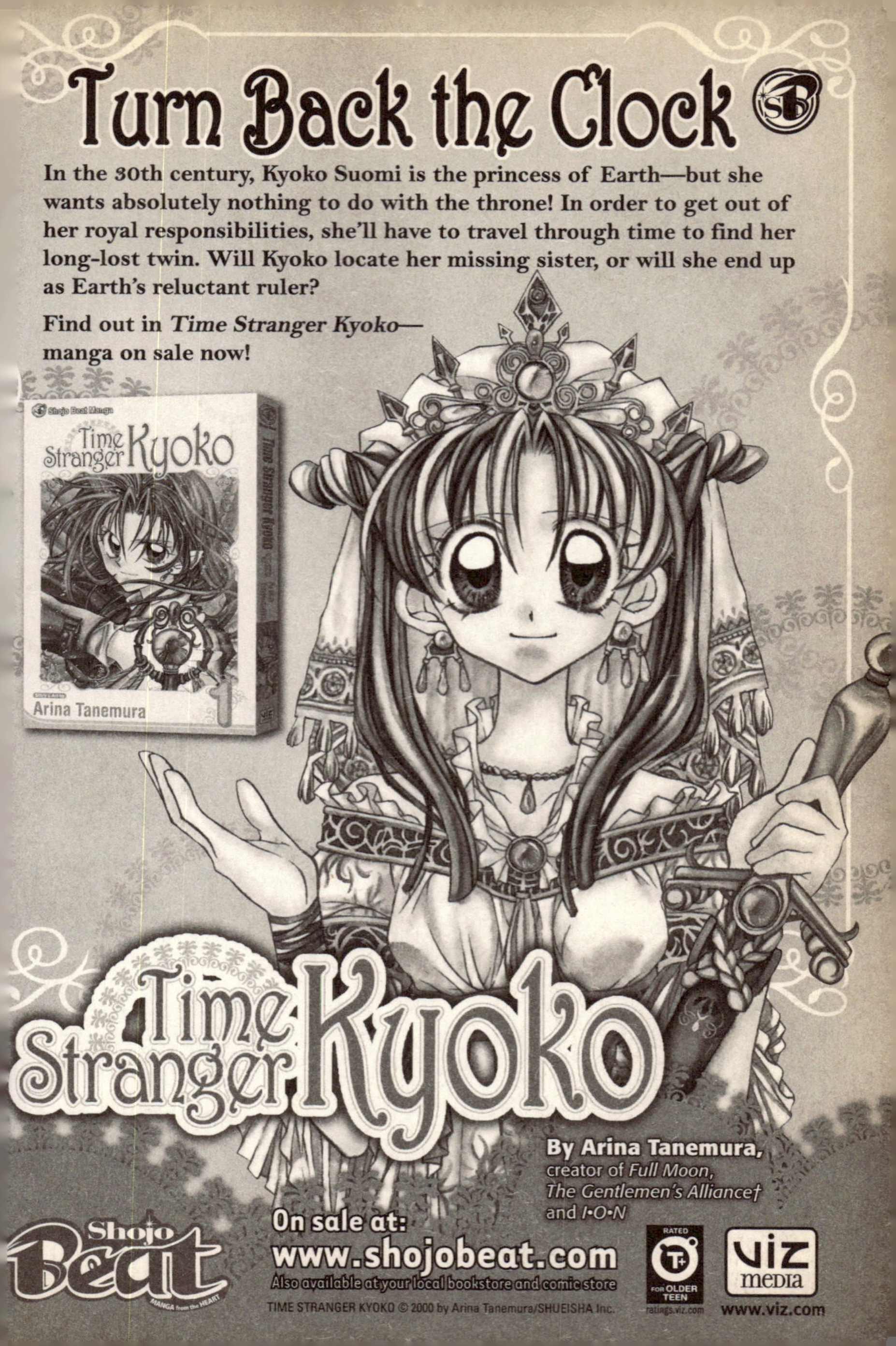
Turn Back the Clock
In the 30th century, Kyoko Suomi is the princess of Earth—but she wants absolutely nothing to do with the throne! In order to get out of her royal responsibilities, she'll have to travel through time to find her long-lost twin. Will Kyoko locate her missing sister, or will she end up as Earth's reluctant ruler?
Find out in Time Stranger Kyoko—manga on sale now!
Shojo Beat Manga
Time Stranger Kyoko
Arina Tanemura
1
Time Stranger Kyoko
By Arina Tanemura,
creator of Full Moon, The Gentlemen's Alliance† and I•O•N
Shojo Beat
MANGA from the HEART
On sale at:
www.shojobeat.com
Also available at your local bookstore and comic store
RATED
T+
FOR OLDER TEEN
ratings.viz.com
VIZ media
www.viz.com
TIME STRANGER KYOKO © 2000 by Arina Tanemura/SHUEISHA Inc.

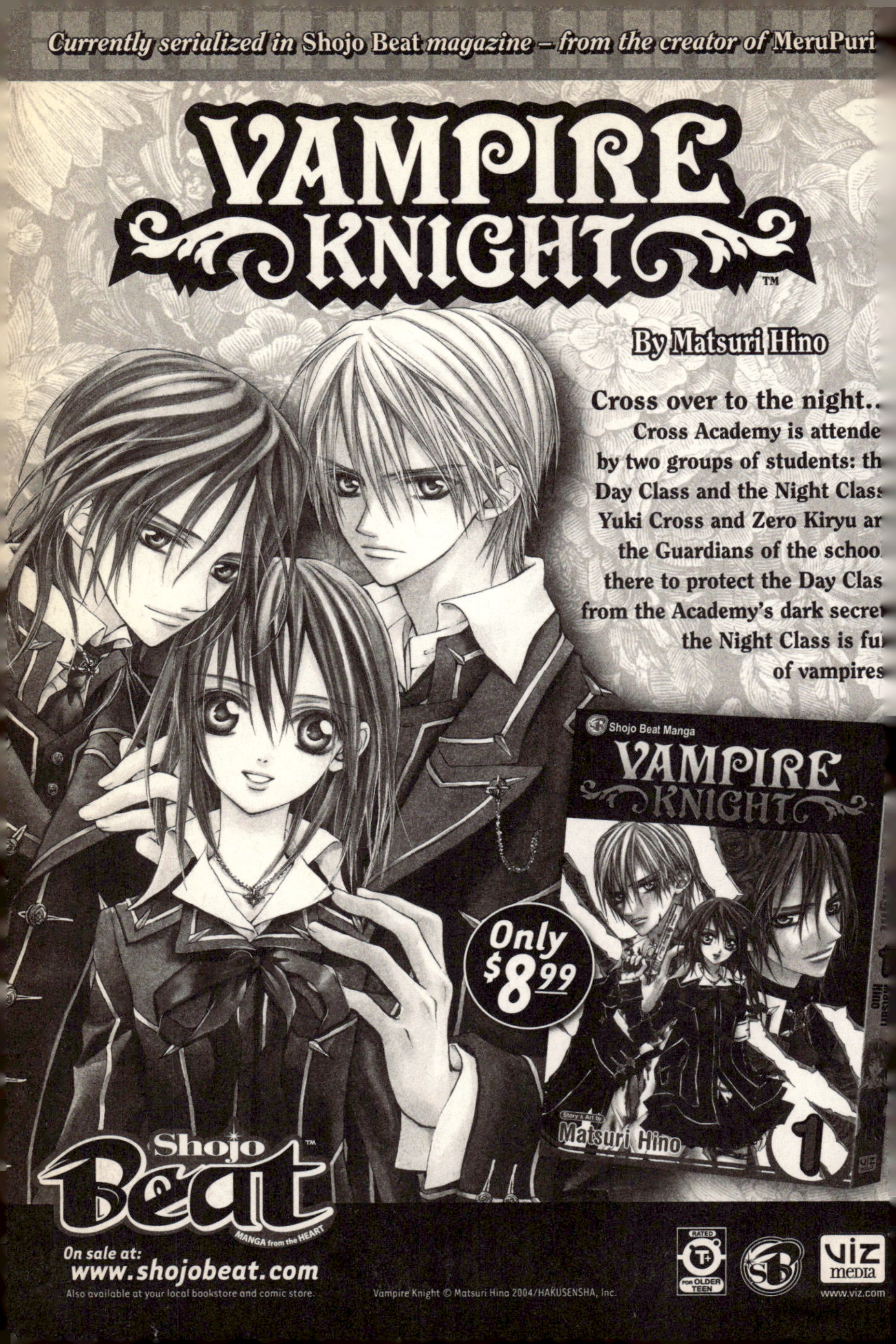
Currently serialized in Shojo Beat magazine – from the creator of MeruPuri
VAMPIRE KNIGHT™
By Matsuri Hino
Cross over to the night..
Cross Academy is attende
by two groups of students: th
Day Class and the Night Class
Yuki Cross and Zero Kiryu ar
the Guardians of the schoo
there to protect the Day Clas
from the Academy's dark secre
the Night Class is fu
of vampires
Shojo Beat Manga
VAMPIRE KNIGHT
Story & Art by
Matsuri Hino
1
Only $8.99
Shojo Beat™
MANGA from the HEART
On sale at:
www.shojobeat.com
Also available at your local bookstore and comic store.
Vampire Knight © Matsuri Hino 2004/HAKUSENSHA, Inc.
RATED T+ FOR OLDER TEEN
viz media
www.viz.com

Tell us what you think about Shojo Beat Manga!

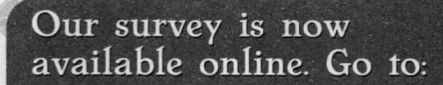

Our survey is now available online. Go to:
shojobeat.com/mangasurvey

Help us make our product offerings better!

FULL MOON WO SAGASHITE © 2001 by Arina Tanemura/SHUEISHA Inc.
Fushigi Yûgi: Genbu Kaiden © 2004 Yuu WATASE/Shogakukan Inc.
Ouran Koko Host Club © Bisco Hatori 2002/HAKUSENSHA, Inc.

Save OVER 50% off the cover price!

Shojo Beat
MANGA from the HEART

The Shojo Manga Authority

This monthly magazine is injected with the most **ADDICTIVE** shojo manga stories from Japan. PLUS, unique editorial coverage on the arts, music, culture, fashion, and much more!

☑ **YES!** Please enter my one-year subscription (12 GIANT issues) to *Shojo Beat* at the LOW SUBSCRIPTION RATE of **$34.99!**

Over 300 pages per issue!

NAME

ADDRESS

CITY   **STATE**   **ZIP**

E-MAIL ADDRESS   P7GNC1

☐ MY CHECK IS ENCLOSED (PAYABLE TO *Shojo Beat*)   ☐ BILL ME LATER

CREDIT CARD: ☐ VISA   ☐ MASTERCARD

ACCOUNT #   **EXP. DATE**

SIGNATURE

CLIP AND MAIL TO → SHOJO BEAT
Subscriptions Service Dept.
P.O. Box 438
Mount Morris, IL 61054-0438

Canada price for 12 issues: $46.99 USD, including GST, HST and QST. US/CAN orders only. Allow 6-8 weeks for delivery. Must be 16 or older to redeem offer. By redeeming this offer I represent that I am 16 or older.

Vampire Knight © Matsuri Hino 2004/HAKUSENSHA, Inc. Nana Kitade © Sony Music Entertainment (Japan), Inc.
CRIMSON HERO © 2002 by Mitsuba Takanashi/SHUEISHA Inc.

RATED T+ FOR OLDER TEEN ratings.viz.com